KOALAS

CONTENTS

*First published in
the United States in 1990 by*
Gloucester Press
387 Park Avenue South
New York NY 10016

Design Rob Hillier, Andy Wilkinson
Editor Fiona Robertson
Photo Research Cecilia Weston-Baker
Illustrations Ron Hayward Associates

Printed in Belgium

Library of Congress Cataloging-in-Publication Data

Bright, Michael.
   Koalas / Michael Bright.
     p. cm. -- (Project Wildlife)
   Summary: Examines the habits and
characteristics of koalas, as well as efforts to
ensure their survival.
   ISBN 0-531-17246-5
   1. Koala--Juvenile literature. [1. Koala.] I. Title.
   II. Series.
QL737.M384B75 1990
599.2--dc20   90-3251   CIP   AC

PROJECT WILDLIFE

KOALAS

Michael Bright

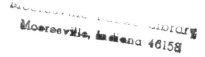
GLOUCESTER PRESS
New York : London : Toronto : Sydney

Introduction

The koala sits in its disappearing habitat.

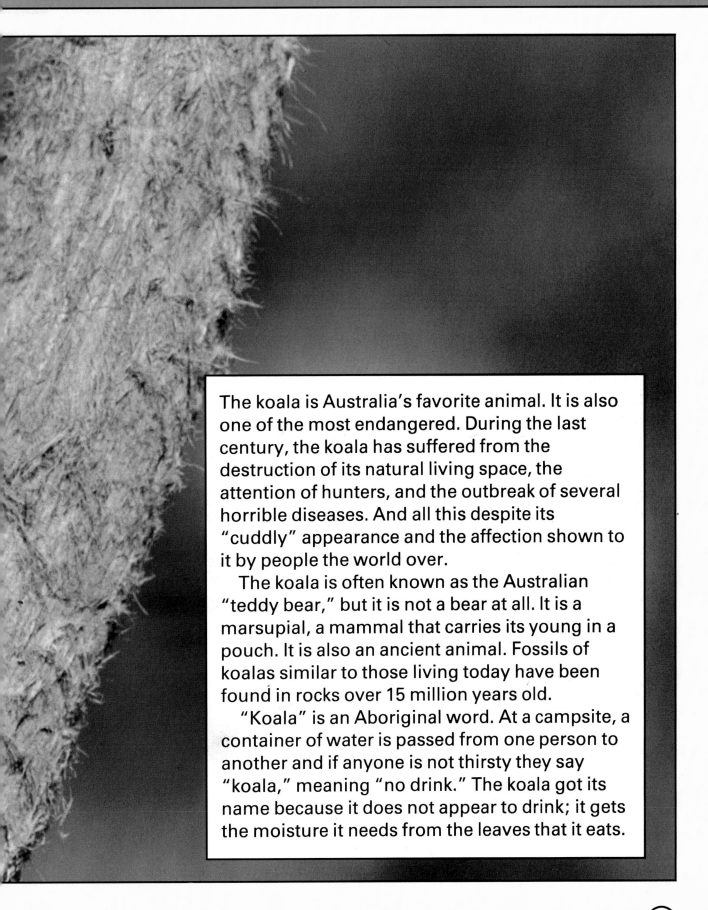

The koala is Australia's favorite animal. It is also one of the most endangered. During the last century, the koala has suffered from the destruction of its natural living space, the attention of hunters, and the outbreak of several horrible diseases. And all this despite its "cuddly" appearance and the affection shown to it by people the world over.

The koala is often known as the Australian "teddy bear," but it is not a bear at all. It is a marsupial, a mammal that carries its young in a pouch. It is also an ancient animal. Fossils of koalas similar to those living today have been found in rocks over 15 million years old.

"Koala" is an Aboriginal word. At a campsite, a container of water is passed from one person to another and if anyone is not thirsty they say "koala," meaning "no drink." The koala got its name because it does not appear to drink; it gets the moisture it needs from the leaves that it eats.

Koala distribution

There were once millions of koalas in eastern Australia, but now there are thought to be no more than 400,000 left. Although the overall population is not threatened with extinction, local isolated populations, such as those in parts of Southern Australia, have disappeared. The distribution of koalas today is very scattered.

Koalas were once found throughout Australia, but changes in climate and vegetation have led to a decline in their numbers. In central Australia forests gave way to desert and so the koalas were confined to the west and east coasts between the desert and the sea. Then, the settlers arrived.

First the Aborigines came, and they wiped out all the koalas in the southwest of Australia. Two hundred years ago, the Europeans arrived and the east coast population came under threat from the wholesale slaughter of animals for their pelts, the destruction of forests for farming and the building of cities and towns, as well as several major epidemics of killer diseases.

▷ The map on the right shows the way populations of koalas have been drastically reduced and isolated from each other by habitat destruction. Much of the forest has been destroyed by man, but some of the losses are due to natural forest fires. The actual decline is unknown because scientists have little idea of the size of the koala population at the time the European settlers arrived.

▽ This is the koala's natural home – young *Eucalyptus* forest at Mt. Irvine in New South Wales. Koalas are restricted to *Eucalyptus* because the shoots and leaves make up a large part of their diet.

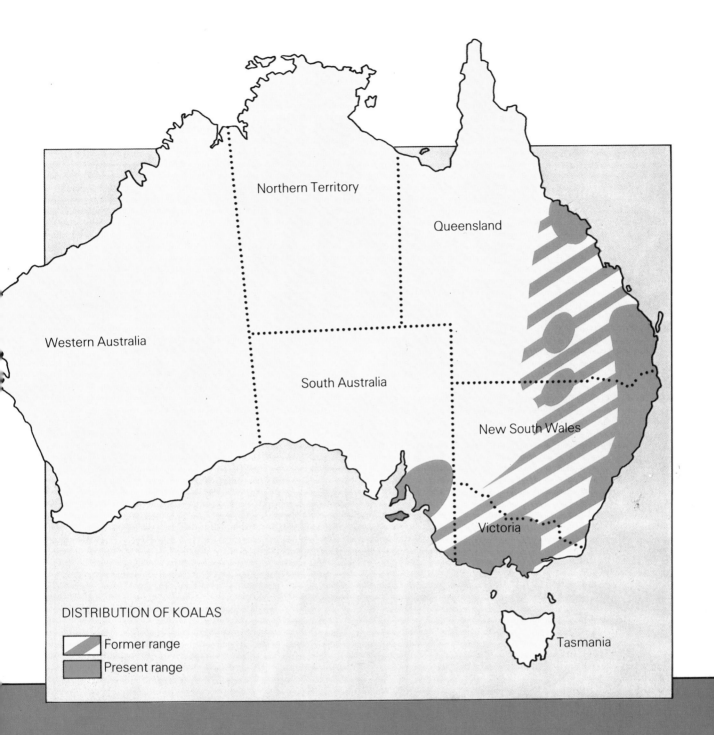

Northern Territory

Queensland

Western Australia

South Australia

New South Wales

Victoria

DISTRIBUTION OF KOALAS

Former range

Present range

Tasmania

Koala populations suffered heavy losses at the turn of the century. In addition to the large-scale hunting which accounted for the disappearance of literally millions of animals, there were huge forest fires between 1850 and 1900. And in the years 1887-89 and 1900-03, there were epidemics of koala diseases which devastated populations. By the 1930s it was thought that the koala was rapidly heading for extinction. Bans on hunting in 1936, and careful management during the 1940s enabled some populations to recover.

Depending on where they came from, each race of European settlers gave the koala a number of alternative names including: colo, colah, cullewine, koolah, kaolah, karboor, bangaroo, buidelbeer, koolewong, narnagoon, native bear, and the New Holland sloth.

The slaughter

Koalas are easy prey for hunters. After the arrival of settlers in Australia, koalas became prime targets. Aborigines, who migrated to southwest Australia, wiped out the koalas living there. In the east, European settlers continued the tradition.

The slaughter started in the late 1870s. Koalas were killed for food, fur and target practice. It was said that they cried like human babies as they were repeatedly fired at until they eventually died. Some old-time hunters claimed to have killed 20-30 koalas a day. By 1918, hunting and forest fires had accounted for most of South Australia's koalas. In Victoria, the situation became so bad, koala management and restocking programs were introduced in the 1920s.

▽ The Aborigines (below) traditionally caught the koala, cooking it with the fur on as a mark of respect. In Aborigine folklore, however, the koala is depicted as a slow-witted villain. In one story, it stole the tribe's water and hid the water bowls at the top of a tree. When the people tried to retrieve their water, the koala threw bowls at them. Another animal showed the men how to kill the koala, and told the tribe to always break its legs and roast it without removing the fur so that it could not steal the bowls.

The authorities in Queensland began to be concerned for the survival of the koala as early as 1906. The state declared it a protected species. Stocks recovered so well that six open seasons were subsequently declared, and the proceeds of the hunt were to go toward the upkeep of koala sanctuaries. In 1919, for instance, one million koalas fell victim to six months of hunting.

The hunting seasons were irregularly spaced and with no sound ecological basis. It was, perhaps, no coincidence that they occurred in times of high rural unemployment. But by 1927, when 10,000 licenses were issued and 584,738 animals were killed within a month, there were few koalas left to protect. There was public outcry, and the open seasons for koalas were stopped.

The Koala was first reported in 1798 by John Price who journeyed into the Blue Mountains near Sydney. Naturalists described it in 1810 when it was given the name "sloth." In 1816 it was given the scientific name *Phascolarctos cinereus*, which literally means a "grey bear-like leather bag."

▽ One legacy of such large-scale hunting was orphaned baby koalas. This one is just five months old. It should be protected in its mother's pouch for at least another two months before fending for itself.

The fur trade

At the height of the koala killing in the 1920s there was a big market for koala fur. The koala's coat is thick, hard-wearing, and long lasting. It is considered to be one of the best insulating furs worn by any of the terrestrial mammals. Many of the pelts exported from Australia found their way to the other side of the world, mainly to Alaska, where they were turned into thick, warm fur hats.

During this time the general public throughout Australia were so appalled by the slaughter of these living "teddy bears," and so concerned about the effect that the enormous trade in their skins was having on population numbers, that the fur traders were forced to label their consignments "wombat" skins (from the name of a burrowing marsupial related to the koala and considered to be an agricultural pest at that time).

> "It is simply unbelievable that a civilized people could slaughter such a harmless indigenous solely for selfish gain."
>
> **Ellis Troughton**
> **Australian zoologist.**

▽ Hunters almost wiped out the koala. Millions were trapped and killed, and wagon-loads of koala skins were transported to eastern ports such as Sydney, before being shipped abroad.

Many millions of koala skins were exported from Australia to all parts of the world. In 1920, a total of 205,679 pelts were exported from the eastern states. By 1924, the trade in exports had increased to over two million skins, and the United States became the first country to ban the import of koala pelts.

In 1927, when Queensland sanctioned its last koala hunt, 600,000 pelts were exported from that state. This final slaughter was introduced at the request of the fur traders who had warehouses filled with koala pelts that had not been sold from previous open seasons. During the intervening years, koalas received total protection and so the dealers could not legally dispose of their stocks. The 1927 open season enabled them to get rid of their remaining pelts.

AUSTRALIAN KOALA ASSOCIATION INC

△ Although the public expressed considerable concern about the fate of koalas, very little funding was put into koala research to assess population sizes and the impact that hunting, disease and the removal of forest have on wild stocks. The Australian Koala Foundation (formerly the Australian Koala Association) was set up in 1986 to right some of these wrongs.

Despite public concern in the 1920s, protection for the koala was slow to materialize. In New South Wales and Victoria it had all but vanished by the late 1920s. Despite Queensland's early attempts to conserve koalas with "The Native Animals Protection Act of 1906," more general protective legislation did not apply throughout the koala's range until 1936. Toy koalas (right) continued to be sold, although the fur from which they were made was not koala, but kangaroo.

Habitat destruction

The greatest threat to the survival of the koala today is the destruction of its native forest habitat. Koalas are very particular about where they live. They need tall and medium-height *Eucalyptus* forests with trees over 30 feet high. The leafy canopy must provide sufficient cover (about 10 percent) in which the animals can hide and feed. In addition, a forest can support only a limited number of koalas.

However, unfortunately for the koala, since the European colonization of Australia, these forest areas have been disappearing quickly. The settlers needed wood for building, land for agriculture, and cleared areas on which to build new towns. Koalas were not included in their plans.

When half the trees have been removed from a forest, those remaining succumb to "dieback," which is the premature death of a tree. Causes can be natural, such as an invasion by insects, or man-made, such as the excessive use of pesticides. In Queensland, 27 out of 42 species of *Eucalyptus* trees favored by koalas are suffering from the effects of dieback.

△ A recent plague of the insect pest, lerps, has devastated *Eucalyptus* forests in New South Wales.

Forest clearance like that shown on the right has reduced considerably the number of places in which koalas can live.

A koala population must be about 500 strong if it is to survive in the long-term. This requires a forest area of between 285 and 960 acres. Any less and the koala population declines. In Victoria, for example, overcrowding of koalas in small forest patches has led to populations gradually becoming extinct. In urban areas, collisions with cars (when animals are trying to get from one tree to another) and attacks by dogs account for two thirds of the deaths.

One hundred years ago, koalas lived in Bega (NSW). However a survey in the 1980s revealed that they had not only disappeared from the town, but also from the nearby coastal forests, where logging still continues.

The extent of forest destruction provides an indication of how fast koala populations are declining. Two thirds of the forest suitable for koalas has been cleared in South Australia. Inevitably, the koalas disappear with the trees.

Native forest

200 years ago

today

Killer diseases

Koala populations in the wild have suffered from recurring epidemics of serious killer diseases. At the turn of the century many koalas died from eye infections and a bone disease, called periostotis, which affected the bones of the skull. Today, one virus-like bacterium, called *Chlamydia psittaci*, is infecting forty percent of all koalas and causing diseases that can kill koalas in large numbers.

When mother koalas succumb to disease, their orphaned babies prove very difficult to rear by hand, and many die. But patience and constant attention, such as frequent feeding by pipette (below) has had some success.

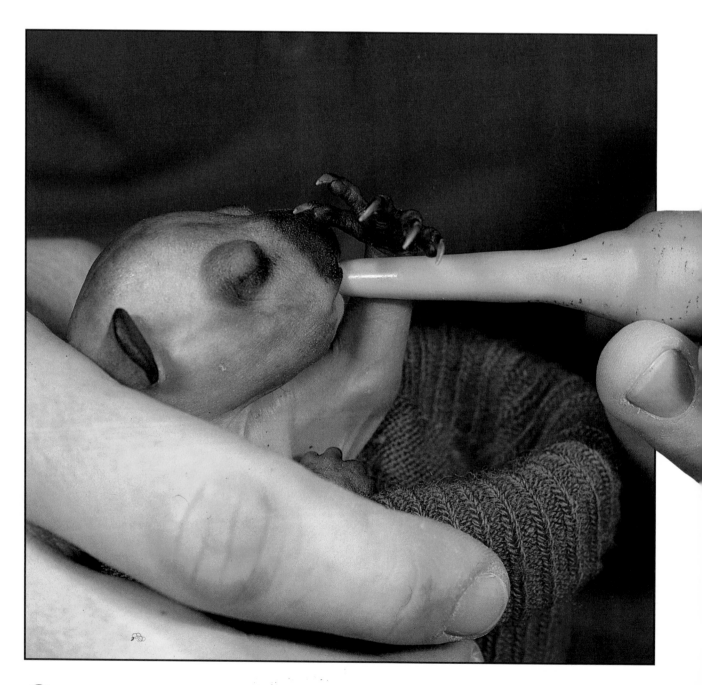

Chlamydia psittaci is thought to cause several different diseases in koalas. The most common areas of infection include the eyes where it causes blindness; the urinary system causing a condition known as "dirty tail;" the lungs causing pneumonia; and the reproductive tract which can make females sterile. *Chlamydia* is a common bacterium that is also found in parrots, cats, dogs, cows and sheep. It causes arthritis in lambs and dogs, and pregnant cows and sheep with the infection may miscarry. Related bacterial organisms can also infect humans. One form of *Chlamydia*, for example, has caused blindness in over 50 million people.

Stress is another major problem that affects koalas, and is caused by shrinking habitat and overcrowding. Stressed koalas more easily succumb to the killer diseases. In a study of two populations of koalas, the group that is visited by tourists, is under pressure from habitat loss and encounters more motor vehicles, has a much lower reproductive rate and suffers more from *Chlamydia* than the group which is undisturbed.

△ The sight of hundreds of dead koalas like the one above, alarmed New South Wales officials so much that koalas were considered to be "endangered." *Chlamydia* was partly responsible for the reduction in Australia's koala population numbers.

"The epidemic is more serious than in earlier times because the remaining koala habitats consist of isolated areas. ... Because *Chlamydia* is extremely small ... it has eluded detection for many years."

Dr. Frank Carrick, leading koala researcher, University of Queensland.

Koala care

In 1974, scientists in Australia discovered and identified the *Chlamydia* bacterium which causes the four lethal diseases in koalas. The bacterium was isolated from swabs taken from the eyes of blind koalas. Having identified the cause, the researchers could then begin to look for a cure.

Recently, an antibiotic has been found and tested. However, there is a major setback. The medicine does not only kill the harmful bacteria, but also destroys the helpful bacteria in the digestive system of the koala which enable it to digest *Eucalyptus* leaves. Treatment for the disease can lead to serious problems of malnutrition and even the death of the animal.

Steve Brown of the Australian Koala Foundation visits many koala sanctuaries to treat sick animals. In a series of 36 autopsies on animals that had died from the four main koala diseases, Brown found that 21 showed signs of the *Chlamydia* infection.

▽ The koala shown below is recovering from a fractured leg after its habitat was bulldozed to make way for a housing development.

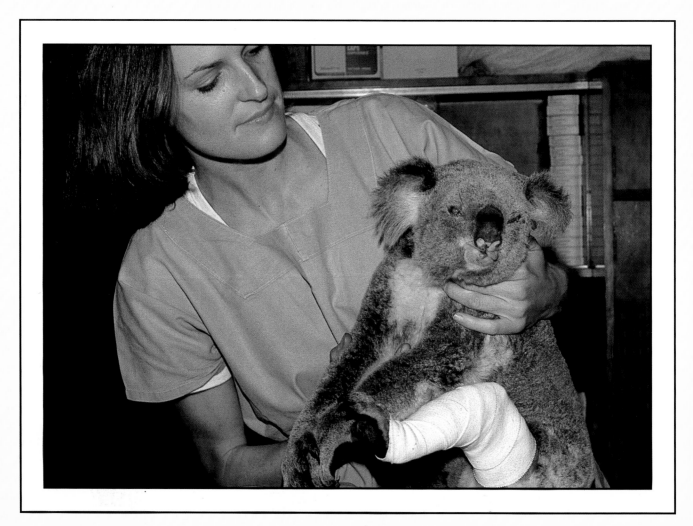

Koalas dislike change, especially changes in diet and habitat. This makes any surgical operation, treatment with antibiotics, or hospitalization extremely difficult. In addition, very few veterinary centers are sufficiently equipped to handle the expensive diagnostic tests necessary to monitor an animal's progress.

But, treatment of diseases is only half the story. Baby orphaned koalas are difficult to wean off their first diet of milk and onto a normal *Eucalyptus* leaf diet. A baby's first solid meal is a special soft, green feces that contains the gut bacteria to help it digest *Eucalyptus*. Providing this in captivity is very difficult.

▽ Supported by the Australian Koala Society, several veterinary teams in southeast Queensland have been working to save sick koalas. Orphaned babies are a particular problem, for they demand constant attention with regular feedings of milk. Few vets have the time the animals require to ensure success. And, the results can be frustrating for the researchers; more than half of those hand-reared eventually die.

Helping koalas in the wild

The key to the conservation of the koala is successful land management. Researchers believe that controls should be introduced to ensure that landowners take account of koala populations on their property. In New South Wales and Queensland, most of the land suitable for koalas is privately owned, and so ways are being sought to encourage landowners to conserve forest areas. In urban areas, property developers are encouraged to leave areas of trees intact, so that a koala refuge could become a feature of a new building development.

▽ There is some reluctance to move koalas from one site to another because the change causes them considerable stress, and they succumb to diseases and die. But in some circumstances, moving animals from a logging area to a place where they will not be disturbed is the only chance they have of survival. There are only a few cases of koalas surviving the trauma of translocation.

In the 1920s, Victoria's koalas were rapidly disappearing. So, some were shipped to Philip and French Islands where they provided a stock from which koalas could be returned to the mainland. But, these islands were also developed and new unsettled islands had to be found.

In eastern Australia, Land Care Committees, backed by the Cattlemen's Union, are attempting to coordinate the way rural lands are used. Included on the agenda are the needs of wildlife. One basic problem for koalas is that large tracts of suitable forest no longer exist.

So, land management experts are suggesting that the small but viable surviving patches of *Eucalyptus* trees be joined together by planting thin corridors of trees, which should be at least 300ft wide to avoid dieback. Koalas can use the corridors to move between the patches. This ensures that a group of animals does not eat out its food supply, and it helps to avoid inbreeding by keeping populations mixed. Already, the planting of trees to stop soil erosion and to provide windbreaks on exposed tracts of land is proving valuable for koalas.

▽ Metal sleeves are fitted around treetrunks to allow the foliage to recover from the effects of overgrazing.

▽ In urban areas frequented by koalas, enlightened local authorities have put up koala warning signs.

Koala research

Koalas are very lethargic and slow-moving animals, so a basic problem for researchers is that they might fall asleep before the koalas do! Koalas are relatively easy to observe as they do not travel far and spend much of the day asleep, starting to move from their sleeping quarters to the tops of the trees where they feed at dusk. Nevertheless, some are tagged so that they may be identified individually.

Although koalas are one of Australia's main emblems, little research had been done until recently. It was estimated that nearly three million dollars had to be spent on research to find out more about these animals. The information obtained will be used to help plan land management programs aimed at protecting and conserving koala populations in the wild.

▽ The koala is a shy animal, and is sensitive to disturbance and disease. In koala habitats near towns and cities, it is important to know just how much stress koalas can tolerate. Much of the present-day research in these areas is directly concerned with this problem, and with trying to find alternative habitats.

In November 1988, a "koala summit" was held. Scientists, conservation groups, government representatives, and the owners of koala refuges gathered in Sydney and presented to the New South Wales government a statement that strongly suggested more research should be carried out on koalas. Top priority, they declared, was to establish what environment would best suit wild koalas. They also recommended that all the surviving koalas should be counted and their numbers and population distribution more accurately recorded. Until then, very little of this information was available. When distribution work was started, the researchers discovered that in some areas where koalas once thrived, there are now none to be seen.

The lack of information about koalas is highlighted by the fact that we do not know how many there once were, how many there should be now, or how many there really are. The International Union for the Conservation of Nature and Natural Resources does not list the koala. It is not labeled "endangered," "vulnerable" or "rare," although clearly its declining numbers do warrant some concern.

Koalas move by night, so to discover in which direction they have headed some are given radio-collars that emit a special radio signal. Researchers with direction-finders (left) can then follow at a discreet distance to avoid disturbing the koalas. They can also use the radio signals to locate the new position of the koalas.

Koalas in captivity

Koalas are difficult to keep in captivity because of their fussy diet. But this has been partly overcome with the help of a special "koala biscuit" that contains many of the necessary ingredients to keep a captive koala content. The biscuit mimics the taste, texture, and smell of *Eucalyptus* leaves and was developed more by trial-and-error than by any scientific analysis.

In the Bronx Zoo a mother koala who was fed the "koala biscuits" showed that the diet was nutritious by giving birth to twins. This is important as there is pressure on world zoos to breed koalas, rather than take them from the wild. Captive-bred specimens would be an insurance policy against any major disaster that might hit wild populations.

The Australian authorities have also banned the export of koalas. Koalas will no longer be an international currency for diplomacy. Instead, Australian koalas will remain in Australia.

In 1980, koalas destined for Japan took part in an auction. Several major Japanese cities participated. The winner was Tokyo where the zoo promised one pair of koalas a $2 million enclosure and 20,000 *Eucalyptus* trees. The Japanese breeding colonies are carefully watched 24 hours a day. If a koala prefers to feed in a particular tree, cells are taken and cloned, and that strain of tree is bred specially for the koalas. Thousands of *Eucalyptus* seedlings are developed and grown in Japanese greenhouses.

▷ This rare albino koala was born at San Diego Zoo. The thriving colony there is the result of Australia relaxing its restrictions on the export of koalas in 1976. In that year the last surviving koala outside Australia died at the zoo. The second attempt at maintaining a colony, which was started with two males and four females, has been more successful. Two of San Diego's koalas have been sent on loan to London Zoo which hopes to start its own breeding program.

◁ These healthy koalas are at the famous Lone Pine Sanctuary in Brisbane. It is the oldest and largest koala sanctuary in Australia. Here, tame koalas are cuddled by visitors. Past "cuddlers" have included Presidents Lyndon B. Johnson and Jimmy Carter, and singers Paul McCartney and Linda Ronstadt. The animals are remarkably tolerant of hugging and rarely bite, even though these nocturnal creatures are asked to perform in daylight. Their *Eucalyptus* diet gives them a slightly medicinal smell, which keeps away fleas.

The future

The koala is Australia's number one mascot. It appears in airline advertisements, on T-shirts, beer mugs, cooking aprons, matchboxes, and other tourist items. Koala "teddy bears" are bedtime companions for children the world over. The real thing draws millions of tourists and millions of tourist dollars each year. Yet until recently, dollars have been slow to materialize for koala conservation.

However, organizations like the Australian Koala Foundation are trying to change all that. Already, $2 million has been raised and invested, and the interest used to fund new koala research projects. Public awareness has increased. Local authorities, mining companies, agricultural concerns, and children in Australian schools are helping to establish *Eucalyptus* forests specially for koalas. Harming a koala in Queensland can result in a $2000 fine. The fight is on to save Australia's marsupial ambassadors.

But, despite the change of attitude, many of the problems remain. *Eucalyptus* forests are still being destroyed by logging operations and land clearance for agriculture and building. And despite medical breakthroughs, diseases are still a threat. One major epidemic, on the scale of those at the turn of the century, could wipe out wild populations.

▷ This mother and baby live at the Lone Pine Koala Sanctuary. They, and the koalas living at the 30 other sanctuaries, are isolated from many of the dangers that face their wild cousins. In these privately run reserves, trees are safe, food is plentiful, and vets are on hand to deal with diseases.

▽ In some parts of eastern Australia, farmers are planting *Eucalyptus* trees for koalas. Even a small forest patch will support a breeding unit of one adult male and two or more female koalas.

"We're not saying that the koalas will be extinct in the next five years, but we are looking at a process of slow but steady wearing away of populations."

Dr. Frank Carrick, leading koala researcher, University of Queensland.

Koala fact file 1

Koalas are marsupials and only live in the wild in the east of mainland Australia. Male koalas can grow up to 2½ft and weigh over 24lbs. Females are smaller at 2ft and weighing up to 17lbs. In favorable conditions in the wild koalas are thought to live to about 13 years of age, while those in captivity can live until they are 18.

Size, shape and color

Koalas living in the northern part of their range are smaller than those living in the south. South-living koalas are browner and shaggier (below left). They have more fur around the face and ears than their northern counterparts. North-living koalas are thinner and more silvery (below right).

The koala is a small bearlike creature that has a heavy body more appropriate for a ground-living animal, but with arms and legs adapted for a life in the trees. Its body is stout and covered with fur. It has a beaklike snout, tufted ears, and small eyes with a vertical pupil slit. It has no tail apart from a small blunt stump. The fur is ash-gray to tawny in color, with a tinge of brown on the upper parts of the body, yellowish-white patches on the hindquarters, and white on the chin, chest and the inner side of the front legs. Males are slightly different to females. Apart from being bigger than the female, the male has a broader face, smaller ears, and a large chest gland. Females do not have the gland, but have a pouch that opens to the back.

Many millions of years ago, the koala was thought to have shared a common ancestor with the wombat. The wombat is a burrowing marsupial, three feet in length and weighing up to 65lbs. Its face and body are very similar to a koala's. It is the biggest burrowing animal in the world. It is interesting that the koala's backward-opening pouch and lack of tail are features more appropriate to an animal that burrows. And curiously, the brain of the wombat is large for its body size, while the brain of the koala is very small and much simpler in structure. The koala's brain is about 60 percent smaller than would be expected in a mammal of comparative size. This might account for its languid lifestyle and very simple social behavior.

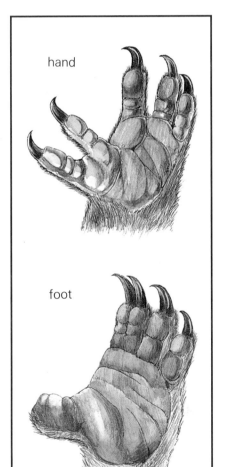

hand

foot

Range

Koalas are solitary animals except for mothers rearing youngsters and during periods of courtship and mating. Males have a home range of 3-5 acres in size. Females have smaller ranges, 1-3 acres. The home range of a male will often overlap with the home ranges of several females. He declares his territorial rights with both sound and smell. A male's loud warning call is known as the "snore-bellow."

Hands and feet

The koala has powerful grasping hands equipped with strong claws. These are used for extra grip during climbing. Special pads on the palms of the hand and soles of the feet also provide extra grip.

A male koala will scent mark his home range, with both urine and secretions from his chest gland. The gland is found in a flat strip of skin down the center of the chest. He marks with it by grasping the trunk of a tree and flattening his chest against it. The gland is activated by rubbing it up and down against the tree. An oily substance is released which leaves a brownish-orange stain on the tree and on his white chest fur. Females also scent mark with urine.

The first two digits of the hand are opposable to the other three (top left), and this enables the koala to hold small branches as it climbs. The second and third digits in the foot (bottom left) are partly fused to form a grooming tool.

Koala fact file 2

Daily life

Koalas are mainly nocturnal. They become mildly active at dusk. They are slow-moving and sleep a lot, an adaptation to a leafy diet which is low in nutrients. Most of their life is spent in *Eucalyptus* trees, although they occasionally descend to move from one tree to another.

During the winter months, a koala living at the southern end of the range spends about 14.5 hours sleeping. It wedges itself in the fork of the tree and even has a pad of gristle and thick fur on its rump so that it can sit in comfort. In very cold weather it curls tightly into a furry ball to reduce heat loss.

A further five hours are spent resting but awake. In hot weather, when the air temperature might reach 90°F, it will lie flat on its back with the white fur of its tummy exposed.

It moves for just a few minutes each day, an activity usually preceded by a bout of intense grooming with the hind feet. Koalas tend to climb to the uppermost branches to feed. They move by reaching up with the arms, clasping the bough with the help of their claws, and then drawing up the hindquarters in a little bound. It progresses upward in a series of these small jumps, moving 4-6 inches at a time.

If a koala changes tree, it is usually in the dark, sometime after midnight. It descends from the tree with its bottom first. On the ground it is rather awkward and usually has one object in mind – getting up the nearest gum tree. If it is not in a hurry it walks with a slow rolling gait. If danger threatens it can put on a momentary spurt of speed and bound along in a similar way to which it climbs. Occasionally, koalas travel long distances.

On the ground the koala is vulnerable and may fall prey to dingoes (Australian wild dogs) and domestic dogs. Those crossing roads are often hit by passing cars and trucks. They sometimes stop to lick earth from the ground or gravel from the road surface. This is thought to help them gain extra salts, particularly calcium.

About four and a half hours of the koala's night is spent eating. One popular myth is that the koala behaves in such a slow-witted and lethargic way because it is under the influence of the drugs that are present in the *Eucalyptus* leaves which it eats. This claim of drug addiction in koalas is now known not to be true. Any toxic plant compounds are detoxified, broken down in the koala's liver, and then safely excreted.

Food and eating

It is a misconception that koalas only eat the leaves of gum trees. In addition to 32 *Eucalyptus* species, they have been known to eat the leaves, buds, and bark of native golden and hop wattles (Australian acacias), coastal tea-tree, box, cherry and kapok trees. They do, however, prefer certain species of *Eucalyptus* for the bulk of their diet. Although the liver can deal with the poisons contained in the koala's regular food tree, it might not be able to cope with the poisons from other species, which could be harmful to the koala.

The koala has many adaptations to cope with such an unusual diet. The cheek teeth, for example, are modified to finely grind each mouthful of leaves. An adult koala will munch its way through about one pound of leaves each night. The most intriguing feature, however, is one part of the gut. The koala's cecum is seven feet long; that is three or four times as long as the koala itself, and is the longest cecum for body size in the animal kingdom. The cecum contains bacteria which break down the poisons, and release the nutrients from the plant material.

The koala's system can also sort out useful material, which is processed in the cecum, and hard, fibrous matter, which passes through the large intestine. Despite the long digestion process, only 25 percent of the nutrients in the leaves is absorbed.

eucalyptus

Koala fact file 3

Courtship and mating

During the breeding season, which peaks in November in the north and December in the south, male koalas can become very aggressive and noisy. They bellow constantly and fight with other males for the right to mate. Each dominant male lords over a clutch of up to eight females that live within his home range. If other males approach this range, they are attacked violently and can be badly bitten. When the females have weaned last year's youngster, they come into heat for just a few days during the mating season. The male koala will try to mate at any time. Unreceptive females snarl their protests, but are ignored and seized by the back of the neck while the male attempts to mate.

The male koala is capable of mating successfully at about two years of age, but it is unlikely that he will command the attention of his own group of females until he is fully grown at about five years old. Only then will he be able to advertise his availability with the loud two-note call that can travel more than a mile through the *Eucalyptus* forest. Receptive females also call when they are ready to mate, but a little more quietly. It is thought the calls are a means by which males and females can find each other quickly. Mating itself is a very brief affair, lasting no more than a couple of minutes. The male grabs the female by the neck with his teeth, and covers her. Mating most often takes place in a tree.

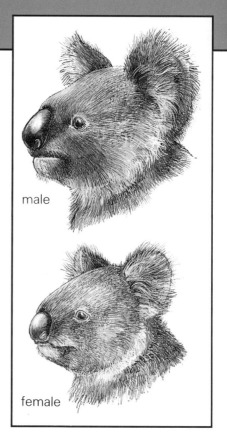

male

female

A male and female koala can be recognized apart, not only by the difference in size, but also by the shape of the head and snout (above).

Babies and young

The gestation period is very short, only 25-35 days. Only one baby is usually born. Twins are rare. The peanut-sized blob is only half an inch long and weighs less than half an ounce. The baby is born with eyes and ears tightly shut and has a pink nose and colorless claws. Using its forelimbs, it clings at first to its mother's fur and hauls itself unaided to the backward opening pouch. Only its forelimbs, smell receptors, and the digestive and excretory systems are working. After this first journey it enters the pouch and latches onto one of the two nipples. Here it sucks small amounts of rich milk almost continuously for about thirteen weeks.

The baby's eyes open at about five to six months and it begins to take a look outside the pouch. At this point the mother starts to feed it with special runny feces called "pap." This is thought to come from her cecum and will supply the youngster with its first batch of bacteria which will live in its own cecum and allow it to digest its first solid meal. By seven or eight months the cub will start to eat leaves. At first it clings to the fur of its mother's belly. Later it will ride on her back. At nine months the youngster begins to wander and feed by itself, returning often to its mother. Koala mothers are tolerant, but not affectionate. They do not groom, train or play with their babies.

On a koala's first birthday, its mother will most likely be expecting a new baby. When it is born, the yearling is rejected. Any attempt to return is met with hostility. Males roam far afield, while females occupy home ranges next to their mother's.

Koalas have no means by which to regulate their population. As more are born and mature they spread out in the forest. If the forest is patchy, as in some parts of Australia, the koalas eat all the leaves, kill the trees, and then die of starvation.

Index

Photographic Credits

Cover and pages 22 and 30: Australian Information Service; pages 4-5, 6, 13, 15, 17, 24, 25, 26 left, 27, 28, 29 and 31: Bruce Coleman Ltd; page 8: Ardea; pages 9, 12, 14, 16, 19 left, 20 and 21: NHPA; page 10: Roger Vlitos with acknowledgement to G. Hitchcock; page 11: Australian Koala Association Inc.; page 12: Steve Brown; pages 18, 19 right and 23: Frank Lane Agency; page 26 right: Planet Earth.

PRINTED IN BELGIUM BY

proost
INTERNATIONAL BOOK PRODUCTION

Cybersecurity

2nd Edition

by Joseph Steinberg

A Wiley Brand

Cybersecurity For Dummies®, 2nd Edition

Published by: **John Wiley & Sons, Inc.**, 111 River Street, Hoboken, NJ 07030-5774, www.wiley.com

Copyright © 2022 by John Wiley & Sons, Inc., Hoboken, New Jersey

Published simultaneously in Canada

For general information on our other products and services, please contact our Customer Care Department within the U.S. at 877-762-2974, outside the U.S. at 317-572-3993, or fax 317-572-4002. For technical support, please visit https://hub.wiley.com/community/support/dummies.

Wiley publishes in a variety of print and electronic formats and by print-on-demand. Some material included with standard print versions of this book may not be included in e-books or in print-on-demand. If this book refers to media such as a CD or DVD that is not included in the version you purchased, you may download this material at http://booksupport.wiley.com. For more information about Wiley products, visit www.wiley.com.

Library of Congress Control Number: 2022933136

ISBN 978-1-119-86718-0 (pbk); ISBN 978-1-119-86719-7 (ebk); ISBN 978-1-119-86720-3 (ebk)

SKY10033633_031222

Contents at a Glance

Table of Contents

PART 4: CYBERSECURITY FOR BUSINESSES, ORGANIZATIONS, AND GOVERNMENT 173

CHAPTER 10: Securing Your Small Business 175

Introduction

In the course of just a single generation, the world has undergone some of the greatest changes since the dawn of mankind. The availability of the Internet as a tool for consumers and businesses alike, coupled with the invention of mobile devices and wireless networking, have ushered in an Information Revolution that has impacted just about every aspect of human existence.

Humanity's reliance on technology, however, has also created enormous risks. It seems that not a day goes by without some new story emerging of a data breach, cyberattack, or the like. Simultaneously, because society's reliance on technology increases on a daily basis, the potential adverse consequences of cyberattacks have grown exponentially to the point that people can now lose their fortunes, their reputations, their health, or even their lives, as the result of cyberattacks.

In fact, since the publication of the first edition of this book, Americans have seen cyberattacks cause fuel shortages, spikes in meat prices, financial losses, and even death. And societal changes resulting from the COVID-19 pandemic — including the dramatic increase in the number of people who, at least sometimes, leverage computers and computer networks in order to work remotely — have upped the stakes even more. While people all around the developed world outsource a large portion of their national security to their countries' respective armed forces, their fire safety to trained fire departments, and their protection from criminals to law enforcement agencies, ensuring that one remains safe from cyber threats requires far more personal involvement.

It is no wonder, therefore, that people living in the modern world understand the need to protect themselves from cyber-dangers. This book shows you how to do so.

About This Book

While many books have been written over the past couple decades on a wide variety of cybersecurity-related topics, most of them don't provide the general population with the information needed to properly protect themselves.

Many cybersecurity books are directed toward highly technical audiences and tend to overwhelm people who are not computer scientists with extraneous information, creating severe challenges for readers seeking to translate the knowledge that they acquire from books into practical actions. On the flip side, various self-published introduction-to-cybersecurity books suffer from all sorts of serious deficiencies, including, in some cases, having been written by non-experts and presenting significant amounts of misinformation. Anyone interested in cybersecurity often shouldn't trust these materials. Likewise, many security tip sheets and the like simply relay oft-repeated clichés and outdated advice, sometimes causing people who follow the recommendations contained within such works to worsen their cybersecurity postures rather than improve them. Furthermore, the nearly constant repetition of various cybersecurity advice by media personalities after news stories about breaches ("Don't forget to reset all your passwords!"), coupled with the lack of consequences to most people after they do not comply with such directives, has led to *cybersecurity fatigue* — a condition in which folks simply don't act when they actually need to because they have heard the "boy cry wolf" one too many times.

I wrote *Cybersecurity For Dummies* to provide people who do not work as cybersecurity professionals with a foundational book that can teach them what they need to know about cybersecurity and explain why they need to know it. This book offers you practical, clear, and straightforward advice that you can easily translate into actions that can help keep you and your children, parents, and small businesses cybersecure. The second edition of this book contains updates to help people understand and address cybersecurity risks created by changes to our world in terms of technological advances, societal changes, and new geopolitical realities.

Cybersecurity For Dummies is divided into several parts. Parts 1, 2, and 3 provide an overview of cybersecurity and give tips on protecting yourself and your loved ones from both external threats and from making dangerous (and potentially disastrous) mistakes. Topics such as how to secure your online accounts, how to select and protect passwords, and how to safely work remotely fall into these parts of the book.

Part 4 offers tips on securing small businesses, which may be especially pertinent for small business owners and employees. Part 4 then also discusses some of the unique security needs that face firms as they grow larger and touches on cybersecurity-in-government related matters.

Part 5 shows you how to identify security breaches. Part 6 covers the process of backing up, something that you should do proactively before the need to recover arises, as well as how to recover from security breaches.

Part 7 looks toward the future — both for those interested in potentially pursuing a cybersecurity-related career (or who have children or other relatives or friends considering doing so) as well as those interested in how emerging technologies are likely to impact their own personal cybersecurity.

Part 8 gives several lists of ten items that you may want to keep as tip sheets.

Please keep in mind that while internalizing all the information in this book, and putting it into practice, will likely dramatically improve your cybersecurity posture, reading this book will no more make you an expert in cybersecurity than reading a book on the workings of the human heart will quickly transform you into a competent cardiologist.

Cybersecurity is a complex, rapidly changing field whose professionals spend years, if not decades, studying and working full-time to develop, sharpen, and maintain the skills and expertise that they utilize on a constant basis. As such, please do not consider the advice within this book as a substitute for hiring a professional for any situation that reasonably warrants the latter.

Also, please keep in mind that technical products change quite often, so any screenshots included within the book may not be identical to the screens that you observe when you perform similar actions to those described in the text. Remember: Cybersecurity threats are constantly evolving, as are the technologies and approaches utilized to combat them.

Foolish Assumptions

In this book, I make some assumptions about your experience with technology:

>> You have experience with using a keyboard and pointer, such as a mouse, on either a Mac or Windows PC and have access to one of those machines.

>> You have experience with using a so-called "smartphone" running the Android or iOS operating systems.

You know how to use an Internet browser, such as Firefox, Chrome, Edge, Opera, or Safari.

>> You know how to install applications on your computer and have adequate rights to do so.

>> You know how to perform a Google search.

Icons Used in This Book

Throughout this book, small images, known as icons, appear in the margins. These icons mark important tidbits of information:

TIP

The Tip icon identifies places where I offer additional tips for making this journey more interesting or clear. Tips cover some neat shortcuts that you may not have known about.

REMEMBER

The Remember icon bookmarks important points that you'll want to keep in mind.

WARNING

The Warning icon helps protect you from common errors and may even give you tips to undo your mistakes.

Beyond the Book

In addition to what you're reading right now, this product also comes with a free access-anywhere Cheat Sheet that covers important cybersecurity actions. To get this Cheat Sheet, simply go to www.dummies.com and search for *Cybersecurity For Dummies Cheat Sheet* in the Search box.

Where to Go from Here

Cybersecurity For Dummies is designed in such a fashion that you don't have to read the book in order or even read the entire book.

If you purchased this book because you suffered a cybersecurity breach of some sort, for example, you can skip to the chapters in Part 5 without reading the prior material (although reading it afterwards may be wise, as it may help you prevent yourself from becoming the victim of another cyberattack).

1
Getting Started with Cybersecurity

Chapter **1**

What Exactly Is Cybersecurity?

To improve your ability to keep yourself and your loved ones cybersecure, you need to understand what cybersecure means, what your goals should be vis-à-vis cybersecurity, and what exactly you're securing against.

While the answers to these questions may initially seem simple and straightforward, they aren't. As you see in this chapter, these answers can vary dramatically between people, company divisions, organizations, and even within the same entity at different times.

Cybersecurity Means Different Things to Different Folks

While *cybersecurity* may sound like a simple enough term to define, in actuality, from a practical standpoint, it means quite different things to different people in different situations, leading to extremely varied relevant policies, procedures, and practices. Individuals who want to protect their social media accounts from hacker takeovers, for example, are exceedingly unlikely to assume many of the approaches and technologies used by Pentagon workers to secure classified networks.

Typically, for example:

>> For **individuals,** *cybersecurity* means that their personal data is not accessible to anyone other than themselves and others they have authorized, and that their computing devices work properly and are free from malware.

>> For **small business owners,** *cybersecurity* may include ensuring that credit card data is properly protected and that standards for data security are properly implemented at point-of-sale registers.

>> For **firms conducting online business,** *cybersecurity* may include protecting servers that untrusted outsiders regularly interact with.

>> For **shared service providers,** *cybersecurity* may entail protecting numerous data centers that house numerous servers that, in turn, host many virtual servers belonging to many different organizations.

>> For **the government,** *cybersecurity* may include establishing different classifications of data, each with its own set of related laws, policies, procedures, and technologies.

REMEMBER

The bottom line is that while the word cybersecurity is easy to define, the practical expectations that enters people's minds when they hear the word vary quite a bit.

Technically speaking, cybersecurity is the subset of information security that addresses information and information systems that store and process data in electronic form, whereas *information security* encompasses the security of all forms of data (for example, securing a paper file and a filing cabinet).

That said, today, many people colloquially interchange the terms, often referring to aspects of information security that are technically not part of cybersecurity as being part of the latter. Such usage also results from the blending of the two in many situations. Technically speaking, for example, if someone writes down a password on a piece of paper and leaves the paper on a desk where other people can see the password instead of placing the paper in a safe deposit box or safe, that person has violated a principle of information security, not of cybersecurity, even though those actions may result in serious cybersecurity repercussions.

Cybersecurity Is a Constantly Moving Target

While the ultimate goal of cybersecurity may not change much over time, the policies, procedures, and technologies used to achieve it change dramatically as the years march on. Many approaches and technologies that were more than adequate to protect consumers' digital data in 1980, for example, are effectively worthless today, either because they're no longer practical to employ or because technological advances have rendered them obsolete or impotent.

While assembling a complete list of every advancement that the world has seen in recent decades and how such changes impact cybersecurity in effectively impossible, we can examine several key development area and their impacts on the ever-evolving nature of cybersecurity: technological changes, economic model shifts, and outsourcing.

Technological changes

Technological changes tremendously impact cybersecurity. New risks come along with the new capabilities and conveniences that new offerings deliver. As the pact of technological advancement continues to increase, therefore, so does the pace of new cybersecurity risks. While the number of such risks created over the past few decades as the result of new offerings is astounding, the areas described in the following sections have yielded a disproportionate impact on cybersecurity.

Digital data

In the last few decades we have witnessed dramatic changes in the technologies that exist, as well as who use such technologies, how they do so, and for what purposes. All of these factors impact cybersecurity.

Consider, for example, that when many of the people alive today were children, controlling access to data in a business environment simply meant that the data owner placed a physical file containing the information into a locked cabinet and gave the key to only people the owner recognized as being authorized personnel and only when they requested the key during business hours. For additional security, the data owner may have located the cabinet in an office that was locked after business hours and which itself was in a building that was also locked and alarmed.

Today, with the digital storage of information, however, simple filing and protection schemes have been replaced with complex technologies that must automatically authenticate users who seek the data from potentially any location at potentially any time, determine whether the users are authorized to access a particular element or set of data, and securely deliver the proper data — all while preventing any attacks against the system servicing data requests, any attacks against the data in transit, and any of the security controls protecting the both of them.

Furthermore, the transition from written communication to email and chat has moved tremendous amounts of sensitive information to Internet-connected servers. Likewise, society's move from film to digital photography and videography has increased the stakes for cybersecurity. Nearly every photograph and video taken today is stored electronically rather than on film and negatives — a situation that has enabled criminals situated anywhere to either steal people's images and leak them, hold people's valuable images ransom with ransomware, or use them to create turmoil in people's personal lives by creating fake profiles on dating sites, for example. The fact that movies and television shows are now stored and transmitted electronically has likewise allowed pirates to copy them and offer them to the masses — sometimes via malware-infested websites.

The Internet

The most significant technological advancement when it comes to cybersecurity impact has been the arrival of the Internet era, and, more specifically, the transformation of the Internet from a small network connecting researchers at a few universities to an enormous worldwide communication system utilized by a tremendous number of people, businesses, and organizations. In recent years, the Internet has also become the conduit for communication both by billions of smart devices and by people remotely connecting to industrial control systems. Just a few decades ago, it was unfathomable that hackers from across the globe could disrupt a business, manipulate an election, create a fuel shortage, pollute drinking water, or steal a billion dollars. Today, no knowledgeable person would dismiss any such possibilities.

Prior to the Internet era, it was extremely difficult for the average hacker to financially profit by hacking. The arrival of online banking and commerce in the 1990s, however, meant that hackers could directly steal money or goods and services — which meant that not only could hackers quickly and easily monetize their efforts, but unethical people had strong incentives to enter the world of cybercrime.

Cryptocurrency

Compounding those incentives severalfold has been the arrival and proliferation of cryptocurrency over the past decade, along with innovation that has dramatically magnified the potential return-on-investment for criminals involved in cybercrime, simultaneously increasing their ability to earn money through cybercrime and improving their ability to hide while doing so. Criminals historically faced a challenge when receiving payments since the account from which they ultimately withdrew the money could often be tied to them. Cryptocurrency effectively eliminated such risks.

In addition, not only has the dramatic rise in the value of cryptocurrencies held by criminals over the past few years enriched many crooks, providing evildoers with the resources to invest in enhancing their cyber-arsenals, but also the public's perception of cryptocurrency as a quick way to get rich has helped scammers perpetuate all sorts of social engineering–based cybercrimes related to cryptocurrency investing.

Furthermore, the availability and global liquidity of cryptocurrency has helped criminals launder money obtained through the perpetration of all sorts of crimes.

Mobile workforces and ubiquitous access

Not that many years ago, in the pre-Internet era, it was impossible for hackers to access corporate systems remotely because corporate networks were not connected to any public networks, and often had no dial-in capabilities. Executives on the road would often call their assistants to check messages and obtain necessary data while they were remote. In later years they may have connected to corporate networks via special dial-up connections using telephone-line–based private lines for extremely limited access to only one or two specific systems.

Connectivity to the Internet, of course, created risk, but initially most firewalls were set up in ways that did not allow people outside the organization to initiate communications — so, short of firewall misconfigurations and/or bugs, most internal systems remained relatively isolated. The dawn of e-commerce and e-banking, of course, meant that certain production systems had to be reachable and addressable from the outside world, but employee networks, for example, usually remained generally isolated.

The arrival of remote access technologies — starting with services like Outlook Web Access and pcAnywhere, and evolving to full VPN and VPN-like access — has totally changed the game.

Likewise, even in the short time since the first edition of this book was published, the dramatic reduction in the cost of cellular-based high-speed Internet access and the availability of mobile data plans supporting data limits sufficient enough to allow effective full-time use have dramatically reduced the need for utilizing public Wi-Fi connections. Risks that one might have deemed reasonable to take a few years ago in order to achieve various business aims have become unnecessary, and as such, policies and procedures regarding public Wi-Fi access must be updated, as is discussed later in this book in Chapters 7 and 21.

Smart devices

Likewise, the arrival of smart devices and the *Internet of Things* (the universe of devices that are connected to the Internet, but that are not traditional computers) — whose proliferation and expansion are presently occurring at a startling rate — means that unhackable solid-state machines are being quickly replaced with devices that can potentially be controlled by hackers halfway around the world. The tremendous risks created by these devices are discussed more in Chapter 18.

Globalization has also meant that cheap Internet of Things (IoT) devices can be ordered by consumers in one country from a supplier in another country halfway around the world — introducing without any oversight all sorts of unknown hardware into personal and corporate environments.

Big data

While big data is helping facilitate the creation of many cybersecurity technologies, it also creates opportunities for attackers. By correlating large amounts of information about the people working for an organization, for example, criminals can more easily than before identify ideal methods for social engineering their way into the organization or locate and exploit possible vulnerabilities in the organization's infrastructure. As a result, various organizations have been effectively forced to implement all sorts of controls to prevent the leaking of information, and the practices of many organizations have invited all sorts of accusations around data misuse and inappropriate protections from both employees and outsiders.

The COVID-19 pandemic

The COVID-19 pandemic served as a watershed moment in the history of cybersecurity. By forcing people to stay home in environments that are unprecedentedly isolated from one another, the novel coronavirus dramatically — and likely permanently — changed the way people in the Western world work, thereby yielding multiple, significant impacts on cybersecurity.

In the short term, the pandemic created all sorts of cybersecurity problems. Organizations that had no work-from-home infrastructures in place, or had such infrastructure but only for a limited portion of their employee populations, were suddenly faced with having to enable people to work from home — often without the ability to prepare users, policies, procedures, and technologies in advance. Many such businesses could not distribute laptops or security devices fast enough to prevent work stoppages, and as a result, relied on users to utilize their personal devices for work purposes without any additional security layers added.

Likewise, few organizations offered their employees separate Internet connections or separate routers for their remote workstations, so remote workers were nearly always sharing physical and logical networks with their other personal devices and possibly with their children who may have been gaming and/or attending virtual school. The security risks of doing such is discussed in detail in Chapter 6.

Compounding COVID-19–inflicted cybersecurity problems was the fact that while many employers did provide some forms of endpoint security software, many did not, and even those that did rarely addressed any hardware-based risks. To this day, for example, many employers have no idea what router models their employees are using for remote access or when such devices were last updated.

Another major cybersecurity concern created by the pandemic has been that communications between employees shifted from conference rooms to remote meetings, opening the doors for hackers to disrupt communications or steal confidential information. The problems were so bad that a new term "zoom bombing" was coined in 2020 to refer to the practice of mischievous folks joining and wreaking havoc in virtual meetings to which they were never invited.

Of course, the fact that people who would otherwise work together in the same location are suddenly unable to communicate quickly in person has also opened the door for many social engineering attacks. For example, a CFO who receives an email from the boss asking that the company pay a certain party for services cannot verify the validity of the request as the CFO has done many times in the past by walking ten feet to the boss's office to confirm that the boss actually sent the message.

Likewise, people working in homes in which children are in virtual school, or quarantined, or simply living, often suffer from far more interruptions than they would had they been working in an office setting. Interruptions often lead to mistakes, and mistakes often lead to cybersecurity problems. The stress of remaining socially isolated for long periods of time also increases the odds of people making dangerous cybersecurity errors.

At a macro level, the sudden shift to work-at-home arrangements has meant that many cybersecurity professionals are increasingly overwhelmed, a problem further exacerbated by organizations having to reallocate resources — sometimes shifting both people and money from security projects to efforts to ensure continuity of operations.

And, of course, being confined to their homes has afforded many hackers more time to work on their crafts as well, perhaps contributing to the significant rise in the number of zero-day attacks and other newer forms of cybersecurity attacks seen since the pandemic's onset. Chapter 2 dives into many of the common cyberattacks that are out there.

REMEMBER

Entire books have been written on the impact of technological advancement. The main point to understand is that technological advancement has had a significant impact on cybersecurity, making security harder to deliver and raising the stakes when parties fail to properly protect their assets. In addition, unforeseen developments, such as pandemics, can bring sudden, huge technological changes that carry with them tremendous cybersecurity dangers.

Social shifts

Various changes in the ways that humans behave and interact with one another have also had a major impact on cybersecurity. The Internet, for example, allows people from all over the world to interact in real-time. Of course, this real-time interaction also enables criminals all over the world to commit crimes remotely. But it also allows citizens of repressive countries and free countries to communicate, creating opportunities for dispelling the perpetual propaganda utilized as excuses for the failure of totalitarianism to produce quality of lives on par with the democratic world. At the same time, it also delivers to the cyberwarriors of governments at odds with one another the ability to launch attacks via the same network.

The conversion of various information management systems from paper to computer, from isolated to Internet-connected, and from accessible-only-in-the-office to accessible from any smartphone or computer has dramatically changed the equation when it comes to what information hackers can steal. And the COVID-19 pandemic has brought many of these issues to the forefront.

Furthermore, in many cases in which technological conversions were, for security reasons, not initially done, the pressure emanating from the expectations of modern people that every piece of data be available to them at all times from anywhere has forced such conversions to occur, creating additional opportunities for criminals. To the delight of hackers, many organizations that, in the past, wisely protected sensitive information by keeping it offline have simply lost the ability to enjoy such protections if they want to stay in business. No modern example portrays this as well as the sudden global shift to remote working arrangements in 2020.

Social media has also transformed the world of information — with people growing accustomed to sharing far more about themselves than ever before — often with audiences far larger than before as well. Today, due to the behavioral shift in this regard, it is trivial for evildoers from anywhere to assemble lists of a target's friends, professional colleagues, and relatives and to establish mechanisms for communication with all those people. Likewise, it is easier than ever before to find out what technologies a particular firm utilizes and for what purposes, discover people's travel schedules, and ascertain their opinions on various topics or their tastes in music and movies. The trend toward increased sharing continues. Most people remain blindly unaware of, and unconcerned with, how much information about them lives on Internet-connected machines and how much other information about them can be extrapolated from the aforementioned data.

All these changes have translated into a scary reality: Due to societal shifts, evildoers can easily launch much larger, more sophisticated social engineering attacks today than they could just a few years.

Economic model shifts

Connecting nearly the entire world has allowed the Internet to facilitate other trends with tremendous cybersecurity ramifications. Operational models that were once unthinkable, such as that of an American company utilizing a call center in India and a software development shop in the Philippines, have become the mainstay of many corporations. These changes, however, create cybersecurity risks of many kinds.

The last 20 years have seen a tremendous growth in the outsourcing of various tasks from locations in which they're more expensive to carry out to regions in which they can be accomplished at much lower costs. The notion that a company in the United States could rely primarily on computer programmers in India or in the Philippines or that entrepreneurs in New York seeking to have a logo made for their business could, shortly before going to bed, pay someone halfway around the globe $5.50 to create it and have the logo in their email inbox immediately upon waking up the next morning, would have sounded like economic science-fiction a generation ago. Today, it's not only common, but also in many cases, it is more common than any other method of achieving similar results.

Of course, many cybersecurity ramifications result from such transformations of how people do business.

Data being transmitted needs to be protected from destruction, modification, and theft, and globalization means that greater assurance is needed to ensure that back doors are not intentionally or inadvertently inserted into code. Greater protections are needed to prevent the theft of intellectual property and other forms of corporate espionage. Code developed in foreign countries, for example, may be at risk of having backdoors inserted by agents of their respective governments. Likewise, computer equipment may have backdoors inserted into hardware components — a problem the U.S. government is struggling with addressing as this book goes to print.

WARNING

Hackers no longer necessarily need to directly breach the organizations they seek to hack; they merely need to compromise one or more of the organizations' providers. And such providers may be far less careful with their information security and personnel practices than the ultimate target, or may be subject to manipulation by governments far less respectful of people's rights than are the powers-that-be in the ultimate targets' location.

Political shifts

As with advances in technology, political shifts have had tremendous cybersecurity repercussions, some of which seem to be permanent fixtures of news headlines. The combination of government power and mighty technology has often proven to be a costly one for ordinary people. If current trends continue, the impact on cybersecurity of various political shifts will continue to grow substantially in the foreseeable future.

Data collection

The proliferation of information online and the ability to attack machines all over the world have meant that governments can spy on citizens of their own countries and on the residents of other nations to an extent never before possible.

Furthermore, as more and more business, personal, and societal activities leave behind digital footprints, governments have much easier access to a much greater amount of information about their potential intelligence targets than they could acquire even at dramatically higher costs just a few years ago. Coupled with the relatively low cost of digital storage, advancing big data technologies, and the expected eventual impotence of many of today's encryption technologies due to the emergence of quantum computing and other cutting-edge developments, governments have a strong incentive to collect and store as much information as they can about as many people as they can, in case it is of use at some later date. It is more likely than not, for example, that hostile governments may have already begun compiling dossiers on the people who will eventually serve as president and vice president of the United States 25 years from now.

The long-term consequences of this phenomenon are, obviously, as of yet unknown, but one thing is clear: If businesses do not properly protect data, less-than-friendly nations are likely to obtain it and store it for use in either the short term, the long term, or both.

Election interference

A generation ago, for one nation to interfere in the elections of another was no trivial matter. Of course, such interference existed — it has occurred as long as there have been elections — but carrying out significant interference campaigns was expensive, resource-intensive, and extremely risky.

To spread misinformation and other propaganda, materials had to be printed and physically distributed or recorded and transmitted via radio, meaning that individual campaigns were likely to reach only small audiences. As such, the efficacy effects of such efforts were often quite low, and the risk of the party running the campaign being exposed was relatively high, and often carried with it the potential for severe repercussions.

Manipulating voter registration databases to prevent legitimate voters from voting and/or to allow bogus voters to vote was extremely difficult and entailed tremendous risks; someone "working on the inside" would likely have had to be nothing short of a traitor in order to have any real significant on election results. In a country such as the United States, in which voter registration databases are decentralized and managed on a county level, recruiting sufficient saboteurs to truly impact a major election would likely have been impossible, and the odds of getting caught while attempting to do so were likely extremely high.

Likewise, in the era of paper ballots cast in person and of manual vote counting, for a foreign power to manipulate actual vote counts on any large scale was impractical, if not impossible.

Today, however, the game has changed. A government can easily spread misinformation through social media at an extremely low cost. If it crafts a well-thought-out campaign, it can rely on other people to spread the misinformation — something that people could not do en masse in the era of radio recordings and printed pamphlets. The ability to reach many more people, at a much lower cost than ever before, has meant that more parties are able to interfere in political campaigns and can do so with more efficacy than in the past. Similarly, governments can spread misinformation to stir up civil discontent within their adversaries nations and to spread hostility between ethnic and religious groups living in foreign lands.

Insecure mail-in ballots as used throughout the United States during the 2020 presidential election aggravated mistrust. And, with voter registration databases stored electronically and sometimes on servers that are at least indirectly connected to the Internet, records may be able to be added, modified, or deleted from halfway across the globe without detection. Even if such hacking is, in reality, impossible, the fact that many citizens today believe that it may be possible has led to an undermining of faith in elections, a phenomenon that we have witnessed in recent years and that has permeated throughout all levels of society. Even Jimmy Carter, a former president of the United States, expressed at one point that that he believed that full investigation into the 2016 presidential election would show that Donald Trump lost the election — despite there being absolutely no evidence whatsoever to support such a conclusion, even after a thorough FBI investigation into the matter. Statements and actions from the other side of the political aisle — including the terrible chaos at the U.S. Capitol after the 2020 presidential election — showed clearly that concerns about election integrity, and the perception that our elections might be manipulatable through cyberattacks and other technology-based techniques, are bipartisan. It is also not hard to imagine that if online voting were ever to arrive, the potential for vote manipulation by foreign governments, criminals, and even political parties within the nation voting — and for removing the ballot auditability that exists today — would grow astronomically.

In an indication of how much concern is growing around potential election manipulation, consider that a decade ago, the United States did not consider election-related computer systems to be critical infrastructure, and did not directly provide federal funding to secure such systems. Today, most people understand that the need for cybersecurity in such areas is of paramount importance, and the policies and behavior of just a few years ago seems nothing short of crazy.

Hacktivism

Likewise, the spread of democracy since the collapse of the Soviet Union a generation ago, coupled with Internet-based interaction between people all over the globe, has ushered in the era of *hacktivism*. People are aware of the goings-on in more places than in the past. Hackers angry about some government policy or activity in some location may target that government or the citizens of the country over which it rules from places far away. Likewise, citizens of one country may target entities in another country with whose policies they disagree, or whose government they consider a national adversary.

Greater freedom

At the same time, repressed people are now more aware of the lifestyles of people in freer and more prosperous countries, a phenomenon that has both forced some governments to liberalize, and motivated others to implement cybersecurity-type controls to prevent using various Internet-based services.

Sanctions

Another political ramification of cybersecurity pertains to international sanctions: Rogue states subject to such sanctions have been able to use cybercrime of various forms to circumvent such sanctions.

For example, North Korea is believed to have spread malware that mines cryptocurrency for the totalitarian state to computers all over the world, thereby allowing the country to circumvent sanctions by obtaining liquid money that can easily be spent anywhere.

Thus, the failure by individuals to adequately secure their personal computers can directly impact political negotiations.

New balances of power

While the militaries of certain nations have long since grown more powerful than those of their adversaries — both the quality and quantity of weapons vary greatly between nations — when it comes to cybersecurity the balance of power is totally different.

While the quality of cyberweapons may vary between countries, the fact that launching cyberattacks costs little means that all militaries have an effectively unlimited supply of whatever weapons they use. In fact, in most cases, launching millions of cyberattacks costs little more than launching just one.

Also, unlike in the physical world in which any nation that bombed civilian homes in the territory of its adversary can reasonably expect to face a severe reprisal, rogue governments regularly hack with impunity people in other countries. Victims often are totally unaware that they have been compromised, rarely report such incidents to law enforcement, and certainly don't know whom to blame.

Even when a victim realizes that a breach has occurred and even when technical experts point to the attackers as the culprits, the states behind such attacks often enjoy plausible deniability (for example, they claim, "we didn't do it, maybe someone else within our country did it" or the like), preventing any government from publicly retaliating. In fact, the difficulty of ascertaining the source of cyberattacks coupled with the element of plausible deniability is a strong incentive for governments to use cyberattacks as a mechanism of proactively attacking an adversary, wreaking various forms of havoc without fear of significant reprisals.

Furthermore, the world of cybersecurity created a tremendous imbalance between attackers and defenders that works to the advantage of less powerful nations.

Governments that could never afford to launch huge barrages against an adversary in the physical world can easily do so in the world of cyber, where launching each attack costs next to nothing. As a result, attackers can afford to keep attacking until they succeed — and they need to breach systems only once to "succeed" — creating a tremendous problem for defenders who must shield their assets against every single attack. This imbalance has translated into a major advantage for attackers over defenders and has meant that even minor powers can successfully breach systems belonging to superpowers.

In fact, this imbalance contributes to the reason why cybersecurity breaches seem to occur so often, as many hackers simply keep attacking until they succeed. If an organization successfully defends against 10 million attacks but fails to stop the

10,000,001, it may suffer a severe breach and make the news. Reports of the breach likely won't even mention the fact that it has a 99.999999 percent success rate in protecting its data and that it successfully stopped attackers one million times in a row. Likewise, if a business installed 99.999 percent of the patches that it should have but neglected to fix a single known vulnerability, it's likely to suffer a breach due to the number of exploits available to criminals. Media outlets will point out the organization's failure to properly patch, overlooking its near perfect record in that area.

As such, the era of cybercrime has also changed the balance of power between criminals and law enforcement.

Criminals know that the odds of being caught and successfully prosecuted for a cybercrime are dramatically smaller than those for most other crimes, and that repeated failed attempts to carry out a cybercrime are not a recipe for certain arrest as they are for most other crimes. They are also aware that law enforcement agencies lack the resources to pursue the vast majority of cyber criminals. Tracking down, taking into custody, and successfully prosecuting someone stealing data from halfway across the world via numerous hops in many countries and a network of computers commandeered from law-abiding folks, for example, requires gathering and dedicating significantly more resources than does catching a thief who was recorded on camera while holding up in a store in a local police precinct. It is also far easier and more lucrative to launch cyberattacks against rich targets from a locale in which law enforcement can be "paid off" to look the other way, than it is to net the same reward via a physical robbery.

With the low cost of launching repeated attacks, the odds of eventual success in their favor, the odds of getting caught and punished miniscule, and the potential rewards growing with increased digitalization, criminals know that cybercrime pays, underscoring the reason that you need to protect yourself.

Looking at the Risks Cybersecurity Mitigates

People sometimes explain the reason that cybersecurity is important as being "because it prevent hackers from breaking into systems and stealing data and money." But such a description dramatically understates the role that cybersecurity plays in keeping the modern home, business, or even world running, and in keeping humans safe from physical harm.

In fact, the role of cybersecurity can be looked at from a variety of different vantage points, with each presenting a different set of goals. Of course the following lists aren't complete, but they should provide food for thought and underscore the importance of understanding how to cybersecure yourself and your loved ones.

The goal of cybersecurity: The CIA Triad

Cybersecurity professionals often explain that the goal of cybersecurity is to ensure the Confidentiality, Integrity, and Availability (CIA) of data, sometimes referred to as the CIA Triad, with the pun lovingly intended:

WARNING

>> **Confidentiality** refers to ensuring that information isn't disclosed or in any other way made available to unauthorized entities (including people, organizations, or computer processes).

Don't confuse confidentiality with privacy: Confidentiality is a subset of the realm of privacy. It deals specifically with protecting data from unauthorized viewers, whereas privacy in general encompasses much more.

Hackers that steal data undermine confidentiality.

>> **Integrity** refers to ensuring that data is both accurate and complete.

Accurate means, for example, that the data is never modified in any way by any unauthorized party or by a technical glitch. *Complete* refers to, for example, data that has had no portion of itself removed by any unauthorized party or technical glitch.

Integrity also includes ensuring *nonrepudiation,* meaning that data is created and handled in such a fashion that nobody can reasonably argue that the data is not authentic or is inaccurate.

Cyberattacks that intercept data and modify it before relaying it to its destination — sometimes known as *man-in-the-middle attacks* — undermine integrity.

>> **Availability** refers to ensuring that information, the systems used to store and process it, the communication mechanisms used to access and relay it, and all associated security controls function correctly to meet some specific benchmark (for example, 99.99 percent uptime). People outside of the cybersecurity field sometimes think of availability as a secondary aspect of information security after confidentiality and integrity. In fact, ensuring availability is an integral part of cybersecurity. Doing so, though, is sometimes more difficult than ensuring confidentiality or integrity. One reason that this is true is that maintaining availability often requires involving many more noncybersecurity professionals, leading to a "too many cooks in the kitchen" type challenge, especially in larger organizations. Distributed denial-of-service attacks attempt to undermine availability. Also, consider that attacks often use large numbers of stolen computer power and bandwidth to launch DDoS attacks, but responders who seek to ensure availability can only leverage the relatively small amount of resources that they can afford.

From a human perspective

The risks that cybersecurity addresses can also be thought of in terms better reflecting the human experience:

>> **Privacy risks:** Risks emanating from the potential loss of adequate control over, or misuse of, personal or other confidential information.

>> **Financial risks:** Risks of financial losses due to hacking. Financial losses can include both those that are direct — for example, the theft of money from someone's bank account by a hacker who hacked into the account — and those that are indirect, such as the loss of customers who no longer trust a small business after the latter suffers a security breach.

>> **Professional risks:** Risks to one's professional career that stem from breaches. Obviously, cybersecurity professionals are at risk for career damage if a breach occurs under their watch and is determined to have happened due to negligence, but other types of professionals can suffer career harm due to a breach as well. C-level executives can be fired, board members can be sued, and so on. Professional damage can also occur if hackers release private communications or data that shows someone in a bad light — for example, records that a person was disciplined for some inappropriate action, sent an email containing objectionable material, and so on.

>> **Business risks:** Risks to a business similar to the professional risks to an individual. Internal documents leaked after breach of Sony Pictures painted various the firm in a negative light vis-à-vis some of its compensation practices.

>> **Personal risks:** Many people store private information on their electronic devices, from explicit photos to records of participation in activities that may not be deemed respectable by members of their respective social circles. Such data can sometimes cause significant harm to personal relationships if it leaks. Likewise, stolen personal data can help criminals steal people's identities, which can result in all sorts of personal problems.

>> **Physical danger risks:** Cyberattacks on sewage treatment plants, utilities, and hospitals in recent years have shown clearly that the failure to maintain cybersecurity can lead to the endangering of human lives. For example, in 2020, a woman in Germany died while being transported between hospitals after the hospital at which she had been a patient was struck by ransomware. And in 2021, a lawsuit was filed arguing that a baby died as a result of medical mistakes made as she was born at a hospital in Alabama during system outages caused by a ransomware attack.

Chapter **2**

Getting to Know Common Cyberattacks

Many different types of cyberattacks exist — so many that I could write an entire series of books about them and add many new chapters every year. In this book, however, I do not cover all types of threats in detail because the reality is, you're likely reading this book to learn about how to keep yourself cybersecure, not to learn about matters that have no impact on you, such as forms of attacks that are normally directed at espionage agencies, industrial equipment, or military armaments.

In this chapter, you find out about the different types of problems that cyberattackers can create through the use of attacks that commonly impact individuals and small businesses.

Attacks That Inflict Damage

Attackers launch some forms of cyberattacks with the intent to inflict damage to victims. The threat posed by such attacks is not that a criminal will directly steal your money or data, but that the attackers will inflict harm to you in some other specific manner — a manner that may ultimately translate into financial, military, political, physical, or other benefit to the attacker and (potentially) damage of some sort to the victim.

Types of attacks that inflict damage include

» Denial-of-service (DoS) attacks

» Distributed denial-of-service (DDoS) attacks

» Botnets and zombies

» Data destruction attacks

Denial-of-service (DoS) attacks

A *denial-of-service (DoS) attack* is one in which an attacker intentionally attempts to either partially cripple or totally paralyze a computer or computer network by flooding it with large amounts of requests or data, which overload the target and make it incapable of responding properly to legitimate requests.

In many cases, the requests sent by the attacker are each, on their own, legitimate — for example, a normal request to load a web page. In other cases, the requests aren't normal requests. Instead, they leverage knowledge of various protocols to send requests that optimize, or even magnify, the effect of the attack.

In any case, denial-of-service attacks work by overwhelming computer systems' central processing units (CPUs) and/or memory, utilizing all the available network communications bandwidth, and/or exhausting networking infrastructure resources such as routers.

Distributed denial-of-service (DDoS) attacks

A *distributed denial-of-service (DDoS) attack* is a DoS attack in which many individual computers or other connected devices across disparate regions simultaneously flood the target with requests. In recent years, nearly all major denial-of-service attacks have been distributed in nature — and some have involved the use of Internet-connected cameras and other devices as attack vehicles, rather than classic computers. Figure 2-1 illustrates the anatomy of a simple DDoS attack.

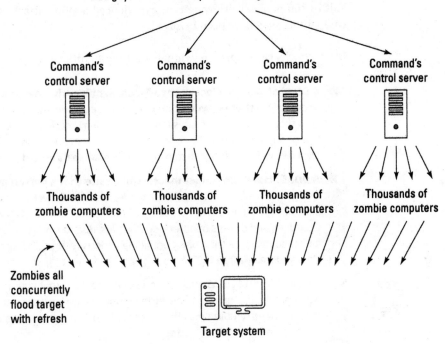

A DDoS ATTACK

Bad guy in front of computer running DDoS attack tool client

| Command's control server | Command's control server | Command's control server | Command's control server |

Thousands of zombie computers | Thousands of zombie computers | Thousands of zombie computers | Thousands of zombie computers

Zombies all concurrently flood target with refresh

FIGURE 2-1:
A DDoS attack.

Target system

The goal of a DDoS attack is to knock the victim offline, and the motivation for doing so varies.

Sometimes the goal is financial: Imagine, for example, the damage that may result to an online retailer's business if an unscrupulous competitor knocked the former's site offline during Black Friday weekend. Imagine a crook who shorts the stock of a major retailer of toys right before launching a DDoS attack against the retailer two weeks before Christmas.

DDoS attacks remain a serious and growing threat. Criminal enterprises even offer DDoS for hire services, which are advertised on the dark web as offering, for a fee, to "take your competitor's websites offline in a cost-effective manner."

In some cases, DDoS launchers may have political, rather than financial, motives. For example, corrupt politicians may seek to have their opponents' websites taken down during an election season, thereby reducing the competitors' abilities to spread messages and receive online campaign contributions. Hacktivists may also launch DDoS attacks in order to take down sites in the name of "justice" — for example, targeting law enforcement sites after an unarmed person is killed during an altercation with police.

In fact, according to a 2017 study by Kaspersky Lab and B2B International, almost half of companies worldwide that experienced a DDoS attack suspect that their competitors may have been involved.

DDoS attacks can impact individuals in three significant ways:

>> **A DDoS attack on a local network can significantly slow down all Internet access from that network.** Sometimes these attacks make connectivity so slow that connections to sites fail due to *session timeout* settings, meaning that the systems terminate the connections after seeing requests take longer to elicit responses than some maximum permissible threshold.

>> **A DDoS attack can render inaccessible a site that a person plans on using.** On October 21, 2016, for example, many users were unable to reach several high-profile sites, including Twitter, PayPal, CNN, HBO Now, The Guardian, and dozens of other popular sites, due to a massive DDoS attack launched against a third party providing various technical services for these sites and many more.

TIP

The possibility of DDoS attacks is one of the reasons that you should never wait until the last minute to perform an online banking transaction — the site that you need to utilize may be inaccessible for a number of reasons, one of which is an ongoing DDoS attack.

>> **A DDoS attack can lead users to obtain information from one site instead of another.** By making one site unavailable, Internet users looking for specific information are likely to obtain it from another site — a phenomenon that allows attackers to either spread misinformation or prevent people from hearing certain information or vantage points on important issues. As such, DDoS attacks can be used as an effective mechanism — at least over the short term — for censoring opposing points of view.

Botnets and zombies

Often, DDoS attacks use what are known as *botnets*. Botnets are a collection of compromised computers that belong to other parties, but that a hacker remotely controls and uses to perform tasks without the legitimate owners' knowledge.

Criminals who successfully infect one million computers with malware can, for example, potentially use those machines, known as *zombies*, to simultaneously make many requests from a single server or server farm in an attempt to overload the target with traffic.

Data destruction attacks

Sometimes attackers want to do more than take a party temporarily offline by overwhelming it with requests — they may want to damage the victim by destroying or corrupting the target's information and/or information systems. A criminal may seek to destroy a user's data through a *data destruction attack* — for example, if the user refuses to pay a ransomware ransom that the crook demands. Of course, all the reasons for launching DDoS attacks (see preceding section) are also reasons that a hacker may attempt to destroy someone's data as well.

Wiper attacks are advanced data destruction attacks in which a criminal uses malware to wipe the data on a victim's hard drive or SSD, in such a fashion that the data is difficult or impossible to recover.

To put it simply, unless the victim has backups, someone whose computer is wiped by a wiper is likely to lose access to all the data and software that was previously stored on the attacked device.

Is That Really You? Impersonation

One of the great dangers that the Internet creates is the ease with which mischievous parties can impersonate others. Prior to the Internet era, for example, criminals could not easily impersonate a bank or a store and convince people to hand over their money in exchange for some promised rate of interest or goods. Physically mailed letters and later telephone calls became the tools of scammers, but none of those earlier communication techniques ever came close to the power of the Internet to aid criminals attempting to impersonate law-abiding parties.

Creating a website that mimics the website of a bank, store, or government agency is quite simple and can sometimes be done within minutes. Criminals can find a near-endless supply of domain names that are close enough to those of legitimate parties to trick some folks into believing that a site that they are seeing is the real deal when it's not, giving crooks the typical first ingredient in the recipe for online impersonation.

WARNING

Sending an email that appears to have come from someone else is simple and allows criminals to perpetrate all sorts of crimes online. I myself demonstrated over 20 years ago how I could defeat various defenses and send an email that was delivered to recipients on a secure system — the message appeared to readers to have been sent from god@heaven.sky.

Phishing

Phishing refers to an attempt to convince a person to take some action by imper-sonating a trustworthy party that reasonably may legitimately ask the user to take such action.

For example, a criminal may send an email that appears to have been sent by a major bank and that asks recipients to click on a link in order to reset their pass-words due to a possible data breach. When users click the link, they are directed to a website that appears to belong to the bank, but is actually a replica run by the criminal. As such, the criminal uses the fraudulent website to collect usernames and passwords to the banking site.

WARNING

While phishing attacks have been around for many years, they show no signs of going away. Some experts believe that a majority of medium- and large-sized businesses in the United States now suffer some form of successful phishing attack every year.

Spear phishing

Spear phishing refers to phishing attacks that are designed and sent to target a specific person, business, or organization. If a criminal seeks to obtain credentials into a specific company's email system, for example, the attacker may send emails crafted specifically for particular targeted individuals within the organization. Often, criminals who spear phish research their targets online and leverage over-shared information on social media in order to craft especially legitimate-sounding emails.

For example, the following type of email is typically a lot more convincing than, "Please login to the mail server and reset your password":

> *Hi, I am going to be getting on my flight in ten minutes. Can you please log in to the Exchange server and check when my meeting is? For some reason, I cannot get in. You can try to call me by phone first for security reasons, but if you miss me, just go ahead, check the information, and email it to me — as you know that I am getting on a flight that is about to take off.*

CEO fraud

CEO fraud is similar to spear phishing (see preceding section) in that it involves a criminal impersonating the CEO or other senior executive of a particular business, but the instructions provided by "the CEO" may be to take an action directly, not to log in to a system, and the goal may not be to capture usernames and passwords or the like.

The crook, for example, may send an email to the firm's CFO with instructions to issue a wire payment to a particular new vendor or to send all the organization's W2 forms for the year to a particular email address belonging to the firm's accountant.

CEO fraud often nets significant returns for criminals and makes employees who fall for the scams appear incompetent. As a result, people who fall prey to such scams are often fired from their jobs. CEO fraud increased during the COVID-19 pandemic as people worked from home and were unable to verify the veracity of communications with as much ease as they could prior to the arrival of the novel coronavirus.

Smishing

Smishing refers to cases of phishing in which the attackers deliver their messages via text messages (SMS) rather than email. The goal may be to capture usernames and passwords or to trick the user into installing malware.

Vishing

Vishing, or voice-based phishing, is phishing via POTS — that stands for "plain old telephone service." Yes, criminals use old, time-tested methods for scamming people. Today, most such calls are transmitted by Voice over Internet Protocol (VoIP) systems, but in the end, the scammers are calling people on regular telephones much the same way that scammers have been doing for decades.

Pharming

Pharming refers to attacks that present much like typical phishing attacks, but exploit different technical vulnerabilities in Internet-based routing in order to do so. Like phishing attacks, pharming attacks involve impersonating a trustworthy party that may legitimately ask the would-be victim to take some particular action. However, in pharming attacks, this is achieved not by tricking users into taking an action that brings them to a rogue clone of a legitimate website, but rather by poisoning routing tables and other network infrastructure so that any user who clicks a link to the legitimate website, or even enters the legitimate website's URL into a browser, will be routed to a criminal's clone.

Whaling: Going for the "big fish"

Whaling refers to spear phishing that targets high-profile business executives or government officials. (I know that whales are mammals and not fish, but this is about phishing not fishing.) For more on spear phishing, see the section earlier in this chapter.

Messing around with Other People's Stuff: Tampering

Sometimes attackers don't want to disrupt an organization's normal activities, but instead seek to exploit those activities for financial gain. Often, crooks achieve such objectives by manipulating data in transit or as it resides on systems of their targets in a process known as *tampering*.

In a basic case of tampering with data in transit, for example, imagine that a user of online banking has instructed the bank to wire money to a particular account, but somehow a criminal intercepted the request and changed the relevant routing and account number to the criminal's own.

A criminal may also hack into a system and manipulate information for similar purposes. Using the previous example, imagine if a criminal changed the payment address associated with a particular payee so that when the Accounts Payable department makes an online payment, the funds are sent to the wrong destination (well, at least it is wrong in the eyes of the payer).

One can also imagine the impact of a criminal modifying an analyst's report about a particular stock before the report is issued to the public, with the criminal, of course, standing by to buy or sell stocks when the report is released in order to exploit the soon-to-be-reversed impact of the misinformation.

Captured in Transit: Interception

Interception occurs when attackers capture information in transit. In the context of cybersecurity, the transit is usually between computers or other electronic devices, but it could also be between a human and a device as well (such as capturing voice spoken to a voice recognition system). If the data isn't properly encrypted, the party intercepting it may be able to misuse it. And, of course, data captured directly from humans — such as the aforementioned voice recordings — often cannot be encrypted.

WARNING

Even properly encrypted data might be at risk. The protection afforded by today's encryption algorithms and mechanisms may be rendered worthless at some point in the future if vulnerabilities are discovered down the road, or as more powerful computers — especially quantum computers — arrive on the scene. As such, encrypted data that is intercepted may be secure from disclosure today, but may be stored and compromised in the future.

Man-in-the-middle attacks

One special type of interception is known as a *man-in-the-middle attack*. In this type of an attack, the interceptor proxies the data between the sender and recipient in an attempt to disguise the fact that the data is being intercepted. *Proxying* in such a case refers to the man-in-the-middle intercepting requests and then transmitting them (either in modified form or unmodified) to their original intended destinations and then receiving the responses from those destination and transmitting them (in modified form or unmodified) back to the sender. By employing proxying, the man-in-the-middle makes it difficult for senders to know that their communications are being intercepted because when they communicate with a server, they receive the responses they expect.

For example, a criminal may set up a bogus bank site (see the earlier "Phishing" section) and relay any information that anyone enters on the bogus site to the actual bank site so that the criminal can respond with the same information that the legitimate bank would have sent. Proxying of this sort not only helps criminals avoid detection — users who provide the crook with their password and then perform their normal online banking tasks may have no idea that anything abnormal occurred during the online banking session — but also helps the criminals ensure that they capture the right password. If a user enters an incorrect password, the criminal will know to prompt for the correct one.

Figure 2-2 shows the anatomy of a man-in-the-middle intercepting and relaying communications.

Man-in-the-middle attack
Joe wants to communicate with his bank

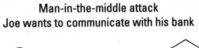

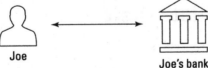

But Bob's evil server is acting as a man-in-the-middle

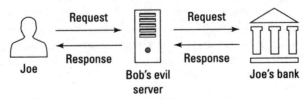

FIGURE 2-2: A man-in-the-middle interception.

Taking What Isn't Theirs: Data Theft

Many cyberattacks involve stealing the victim's data. An attacker may want to steal data belonging to individuals, businesses, or a government agency for one or more of many possible reasons.

People, businesses, nonprofits, and governments are all vulnerable to data theft.

Personal data theft

Criminals often try to steal people's data in the hope of finding items that they can monetize, including:

» Data that can be used for identity theft or sold to identity thieves

» Compromising photos or health-related data that may be sellable or used as part of blackmail schemes

» Information that is stolen and then erased from the user's machine that can be ransomed to the user

» Password lists that can be used for breaching other systems

» Confidential information about work-related matters that may be used to make illegal stock trades based on insider information

» Information about upcoming travel plans that may be used to plan robberies of the victim's home

Business data theft

Criminals can use data stolen from businesses for a number of nefarious purposes:

» **Making stock trades:** Similar to the criminals mentioned earlier in this chapter who tamper with data in order to manipulate financial markets, criminals may also seek to steal data in order to have advance knowledge of how a particular business's current and yet unreported quarter is going. They then use that insider information to illegally trade stocks or options, thereby potentially making a significant profit.

» **Selling data to unscrupulous competitors:** Criminals who steal sales pipeline information, documents containing details of future products, or other sensitive information can sell that data to unscrupulous competitors or to unscrupulous employees working at competitors whose management may never find out how such employees suddenly improved their performance.

» **Leaking data to the media:** Sensitive data can embarrass the victim and cause its stock to decline (perhaps after selling short some shares).

» **Leaking data covered by privacy regulations:** The victim may be potentially fined.

» **Recruiting employees:** By recruiting employees or selling the information to other firms looking to hire employees with similar skills or with knowledge of competitions' systems, criminals who steal emails and discover communication between employees that indicates that one or more employees are unhappy in their current positions can sell that information to parties looking to hire.

» **Stealing and using intellectual property:** Parties that steal the source code for computer software may be able to avoid paying licensing fees to the software's rightful owner. Parties that steal design documents created by others after extensive research and development can easily save millions of dollars — and, sometimes, even billions of dollars — in research and development costs. For more on the effects of this type of theft, see the nearby sidebar "How a cyberbreach cost one company $1 billion without 1 cent being stolen."

Data exfiltration

Data exfiltration is a somewhat complicated term for a simple concept, and refers to situations in which a party, through the use of malware or other automated means, or by manually issuing commands to a remote computer, causes data to be transferred without authorization from some information system or repository to somewhere else.

Anytime you hear of a data breach in which sensitive data has been copied by criminals, that is an example of data exfiltration. Depending on what data leaks and from whom, data exfiltration can easily harm the confidence of a business's customers, reduce trust in a government entity, undermine the confidentiality of proprietary information, and/or undermine national security.

Compromised credentials

Compromised credentials refers to account authentication information that someone else other than you is privy to, such as your username and/or password. Abusing compromised credentials almost always refers to situations in which a criminal uses a login and password combination that was obtained from one cybersecurity breach in order to gain unauthorized access to a system and carry out another cybersecurity breach. Such attacks with compromised credentials are common, as criminals know that people commonly reuse login username/password combinations.

Likewise, use by a rogue employee of another employee's credentials for any nefarious purpose (and even for most non-nefarious purposes) is also an example of such an attack.

Forced policy violations

Any attack in which a user or device is forced to violate cybersecurity policies is considered a forced policy violation attack.

Cyberbombs That Sneak into Your Devices: Malware

Malware, or malicious software, is an all-encompassing term for software that intentionally inflicts damage on its users who typically have no idea that they are running it. Malware includes computer viruses, worms, Trojans, ransomware, scareware, spyware, cryptocurrency miners, adware, and other programs intended to exploit computer resources for nefarious purposes.

Viruses

Computer viruses are instances of malware that, when executed, replicate by inserting their own code into computer systems. Typically, the insertion is in data files (for example, as rogue macros within a Word document), the special portion of hard drives or solid state drives that contain the code and data used to boot a computer or disk (also known as *boot sectors*), or other computer programs.

Like biological viruses, computer viruses can spread like wildfire, but they cannot spread without having hosts to infect. Some computer viruses significantly impact the performance of their hosts, while others are, at least at times, hardly noticeable.

REMEMBER

While computer viruses still inflict tremendous damage worldwide, the majority of serious malware threats today arrive in the form of worms and Trojans.

Worms

Computer worms are stand-alone pieces of malware that replicate themselves without the need for hosts in order to spread. Worms often propagate over connections by exploiting security vulnerabilities on target computers and networks. Because they normally consume network bandwidth, worms can inflict harm even without modifying systems or stealing data. They can slow down network connections — and few people, if any, like to see their internal and Internet connections slow down.

Trojans

Trojans (appropriately named after the historical Trojan horse) is malware that is either disguised as nonmalicious software or hidden within a legitimate, nonmalicious application or piece of digital data.

Trojans are most often spread by some form of social engineering — for example, by tricking people into clicking on a link, installing an app, or running some email attachment. Unlike viruses and worms, Trojans typically don't self-propagate using technology — instead, they rely on the effort (or more accurately, the mistakes) of humans.

Ransomware

Ransomware is malware that demands that a ransom be paid to some criminal in exchange for the infected party not suffering some harm. Ransomware often encrypts user files and threatens to delete the encryption key if a ransom isn't paid within some relatively short period of time, but other forms of ransomware involve a criminal actually stealing user data and threatening to publish it online if a ransom is not paid.

Some ransomware actually steals the files from users' computers, rather than simply encrypting data, so as to ensure that users have no possible way to recover their data (for example, using an anti-ransomware utility) without paying the ransom.

Ransomware is most often delivered to victims as a Trojan or a virus, but has also been successfully spread by criminals who packaged it in a worm. In recent years sophisticated criminals have even crafted targeted ransomware campaigns that leverage knowledge about what data is most valuable to a particular target and how much that target can afford to pay in ransoms.

Figure 2-3 shows the ransom demand screen of WannaCry — a flavor of ransomware that inflicted at least hundreds of millions of dollars in damage (if not billions), after initially spreading in May 2017. Many security experts believe that the North Korean government or others working for it created WannaCry, which, within four days infected hundreds of thousands of computers in about 150 countries.

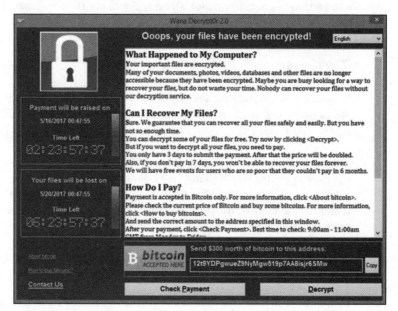

Since publication of the first edition of this book, ransomware has both emerged as one of the largest sources of financial losses due to cyberattacks for American businesses, as well as led to interruptions in the life of ordinary civilians. For example, in 2021, ransomware attacks on an American fuel pipeline operator led to shortages of gas and price increases, and attacks on a meat processing facility led to shortages of meat in some locations (see Chapter 21).

Scareware

Scareware is malware that scares people into taking some action. One common example is malware that scares people into buying security software. A message appears on a device that the device is infected with some virus that only a particular security package can remove, with a link to purchase that "security software." This topic is also explored in the discussion about fake malware later in this chapter.

Spyware

Spyware is software that surreptitiously, and without permission, collects information from a device. Spyware may capture a user's keystrokes (in which case it is called a *keylogger*), video from a video camera, audio from a microphone, screen images, and so on.

It is important to understand the difference between spyware and invasive programs. Some technologies that may technically be considered spyware if users had not been told that they were being tracked online are in use by legitimate businesses; they may be invasive, but they are not malware. These types of *nonspyware that also spies* includes beacons that check whether a user loaded a particular web page and tracking cookies installed by websites or apps. Some experts have argued that any software that tracks a smartphone's location while the app is not being actively used by the device's user also falls into the category of *nonspyware that also spies* — a definition that would include popular apps, such as Uber.

Cryptocurrency miners

Cryptocurrency miners, or cryptominers, are malware that, without any permission from devices' owners, commandeers infected devices' brainpower (its CPU cycles) to generate new units of a particular cryptocurrency (which the malware gives to the criminals operating the malware) by completing complex math problems that require significant processing power to solve.

The proliferation of cryptocurrency miners exploded in 2017 with the rise of cryptocurrency values. Even after price levels subsequently dropped, the miners are still ubiquitous as once criminals have invested in creating the miners, there is little cost in continuing to deploy them. Not surprisingly, as cryptocurrency prices began to rise again in 2019, new strains of cryptominers began to appear as well — some of which specifically target Android smartphones.

Many low-end cybercriminals favor using cryptominers. Even if each miner, on its own, pays the attacker very little, miners are easy to obtain and directly monetize cyberattacks without the need for extra steps (such as collecting a ransom) or the need for sophisticated command and control systems.

Adware

Adware is software that generates revenue for the party operating it by displaying online advertisements on a device. Adware may be malware — that is, installed and run without the permission of a device's owner — or it may be a legitimate component of software (for example, installed knowingly by users as part of some free, ad-supported package).

Some security professionals refer to the former as *adware malware,* and the latter as adware. Because no consensus exists, it's best to clarify which of the two is being discussed when you hear someone mention just the generic term adware.

Blended malware

Blended malware is malware that utilizes multiple types of malware technology as part of an attack — for example, combining features of Trojans, worms, and viruses.

Blended malware can be quite sophisticated and often stems from skilled attackers.

Zero-day malware

Zero-day malware is any malware that exploits a vulnerability not previously known to the public or to the vendor of the technology containing the vulnerability, and is, as such, often extremely potent.

Regularly creating zero-day malware requires significant resource and development. It's quite expensive and is often crafted by the cyber armies of nation states rather than by other hackers.

Commercial purveyors of zero day malware have been known to charge over $1 million for a single exploit.

Fake malware on computers

Ironically, some attackers don't even bother to actually hack computers. Instead, they just send messages to would-be victims that the would-be victims' computers are infected and that to re-secure the device the intended victims must pay some fee or purchase some security software. Sometimes criminals are able to display messages to such an effect in a pop-up window, and sometimes they keep things simple, and just send the messages via email.

Fake malware on mobile devices

Fake malware may be even more common on mobile devices than on laptops and other computers. For various technical reasons, it is harder to hack mobile devices, so many criminals go for the "low hanging fruit" and just pretend to have compromised devices in order to get would-be victims to pay up. There are even flavors of "mobile device ransomware" that display ransomware-type demands without ever having encrypted anything on the mobile device.

Fake security subscription renewal notifications

A type of social-engineering attack that exploits people's desire to remain cyber-secure (and that I have included in the malware section because it is directly related to protection against malware), is fake "renewal notices" from anti-malware product vendors. Email that says one's security software subscription is expiring and asks users to click a link (don't do it!) or to otherwise submit payment for a renewal, can closely parallel their legitimate counterparts. This sort of attack has become extremely common during the COVID-19 pandemic era during which many people worked from home and, more often than ever before, were responsible for making sure they had current security software subscriptions.

Poisoned Web Service Attacks

Many different types of attacks leverage vulnerabilities in servers, and new weaknesses are constantly discovered, which is why cybersecurity professionals have full-time jobs keeping servers safe. Entire books — or even several series of books — can be written on such a topic, which is, obviously, beyond the scope of this work.

That said, it is important for you to understand the basic concepts of server-based attacks because some such attacks can directly impact you.

One such form of attack is a *poisoned web service attack*, or a *poisoned web page attack*. In this type of attack, an attacker hacks into a web server and inserts code onto it that causes it to attack users when they access a page or set of pages that the server is serving.

For example, a hacker may compromise the web server serving www.abc123.com and modify the home page that is served to users accessing the site so that the home page contains malware.

But a hacker does not even need to necessarily breach a system in order to poison web pages!

If a site that allows users to comment on posts isn't properly secured, for example, it may allow a user to add the text of various commands within a comment — commands that, if crafted properly, may be executed by users' browsers any time they load the page that displays the comment. A criminal can insert a command to run a script on the criminal's website, which can receive the authentication credentials of the user to the original site because it is called within the context of one of that site's web pages. Such an attack is known as *cross-site scripting*, and it continues to be a problem even after over a decade of being addressed.

Network Infrastructure Poisoning

As with web servers, many different types of attacks leverage vulnerabilities in network infrastructure, and new weaknesses are constantly discovered. The vast majority of this topic is beyond the scope of this book. That said, as is the case with poisoned web servers, you need to understand the basic concepts of server-based attacks because some such attacks can directly impact you. For example, criminals may exploit various weaknesses in order to add corrupt domain name system (DNS) data into a DNS server.

DNS is the directory of the Internet that translates human readable addresses into their numeric, computer-usable equivalents (IP addresses). For example, if you enter `https://JosephSteinberg.com` into your web browser, DNS directs your connection to an address taking the form of four numbers less than 256 and separated by periods, such as `104.18.45.53`.

By inserting incorrect information into DNS tables, a criminal can cause a DNS server to return an incorrect IP address to a user's computer. Such an attack can easily result in a user's traffic being diverted to a computer of the attacker's choice instead of the user's intended destination. If the criminal sets up a phony bank site on the server to which traffic is being diverted, for example, and impersonates on that server a bank that the user was trying to reach, even a user who enters the bank URL into a browser (as opposed to just clicking on a link) may fall prey after being diverted to the bogus site. (This type of attack is known as *DNS poisoning* or *pharming*.)

REMEMBER

Network infrastructure attacks take many forms. Some seek to route people to the wrong destinations. Others seek to capture data, while others seek to effectuate denial-of-service conditions. The main point to understand is that the piping of the Internet is quite complex was not initially designed with security in mind, and is vulnerable to many forms of misuse.

Malvertising

Malvertising is an abbreviation of the words malicious advertising and refers to the use of online advertising as a vehicle to spread malware or to launch some other form of a cyberattack.

Because many websites display ads that are served and managed by third-party networks and that contain links to various other third parties, online advertisements are a great vehicle for attackers. Even companies that adequately secure their websites may not take proper precautions to ensure that they do not deliver problematic advertisements created by, and managed by, someone else.

As such, malvertising sometimes allows criminals to insert their content into reputable and high-profile websites with large numbers of visitors (something that would be difficult for crooks to achieve otherwise), many of whom may be security conscious and who would not have been exposed to the criminal's content had it been posted on a less reputable site.

Furthermore, because websites often earn money for their owners based on the number of people who click on various ads, website owners generally place ads on their sites in a manner that will attract users to the ads. As such, malvertising allows criminals to reach large audiences via a trusted site without having to hack anything.

Some malvertising requires users to click on the ads in order to become infected with malware; others do not require any user participation — users' devices are infected the moment the ad displays.

Drive-by downloads

Drive-by downloads is somewhat of a euphemism that refers to software that users download without understanding what they are doing. A drive-by download may occur, for example, if users download malware by going to a poisoned website that automatically sends the malware to the users' device when they open the site.

Drive-by downloads also include cases in which users know that they are downloading software, but is not aware of the full consequences of doing so. For example, if a user is presented with a web page that says that a security vulnerability is present on their computer and that tells the user to click on a button that says "Download to install a security patch," the user has provided authorization for the (malicious) download — but only because the user was tricked into believing that the nature of the download was far different than it truly is.

Stealing passwords

Criminals can steal passwords many different ways. Two common methods include

>> **Thefts of password databases:** If a criminal steals a password database from an online store, anyone whose password appears in the database is at risk of having their password compromised. (If the store properly encrypted its

passwords, it may take time for the criminal to perform what is known as a *hash attack,* but nonetheless, passwords — especially those that are likely to be tested early on — may still be at risk. To date, stealing passwords is the most common way that passwords are undermined.

>> **Social engineering attacks:** *Social engineering attacks* are attacks in which a criminal tricks people into doing something they would not have done had they realized that the person making the request was tricking them in some way. One example of stealing a password via social engineering is when a criminal pretends to be a member of the target's tech support department and tells the target that the target must reset a particular password to a particular value to have the associated account tested as is needed after the recovery from some breach, and the target obeys. (For more information, see the earlier section on phishing.)

>> **Credential attacks:** Credential attacks are attacks that seek to gain entry into a system by entering, without authorization, a valid username and password combination (or other authentication information as needed). These attacks fall into four primary categories:

- *Brute force:* Criminals use automated tools that try all possible passwords until they hit the correct one.

- *Dictionary attacks:* Criminals use automated tools to feed every word in the dictionary to a site until they hit the correct one.

- *Calculated attacks:* Criminals leverage information about a target to guess the target's password. Criminals may, for example, try someone's mother's maiden name because they can easily garner it for many people by looking at the most common last names of their Facebook friends or from posts on social media. (A Facebook post of "Happy Mother's Day to my wonderful mother!" that includes a user tag to a woman with a different last name than the user is a good giveaway.)

- *Blended attacks:* Some attacks leverage a mix of the preceding techniques — for example, utilizing a list of common last names, or performing a brute force attack technology that dramatically improves its efficiency by leveraging knowledge about how users often form passwords.

>> **Malware:** If crooks manage to get malware onto someone's device, it may capture passwords. (For more details, see the section on malware, earlier in this chapter.)

>> **Network sniffing:** If users transmit their password to a site without proper encryption while using a public Wi-Fi network, a criminal using the same network may be able to see that password in transit — as can potentially other criminals connected to networks along the path from the user to the site in question.

>> **Credential stuffing:** In credential stuffing, someone attempts to log in to one site using usernames and passwords combinations stolen from another site.

Exploiting Maintenance Difficulties

Maintaining computer systems is no trivial matter. Software vendors often release updates, many of which may impact other programs running on a machine. Yet, some patches are absolutely critical to be installed in a timely fashion because they fix bugs in software — bugs that may introduce exploitable security vulnerabilities. The conflict between security and following proper maintenance procedures is a never-ending battle — and security doesn't often win.

As a result, the vast majority of computers aren't kept up to date. Even people who do enable automatic updates on their devices may not be up to date — both because checks for updates are done periodically, not every second of every day, and because not all software offers automatic updating. Furthermore, sometimes updates to one piece of software introduce vulnerabilities into another piece of software running on the same device.

Advanced Attacks

If you listen to the news during a report of a major cyberbreach, you'll frequently hear commentators referring to advanced attacks. While some cyberattacks are clearly more complex than others and require greater technical prowess to launch, no specific, objective definition of an advanced attack exists. That said, from a subjective perspective, you may consider any attack that requires a significant investment in research and development to be successfully executed to be advanced. Of course, the definition of significant investment is also subjective. In some cases, R&D expenditures are so high and attacks are so sophisticated that there is near universal agreement that an attack was advanced. Some experts consider any zero-day attack to be advanced, but others disagree.

Advanced attacks may be opportunistic, targeted, or a combination of both.

Opportunistic attacks are attacks aimed at as many possible targets as possible in order to find some that are susceptible to the attack that was launched. The attacker doesn't have a list of predefined targets — the attacker's targets are effectively any and all reachable systems that are vulnerable to the launched attack. These attacks are similar to someone firing a massive shotgun in an area with many targets in the hope that one or more pellets will hit a target that it can penetrate.

Targeted attacks are attacks that target a specific party and typically involve utilizing a series of attack techniques until one eventually succeeds in penetrating into the target. Additional attacks may be launched subsequently in order to move around within the target's systems.

Opportunistic attacks

The goal of most opportunistic attacks is usually to make money — which is why the attackers don't care whose systems they breach; money is the same regardless of whose systems are breached in order to make it.

Furthermore, in many cases, opportunistic attackers may not care about hiding the fact that a breach occurred — especially after they've had time to monetize the breach, for example, by selling lists of passwords or credit card numbers that they stole.

While not all opportunistic attacks are advanced, some certainly are. Opportunistic attacks are quite different than targeted attacks.

Targeted attacks

When it comes to targeted attacks, successfully breaching any systems not on the target list isn't considered even a minor success.

For example, if a Russian operative is assigned the mission to hack into the Democratic and Republican parties' email systems and steal copies of all the email on the parties' email servers, the mission is going to be deemed a success only if the operative achieves those exact aims. If the operative manages to steal $1 million from an online bank using the same hacking techniques that were directed at the targets, it will not change a failure to breach the intended targets into even a small success. Likewise, if the goal of an attacker launching a targeted attack is to take down the website of a former employer the attacker had issues with, taking down other websites doesn't accomplish anything in the attacker's mind.

Because such attackers need to breach their targets no matter how well defended those parties may be, targeted attacks often utilize advanced attack methods — for example, exploiting vulnerabilities not known to the public or to the vendors who would need to fix them.

As you may surmise, advanced targeted attacks are typically carried out by parties with much greater technical prowess than those who carry out opportunistic attacks. Often, but not always, the goal of targeted attacks is to steal data undetected or to inflict serious damage — not to make money. After all, if one's goal is to make money, why expend resources targeting a well-defended site? Take an opportunistic approach and go after the most poorly defended, relevant sites.

Some advanced threats that are used in targeted attacks are described as *advanced persistent threats* (APTs):

>> **Advanced:** Uses advanced hacking techniques, likely with a major budget to support R&D

>> **Persistent:** Keeps trying different techniques to breach a targeted system and won't move on to target some other system just because the initial target is well protected

>> **Threat:** Has the potential to inflict serious damage

Blended (opportunistic and targeted) attacks

Another type of advanced attack is the opportunistic, semi-targeted attack. If criminals want to steal credit card numbers, for example, they may not care whether they successfully steal an equivalent number of active numbers from Best Buy, Walmart, or Barnes & Noble. All that the criminals likely care about is obtaining credit card numbers — from whom the numbers are pilfered isn't relevant.

At the same time, launching attacks against sites that don't have credit card data is a waste of the attacker's time and resources.

Some Technical Attack Techniques

While it is not necessary for most people to understand the details of how technical cyberattacks exploit system vulnerabilities, it is often interesting for people to understand the basic ideas behind popular methods utilized by hackers. The following sections outline some common ways of breaching and exploiting technical systems.

Rootkits

Rootkits are software toolsets that allow attackers to perform unauthorized activities at a privileged level on a compromised computer. ("Root" refers to the administrator account on UNIX systems.) Rootkits typically also contain features that seek to ensure that the attacker maintains access while that access remains secret from the authorized user or users of the compromised device.

Brute-force attacks

Brute-force attacks are simply attacks in which an attacker tries many possible values until the tools the attacker is using guess the correct value. A brute-force attack, for example, might consist of an attacker trying to log in to a user's account by trying every possible password combination until the attacker (or the attacker's brute-force attack tool, as the case may be) submits the correct one. Or the attacker may try different decryption keys until successfully decrypting an encrypted message.

Injection attacks

Injection attacks are attacks in which a system is expecting some sort of input from a user, but instead of submitting such input, an attacker submits malicious material such as code, which the receiving system then either executes or distributes to others to execute. Even though proper coding of applications can, at least in theory, prevent most forms of injection attacks, the reality is that many (if not most) systems remain vulnerable to such attacks, and as a result, injection attacks are an extremely commonly used tool within hacker arsenals.

Cross-site scripting

Cross-site scripting (XSS) is a specific type of injection attack in which an attacker adds malicious code into a legitimate web site so that when a user visits the relevant website (via a web browser or app), the malicious code is delivered to the user's device and is executed there. The attacker is able to insert the malicious code into the legitimate server because the server allows users to submit material that will then be displayed to other users.

Online user forums and social media platforms are prime candidates for cross-site scripting attacks if they are not properly secured against such attacks. So are websites that allow users to comment on information such as a news article. For example, an XSS attack may occur if a hacker submits malicious code within a comment in such a fashion that when a subsequent user's browser tries to display the comment, it will end up executing the code.

SQL injection

SQL injection attacks are a specific type of injection attacks that exploit the way most computer systems store data, which is in relational databases that provide access to people and systems through the use of what is known as standard Structured Query Language (SQL) interfaces. When an attacker launches a SQL injection attack, the attacker simply submits data to the system that includes SQL commands rather than regular data. For example, if the system asks the user to submit a user ID in order to search on it, and the attacker, aware of the SQL command likely to be used by the system to its database in order to perform that search, instead submits a user ID that consists of code to both complete that command and to issue another command to display all records in the database, the system, if not protected against SQL injection, might do exactly what the attacker wants.

Even if the SQL injection attack does not fully work — and the system being attacked does not display the data — the system's response to the SQL injection attack may still reveal information about how it handles SQL injection, thereby providing the hacker with information about the system, the database, and the security mechanisms in place (or information as to what is not in place that should be).

Session hijacking

Session hijacking refers to situations in which an attacker takes over the communications session between two or more parties. For example, during an online baking session, if an attacker is able to come between the user and the user's bank in such a fashion that the bank continues its session with the attacker rather than with the legitimate user, that would be an example of a successful session hijacking attack.

In a session hijacking situation, the attacker effectively becomes the authenticated and authorized user as far as the other party is concerned, and the attacker can do anything on the relevant system that the legitimate user would have been authorized to do. Session hijacking often occurs when session management is mishandled by an application, especially in cases in which trust that communications are from a particular session with a particular user is established through technical mechanisms that should not be trusted for such purposes.

Malformed URL attacks

Malformed URL attacks are attacks in which an attacker crafts a URL that appears to link to a particular legitimate website, but because of special characters utilized within the URL text, actually does something nefarious. The attacker may then distribute the nefarious URL in email and text messages and/or by posting it within a comment on a blog or via other social media.

Another form of malformed URL attack is an attack in which an attacker crafts a URL that contains elements within it that will cause a system being accessed to malfunction.

Buffer overflow attacks

Buffer overflow attacks are attacks in which an attacker submits data to a system that exceeds the storage capacity of the memory buffer in which that data is supposed to be stored, thereby causing the system to overwrite other memory with the data the user submitted. Carefully crafted buffer overflow input by an attacker, for example, could overwrite memory space in which the system is storing commands that it will execute per the instructions of its authorized user — perhaps even replacing such commands with commands the attacker wants the system to execute.

Chapter **3**

The Bad Guys You Must Defend Against

Many centuries ago, the now world-famous Chinese military strategist and philosopher, Sun Tzu, wrote:

If you know the enemy and know yourself,

   you need not fear the result of a hundred battles.

If you know yourself but not the enemy,

   for every victory gained you will also suffer a defeat.

If you know neither the enemy nor yourself,

   you will succumb in every battle.

As has been the case since ancient times, knowing your enemy is necessary in order to ensure that you can properly protect yourself.

Such wisdom remains true in the age of digital security. While Chapter 2 covers many of the threats posed by cyber-enemies, this chapter covers the enemies themselves:

>> Who are they?

>> Why do they launch attacks?

>> How do they profit from attacks?

You also find out about nonmalicious attackers — both people and inanimate parties who can inflict serious damage even without any intent to do harm.

Bad Guys and Good Guys Are Relative Terms

Albert Einstein famously said that "everything is relative," and that concept certainly holds true when it comes to understanding who the "good" guys and "bad" guys are online. As someone seeking to defend yourself against cyberattacks, for example, you may view Russian hackers seeking to compromise your computer in order to use it to hack U.S. government sites as bad guys, but to patriotic Russian citizens, they may be heroes.

If you're an American enjoying free speech online and make posts promoting atheism, Christianity, Buddhism, or Judaism and an Iranian hacker hacks your computer, you'll likely consider the hacker to be a bad guy, but various members of the Iranian government and other fundamentalist Islamic groups may consider the hacker's actions to be a heroic attempt to stop the spread of blasphemous heresy.

In many cases, determining who is good and who is bad may be even more complicated and create deep divides between members of a single culture. For example, how would you view someone who breaks the law and infringes on the free speech of neo-Nazis by launching a crippling cyberattack against a neo-Nazi website that preaches hate? Or someone outside of law enforcement who illegally launches attacks against sites spreading child pornography, malware, or jihadist material that encourages people to kill Americans? Do you think that everyone you know would agree with you? Would U.S. courts agree?

Before answering, please consider that in the 1977 case, *National Socialist Party of America v. Village of Skokie,* the U.S. Supreme Court ruled that freedom of speech goes so far as to allow Nazis brandishing swastikas to march freely in a neighborhood in which many survivors of the Nazi Holocaust lived. Clearly, in the world of cyber, only the eye of the beholder can measure good and bad — and the eyes of different beholders can be quite different in such regards.

For the purposes of this book, therefore, you need to define who the good and bad guys are, and, as such, you should assume that the language in the book operates from your perspective as you seek to defend yourself digitally. Anyone seeking to harm your interests, for whatever reason, and regardless of what you perceive your interests to be, is, for the purposes of this book, bad.

Bad Guys Up to No Good

A group of potential attackers that is likely well-known to most people are the bad guys who are up to no good. This group consists of multiple types of attackers, with a diverse set of motivations and attack capabilities, who share one goal in common: They all seek to benefit themselves at the expense of others, including, potentially, you.

Bad guys up to no good include

>> Script kiddies

>> Kids who are not kiddies

>> Nations and states

>> Corporate spies

>> Criminals

>> Hacktivists

Script kiddies

The term *script kiddies* (sometimes shortened to skids or just kiddies) refers to people — often (but not always) young — who hack, but who are able to do so only because they know how to utilize scripts and/or programs developed by others to attack computer systems. These folks lack the technological sophistication needed in order to create their own tools or to hack without the assistance of others.

Kids who are not kiddies

While script kiddies are technologically unsophisticated (see preceding section), plenty of other kids are not. For many years, the caricature of a hacker has been a young, nerdy male interested in computers, who hacks from his parents' home or from a dorm room at college. In fact, the first crop of hackers targeting civilian systems included many technologically sophisticated kids interested in exploring or carrying out various mischievous tasks for bragging rights or due to curiosity.

While such attackers still exist, the percentage of attacks emanating from these attackers has dropped dramatically from a huge portion to a minute fraction of a percentage of all attacks.

Simply put, teenage hackers similar to those depicted in movies from the 1980s and 1990s may have been a significant force in the pre-commercial Internet era, but once hacking could deliver real money, expensive goods, and valuable, monetizable data, criminals seeking to profit joined the fray en masse. Furthermore, as the world grew increasingly reliant on data and more government and industrial systems were connected to the Internet, nation and states began to dramatically increase the resources that they allocated to cyber-operations from both espionage and military standpoints, further diluting the classic teenage hacker to a minute portion of today's cyberattackers.

Terrorists and other rogue groups

To date, terrorist groups and other parties intent on wreaking havoc and inflicting harm on innocent people have focused much of their online activities on brainwashing vulnerable people, recruiting members, and assembling supporters. There is little doubt, however, that such nefarious parties also understand the potential damage that can be inflicted by cyberattacks — and are actively building and seeking to exploit cyberattack capabilities — and that Western nations are beginning to react accordingly. In May 2019, for example, the Israeli military bombed a building in Gaza from which the Hamas terrorist organization — a group then receiving both financial aid and technology know-how from Iran — was allegedly launching cyberattacks against civilian targets.

Nations and states

Hacking by nations and states has received significant press coverage in recent years. The alleged hackings of the Democratic party email systems by Russian agents during the 2016 Presidential election campaign and the Republican party email system during the 2018 midterm elections are high profiles examples of nation state hacking.

That said, most nation and state cyberattacks are not nearly as high profile as those examples, do not receive media coverage, and do not target high profile targets. Often, they're not even discovered or known to anyone but the attackers!

Furthermore, in some countries, it is difficult, if not impossible, to distinguish between nation or state hacking and commercial espionage. Consider countries in which major companies are owned and operated by the government, for example. Are hackers from such companies nation or state hackers? Are such companies legitimate government targets, or is hacking them an example of corporate espionage?

Of course, nations and states that hack may also be seeking to impact public sentiment, policy decisions, and elections in other nations. Discussions of this topic have been aired via major media outlets on a regular basis since the 2016 presidential election. In fact, since then, accusations of foreign meddling in U.S. elections through the use of both cyber misinformation campaigns and hacking, only continue to grow.

CHINESE FIRMS STEAL AMERICAN INTELLECTUAL PROPERTY

In May 2014, United States federal prosecutors charged five members of the People's Liberation Army (PLA) of China with hacking four U.S. businesses and one labor union as part of their service in Unit 61398, China's cyber-warrior unit. The allegedly hacked parties included Alcoa, Allegheny Technologies, SolarWorld, and Westinghouse, all of which are major suppliers of goods to utilities, and the United Steel Workers labor union.

While the full extent of the damage to American businesses caused by the hacking remains unknown to this day, SolarWorld claimed that as a result of confidential information stolen by the hackers, a Chinese competitor appeared to have gained access to SolarWorld's proprietary technology for making solar cells more efficient. This particular case illustrates the blurred lines between nation and state and corporate espionage when it comes to Communist nations and also highlights the difficulty in bringing hackers who participate in such attacks to justice; none of the indicted parties were ever tried, because none have left China to any jurisdiction that would extradite them to the United States.

Corporate spies

Unscrupulous companies sometimes utilize hacking as a way to gain competitive advantages or steal valuable intellectual property. The United States government, for example, has repetitively accused Chinese corporations of stealing the intellectual property of American businesses, costing Americans billions of dollars per year. Sometimes the process of stealing intellectual property involves hacking the home computers of employees at targeted companies with the hope that those employees will use their personal devices to connect to their employers' networks.

Criminals

Criminals have numerous reasons for launching various forms of cyberattacks:

>> **Stealing money directly:** Attacking to gain access to someone's online banking account and issue a wire transfer of money to themselves.

>> **Stealing credit card numbers, software, video, music files, and other goods:** Attacking to purchase goods or add bogus shipping instructions into a corporate system leading to products being shipped without payment ever being received by the shipper, and so on.

>> **Stealing corporate and individual data:** Attacking to obtain information that criminals can monetize in multiple ways (see the section "It's All About the Money: How Cybercriminals Monetize Their Actions," later in this chapter).

Over the years, the type of criminals who commit online crimes has evolved from being strictly solo actors to a mix of amateurs and organized crime.

Hacktivists

Hacktivists are activists who use hacking to spread the message of their "cause" and to deliver justice to parties whom they feel aren't being otherwise punished for infractions that the activists view as crimes. Hacktivists include terrorists and rogue insiders.

Terrorists

Terrorists may hack for various purposes, including to

>> Directly inflict damage (for example, by hacking a utility and shutting off power)

>> Obtain information to use in plotting terrorist attacks (for example, hacking to find out when weapons are being transported between facilities and can be stolen)

>> Finance terrorist operations (see the earlier section on criminals)

>> Build credibility and invigorate supporters by demonstrating cyberattack prowess.

Rogue insiders

Disgruntled employees, rogue contractors, and employees who have been financially incentivized by an unscrupulous party pose serious threats to businesses and their employees alike.

WARNING

Insiders intent on stealing data or inflicting harm are normally considered to be the most dangerous group of cyberattackers. They typically know far more than do any outsiders about what data and computer systems a company possesses, where those systems are located, how they are protected, and other information pertinent to the target systems and their potential vulnerabilities. Rogue insiders may target a businesses for one or more reasons:

>> They may seek to disrupt operations in order to lighten their own personal workloads or to help a competitor.

>> They may seek revenge for not receiving a promotion or bonus.

>> They may want to make another employee, or team of employees, look bad.

>> They may want to cause their employer financial harm.

>> They may plan on leaving and want to steal data that will be valuable in their next job or in their future endeavors.

Cyberattackers and Their Colored Hats

Cyberattackers are typically grouped based on their goals:

>> **Black hat hackers** have evil intent and hack in order to steal, manipulate, and/or destroy. When typical people think of a hacker, they are thinking of a black hat hacker.

>> **White hat hackers** are ethical hackers who hack in order to test, repair, and enhance the security of systems and networks. These folks are typically computer security experts who specialize in penetration testing, and who are hired by businesses and governments to find vulnerabilities in their IT systems. Hackers are considered to be white hat hackers only if they have explicit permission to hack from the owner of the systems that they are hacking.

>> **Grey hat hackers** are hackers who do not have the malicious intent of black hat hackers, but who, at least at times, act unethically or otherwise violate anti-hacking laws. Hackers who attempt to find vulnerabilities in a system without the permission of the system's owner and who report their findings to the owner without inflicting any damage to any systems that they scan are acting as grey hat hackers. Grey hat hackers sometimes act as such to make money. For example, when they report vulnerabilities to system owners, they may offer to fix the problems if the owner pays them some consulting fees. Some of the hackers who many people consider to be black hat hackers are actually grey hats.

>> **Green hat hackers** are novices who seek to become experts. Where green hats fall within the white-grey-black spectrum may evolve over time, as does their level of experience.

>> **Blue hat hackers** are paid to test software for exploitable bugs before the software is released into the market.

For the purposes of this book, black and gray hat hackers are the hackers that should primarily concern you as you seek to cyberprotect yourself and your loved ones.

How Cybercriminals Monetize Their Actions

Many, but not all, cyberattackers seek to profit financially from their crimes. Cyberattackers can make money through cyberattacks in several ways:

>> Direct financial fraud

>> Indirect financial fraud

>> Ransomware

>> Cryptominers

Direct financial fraud

Hackers may seek to steal money directly through attacks. For example, hackers may install malware on people's computers to capture victims' online banking sessions and instruct the online banking server to send money to the criminals' accounts. Of course, criminals know that bank systems are often well-protected against such forms of fraud, so many have migrated to target less well-defended systems. For example, some criminals now focus more on capturing login credentials (usernames and passwords) to systems that store credits — for example, coffee shop apps that allow users to store prepaid card values — and steal the money effectively banked in such accounts by using it elsewhere in order to purchase goods and services. Furthermore, if criminals compromise accounts of users that have auto-refill capabilities configured, criminals can repetitively steal the value after each auto-reload. Likewise, criminals may seek to compromise people's frequent traveler accounts and transfer the points to other accounts, purchase goods, or obtain plane tickets and hotel rooms that they sell to other people for cash. Criminals can also steal credit card numbers and either use them or quickly sell them to other crooks who then use them to commit fraud.

REMEMBER

Direct is not a black-and-white concept; there are many shades of grey.

Indirect financial fraud

Sophisticated cybercriminals often avoid cybercrimes that entail direct financial fraud because these schemes often deliver relatively small dollar amounts, can be undermined by the compromised parties even after the fact (for example, by reversing fraudulent transactions or invalidating an order for goods made with stolen information), and create relatively significant risks of getting caught. Instead, they may seek to obtain data that they can monetize for indirect fraud. Several examples of such crimes include

>> Profiting off illegal trading of securities

>> Stealing credit card, debit card, or other payment-related information

>> Stealing goods

>> Stealing data

Profiting off illegal trading of securities

Cybercriminals can make fortunes through illegal trading of securities, such as stocks, bonds, and options, in several ways:

>> **Pump and dump:** Criminals hack a company and steal data, short the company's stock, and then leak the company's data online to cause the company's stock price to drop, at which point they buy the stock (to cover the short sale) at a lower price than they previously sold it.

» **Bogus press releases and social media posts:** Criminals either buy or sell a company's stock and then release a bogus press release or otherwise spread fake news about a company by hacking into the company's marketing systems or social media accounts and issuing false bad or good news via the company's official channels.

» **Insider information:** A criminal may seek to steal drafts of press releases from a public company's PR department in order to see whether any surprising quarterly earnings announcements will occur. If the crook finds that a company is going to announce much better numbers than expected by Wall Street, the criminal may purchase *call options* (options that give the crook the right to purchase the stock of the company at a certain price), which can skyrocket in value after such an announcement. Likewise, if a company is about to announce some bad news, the crook may short the company's stock or purchase *put options* (options that give the crook the right to sell the stock of the company at a certain price), which, for obvious reasons, can skyrocket in value if the market price of the associated stock drops.

Discussions of indirect financial fraud of the aforementioned types is not theoretical or the result of paranoid or conspiracy theories; criminals have already been caught engaging in precisely such behavior. These types of scams are often also less risky to criminals than directly stealing money, as it is difficult for regulators to detect such crimes as they happen, and it is nearly impossible for anyone to reverse any relevant transactions. For sophisticated cybercriminals, the lower risks of getting caught coupled with the relatively high chances of success translate into a potential gold mine.

Stealing credit card, debit card, and other payment-related information

As often appears in news reports, many criminals seek to steal credit card or debit card numbers. Thieves can use these numbers to purchase goods or services without paying. Some criminals tend to purchase electronic gift cards, software serial numbers, or other semi-liquid or liquid assets that they then resell for cash to unsuspecting people, while others purchase actual hard goods and services that they may have delivered to locations such as empty houses, where they can easily pick up the items.

Other criminals don't use the credit cards that they steal. Instead, they sell the numbers on the dark web (that is, portions of the Internet that can be accessed only when using technology that grants anonymity to those using it) to criminals who have the infrastructure to maximally exploit the credit cards quickly before people report fraud on the accounts and the cards are blocked.

Stealing goods

Besides the forms of theft of goods described in the preceding section, some criminals seek to find information about orders of high-value, small, liquid items, such as jewelry. In some cases, their goal is to steal the items when the items are delivered to the recipients rather than to create fraudulent transactions.

Stealing data

Some criminals steal data so they can use it to commit various financial crimes. Other criminals steal data to sell it to others or leak it to the public. Stolen data from a business, for example, may be extremely valuable to an unscrupulous competitor.

Ransomware

Ransomware is computer malware that prevents users from accessing their files until they pay a ransom to some criminal or criminal enterprise. This type of cyberattack alone has already netted criminals billions of dollars (yes, that is billions with a *b*) and endangered many lives as infected hospital computer systems became inaccessible to doctors. In fact, there are multiple cases known today in which ransomware may have directly contributed to a person dying prematurely or unnecessarily.

Ransomware remains a growing threat, with criminals constantly improving the technical capabilities and earning potential of their cyberweapons. Criminals are, for example, crafting ransomware that, in an effort to obtain larger returns on investment, infects a computer and attempts to search through connected networks and devices to find the most sensitive systems and data. Then, instead of kidnapping the data that it first encountered, the ransomware activates and prevents access to the most valuable information.

REMEMBER

Criminals understand that the more important the information is to its owner, the greater the likelihood that a victim will be willing to pay a ransom, and the higher the maximum ransom that will be willingly paid is likely to be.

Ransomware is growing increasingly stealthy and often avoids detection by antivirus software. Furthermore, the criminals who use ransomware are often launching targeted attacks against parties that they know have the ability to pay decent ransoms. Criminals know, for example, that the average American is far more likely to pay $200 for a ransom than the average person living in China. Likewise, they often target environments in which going offline has serious consequences — a hospital, for example, can't afford to be without its patient records system for any significant period of time.

Cryptominers

A *cryptominer*, in the context of malware, refers to software that usurps some of an infected computer's resources in order to use them to perform the complex mathematical calculations needed to create new units of cryptocurrency. The currency that is created is transferred to the criminal operating the cryptominer. Many modern day cryptominer malware variants utilize groups of infected machines working in concert to do the mining.

Because cryptominers create money for criminals without the need for any involvement by their human victims, cybercriminals, especially those who lack the sophistication to launch high-stakes targeted ransomware attacks, have increasingly gravitated to cryptominers as a quick way to monetize cyberattacks.

While the value of cryptocurrencies fluctuates wildly (at least as of the time of the writing of this chapter), some relatively unsophisticated cryptocurrency mining networks are believed to net their operators more than $30,000 per month.

Not All Dangers Come From Attackers: Dealing with Nonmalicious Threats

While some potential attackers are intent on benefiting at your expense, others have no intentions of inflicting harm. However, these parties can innocently inflict dangers that can be even greater than those posed by hostile actors.

Human error

Perhaps the greatest cybersecurity danger of all — whether for an individual, business, or government entity — is the possibility of human error. Nearly all major breaches covered in the media over the past decade were made possible, at least in part, because of some element of human error. In fact, human error is often necessary for the hostile actors to succeed with their attacks — a phenomenon about which they're well aware.

Humans: The Achilles' heel of cybersecurity

Why are humans so often the weak point in the cybersecurity chain — making the mistakes that enable massive breaches? The answer is quite simple.

Consider how much technology has advanced in recent years. Electronic devices that are ubiquitous today were the stuff of science-fiction books and movies just one or two generations ago. In many cases, technology has even surpassed predictions about the future — today's phones are much more powerful and convenient than Maxwell Smart's shoe-phone, and Dick Tracy's watch would not even be perceived as advanced enough to be a modern day toy when compared with devices that today cost under $100.

Security technology has also advanced dramatically over time. Every year multiple new products are launched, and many new, improved versions of existing technologies appear on the market. The intrusion detection technology of today, for example, is so much better than that of even one decade ago that even classifying them into the same category of product offering is questionable.

On the flip side, however, consider the human brain. It took tens of thousands of years for human brains to evolve from that of earlier species — no fundamental improvement takes place during a human lifetime, or even within centuries of generations coming and going. As such, security technology advances far more rapidly than the human mind.

Furthermore, advances in technology often translate into humans needing to interact with, and understand how to properly utilize a growing number of increasingly complex devices, systems, and software. Given human limitations, the chances of people making significant mistakes keep going up over time.

The increasing demand for brainpower that advancing technology places on people is observable even at a most basic level. How many passwords did your grandparents need to know when they were your age? How many did your parents need? How many do you need? And, how easily could remote hackers crack passwords and exploit them for gain in the era of your grandparents? Your parents? Yourself?

Add to the mix that many people today work from home — often at the same time during which their children attend school remotely from the same location — and the possibility of human errors made either due to interruptions mid-task, or due to the inability to speak in-person with a colleague, grow dramatically.

TIP

The bottom line: You must internalize that human error poses a great risk to your cybersecurity — and act accordingly.

Social engineering

In the context of information security, *social engineering* refers to the psychological manipulation of human beings into performing actions that they otherwise would not perform and which are usually detrimental to their interests.

Examples of social engineering include

>> Calling someone on the telephone and tricking that person into believing that the caller is a member of the IT department and requesting that the person reset their email password

>> Sending phishing emails (see Chapter 2)

>> Sending CEO fraud emails (see Chapter 2)

While the criminals launching social engineering attacks may be malicious in intent, the actual parties that create the vulnerability or inflict the damage typically do so without any intent to harm the target. In the first example, the user who resets their password believes that they are doing so to help the IT department repair email problems, not that they are allowing hackers into the mail system. Likewise, someone who falls prey to a phishing or CEO fraud scam is obviously not seeking to help the hacker who is attacking them.

Other forms of human error that undermine cybersecurity include people accidentally deleting information, accidentally misconfiguring systems, inadvertently infecting a computer with malware, mistakenly disabling security technologies, and other innocent errors that enable criminals to commit all sorts of mischievous acts.

WARNING

The bottom line is never to underestimate both the inevitability of, and power of, human mistakes — including your own. You will make mistakes, and so will I — everyone does. So on important matters, always double-check to make sure that everything is the way it should be. It is better to check many times when there was, in fact, no social engineering attack, than to fail to check the one time that there was such an attack.

External disasters

As described in Chapter 2, cybersecurity includes maintaining your data's confidentiality, integrity, and availability. One of the greatest risks to availability — which also creates secondhand risks to its confidentiality and integrity — is external disasters. These disasters fall into two categories: naturally occurring and man-made.

Natural disasters

A large number of people live in areas prone to some degree to various forms of natural disasters. From hurricanes to tornados to floods to fires, nature can be brutal — and can corrupt, or even destroy, computers and the data that the machines house.

Continuity planning and disaster recovery are, therefore, taught as part of the certification process for cybersecurity professionals. The reality is that, statistically speaking, most people will encounter and experience at least one form of natural disaster at some point in their lives. As such, if you want to protect your systems and data, you must plan accordingly for such an eventuality. It is not surprising that organizations with proper continuity plans in place often fared far better than their unprepared counterparts when the COVID-19 pandemic hit and forced people to work from home.

A strategy of storing backups on hard drives at two different sites may be a poor strategy, for example, if both sites consist of basements located in homes within flood zones.

Pandemics

One particular form of natural disaster is a pandemic or other medical issue. As people around the world saw clearly in 2020, the arrival of a highly contagious disease can cause a sudden shutdown of many in-person working facilities and schools, and cause a sudden migration to online platforms — creating all sorts of cybersecurity-related issues.

Man-made environmental problems

Of course, nature is not the only party creating external problems. Humans can cause floods and fires, and man-made disasters can sometimes be worse than those that occur naturally. Furthermore, power outages and power spikes, protests and riots, strikes, terrorist attacks, and Internet failures and telecom disruptions can also impact the availability of data and systems.

Businesses that backed up their data from systems located in New York's World Trade Center to systems in the nearby World Financial Center learned the hard way after 9/11 the importance of keeping backups outside the vicinity of the corresponding systems, as the World Financial Center remained inaccessible for quite some time after the World Trade Center was destroyed.

Cyberwarriors and cyberspies

Modern-day governments often have tremendous armies of cyberwarriors at their disposal. Such teams often attempt to discover vulnerabilities in software products and systems to use them to attack and spy on adversaries, as well as to use as a law enforcement tool. Doing so, however, creates risks for individuals and businesses. Instead of reporting vulnerabilities to the relevant vendors, various government agencies often seek to keep the vulnerabilities secret — meaning that they leave their citizens, enterprises, and other government entities vulnerable to attack by adversaries who may discover the same vulnerability.

In addition, governments may use their teams of hackers to help fight crime — or, in some cases, abuse their cyber-resources to retain control over their citizens and preserve the ruling party's hold on power. Even in the United States, in the aftermath of 9/11, the government implemented various programs of mass data collection that impacted law-abiding U.S. citizens. If any of the databases that were assembled had been pilfered by foreign powers, U.S. citizens may have been put at risk of all sorts of cyberproblems.

The dangers of governments creating troves of data exploits are not theoretical. In recent years, several powerful cyberweapons believed to have been created by a U.S. government intelligence agency surfaced online, clearly having been stolen by someone whose interests were not aligned with those of the agency. To this day, it remains unclear whether those weapons were used against American interests by whoever stole them.

The impotent Fair Credit Reporting Act

Many Americans are familiar with the Fair Credit Reporting Act (FCRA), a set of laws initially passed nearly half a century ago and updated on multiple occasions. The FCRA regulates the collection and management of credit reports and the data used therein. The FCRA was established to ensure that people are treated fairly, and that credit-related information remains both accurate and private.

According to the Fair Credit Reporting Act, credit reporting bureaus must remove various forms of adverse information from people's credit reports after specific time frames elapse. If you don't pay a credit card bill on time while you're in college, for example, it's against the law for the late payment to be listed on your report and factored against you into your credit score when you apply for a mortgage two decades later. The law even allows people who declare bankruptcy in order to start over to have records of their bankruptcy removed. After all, what good would starting over be if a bankruptcy forever prevented someone from having a clean slate?

Today, however, various technology companies undermine the protections of the FCRA. How hard is it for a bank's loan officer to find online databases of court filings related to bankruptcies by doing a simple Google search and then looking into such databases for information relevant to a prospective borrower? Or to see whether any foreclosure records from any time are associated with a name matching that of someone seeking a loan? Doing either takes just seconds, and no laws prohibit such databases from including records old enough to be gone from credit reports, and, at least in the United States, none prohibit Google from showing links to such databases when someone searches on the name of someone involved with such activities decades earlier.

Expunged records are no longer really expunged

The justice system has various laws that, in many cases, allow young people to keep minor offenses off of their permanent criminal records. Likewise, our laws afford judges the ability to seal certain files and to expunge other forms of information from people's records. Such laws help people start over; it is not a secret that many wonderful, productive members of modern society may not have turned out as they did without these protections.

But what good are such laws if a prospective employer can find the supposedly purged information within seconds by doing a Google search on a candidate's name? Google returns results from local police blotters and court logs published in local newspapers that are now archived online. People who were cited for minor offenses and then had all the charges against them dropped can still suffer professional and personal repercussions decades later — even though they were never indicted, tried, or found guilty of any offense.

Social Security numbers

A generation ago, it was common to use Social Security numbers as college ID numbers. The world was so different back then that for privacy reasons, many schools even posted people's grades using Social Security numbers rather than using students' names! Yes, seriously.

Should all students who went to college in the 1970s, 1980s, or early 1990s really have their Social Security numbers exposed to the public because college materials that were created in the pre-web world have now been archived online and are indexed in some search engines? To make matters worse, some parties authenticate users by asking for the last four digits of people's phone numbers, which can often be found in a fraction of a second via a cleverly crafted Google or Bing search. If it is common knowledge that such information has been rendered insecure by previously acceptable behaviors, why does the government still utilize Social Security numbers and treat them as if they were still private?

Likewise, online archives of church, synagogue, and other community newsletters often contain birth announcements listing not only the name of the baby and the baby's parents, but the hospital in which the child was born, the date of birth, and the grandparents' names. How many security questions for a particular user of a computer system can be undermined by a crook finding just one such announcement? All of these examples show how advances in technology can undermine our privacy and cybersecurity — even legally undermining laws that have been established to protect us.

Social media platforms

One group of technology businesses that generate serious risks to cybersecurity are social media platforms. Cybercriminals increasingly scan social media — sometimes with automated tools — to find information that they can use against companies and their employees. Attackers then leverage the information that they find to craft all sorts of attacks, such as one involving the delivery of ransomware. For example, they may craft highly effective spear-phishing emails credible enough to trick employees into clicking on URLs to ransomware-delivering websites or into opening ransomware-infected attachments.

The number of virtual kidnapping scams — in which criminals contact the family of a person who is off the grid due to being on a flight or the like and demand a ransom in exchange for releasing the person they claim to have kidnapped — has skyrocketed in the era of social media, as criminals often can discern from looking at users' social media posts both when to act and whom to contact.

Google's all-knowing computers

One of the ways computer systems verify that people are who they claim to be is by asking questions to which few people other than the legitimate party would know the correct answers. In many cases, someone who can successfully answer "How much is your current mortgage payment?" and "Who was your seventh grade science teacher?" is more likely to be the authentic party than an impersonator.

But the all-knowing Google engine undermines such authentication. Many pieces of information that were difficult to obtain quickly just a few year ago can now be obtained almost instantaneously via a Google search. In many cases, the answers to security questions used by various websites to help authenticate users are, for criminals, "just one click away."

While more advanced sites may consider the answer to security questions to be wrong if entered more than a few seconds after the question is posed, most sites impose no such restrictions — meaning that anyone who knows how to use Google can undermine many modern authentication systems.

Mobile device location tracking

Likewise, Google itself can correlate all sorts of data that it obtains from phones running Android or its Maps and Waze applications — which likely means from the majority of people in the Western World. Of course, the providers of other apps that run on millions of phones and that have permission to access location data can do the same as well. Any party that tracks where a person is and for how long that person is there may have created a database that can be used for all sorts of nefarious purposes — including undermining knowledge-based authentication, facilitating social engineering attacks, undermining the confidentiality of secret projects, and so on. Even if the firm that creates the database has no malicious intent, rogue employees or hackers who gain access to, or steal, the database pose serious threats.

Such tracking also undermines privacy. Google knows, for example, who is regularly going into a chemotherapy facility, where people sleep (for most people, the time that they are asleep is the only time that their phones do not move at all for many hours) and who else is sleeping near them when they do, and various other information from which all sorts of sensitive extrapolations can be made.

Defending against These Attackers

REMEMBER

It is important to understand that there is no such thing as 100 percent cybersecurity. While people used to joke that you could get a 100 percent cybersecure computer by using a manual typewriter, even that was not true; if you used a manual typewriter instead of a computer, someone could potentially decipher what you would be typing by closely listening to the sounds of the letters striking paper, as each letter produces a slightly different sound when inking the page.

Rather than 100 percent cybersecurity, we must pursue *adequate cybersecurity*, which is defined by understanding what risks exist, which ones are adequately mitigated, and which ones persist.

Defenses that are adequate to shield against some risks and attackers are inadequate to protect against others. What may suffice for reasonably protecting a home computer, for example, may be wildly inadequate to shield an online banking server. The same is true of risks that are based on who uses a system: A cellphone used by the President of the United States to speak to advisors, for example, obviously requires better security than the cellphone used by the average sixth grader.

2

Improving Your Own Personal Security

IN THIS PART . . .

Understand why you may be less cybersecure than you think.

Find out how to protect yourself against various cyberdangers.

Learn about physical security as it relates to cybersecurity.

» Understanding how to protect against cyber risks

» Evaluating your current cybersecurity measures

» Taking a look at privacy

» Adopting best practices

Chapter **4**

Evaluating Your Current Cybersecurity Posture

The first step in improving your protection against cyberthreats is to understand exactly what it is that you need to protect. Only after you have a good grasp on that information can you evaluate what is actually needed to deliver adequate security and determine whether you have any gaps to address.

You must consider what data you have, from whom you must protect it, and how sensitive it is to you. What would happen if, for example, it were publicized on the Internet for the world to see? Then you can evaluate how much you're willing to spend — timewise and moneywise — on protecting it.

Don't be Achilles: Identifying Ways You May Be Less than Secure

One lesson we can all learn from the Greek hero Achilles is that if you suffer from a vulnerability, attackers may eventually exploit it to your detriment. As such, it is important to understand the various areas in which your current cybersecurity posture may be less than ideal so that you can figure out how to address any relevant issues, and thereby, ensure that you're adequately protected. You should, for example, inventory all items that could contain sensitive data, become launching pads for attacks, and so on.

Your home computer(s)

Your home computers may suffer from one or major types of potential problems relevant to cybersecurity:

» **Breached:** A hacker may have penetrated your home computer and be able to use it much as you can — view its contents, use it to contact other machines, leverage it as a staging ground from which to attack other computers, phones, and smart devices and penetrate them, mine cryptocurrency, view data on your network, and so on.

» **Malware:** Similar to the dangers created by human invaders, a computer-based attacker — that is *malware* — may be present on your home computer, enabling a criminal to use the computer much as you can — view the computer's contents, contact other electronic devices, mine cryptocurrency, and so on — as well as read data from your network traffic and to infect other computers on your network and outside of it.

» **Shared computers:** When you share a computer with other people — including your significant other and/or your children — you expose your device to the risk that one or more of the other folks using it won't practice proper cyber-hygiene to the same level you do, and as a result, that person or people may expose the device to infection by malware or a breach by some hacker, or they may unintentionally inflict self-damage.

» **Connections to other networks and storage applications:** If you connect your computer via a virtual private network (VPN) to other networks, such as the network at your place of employment, network-borne malware on those remote networks or hackers lurking on devices connected to those networks can potentially attack your network and your local devices as well. In some cases, similar risks may exist if you run applications that connect your computer to remote services, such as remote storage systems.

» **Physical security risks:** As discussed in detail in Chapter 5, the physical location of your computer may either increase or decrease the danger to it and its contents.

Your mobile devices

From an information security standpoint, mobile devices are inherently risky because they

>> Are constantly connected to the Internet, which is a highly insecure, public network on which many hackers are known to lurk, and over which nearly all cyberattacks take place

>> Often have significant amounts of confidential information stored on them

>> Are used to communicate with many people and systems, both of which are groups that include parties who aren't always trustworthy, via the Internet (which is also inherently not trustworthy)

>> Can receive inbound messages from parties with whom you have never interacted prior to receiving the messages in question, and some such parties may be up to no good

>> Often don't run full-blown security software due to resource limitations, or run security software that comes with the device and that you cannot manually upgrade or otherwise change if you find it doesn't meet your needs

>> Can easily be lost or stolen

>> Can easily be accidentally damaged or destroyed

>> Often connect to insecure and untrusted Wi-Fi networks

>> Are replaced on a regular basis, and are often not properly decommissioned when being disposed of

>> Are often traded in for upgraded devices — often without being properly decommissioned

Your Internet of Things (IoT) devices

As discussed in detail in Chapter 18, the world of the connected computing has changed dramatically in recent years. Not that long ago, the only devices that were connected to the Internet were what people classically called computers — desktops, laptops, and servers that could be used for many different computing purposes. Today, however, we live in an entirely different world in which computers form only a small percentage of connected devices.

From smartphones to security cameras, refrigerators to cars, and coffeemakers to exercise equipment, numerous types of electronic devices now often have powerful computers embedded within them, and many of these computers are perpetually connected to the Internet.

The Internet of Things (IoT), as the ecosystem of connected devices is commonly known, has been growing exponentially over the past few years, yet the security of such devices is often, at best, inadequate. Many IoT devices do not contain security technology to secure themselves against breaches. Even those that do are often not properly configured to be secure. Hackers can exploit IoT devices to spy on you, steal your data, attack other systems and/or devices, launch denial-of-service attacks against networks or devices, and inflict various other forms of damage.

Your networking equipment

Networking equipment can be hacked to route traffic to bogus sites, capture data, launch attacks, block Internet access, and so on.

Your work environment

You may have sensitive data in your work environment — and you can be put at risk by colleagues at work as well. For example, if you bring any electronic devices to work, connect them to a network at work, and then bring those devices home and connect them to your home network, malware and other problems can potentially spread to your device from a device belonging to your employer or to any one or more of your colleagues using the same infrastructure and then later spread from your device to other machines on your home network.

Of course, the COVID-19 pandemic led to the blending of many work and home environments, and the cybersecurity effects of such developments have often been troubling.

Identifying Risks

To secure anything, you must know what it is that you're securing; securing an environment is difficult to do, if not impossible, to do if you do not know what is in that environment. (This concept is age-old wisdom; refer to the Sun Tzu quote at the beginning of Chapter 3.)

To secure yourself, therefore, you must understanding what assets you have — both those that are in digital formats and those in related physical formats — and what it is that you seek to protect. Those assets may or may not be in one location. In fact, some or all of them may be in locations that you cannot physically access. For example, you may have data stored in a cloud storage service such as Google Drive, Apple iCloud, or Microsoft OneDrive. You must also understand what risks you face to those assets.

TIP

Inventorying such assets is usually pretty simple for individuals: Make a written list of all devices that you attach to your network. You can often get a list by logging into your router and looking at the Connected devices section. Of course, you may have some devices that you connect to your network only occasionally or that must be secured even though they do not attach to your network, so be sure to include those on your list as well.

Add to that list — in a separate section — all storage devices that you use, including external hard drives, flash drives, and memory cards, as well as any storage or computing services that you use from third parties. Write or print the list; forgetting even a single device can lead to problems.

Protecting against Risks

After you identify what you must protect (see preceding section), you must develop and implement appropriate safeguards for those items to keep them as secure as appropriate and limit the impact of a potential breach.

In the context of home users, protecting includes providing barriers to anyone seeking to access your digital and physical assets without proper authorization to do so, establishing (even informal) processes and procedures to protect your sensitive data, and creating backups of all configurations and basic system restore points.

Basic elements of protection for most individuals include

>> Perimeter defense

>> Firewall/router

>> Security software

>> Your physical computer(s) and any other endpoints

>> Backups

And part of learning how to protect against risks is knowing how to detect cyber-security events, respond to them appropriately, recover the affected devices, and improve defenses to reduce risk even more.

Perimeter defense

Defending your cyber-perimeter is essentially the digital equivalent of building a moat around a castle — attempting to stop anyone from entering except through authorized pathways while under the watchful eyes of guards.

You can build that digital moat by never connecting any computer directly to your Internet modem. Instead connect a firewall/router to the modem and connect computers to the firewall/router. (If your modem contains a firewall/router, then it serves both purposes; if your connection is to the firewall/router portion, not to the modem itself, that is okay.) Normally, the connections between firewalls and modems are wired — that is, are achieved using a physical network cable. In some cases both the modem and the firewall/router might even be contained within the same physical device.

Firewall/router

Modern routers used in home environments include firewalling capabilities that block most forms of inbound traffic when such traffic isn't generated as the result of activities initiated by devices protected by the firewall. That is, a firewall will block outsiders from trying to contact a computer inside your home, but it will not block a web server from responding if a computer inside your home requests a web page from the server. Routers use multiple technologies to achieve such protection.

One important technology of note is Network Address Translation (NAT), which allows computers on your home network to use Internet Protocol (IP) addresses that are invalid for use on the Internet, but can be used on private networks. To the Internet, all the devices on networks using NAT appear to use one address, which is the address of the firewall that is situated between them and the Internet and is handling the NAT function.

The following recommendations help your router/firewall protect you:

REMEMBER

>> **Keep your router up to date.** Make sure to install all updates before initially putting your router into use and regularly check for new updates (unless your router has an auto-update feature, in which case you should leverage that feature).

An unpatched vulnerability in your router can allow outsiders to enter your network.

>> **Replace your router when it is no longer supported.** If the vendor is no longer providing support (including updates) for your router, it is probably time to replace it. Considering the lifecycle of such devices and the lifecycle of networking protocols, you may also benefit from improved performance by doing so.

>> **Change the default administrative password on your firewall/router to a strong password that only you know.** Write the default and new passwords down, and put the paper on which you write them in a safe or safe deposit box. Do not store such passwords on devices that connect to that network. Practice logging into the router — and continue doing so on a regular basis so that you do not forget the relevant password.

>> **Don't use the default name provided by your router for your Wi-Fi network name (its SSID).** Create a new name.

>> **Configure your Wi-Fi network to use encryption of at least the WPA2 standard, and use WPA3 if possible** These are the current standards at the time of the writing of this book.

>> **Establish a password that any device is required to know to join your Wi-Fi network.** Make that password a strong one. For information on creating strong passwords that you can easily remember, see Chapter 8.

>> **If all your wireless devices know how to use the modern Wi-Fi 6 and/or Wi-Fi 5 wireless networking protocols, disable older Wi-Fi protocols that your router supports.** Disabling protocols such as 802.11b, 802.11g, and 802.11n may help improve performance and offers security benefits.

>> **Enable MAC address filtering or make sure all members of your household know that nobody is to connect anything to the wired network without your permission.** At least in theory, MAC address filtering prevents any device from connecting to the network if you do not previously configure the router to allow it to connect. Do not allow people to connect insecure devices to the network without first securing them.

>> **Locate your wireless router centrally within your home.** Doing so will provide better signal for you and will also reduce the strength of the signal that you provide to people outside your home who may be seeking to piggyback onto your network. If you have a mesh routing system that comes with multiple access points, follow the relevant instructions regarding locating the devices.

>> **Do not enable remote access to your router.** You want the router to be manageable only via connections from devices that it is protecting, not from the outside world. The convenience of remote management of a home firewall is rarely worth the increase in security risk created by enabling such a feature.

>> **Maintain a current list of devices connected to your network.** Also include on that list devices that you allow to connect to your network but that are not currently connected.

>> **For any guests for whom you want to give network access, turn on the guest network capability of the router and, as with the private network, activate encryption and require strong password.** Give guests access to that guest network and not to your primary network. The same applies for anyone else to whom you must give Internet access but whose security you do not fully trust, including family members, such as children.

>> **If you're sufficiently technically knowledgeable to turn off DHCP and change the default IP address range used by the router for the internal network, do so.** Doing so interferes with some automated hacking tools and provides other security benefits. If you're not familiar with such concepts or don't have a clue what the aforementioned sentence means, simply ignore this paragraph. In this case, the security benefits of the recommendation are likely going to be outweighed by the problems that you may encounter due to the additional technical complexity that turning off DHCP and changing the default IP address range can create.

Security software

How should you use security software to protect yourself?

>> Use security software on all your computers and mobile devices. The software should contain at least antivirus and personal device firewall capabilities.

>> Use antispam software on any device on which you read email.

>> Enable remote wipe on any and every mobile device.

>> Require a strong password to log in to any computer and mobile device.

>> Enable auto-updates whenever possible and keep your devices updated.

Your physical computer(s) and any other endpoints

To physically secure your computers and other endpoints:

>> **Control physical access to your computer and keep it in a safe location.** If anyone entering your home can get to a machine, for example, that device can be relatively easily stolen, used, or damaged without your knowledge.

>> **If possible, do not share your computer with family members.** If you must share your computer, create separate accounts for each family member and do not give any other users of the device administrative privileges on it.

>> **Do not rely on deleting data before throwing out, recycling, donating, or selling an old device.** Use a multiwipe erasure system for all hard drives and solid state drives. Ideally, remove the storage media from the computer before getting rid of the device — and physically destroy the storage media.

Also, keep in mind that that some computing devices that need to be secured might not be true "endpoints" in that they may have other devices connected to them. A smart home hub or smart wireless camera system, for example, may have smart devices and/or cameras connected to them using proprietary communication mechanisms; they still, of course, need to be properly secured.

Backups

Back up regularly. If you are not sure what "regularly" means in your case, the odds are pretty good that you are not backing up often enough.

For more on backups, see Chapter 14.

Detecting

Detecting refers to implementing mechanisms by which you can detect cybersecurity events as quickly as possible after they commence. While most home users do not have the budget to purchase specialized products for the purpose of detection, that does not mean that the detection phase of security should be ignored.

Today, most personal computer security software has detection capabilities of various types. Make sure that every device that you manage has security software on it that looks for possible intrusions, for example. See Chapter 12 for more details on detecting possible breaches.

Responding

Responding refers to acting in response to a cybersecurity incident. Most security software will automatically either act, or prompt users to act, if it detects potential problems. For more on responding, see Chapter 13.

Recovering

Recovering refers to restoring an impacted computer, network, or device — and all of its relevant capabilities — to its fully functioning, proper state after a cybersecurity event occurs. See Chapters 13, 15, and 16 for more on recovering.

REMEMBER

Ideally, a formal, written, simple and straightforward, prioritized plan for how to recover should be documented before it is needed. Most home users do not actually create one, but doing so can be extremely beneficial. In most home cases, such a plan will be less than one page long.

Improving

Shame on any of us if we do not learn from our own mistakes. Every cybersecurity incident offers lessons learned that can be put into action to reduce risk in the future. For examples of learning from mistakes, see Chapter 20.

Evaluating Your Current Security Measures

After you know what you need to protect and how to protect such items, you can determine the difference between what you need and what you currently have in place.

The following sections cover some things to consider. Not all of the following apply in every case:

Software

When it comes to software and cybersecurity, think about the following questions for each device:

>> Are all the software packages (including the operating system itself) on your computer legally obtained?

>> Were the software packages (including the operating system itself) obtained from reliable sources that always (or at least as close to always as is humanly possibly) provide legitimate versions?

>> Are all the software packages (including the operating system itself) currently supported by their respective vendors?

>> Are all the software packages (including the operating system itself) up-to-date?

>> Are all the software packages (including the operating system itself) set to automatically update?

>> Is security software on the device?

>> Is the security software configured to auto-update?

>> Is the security software up-to-date?

>> Does the security software include anti-malware technology — and is that capability fully enabled?

>> Are virus scans configured to run after every update is applied?

>> Does the software include firewall technology — and is that capability fully enabled?

>> Does the software include anti-spam technology — and is that capability fully enabled? If not, is other anti-spam software present, and is it running?

>> Does the software include remote lock and/or remote wipe technology — and is that capability fully enabled? If not, is other remote lock/remote wipe software present, and is it running?

>> Are all other aspects of the software enabled? If not, what is not?

>> Is backup software running that will back up the device as part of a backup strategy?

>> Is encryption enabled for at least all sensitive data stored on the device?

>> Are permissions properly set for the software — locking out people who may have access to the device, but who should not have access to the software?

>> Have permissions been set to prevent software from making changes to the computer that you may not want done (for example, is any software running with administrator privileges when it should not be)?

Of course, all these questions refer to software on a device that you use, but that you don't expose to use by untrusted, remote outsiders. If you have devices that are used as in the latter case — for example, a web server — you must address many other security issues, which are beyond the scope of this book.

Hardware

For all your hardware devices, consider the following questions:

>> Was the hardware obtained from a trusted party? (If you bought an IP-based camera directly from China via some online retailer than you never of heard of prior to making the purchase, for example, the answer to this question may not be yes.)

>> How sure are you of the answer to the previous question — and if you are highly confident, why are you so confident?

>> Is the hardware from a brand that the U.S. Government prohibits its own agencies from using because it does not trust that brand to be sufficiently secure from foreign spying or cyber risks?

>> Is all your hardware adequately protected from theft and damage (rain, electrical spikes, and so on) as it resides in its home location?

>> What protects your hardware when it travels?

>> Do you have an uninterruptible power supply or built-in battery protecting the device from a hard, sudden shut-off if power fails even momentarily?

>> Is all your hardware running the latest firmware — and did you download that firmware from a reliable source, such as the vendor's website or via an update initiated from within the device's configuration tool?

>> For routers (and firewalls), does your device meet the criteria listed as recommendations in the "Firewall/router" section earlier in this chapter?

>> Do you have a BIOS password, locking a device from use until a password is entered?

>> Have you disabled all wireless protocols that you do not need? If you're not using Bluetooth on a laptop, for example, turn off the Bluetooth radio, which not only improves security, but also helps your battery last longer.

Insurance

While cybersecurity insurance is often overlooked, especially by smaller businesses and individuals, it is a viable way of mitigating some cyber-risks. Depending on the particulars of your situation, purchasing a policy protecting against specific risks may make sense.

If you own a small business that may go bankrupt if a breach occurs, you will, of course, want to implement strong security. But, as security measures can never be 100 percent perfect and foolproof, purchasing a policy to cover catastrophic situations may be wise.

While cyber insurance used to be something that only large enterprises could obtain, in recent years, cybersecurity policies have started to become available to both individuals and small businesses.

Education

A little bit of education can go a long way in helping to prevent the people in your household (or other entity, as the case may be) from becoming the Achilles' heels of your cybersecurity. The following list covers some things to think about and discuss:

>> Do all you family members know what their rights and responsibilities are regarding vis-à-vis technology in the house, vis-à-vis connecting devices to the home network, and vis-à-vis allowing guest to connect to the home network (or the guest network)?

>> Have you taught your family members about the risks they need to be aware — for example, phishing emails. Do you have confidence that they "get it"?

>> Have you ensured that everyone in the family who uses devices knows about cybersecurity hygiene (for example, not clicking on links in emails)?

>> Have you ensured that everyone in the family who uses devices knows about password selection and protection?

>> Have you ensured that everyone in the family who uses social media grasps the risks associated with oversharing and understands what can and what can't be safely shared?

>> Have you ensured that everyone in the family understands the concept on thinking before acting?

Privacy 101

Technology threatens personal privacy in many ways: Ubiquitous cameras watch you on a regular basis, technology companies track your online behaviors via all sorts of technical methods, and mobile devices track your location.

While technology has certainly made the task of maintaining privacy far more challenging than doing so was just a few years ago, privacy is not dead. You can do many things to improve your level of privacy, even in the modern, connected era.

Think before you share

People often willingly overshare information when asked for it.

Yes, you and me included.

Consider the paperwork patients are given at a typical doctor's office in the United States that you have likely been asked to complete at more than one facility at your initial appointment with the doctor in question. While the answers to many of the questions are relevant and may contain information that is valuable for the doctor to know to properly evaluate and treat you, other portions are probably not. Many (if not most) such forms ask patients for their Social Security numbers. Such information was needed decades ago when medical insurance companies regularly used Social Security numbers as insurance ID numbers, but that dangerous practice has long since ended. Perhaps some facilities use the Social Security number to report your account to credit bureaus if you don't pay your bills, but in most cases, the reality is that the question is an unsafe vestige of the past, and you can leave the field blank.

REMEMBER

Even if you don't believe that a party asking you for personal data would ever abuse the information that it collected about you, as the number of parties that have private information about you increases, and as the quantity and quality of that data grows, the odds rise that you will suffer a privacy violation due to a data breach occurring somewhere.

If you want to improve your privacy, the first thing to do is to consider what information you may be disclosing about yourself and your loved ones before you disclose it. This is true when interacting with government agencies, corporations, medical facilities, and other individuals. If you do not need to provide private information, don't. All other factors being identical, the less private information that is "out there," and the fewer places it resides, the lower the risk to you of a privacy compromise.

Think before you post

Consider the implications of any social media post before making it — there could be adverse consequences of many sorts, including effectively compromising the privacy of information. For example, criminals can leverage shared information about a person's family relationships, place of employment, and interests as part of identity theft and to social engineer their way into your accounts.

WARNING

If, by choice or due to the negligent policies of a provider, you use your mother's maiden name as a de facto password, make sure that you do not make it easy for criminals to find out that name by listing your mother as your mother on Facebook or by being friends on Facebook with many cousins whose last name is the same as your mother's maiden name. Often, people can obtain someone's mother's maiden name simply by selecting from another person's Facebook friends list the most common last name that is not the same as the account holder's name.

Sharing information about a person's children and their schedules may help facilitate all sorts of problems — including potentially kidnapping, break-ins into the person's home while the person is carpooling to work, or other harmful actions.

Sharing information related to medical activities may lead to disclosure of sensitive and private information. For example, photographs or location data placing a person at a particular medical facility may divulge that the person suffers from a condition that the facility is known to specialize in treating.

Sharing various types of information or images may impact a user's personal relationships and leak private information about such.

Sharing information or images may leak private information about potentially controversial activities in which a person has engaged — for example, consuming alcohol or using recreational drugs, using various weapons, participating in certain controversial organizations, and so on. Even disclosing that one was at a particular location at a certain time may inadvertently compromise the privacy of sensitive information.

REMEMBER

Also, keep in mind that the problem of oversharing is not limited to social networks. Oversharing information via chat, email, group chats, and so on is a serious modern day problem as well. Sometimes people do not realize that they are oversharing, and sometimes they accidentally paste the wrong data into emails or attach the wrong files to emails.

General privacy tips

In addition to thinking before you share, you can do a few other things to reduce your exposure to risks of oversharing:

>> **Use social media privacy settings.** In addition to not sharing private information (see preceding section), make sure that your privacy settings on social media are set to protect your data from viewing by members of the public — unless the post in question is intended for public consumption.

>> **But do not rely on them.** Nonetheless, never rely on social media security settings to ensure the privacy of information. Significant vulnerabilities that undermine the effectiveness of various platforms' security controls have been repetitively discovered.

>> **Keep private data out of the cloud unless you encrypt the data.** Never store private information in the cloud unless you encrypt it. Do not rely on the encryption provided by the cloud provider to ensure your privacy. If the provider is breached, in some cases the encryption can be undermined as well. So, if you must store sensitive information in the cloud, encrypt it yourself before uploading it — regardless of whatever encryption the cloud provider uses. There are applications available that simplify doing so for major cloud storage providers, such as by automatically encrypting and copying to the cloud any files placed in a special folder on your computer.

   Do not store private information in cloud applications designed for sharing and collaboration. For example, do not store a list of your passwords, photos of your driver's license or passport, or confidential medical information in a Google doc. This may seem obvious, but many people do so anyway.

>> **Leverage the privacy settings of a browser — or better yet, use Tor.** If you're using the a web browser to access material that you don't want associated with you, at a minimum, turn on Private/Incognito Mode (which offers only partial protection), or, if possible, use a web browser like the Tor Browser Bundle (which contains obfuscated routing, default strong privacy settings, and various, preconfigured, privacy add-ons).

   If you do not take precautions when using a browser, you may be tracked. If you search for detailed information on a medical condition in a normal browser window, various parties will likely capitalize on that data. You have probably seen the effects of such tracking — for example, when ads appear on one web page related to something that you searched for on another.

>> **Do not publicize your real cellphone number.** Get a forwarding number from a service like Google Voice and, in general, give out that number rather than your actual cellphone number. Doing so helps protect against many risks — SIM swapping, spam, and so on.

>> **Store private materials offline.** Ideally, store highly sensitive materials offline, such as in a fireproof safe or in a bank safe deposit box. If you must store them electronically, store them on a computer with no network connection.

>> **Encrypt all private information,** such as documents, images, videos, and so on. If you're not sure if something should be encrypted, it probably should.

>> **If you use online chat, use end-to-end encryption.** Assume that all your text messages sent via regular cellphone service (SMS messages) can potentially be read by outsiders. Ideally, do not share sensitive information in writing. If you must share some sensitive item in writing, encrypt the data.

TIP

The simplest way to encrypt data is to use a chat application that offers end-to-end encryption. *End-to-end* means that the messages are encrypted on your device and decrypted on the recipient's device and vice versa — with the provider effectively unable to decrypt the messages; as such, it takes far more effort by hackers who breach the provider's servers to read your messages if end-to-end encryption is utilized. (Sometimes, providers claim that hackers can't read such messages altogether, which isn't correct. for two reasons: 1. Hackers may be able to see the metadata — for example, with whom you chatted and when you did so, and 2. If hackers breach enough internal servers, they may be able to upload to the app store a poisoned version of the app containing a backdoor of some sort.) WhatsApp is probably the most popular chat application that uses end-to-end encryption.

>> **Practice proper cyberhygiene.** Because so much of the information that you want to keep private is stored in electronic form, practicing proper cyberhygiene is critical to preserving privacy. See the tips in Chapter 18.

TURNING ON PRIVACY MODE

To turn on privacy mode:

- **Chrome:** Control + Shift-N or choose New incognito window from the menu

- **Firefox:** Control + Shift + P or choose New private window from the menu

- **Opera:** Control + Shift + N or choose New private window from the menu

- **Edge:** Control + Shift + P or choose New private window from the menu

- **Vivaldi:** Control + Shift + N or choose New private window from the menu

- **Safari:** Command + Shift + N or choose New private window from the File menu

- **Tor Browser Bundle:** Privacy Mode is on by default in this version of Firefox (and Tor enhances privacy as well, as discussed in Chapter 21)

Banking Online Safely

Eschewing online banking due to the security concerns that it creates is simply not practical for most people living in the modern age. Doing so would also increase the risks of other dangers that emanate from phone-based banking or from banking in person.

Fortunately, you don't have to give up the conveniences of online banking in order to stay secure. In fact, I'm keenly aware of the risks involved because I have been banking online since online banking was first offered by several major financial institutions in the mid-1990s as a replacement for direct-dial-up banking services.

Here are some suggestions of what you can do to improve your security as you bank online:

>> **Your online banking password should be strong, unique, and committed to memory.** It should not be stored in a database, password manager, or anywhere else electronic. (If you want to write it down and keep the paper in a safe deposit box, that may be okay — but doing so is rarely necessary.)

>> **Choose a random Personal Identification Number (PIN) for your ATM card and/or phone identification.** Any PIN that you use for banking-related purposes should be unrelated to any information that you know. Don't use a PIN that you have used for some other purpose and don't establish any PINs or passwords based on the one you chose for your ATM card. Never write down your PIN. Never add it to any computer file. Never tell your PIN to anyone, including bank employees.

>> **Consider asking your bank for an ATM card that can't be used as a debit card.** While such cards may lack the ability to be used to buy goods and services, if you make your purchases using credit cards, you don't need the purchase feature on your ATM card. By preventing the card from being used as a debit card, you make it more likely that only someone who knows your PIN number can take money out of your account. Perhaps equally as important is that "crippled" ATM cards can also not be used by crooks to make fraudulent purchases.

REMEMBER

If your debit card is used fraudulently, you're out money and need to get it back. If your credit card is used fraudulently, you're not out any money unless an investigation reveals that you were the one doing the defrauding.

» **Log in to online banking only from trusted devices that you control, that have security software on them, and that are kept up to date.**

» **Log in to online banking only from secure networks that you trust.** If you're on the road, use your cellular provider's connection, not public Wi-Fi. (For more details on this, see Chapter 21.) Do not login to online banking or any other sensitive apps from locations in which communication providers are believed to target with malware devices connecting to their networks.

» **Log in to online banking using a web browser or the official app of the bank.** Never log in from a third-party app or an app obtained from anywhere other than the official app store for your device's platform.

» **Sign up for alerts from your bank.** You should configure to be alerted by text message and/or email any time a new payee is added, a withdrawal is made, and so on.

» **Use multifactor authentication and protect any device used for such authentication.** If you generate one-time passwords on your phone, for example, and your phone is stolen, your second factor becomes (at least temporarily) usable by the crook and not by you.

» **Do not allow your browser to store your online banking password.** Your online banking password should not be written down anywhere — certainly not in a system that will enter it on behalf of someone using a web browser.

» **Enter the URL of your bank every time you visit the bank on the web.** Never click links to it.

» **Ideally, use a separate computer for online banking than you use for online shopping, email access, and social media.** If that isn't possible or practical, use a different web browser — and be sure to keep that browser up to date.

TIP

As an extra precaution, you can configure your browser to remember the wrong password to a site so that if someone ever does get into your laptop or phone, that person will be less likely to successfully log into that site using your credentials.

» **Make sure to secure any devices from which you bank online.** That includes physically securing them (don't leave them on a table in a restaurant while going to the restroom), requiring a password to unlock them, and enabling remote wipe.

» **Monitor your account for unauthorized activity.**

Safely Using Smart Devices

As I discuss in detail in Chapter 18, smart devices and the so-called Internet of Things create all sorts of cybersecurity risks. Here are some recommendations as to how to improve your security as you use such devices:

» **Make sure that none of your IoT devices create security risks in the event of a failure.** Never create a situation in which a smart lock prevents you from leaving a room during a fire, for example, or lets robbers into your house during a power outage or network failure.

» **If possible, run your IoT devices on a separate network than your computers.** The IoT network should have a firewall protecting it.

» **Keep all IoT devices up to date.** Hackers have exploited vulnerabilities in IoT devices to commandeer the devices and use them to carry out major attacks. If a device has a firmware auto-update capability, consider enabling it.

» **Keep a full, current list of all devices connected to your network.** Also keep a list of all devices that are not currently connected but that are authorized to connect and sometimes do connect.

» **If possible, disconnect devices when you're not using them.** If a device is offline, it is obviously not hackable by anyone not physically present at the device.

» **Password-protect all devices.** Never maintain the default passwords that come with the devices. Each device should have a unique login and password.

» **Check your devices' settings.** Many devices come with default setting values that are terrible from a security perspective.

» **Keep your smartphone physically and digitally secure.** It likely runs apps with access to some or all of your devices.

» **If possible, disable device features that you do not need.** Doing so reduces the relevant attack surface — that is, it reduces the number of potential points at which an unauthorized user can attempt to hack into the device — and simultaneously lowers the chances of the device exposing an exploitable software vulnerability.

Universal Plug and Play (UPnP) simplifies device setup, but it also makes it easier for hackers to discover devices and attack them for many reasons, including that many implementations of UPnP contain vulnerabilities, UPnP can sometimes allow malware to bypass firewall security routines, and UPnP can sometimes be exploited by hackers to run commands on routers.

» **Do not connect your IoT devices to untrusted networks.**

Cryptocurrency Security 101

In simplified terms, *cryptocurrency* refers to "money" that is tracked using a ledger of accounts whose copies are distributed to *nodes* running the cryptocurrency network (which means numerous parties all over the world have copies of the ledger containing a list of all transactions that have ever occurred using that particular cryptocurrency). Most cryptocurrencies are managed not by a central party, but rather, by a majority consensus, with the definition of who is included in calculating the majority consensus varying by cryptocurrency.

The most well-known cryptocurrency is Bitcoin, which was also the first cryptocurrency to arrive on the scene. When someone owns a Bitcoin (or a fraction thereof), that information is stored in a ledger — not with the person's name, but with an address. For example, address 123 received one Bitcoin from address 321, which means that now address 123 has one Bitcoin.

The owner of the Bitcoin does not actually own anything; instead, the owner simply has control over the relevant Bitcoin address. In the previous example, the person who possesses the secret key needed to authorize any transactions made from address 321 controls any Bitcoins stored at that address.

While going into a discussion about the technology used by Bitcoin is beyond the scope of this book, one important security concern for people to be aware of is that when it comes to cryptocurrency, the secret key needed to perform transactions effectively defines ownership. If the owner of the Bitcoin at address 321 lost the key to that address, the owner would no longer be able to access the Bitcoin stored there, and would likely permanently lose whatever money was stored at that address.

Likewise, if someone else obtained the key for 321 and utilized it without authorization from the owner to transfer the Bitcoin to another address, that transaction would, in nearly all cases, be deemed valid, and the rightful owner will lose the Bitcoin.

As such, it is critical to protect the secret keys associated with cryptocurrency holdings.

One way to do so is to store secret keys on a special hardware device called a hardware "wallet." Such a device keeps the keys offline so that no Internet-connected devices hold the keys anywhere where the keys could potentially be stolen by a hacker. When the rightful owner wants to perform a transaction with the cryptocurrency, the owner must connect the relevant hardware wallet to a computer (often by USB connection), and unlock the wallet (usually by using a passcode of some sort), in order to utilize the keys stored on the wallet.

REMEMBER

Note that hardware cryptocurrency wallets do not store cryptocurrency — they store keys used to authorize actions on particular cryptocurrency addresses on ledgers.

Also, keep in mind that when people store cryptocurrency at a cryptocurrency exchange, it is the exchange that stores the keys for the cryptocurrency. If the user's credentials to the exchange are stolen, the cryptocurrency may be stolen as well.

Chapter **5**

Enhancing Physical Security

You may be tempted to skip this chapter — after all, you are reading this book to learn about cybersecurity, not physical security.

But, please don't.

Seriously.

Certain aspects of physical security are *essential* ingredients of any cybersecurity program, whether formal or informal. Without them, all of the policies, procedures, and technical defenses can prove to be worthless. In fact, just a few decades ago, the teams responsible for protecting computers and the data housed within them focused specifically on physical security. Locking a computer in a secured area accessible by only authorized personnel was often sufficient to protect it and its contents. Of course, the dawn of networks and the Internet era, coupled with the mass proliferation of computing devices, totally transformed the risks. Today, even computers locked in a physical location can still be accessed electronically by billions of people around the world. That said, the need for physical security is as important as ever.

This chapter covers elements of physical security that are necessary in order to implement and deliver proper cybersecurity. I cover the "what and why" that you need to know about physical security in order to keep yourself cyber-secure. Ignoring the concepts discussed in this chapter may put you at risk of a data breach equivalent to, or even worse than, one carried out by hackers.

Understanding Why Physical Security Matters

Physical security means protecting something from unauthorized physical access, whether that access is by man or by nature. Keeping a computer locked in an office server closet, for example, to prevent people from tampering with it is an example of physical security.

The goal of physical security is to provide a safe environment for the people and assets of a person, family, or organization. Within the context of cybersecurity, the goal of physical security is to ensure that digital systems and data are not placed at risk because of the manner in which they're physically housed.

REMEMBER

Classified information contains secrets whose compromise can endanger American intelligence agents and operations, undermine diplomatic and military operations, and harm national security.

I hope that you're not storing highly sensitive classified files in your home. If you are, you had better know a lot more about information security than is taught in this book. Also, because removing classified information from its proper storage location is often a serious crime, I suggest that you get yourself a good lawyer.

Taking Inventory

Before you implement a physical security plan, you need to understand what it is that you have to secure. You likely possess more than one type of electronic device and have data that varies quite a bit in terms of the level of secrecy and sensitivity that you attach to it. Step 1 in implementing proper physical security is to understand what data and systems you have and determine what type of security level each one demands.

SECRETARY OF STATE HILLARY CLINTON'S EMAIL PROBLEM

Whenever politicians or journalists attack former U.S. Secretary of State Hillary Clinton for storing sensitive information on a server located inside a spare closet in her home in Chappaqua, New York, they're effectively accusing her of endangering national security by placing sensitive digital data in an insufficiently secure physical location. After all, as far as the risks of Internet-based hackers are concerned, digital security is what matters; to hackers from China and Russia, for example, whether her server was located in her spare closet or in a data center protected by armed guards is irrelevant.

The security experts who devised our national security procedures for the handling of classified information understood the necessity of keeping such data physically secure — it is, generally speaking, against the law to remove classified information from the secure locations in which it's intended to be handled. While many modern-day workers may telecommute and bring work home with them at times, folks who handle classified information can be sentenced to serve time in prison for even attempting to do the same with classified data.

The laws governing the protection of classified information prohibit removing it from classified networks, which are never supposed to be connected to the Internet. All people who handle classified information are required to obtain clearances and be trained on the handling of sensitive information; they are required by federal law to understand, and to adhere to, strict rules. As such, Sec. Clinton should have never removed classified information from classified networks and should never have brought it home or accessed it via a server in her home.

In fact, people can be charged with a crime for mishandling classified information — even if they do so inadvertently, which is a point that the Republicans mentioned repetitively during the 2016 Presidential election. Sec. Clinton's email security challenges likely impacted world history in a big way — something to keep in mind when people ask how important cybersecurity can be.

In all likelihood, your computer devices fall into two categories:

> » **Stationary devices,** such as a desktop computer sitting in your family room on which your teenagers play video games
> » **Mobile devices,** such as laptops, tablets, and cellphones

REMEMBER

Don't forget to inventory the equipment to which your devices are connected. When you inventory your devices, pay attention to networks and networking equipment. To what networks are stationary devices attached? How many networks are in place? Where do they connect to the outside world? Where is the relevant network equipment located? What mobile devices connect to wirelessly?

Stationary devices

Stationary devices, such as desktop computers, networking equipment, and many Internet of Things (IoT) devices, such as wired cameras, are devices that don't move from location to location on a regular basis.

These devices can, of course, still be stolen, damaged, or misused, and, therefore, must be adequately protected. Damage need not be intentionally inflicted — early in my career I helped troubleshoot a server problem that began when a nighttime custodian unplugged an improperly secured server from its uninterruptible power supply in order to plug in a vacuum cleaner. Yes, seriously. As it is imperative to secure stationary devices in the locations in which they "live," you must inventory all such devices. Securing something that you do not know that you possess is difficult, if not impossible.

SMARTPHONES ARE A LOT MORE THAN SMART PHONES

The term *smartphone* is extremely misleading — the device in your pocket is a full-blown computer with more processing power than all the computers used to first put a man on the moon combined. It is only a smartphone in the same way that a Ferrari is a fast, horseless carriage — a technically correct description, but one that is highly misleading. Why do you call these devices smartphones — well, think of where you encountered your first smartphone.

Most people's first experience with a smartphone was when they upgraded from a regular cellphone — and they obtained the new devices from cellphone providers who (likely correctly) reasoned that people would be more likely to upgrade their cellphone to "smartphones" than to replace their cellphones with "pocket computers that have a phone app."

Smartphone is, as such, a marketing term. "Easily lost or stolen, and potentially hackable, pocket-sized computer with lots of sensitive information on it" provides a more accurate understanding.

In many cases, anyone who can physically access a computer or other electronic device can access all the data and programs on that device, regardless of security systems in place. The only question is how long it will take that party to gain the unauthorized access that it desires. Never mind that anyone who can access a device can physically damage it — whether by physically striking it, sending into it a huge power surge, dumping water on it, or setting it ablaze. In case you think that these scenarios are far-fetched, know that I have seen all four of these options utilized by people intent on damaging computers.

Mobile devices

Mobile devices are computerized devices that are frequently moved. Laptops, tablets, and smartphones are all mobile devices. In some ways mobile devices are inherently more secure than stationary devices — you likely always have your cellphone with you, so that device not sitting at home unwatched for long periods of time as a computer may be.

That said, in reality, experience shows that portability dramatically increases the chances of an electronic device being lost or stolen. In fact, in some ways, mobile devices are the stuff of security professionals' nightmares. The "smartphone" in your pocket is constantly connected to an insecure network (the Internet), contains highly sensitive data, has access tokens to your email, social media, and a whole host of other important accounts, likely lacks security software of the sophistication that is on desktop computers, is frequently in locations in which it is likely to be stolen, is often out of sight, is taken on trips that cause you to deviate from your normal routine, and so on.

Properly inventorying every mobile device so that you can properly secure all such devices is critical.

Locating Your Vulnerable Data

Review what data your devices house. Think of the worst-case consequences if an unauthorized person obtained your data or it leaked to the public on the Internet. No list of items to search for can possibly cover all possible scenarios, but here are some things to think about. Do you have

>> Private photos and videos

>> Recordings of your voice

>> Images of your handwriting (especially of your signature)

- >> Financial records
- >> Medical records
- >> School-related documents
- >> Password lists
- >> Repositories of digital keys
- >> Documents containing:
- >> Credit card numbers
- >> SSNs/EINs/taxpayer identification numbers
- >> Maiden names
- >> Codes to physical locks or other passcodes
- >> Correspondence with the IRS and state tax authorities
- >> Lawsuit-related information
- >> Employment-related information
- >> Mother's maiden name
- >> Birth dates
- >> Passport numbers
- >> Driver's license numbers
- >> Information about your vehicles
- >> Information about your former addresses
- >> Biometric data (fingerprints, retina scan, facial geometry, keyboard dynamics, and so on)

These items will need to be protected against cyberthreats, as described in multiple later chapters. But the data stores in which they reside also need to be protected physically, as described in the next section.

Creating and Executing a Physical Security Plan

In order to adequately physically protect your technology and data, you should not attempt to simply deploy various security controls on an ad hoc basis. Rather, it is far better to develop and implement a physical security plan — doing so, will help you avoid making costly mistakes.

In most cases, physically securing computing systems relies on applying a well-known established principal of crime prevention, known as Crime Prevention Through Environmental Design (CPTD), that states that you can reduce the likelihood of certain crimes being committed if you create a physical environment that allows legitimate users to feel secure, but makes ill-doers unconformable with actually carrying out any planned problematic activities.

Understanding this high-level concept can help you think about ways to keep your own systems and data safe. Three components of CPTD as they apply in general to preventing crime include access control, surveillance, and marking:

>> **Access control:** Limiting access to authorized parties, by using fences, monitored entrances and exits, proper landscaping, and so on makes it harder for criminals to penetrate a building or other facility, and increases the risk to crooks that they will be noticed, thus discouraging potential criminals from actually carrying out crimes.

>> **Surveillance:** Criminals often avoid committing crimes that are likely to be seen and recorded; as such, they gravitate away from environments that they know are well-watched. Cameras, guards, and motion-sensitive-lighting all discourage crime.

>> **Marking:** Criminals tend to avoid areas that are clearly marked as belonging to someone else — for example, through the use of fences and signs — as they do not want to stand out and be easily noticeable when committing crimes. Likewise, they avoid environments in which authorized parties are marked. Consider, for example, that an unauthorized person not wearing a post office uniform while walking around in an area marked "U.S. Postal Service Employees Only" is far more likely to be noticed and stopped than someone else walking in a similar unmarked environment belonging to a business that does not require uniforms.

TIP

You can apply these same principles in your own home — for example, placing a computer in a parent's home office sends a message to children, babysitters, and guests that the device is off limits, far stronger than the message would be delivered if the same machine were located in a family room or den. Likewise, curious babysitters or houseguests are far less likely to go into one's private home office without permission after being told not to if they are aware that the area is monitored with cameras.

You know your own environment. By applying these concepts you can improve the likelihood that unauthorized parties will not attempt to gain unauthorized access to your computers and data.

Implementing Physical Security

You can use many techniques and technologies to help secure an object or facility. How much physical security you implement for a device depends heavily on the purpose for which it is being used and what types of information it houses.

Here are some examples of methods of securing devices — based on your tolerance level for risk and your budget, you may choose variants of all, some, or none of these techniques:

>> **Locks:** For example, store devices in a locked room, with access to the room provided to only those people who need to use the device. In some environments, you may be able to utilize a smart lock to record or monitor all entrances and exits from the room. Another popular variant is to store laptops in a safe located in one's master bedroom or home office when the computers are not in use.

>> **Video cameras:** For example, consider having a video camera focused on the devices to see who accesses them and when they do so.

>> **Security guards:** Obviously, security guards are not a practical solution in most home environments, but human defenders do have a time and place. For example, consider posting guards inside the room where the device is located, outside the room, in halls around the entrance to the room, outside the building, and outside the perimeter fence.

>> **Alarms:** Alarms not only serve as a reactive force that scare away criminals who actually attempt to enter a home or office, they also serve as a strong deterrent, pushing many opportunistic evildoers to "look elsewhere" and target someone else.

>> **Perimeter security:** Traffic posts prevent people from crashing cars into a facility, and proper fences and walls prevent people from approaching a home or office building. You should note that most experts believe that a fence under 8 feet tall does not provide any significant security value when it comes to potential human intruders.

>> **Lighting:** Criminals tend to avoid well-lit places. Motion-triggered lighting is even more of a deterrent than static lighting. When lights go on suddenly, people in the area are more likely to turn and look at what just happened — and see the criminals just as they are illuminated.

>> **Environmental risk mitigation:** If you're in an area that is likely to be hit by floods, for example, ensure that computing resources are stationed somewhere not likely to flood. If such advice seems obvious, consider that residents of northern New Jersey lost telephone service after a storm in the late 1990s when telephone switching equipment flooded — because it was situated in

the basement of a building standing next to a river. Having proper defenses against fires is another critical element of environmental risk mitigation.

>> **Backup power and contingencies for power failures:** Power failures impact not only your computers, but many security systems as well.

>> **Contingencies during renovations and other construction, and so forth:** The risks to data and computers during home renovations are often overlooked. Leaving your cellphone unattended when workers are routinely entering and exiting your home, for example, can be a recipe for a stolen device and/or the compromise of data on the device.

>> **Risks from backups:** Remember to protect backups of data with the same security precautions as you do the original copies of the data. Spending time and money protecting a computer with a safe and cameras because of the data on its hard drive, for example, is silly if you leave backups of that same data on portable hard drives stored on a family room shelf in plain sight of anyone visiting your home.

Of course, you should not consider the preceding list to be comprehensive. But, if you think about how you can apply each of these items to help keep your devices safe within the context of a CPTD approach, you will likely benefit from much greater odds against an "unfortunate incident" occurring than if you do not. (For more on CPTD, see the earlier section "Creating and Executing a Physical Security Plan.")

Security for Mobile Devices

TIP

Of course, mobile devices — that is, computers, tablets, smartphones, and other electronic devices that are moved from location to location on a regular basis — pose additional risks because these devices can be easily lost or stolen. As such, when it comes to mobile devices, one simple, yet critically important, physical security principle should be added: Keep your devices in sight or locked up.

Such advice may sound obvious; sadly, however, a tremendous number of devices are stolen each year when left unattended, so you can be sure that the advice is either not obvious or not followed — and, in either case, you want to internalize it and follow it.

In addition to watching over your phone, tablet, or laptop, you should enable location broadcasting, remotely triggerable alarms, and remote wipe — all of which can be invaluable at quickly reducing the risk posed if the device is lost or stolen. Some devices even offer a feature to photograph or video record anyone using a mobile device after the user flags it as stolen — which can not only help you locate the device, but can also help law enforcement catch any thieves involved in stealing it.

Realizing That Insiders Pose the Greatest Risks

According to most experts, the majority of information-security incidents involve insider threats — meaning that the biggest cyber risk to businesses are posed by their own employees. Likewise, if you share a home computer with family members who are less cyber-aware, they may pose the greatest risk to your cybersecurity. You may take great care of your machine and be diligent with cybersecurity every single day, but if your teen downloads malware-infected software onto the device on even a single occasion, you may be in for a nasty surprise.

One critical rule from "the old days" that rings true today — even though it is often dismissed as outdated due to the use of technologies such as encryption — is that anyone who can physically access a computer may be able to access the data on that computer.

REMEMBER

Anyone who can physically access a computer may be able to access the data on that computer.

This rule is true even if encryption is utilized, for at least two reasons: Someone who accesses your device may not be able to access your data, but that person can certainly destroy it and may even be able to access it due to one or more of the following reasons:

>> You may not have set up the encryption properly.

>> Your machine may have an exploitable vulnerability.

>> The encryption software may have a bug in it that undermines its ability to properly protect your secrets.

>> Someone may have obtained the password to decrypt.

>> Someone may be willing to copy your data and wait until computers are powerful enough to break your encryption. This is especially true today, as experts believe that in the not-so-distant future we will see the next generation of computers (known as quantum computers) that will be able to undermine most of today's encryption mechanisms.

WARNING

Here is the bottom line: If you do not want people to access data, not only should you secure it logically (for example, with encryption), you should also secure it physically in order to prevent them from obtaining a copy of the data, even in encrypted form.

On that note, if your computer contains files that you do not want your children to have access to, do not share your computer with your children. That may seem like obvious advice, but you would be amazed at how often it is ignored for financial reasons. (Why should I buy a second computer for my children when I already have a perfectly good computer at home?)

REMEMBER

Do not rely solely on digital security. Utilize a physical defense. While it is true that crafty, skilled children may be able to hack your computer across your LAN, the risks of such an attack occurring are miniscule compared with the temptation of a curious child who is actually using your computer. That said, ideally you should keep your most sensitive data and machines on a network physically isolated from the one that your children use.

Chapter **6**

Cybersecurity Considerations When Working from Home

I n early 2020, the spread of a new, deadly and highly contagious disease — COVID-19 — began to facilitate a worldwide change in the way many people work. For the first time in generations, the need to stop a global pandemic led to governments enforcing lockdowns that prohibited people from working together in offices. Unlike during all prior such lockdowns in human history, however, technological advances made over the past few decades meant that many people who would otherwise have been unable to work, could, in fact, continue to do their jobs — albeit remotely.

Naturally, the sudden transition of a tremendous number of in-office workers to remote workers, and on such short notice, translated into a whole host of cybersecurity challenges. In addition, while many business leaders initially thought that the remote-working phase would be short-lived, that was not to be the case. Remote working in some fashion is here to stay, and, therefore, in the second edition of this book, I dedicate a chapter to discussing cybersecurity issues related specifically to working from home.

Network Security Concerns

A major cybersecurity concern with working remotely involves the networks from which remote employees access sensitive data. If those networks aren't properly secured, two really bad things can occur:

>> Someone may steal sensitive information — and neither the employee, nor the employer, may ever know that it happened.

>> Malware or a hacker may compromise some user's device and leapfrog from it to other corporate devices and networks — and, once inside corporate resources, wreak havoc in any one or more of many possible ways.

Why are remote-worker networks often unsafe?

Businesses often have much better firewalls than those offered in consumer products — and most remote workers are using consumer-grade routers and no additional firewalls. Should your employer really be trusting its cybersecurity to the router you bought for $19.99 on Black Friday five years ago? Likewise, most consumers have no idea how to configure their routers or firewalls, and utilize only basic options. Even when they are more sophisticated, people rarely deploy true intrusion detection systems and other security technologies at home. Such offerings are simply not available in inexpensive routers.

Businesses often have all sorts of security technologies deployed at their perimeters. An organization's firewalls, for example, may block certain types of outbound requests, and data loss prevention systems may stop emails that contain sensitive materials that appear to have been inadvertently attached to the messages. Remote workers rarely, if ever, have such security functionality available from their routers. On that note, how many employers even know what routers their employees are using when their employees work from home, never mind know if those routers have had their firmware kept up to date? Do managers of businesses really know if an employee working from home has properly conducted vulnerability scans?

Besides the issue of the router's patch level and firmware, how many employers have verified that their employees have properly secured their personal home-based Wi-Fi access points? And how many employers know who else is using the home network — and for what they are using it? Kids downloading games can easily infect computers with malware, and malware can spread via network connections.

While some have suggested that employers can utilize a full tunneling virtual private network (VPN) to address such risks — such a VPN would force all Internet traffic from the user to the employer's network and would route all Internet requests through the employer's security systems at the perimeter. Doing so is often highly risky as it essentially means that malware and other cyber-problems present on the employee's home network can potentially propagate to the employer's network. It also means that if something goes wrong with the employer's connectivity, the employee cannot work — even remotely.

How can you address such risks?

Ideally, your employer should provide you with a second router that connects to your home router — the second router would effectively form a separate work environment, with a different network segment, that is logically (somewhat) isolated from all of the other devices on the network.

If properly set up, the work network will be able to initiate outbound requests to the Internet, but your home network will not be able to initiate requests to the work network. One way to do this is shown in Figure 6-1. This type of configuration is better than using one router, but still not ideal as the work network can still communicate with the home network. While, in theory, there are ways to ensure that such a configuration is still secure, the opportunity increases for making configuration mistakes undermining security. Ideally, therefore, use two internal routers as shown Figure 6-2. It should be noted however, that deploying the third network segment as shown in Figure 6-2 can complicate printing and various other tasks, but as printers are inexpensive and do not take up a lot of space, ask your employer to supply you with a work-related printer.

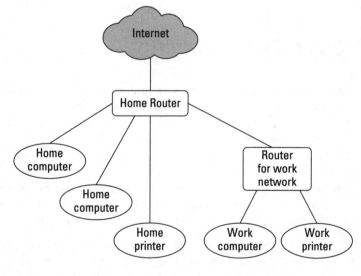

FIGURE 6-1: Network setup in which the work router communicates through the home router.

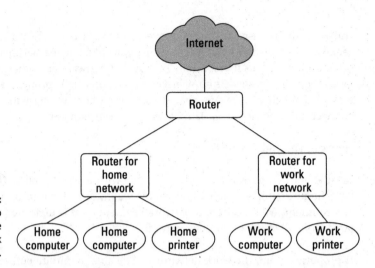

FIGURE 6-2:
Network setup
using separate
routers for work
and home.

TIP

In addition, because the work network router is supplied by your employer, your employer can select an appropriately equipped and remotely manageable device — and can keep it updated and patched.

Ideally, employees should also use computers owned by their employers — both for legal reasons (to prevent various privacy-related matters if private devices are used) and to prevent data leaks and prevent corporate data from ending up on computers that could be used by others and/or connected to insecure networks. In a perfect world, the only devices that ever connect to a work network are those owned by the employer.

Device Security Concerns

Insecure devices can lead to the same problems as insecure networks — data can potentially be pilfered and/or hackers can penetrate the organization and wreak havoc of all sorts. As I mention in the previous section, ideally, all devices used for work should be owned and managed by your employer. There are many reasons for this:

» Employers should know what is on workers' devices so that workers can work efficiently and with minimal distractions and without potential spyware or the like capturing data or otherwise performing nefarious actions.

» Employers can be liable if they ask an employee to install an app on the employee's personal device and the app creates vulnerabilities or otherwise causes problems, such as conflicting with other software on the device.

>> If an employee suddenly leaves the organization and has work-related data on a personal device, that data may remain intact and put the employer at risk intentionally or inadvertently. The same holds true of the device is stolen from the employee. Likewise, in a more extreme case, if an employee were to die, who knows where the employee's laptop containing sensitive work-related information will end up.

That said, issuing employer devices for employees to use from home is not always a practical possibility.

REMEMBER

In any case, all computing devices — whether laptops, tablets, and/or smartphones — need appropriate security software installed, enabled, and kept up to date. Such devices should also have the ability to be remotely wiped if lost or stolen, and all relevant data on them must be both encrypted and appropriately backed up.

Location Cybersecurity

While we often think of the technology handing data as being the primary factor impacting the security of that data, the reality is that other factors play at least as great a role. As described throughout this book, people themselves are a significant factor. Another important element is the location in which systems are used and data is accessed. This factor has dramatically increased in significance as a result of the migration from in office working to remote working, which means that location-based dangers are more important than ever to understand.

Shoulder surfing

One of the greatest risks created by employees working remotely to the security and privacy of employer data is actually a quite old-fashioned danger. If an employee works in a place in which other people or cameras can see sensitive information as it is displayed on the screen of the user's device, the confidentiality of the data may be compromised.

Such a problem is known colloquially as *shoulder surfing*. It is hardly a new concept, but it still remains a problem. Especially when large numbers of workers are expected to work outside of their usual professional workspaces. So, ideally, if you are going to work from home, do exactly that — work from *home* — and not from coffee shops, public parks, or the like.

Also, if possible, work in an environment that is configured in such a manner that your significant others and/or kids are not able to view sensitive information either. If need be, employers may even purchase furniture or equipment to help you ensure such privacy.

Eavesdropping

Similar risks apply in regard to voice communication — don't discuss sensitive information over the phone or other voice communication system from a location in which other people can hear you. This may sound obvious, but prior to the pandemic, I heard many sensitive work-related calls transpiring on buses to and from New York City, while the bus-riding employee was oblivious to the fact that they were compromising the privacy of information that was clearly intended not to become public.

TIP

When working from home, a simple sound machine that generates white background noise — such as those used by many psychologists and psychiatrists to prevent people in waiting rooms from hearing the conversations taking place in treatment rooms — can be of great assistance.

Theft

Home offices are rarely as well secured as professional office spaces, and public locations — such as parks, libraries, and coffee shops — are even less secure. Remote workers, therefore, often stand a greater chance of having a laptop stolen from them than do their counterparts whose devices never leave their normal at-work offices.

Human errors

It is important to understand that if people are repetitively interrupted, they are more likely to make mistakes than if that were not the case, and mistakes, of course, can easily lead to data leaks. If you are working remotely, create a workspace where you can keep disruptions to a minimum. Of course, remote working locations are often much more problematic than professional offices in such regard — especially during a pandemic when children are home all day and attend school virtually. So, seek to create a workspace in which you can work efficiently while staying focused and keeping data as private as is reasonably possible.

Video Conferencing Cybersecurity

As a result of the transition from in-office work to remote work that began in 2020 as a result of the COVID-19 pandemic, the use of video call and video conferencing technology has skyrocketed, with the number of people who regularly make work-related video calls from outside of their official places of work growing by orders of magnitude in just a short period of time. With the sudden and rapid adoption of such a transformative and unfamiliar technology comes risks, and, in the case of video conferencing, those risks include serious risks to information security and privacy.

Keep private stuff out of camera view

When you video conference, make sure you do not have any sensitive information or other private material on display in your camera's frame. Keep in mind that mirrors and reflective surfaces in frame can also allow people in a video conference to see materials that are technically out of the camera's view. If the preceding two points sound obvious, feel free to search online for how many significant cases are known of people not being careful as such.

TIP

Consider using a virtual background (preferably with a physical green screen) to keep inquisitive eyes focused on you rather than on background elements. At a minimum, utilize blur background features made available to you by your particular video conferencing tool.

WARNING

When participating in a video conference from home in which your camera and/or microphone are on (for even part of the time), make sure that any and all other people in the home are aware that you are engaging in such a session. Warn them that you are sharing your camera feed and microphone, and that if they speak near you or walk near you, they may be heard or seen by others. Sadly, there have been many embarrassing incidents in which people walked half naked into the field of view of someone else's video conference session.

Keep video conferences secure from unauthorized visitors

Video conferencing cybersecurity is about much more than just keeping sensitive data out of frame. In fact, the tremendous number of security violations that occurred during the earlier months of the COVID-19 pandemic — in which unauthorized parties regularly joined Zoom meetings and wreaked havoc — led to the creation and proliferation of a new term: *Zoom bombing*. To reduce the chances that your video communications will be Zoom bombed, consider the following advice:

>> **Never use video conferencing for secret conversations.** No modern commercial video conferencing services are appropriate for truly secret conversations. Remember, video conferencing software, like all other software packages, may have exploitable vulnerabilities within it.

>> **Password-protect your sessions.** If unauthorized users try to join your video calls without authorization, they will find doing so challenging, as without the password to your calls, they will not be able to easily join you.

>> **Create a new room name for every meeting.** Some video call services allow you to use the same meeting room name over and over. Do not do so, as this makes it much easier for someone who obtains information about one of your calls to join another call.

>> **Use a waiting room.** Many popular video-conferencing apps allow you to automatically redirect all participants into a virtual waiting room after they join the call. You, the host, get to decide who gets admitted from the waiting room into the actual call meeting room; you can usually either admit everyone in one shot, or select participants individually to admit into the session. You may also have the option of having pre-registered participants placed directly into the meeting room upon their joining the session, but forcing unknown parties seeking to join to wait for admission from the waiting room.

>> **Lock your sessions.** Once all of the expected participants have joined a session, or after some period of time after the start of a session if some such folks have not joined, lock the session so that no additional parties can join.

>> **"Throw the bums out."** Periodically scan the list of who is participating in your meeting. If you see anyone who does not belong, remove them immediately! Likewise, if an authorized participant is causing problems during a video call session, consider removing them as well. If you locked the session, you should only need to review the list of participants once — right after you lock the session. Of course, if you have cohosts, your locking may be undone by them, so make sure to scan the participant list periodically.

>> **Disable private chatting.** If possible, disable the ability of participants to private message one another via the video conferencing app. If they want to chat, let them use their regular chat apps.

>> **Do not allow general participants to share their screens.** Unless there is a need for a particular party in a virtual meeting to share their device's screen with other participants, either disable screen sharing altogether or set screen sharing to be available to only yourself, the host.

>> **Do not overshare meeting login information on social media.** When possible — and I know that it is not always possible — do not share on public social platforms any login details for meetings. Instead, if necessary, advertise about the meeting, but require people to sign up for it, check the list of registered participants, and email the relevant login information to the folks who both signed up and you want to attend. And, in any event, private meetings should *never* be announced on public social media.

Social Engineering Issues

People who work from home, in environments separate from those in which their colleagues do their own jobs, are more likely to fall for some types of social engineering attacks than are people who work together, in person, with their colleagues. People in distinct locations cannot as easily verify the authenticity of a request. A homebound CFO who receives a request from a CEO to issue a payment, for example, cannot simply walk to the office next door and ask the CEO in person if the request is legitimate.

In addition, as we saw during the early weeks of the COVID-19 pandemic, many businesses that were forced to suddenly convert to a remote work model did not have the chance to properly prepare for such a situation, and as a result, various technologies that they had in place in their professional offices to reduce the likelihood of users being exposed to social engineering attacks were not successfully extended to remote locations prior to the commencement of remote work.

REMEMBER

The most important element in a defense against social engineering attacks is to ensure that any and every remote worker understands that they are a target. People who internalize such a belief tend to act differently in situations that could lead to a data breach than do those who do not truly accept that reality. Of course, training and assessments can also help in this regard.

Regulatory Issues

The fact that people need to work remotely due to the rapid spreading of a dangerous virus does not negate the requirements of various laws and other regulations related to information security and privacy. Businesses subject to Europe's General Data Protection Regulation (GDPR), for example, still must ensure that remote working does not undermine efforts to protect the privacy of personal information. Likewise, the fact that a medical facility might have allowed its clerical staff to work remotely on tasks such as billing insurance companies for services, does not excuse it from compliance with the relevant data protection requirements of the Health Insurance Portability and Accountability Act of 1996 (HIPAA). U.S. Securities and Exchange Commission (SEC) rules still apply as well — so insider information cannot be allowed to leak, or otherwise be provided even to authorized parties at inappropriate times. The same holds true for other regulations and industry guidelines.

Make sure your remote working program is not going to get you or others into regulatory hot water.

3

Protecting Yourself from Yourself

IN THIS PART . . .

Understand how to secure your accounts.

Learn all about passwords, including how to create strong passwords that you can actually remember.

Protect yourself and your loved ones against social engineering.

Chapter **7**

Securing Your Accounts

The weakest link in the cybersecurity chain is almost always people, and the greatest threat to your own cybersecurity is likely yourself, with the members of your family being a close second. As such, all of the technology and technical knowledge in the world won't deliver much value if you don't also address various human shortcomings.

Realizing You're a Target

Perhaps the most significant first step in securing yourself digitally is to understand that you're a target and that nefarious parties have the desire to breach your computer systems, electronically accessible accounts, and anything else they can get their hands on.

Even if you already realize that you're a target, it is important that you truly internalize such a notion. People who believe that criminals want to breach their computers and phones act differently than people who do not appreciate this reality, and whose lack of skepticism sometimes leads them into trouble. There is a difference between knowing something in theory and truly believing it. If you want to stay secure you must convince yourself that you really are a target, not just simply understand that in theory you may be.

WARNING

Because your family members can also impact your digital security, they also need to be aware that they are potential targets. If your children take unwise risks online, they may inadvertently inflict harm not only on themselves, but upon you and other members of the family as well. In some cases, attackers have managed to attack people's employers via remote connections that were compromised because children misused computers on the same networks as computers that the employees were using for working remotely. Think about how dangerous such attacks can be and how much damage they can cause during an era in which large portions of the population work from home.

The threat posed by such attacks is usually not that a criminal will directly steal someone's money or data, but rather that some party will seek to harm the target in some other manner — a manner that may ultimately translate into some form of financial, military, political, or other benefit to the attacker and (potentially) damage of some sort to the victim. Often the damage is far greater than if the criminal were just seeking to "make a quick buck."

Securing Your External Accounts

Chapter 4 discusses how you can acquire your own technology products. But using these products isn't enough to keep you cybersecure as you, no doubt, have digital data of significant value that is stored outside of your own physical possession — that is, outside of data systems and data stores under your control.

In fact, data about every person living in the western world today is likely stored on computer systems belonging to many businesses, organizations, and governmental agencies. Sometimes those systems reside within the facilities of the organizations to which they belong, sometimes they're located at shared data centers, and, sometimes the systems themselves are virtual machines rented from a third-party provider. Additionally, some such data may reside in cloud-based systems offered by a third party. Not always is the data (or every copy of the data) even located within the same country as the people who are the subjects of the data.

In any event, such data can be broken down and divided into many different categories, depending on which aspects of it a person is interested in. One way of examining the data for the purposes of discovering how to secure it, for example, is to group it according to the following scheme:

>> Accounts, and the data within them, that a user established and controls

>> Data belonging to organizations that a user has willingly and knowingly interacted with, but the user has no control over the data

>> Data in the possession of organizations that the user has never knowingly established a relationship with

Addressing the risks of each type of data requires a different strategy.

Securing Data Associated with User Accounts

When you bank online, shop online, use social media, or even simply browse the web, you provide all sorts of data to the parties that you interact with. When you establish and maintain an account with a bank, store, social media provider, or other online party, you gain control over significant amounts of data related to yourself that the party maintains on your behalf. Obviously, you can't fully control the security of that data because the data is not in your possession. That said, you should have a strong interest in protecting that data — and, in not undermining the protections for the data that the party hosting your account has established.

While every situation and account has its unique attributes, certain strategies can help keep your data secure at third parties. Obviously, not all the ideas in the following sections apply to every situation, but applying the appropriate items from the menu to your various accounts and online behavior can dramatically improve your odds of remaining cybersecure.

Conduct business with reputable parties

There is nothing wrong with supporting small businesses — in fact, doing so is quite admirable. And, it is certainly true that many large firms have suffered serious security breaches. But if you search for the latest electronic gizmo, for example, and one store that you have never heard of is offering it at a substantial discount from the prices offered at all well-known stores, be wary. There may be a legitimate reason for the discount — or there may be a scam in the works.

WARNING

Always check the websites of stores that you're conducting business with to see whether something looks off — and beware if it does.

Use official apps and websites

Clones of official apps have been found in various app stores. If you install a banking, credit card, or shopping app for a particular company, make sure that you install the official app and not some malicious impersonator. Install apps only from reputable app stores, such as Google Play, Amazon AppStore, and Apple App Store.

Don't install software from untrusted parties

Malware that infects a computer can capture sensitive information from both other programs and web sessions running on the device. If a website is offering free copies of movies, software, or other items that normally cost money, not only may the offerings be stolen copies, but ask yourself how the operator is making money — it may be by distributing malware.

Don't root your phone

You may be tempted to *root* your phone (especially if your phone runs the Android operating system). *Rooting* is a process that allows you greater control over your device — but rooting also undermines various security capabilities, and may allow malware to capture sensitive information from other apps on the device, leading to account compromises.

Don't provide unnecessary sensitive information

Don't provide private information to anyone who doesn't need that particular data. For example, don't give your Social Security number to any online stores or doctors. While they often ask for it, they have no need for it.

REMEMBER

Keep in mind that the less information about you that a specific party has, the less data that can be compromised, and correlated, in case of a breach.

Use payment services that eliminate the need to share credit card numbers

Services like PayPal, Samsung Pay, Apple Pay, and so on let you make online payments without having to give vendors your actual credit card number. If a vendor is breached, the information about your account that is likely to be stolen is significantly less likely to lead to fraud (and, perhaps, even various forms of identity theft) than if actual credit card data were stored at the vendor. Moreover, major payment sites have armies of skilled information security professionals working to keep them safe that vendors accepting such payments can rarely, if ever, match.

TIP

In addition, many stores now accept such payments using near-field communication (NFC), which is another form of contactless communication between devices in which you hold your phone against or near a payment processing device to wirelessly make payment. Not only is such a payment scheme safer from a cybersecurity standpoint than handing credit cards to a clerk, but it also avoids exposing both payers and cashiers to the biological risks posed by passing cash or payment cards between potentially germ-infected people.

Use one-time, virtual credit card numbers when appropriate

Some financial institutions allow you to use an app (or website) to create disposable, one-time *virtual credit card numbers* that allow you to make a charge to a real credit card account (associated with the virtual number) without having to give the respective merchant your real credit card number. As seen in Figure 7-1, some virtual credit card systems also allow you to specify the maximum allowable charge size on a particular virtual card number at a figure much lower than it would be on the real corresponding card.

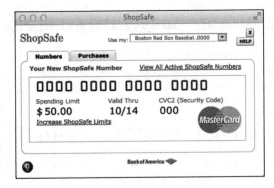

FIGURE 7-1:
A (slightly edited image of) a one-time credit card number generator.

While creating one-time numbers takes time and effort, and, in fact, may be overkill when doing repeated deals with a reputable vendor in whose information-security practices you have confidence, virtual credit card numbers do offer benefits for defending against potential fraud and may be appropriately used when dealing with less familiar parties.

Besides minimizing the risk to yourself if a vendor turns out to be corrupt, virtual credit card numbers offer other security benefits. If criminals hack a vendor and steal your virtual credit card number that was previously used, not only can they not make charges with it, their attempts to do so may even help law enforcement track them down, as well as help relevant forensics teams identify the source of the credit card number data leak.

Monitor your accounts

TIP

You should regularly check your payment, banking, shopping, and other financial accounts for any unrecognized activities. Ideally, do this check by not only looking at online transaction logs, but also by checking relevant monthly statements (no matter whether such statements are physically delivered in the mail, sent to you electronically over email, displayed in apps, or posted on a web portal for you to download) for anything that does not belong.

Report suspicious activity ASAP

REMEMBER

The faster a case of fraud is reported to the parties responsible for addressing it, the greater the chance of reversing it, and of preventing further abuse of whatever materials were abused in order to commit it. Also, the sooner the fraud is reported, the greater the chance of catching the parties committing it. It is important, therefore, to quickly report potential cases of fraud and other forms of suspicious activity.

Employ a proper password strategy

While conventional wisdom may be to require complex passwords for all systems, such a password strategy fails in practice. Be sure to implement a proper password strategy. For more on choosing passwords, see Chapter 8.

Utilize multifactor authentication

Multifactor authentication means authentication that requires a user to authenticate using two or more of the following methods:

>> Something that the user knows, such as a password

>> Something that the user is, such as a fingerprint

>> Something that the user has, such as a hardware token

For extremely sensitive systems, you should use forms of authentication that are stronger than passwords alone. The following forms of authentication all have their places:

>> **Biometrics,** which means using measurements of various human characteristics to identify people. Fingerprints, voiceprints, iris scans, facial structures, the speed at which people type different characters on a keyboard, and the like are all examples of features that differ between people, and that can be compared in order to distinguish between folks and establish someone's identity.

>> **Digital certificates,** which effectively prove to a system that a particular public key represents the presenter of the certificate. If the presenter of the certificate is able to decrypt messages encrypted with the public key in the certificate, it means that the presenter possesses the corresponding private key, which only the legitimate owner should have.

>> **One-time passwords,** or one-time tokens, generated by apps, read from a list of codes on a sheet of paper, or sent via SMS to your cellphone.

>> **Hardware tokens,** which are typically small electronic devices that either plug into a USB port, display a number that changes every minute or so, or allow users to enter a challenge number and receive a corresponding response number back. Today, smartphone apps perform such functions, allowing, at least theoretically, the smartphone to assume the role of a hardware token. Figure 7-2 shows you an example of using such an app to generate a one-time code for logging into Snapchat. (Note that smartphones can suffer from all sorts of security vulnerabilities that hardware tokens can't suffer from, so hardware tokens are still likely more appropriate for certain high-risk situations.)

TIP

>> **Knowledge-based authentication,** which is based on real knowledge, not simply answering questions with small numbers of possible answers that are often guessable like "What color was your first car?" Note that technically speaking, adding knowledge-based authentication questions to password authentication doesn't create multifactor authentication since both the password and the knowledge-based answer are examples of things that a user knows. However, doing so certainly does improve security when the questions are chosen properly.

Most financial institutions, social media companies, and major online retailers offer multifactor authentication — use it.

Also, note that while sending one-time passwords to users' smartphones via text messages theoretically verifies that a person logging in possesses the smartphone that the user is supposed to possess (something that the user has), various vulnerabilities undermine that supposition. It is potentially possible, for example, for a sophisticated criminal to intercept text messages even without possessing the relevant phone, or to hack into another chat application used for transmitting such codes.

FIGURE 7-2:
One-time
password for
Snapchat
generated by the
app Authy — an
example of an
app-generated
multifactor
authentication
token.

> Snapchat: john
>
> SNAPCHAT TOKEN IS:
>
> # 538 144
>
> YOUR TOKEN EXPIRES IN   28

Log out when you're finished

Don't rely on automatic timeouts, closing the browser, or shutting down a computer to log you out of accounts. Manually log out every time you're finished. Don't leave yourself logged in between sessions unless you're on a device that you know with — as close as possible to — certainty will remain secure.

Use your own computer or phone

You don't know how well others have secured any one of more of their devices — a particular computer may, for example, have malware on it that can capture your passwords and other sensitive information or that can hijack sessions and/or perform all sorts of other nefarious activities.

Furthermore, despite the fact that doing so is severely problematic, some applications and websites — to this day — cache data on endpoints that are used for accessing them. You don't want to leave other people souvenirs consisting of data from your sensitive sessions.

Lock your computer

Lock any computer that you use for accessing sensitive accounts, and keep it physically secure as well.

Use a separate, dedicated computer for sensitive tasks

Consider purchasing a special computer that you use for online banking and other sensitive tasks. For many people, a second computer isn't practical, but if it is, having such a machine — on which you never read email, access social media, browse the web, and so on — offers security benefits.

Use a separate, dedicated browser for sensitive web-based tasks

If you can't obtain a separate computer, at least use a separate browser for sensitive tasks. Don't use the same browser that you use for reading the news, accessing social media, checking out blog posts, and/or most other activities.

Secure your access devices

Every phone, laptop, tablet, and desktop used for accessing secure systems should have security software on it, and that security software should be configured to regularly scan applications when they're added, as well as to run periodic general scans. Also, make sure to keep the security software up to date — most antivirus technology products perform far better against newer strains of malware when they're kept up to date than they do when they're not.

Keep your devices up to date

Besides keeping your security software up to date, be sure to install operating system and program updates to reduce your exposure to vulnerabilities. Windows AutoUpdate and its equivalent on other platforms can simplify this task for you.

Don't perform sensitive tasks over public Wi-Fi

If you must perform a sensitive task while you're in a location where you don't have access to a secure, private network, do what you need to do over the cellular system, not over public Wi-Fi. Public Wi-Fi simply poses too many risks. (To find out more about how to use public Wi-Fi safely, please see Chapter 21.)

Never use public Wi-Fi in high-risk places

Don't connect any device from which you plan to perform sensitive tasks to a Wi-Fi network in areas that are prone to *digital poisoning* — that is, to the hacking of, or distribution of malware, to devices that connect to a network.

Hacker conferences and certain countries, such as China, that are known for performing cyberespionage are examples of areas that are likely to experience digital poisoning. Many cybersecurity professionals recommend keeping your primary computer and phone off and using a separate computer and phone when working in such environments. Such advice appeared in the media on a regular basis in the lead-up to the 2022 Winter Olympics in Beijing, during which both journalists covering the games, as well as athletes participating in them, discussed how they planned to address such concerns.

Access your accounts only in safe locations

Even if you're using a private network, don't type passwords to sensitive systems or perform other sensitive tasks while in a location where people can easily watch what you type and see your screen.

Use appropriate devices

Don't try to save money by using dangerous equipment. Do not, for example, purchase electronics directly from sellers overseas and install unbranded networking devices that are not certified by any U.S. authorities. Such devices could have poisoned hardware within them.

Set appropriate limits

Various online venues let you set limits — for example, how much money can be transferred out of a bank account, the largest charge that can be made on a credit card with the card not physically present (as in the case of online purchases), or the maximum amount of goods that you can purchase in one day.

TIP

Set these limits. Not only will they limit the damage if a criminal does breach your account, but in some cases, they may trigger fraud alerts in real time as a crook tries to use the cards, and thereby both prevent theft and increase the odds of law enforcement apprehending the relevant criminals.

Use alerts

If your bank, credit card provider, or a store that you frequent offers the ability to set up text or email alerts, you should seriously consider taking advantage of those services. Theoretically, it is ideal to have the issuer send you an alert every time activity occurs on your account. From a practical standpoint, however, if doing so would overwhelm you and cause you to ignore all the messages (as is the case for most people), consider asking to be notified when transactions are made over a certain dollar amount (which may be able to be set to different thresholds for different stores or accounts) or otherwise appear to the issuer to be potentially fraudulent.

Periodically check access device lists

Some websites and apps — especially those of financial institutions — allow you to check the list of devices that have accessed your account. Checking this list each time that you log in can help you identify potential security problems quickly.

Check last login info

After you log in to some websites and via some apps — especially those of financial institutions — you may be shown information as to when and from where you last successfully logged in prior to the current session. Whenever any entity shows you such information, take a quick glance. If something is amiss and a criminal recently logged in while pretending to be you, it may stand out like a sore thumb.

Respond appropriately to any fraud alerts

If you receive a phone call from a bank, credit card company, or store about potential fraud on your account, respond quickly. But do not do so by speaking with the party who called you. Instead, contact the outlet at a known valid number that is advertised on its website.

Never send sensitive information over an unencrypted connection

When you access websites, look for the padlock icon (see Figure 7-3), indicating that encrypted HTTPS is being used. Today, HTTPS is ubiquitous; even many websites that do not ask users to submit sensitive data utilize it. If you don't see the icon, unencrypted HTTP is being used. In such a case, don't provide sensitive information or log in.

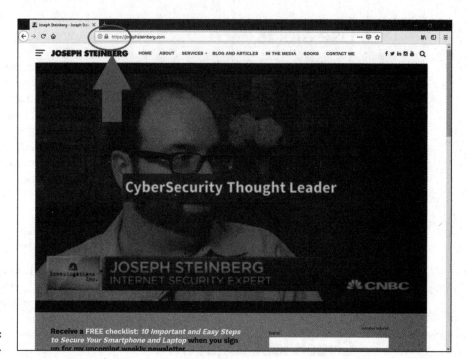

FIGURE 7-3:
A secure website.

TIP

The lack of a padlock on a site that is prompting for a login and password or handling financial transactions is a huge red flag that something is seriously amiss. However, contrary to what you've likely heard in the past, the presence of the lock doesn't necessarily mean that the site is safe.

Beware of social engineering attacks

In the context of cybersecurity, social engineering refers to the psychological manipulation by cyberattackers of their intended victims into performing actions that without such manipulation the targets would not perform or into divulging confidential information that they otherwise would not divulge. A huge portion of successful data breaches begin with social engineering attacks.

To help prevent yourself from falling prey to social engineering attacks, consider any and all emails, text messages, phone calls, or social media communications from all banks, credit card companies, healthcare providers, stores, and so on to be potentially fraudulent.

WARNING

Never click on links in any such correspondence. Always connect with such parties by entering the URL in the URL bar of the web browser.

Establish voice login passwords

Online access isn't the only path that a criminal can use to breach your accounts. Many crooks do reconnaissance online and subsequently social engineer their ways into people's accounts using old-fashioned phone calls to the relevant customer service departments at the target organizations.

TIP

To protect yourself and your accounts, establish voice login passwords for your accounts whenever possible — that is, set up passwords that must be given to customer service personnel in order for them to be able to provide any information from your accounts or to make changes to them. Many companies offer this capability, but relatively few people actually use it.

Protect your cellphone number

If you use strong authentication via text messages, ideally set up a forwarding phone number to your cellphone and use that number when giving out your cell number. Doing so reduces the chances that criminals will be able to intercept one-time passwords that are sent to your phone and also diminishes the chances of various other attacks succeeding.

For example, Google Voice allows you to establish a new phone number that forwards to your cellphone so that you can give out a number other than your real cellphone number and reserve the real number for use within the authentication process.

WARNING

If you use Google Voice or another free service, be sure to occasionally use the number for calls as well, as if you fail to do so, some providers may ultimately "reclaim" the number due to non-usage.

Don't click on links in emails or text messages

Clicking on links is one of the primary ways that people get diverted to fraudulent websites. For example, I recently received an email message that contained a link. If I had clicked the link in the message shown in Figure 7-4, I would have been brought to a phony LinkedIn login page that collects LinkedIn username and password combinations and provides them to criminals. Phishing emails and the like are examples of social engineering attacks, which are described earlier.

From: LinkedIn connections <noreply@linkedin.com> <Rob@athleticclubofbend.com>
To:
Cc:
Subject: Your connection sent you a message

A user replied to your message on LinkedIn

Subject - RE: Follow Up

Login with your LinkedIn Credentials below to read and reply.

Read Your Message Now

Unsubscribe | Help

FIGURE 7-4:
Email with a link to a phony page.

Securing Data with Parties You've Interacted With

When you interact online with a party, not all of the data related to your interaction is under your control. If you browse a website with typical web browser settings, that site may track your activity. Because many sites syndicate content from third parties — for example from advertising networks — sites may even be able to track your behavior on other sites.

To understand how this works, consider two different businesses with two different websites that are using the same advertising network. When the businesses add code to their discrete, separate sites, that code loads advertisements directly from the ad network. When a user visits the first site, the ad network may send a cookie to the user's device, which the same ad network can read back when the user visits the second site, since both sites cause the user to interact with the same ad network.

If you have an account on any sites that do such tracking and log in, all the sites utilizing the syndicated content may know your true identity and plenty of information about you — even though you never told them anything about yourself. Even if you don't have such an account or don't log in, profiles of your behavior may be established and used for marketing purposes, even without knowing who you are. (Of course, if you ever log in in the future to any site using the network, all the sites with the profiles may correlate them to your true identity.)

It is far more difficult to protect data about you that is in the possession of third parties but that is not under your control than it is to protect data in your accounts.

That does not mean, however, that you're powerless. (Ironically, and sadly, most owners of such data likely do a better job protecting data about people than do the people themselves.)

TIP

Besides employing the strategies in the previous section, you may want to browse in private sessions. For example, by using a Tor browser — which, as shown in Figure 7-5, automatically routes all your Internet traffic through computers around the world before sending it to its destination — you make it difficult for third parties to track you. As discussed in Chapter 4, the Tor browser bundle is free and comes with all sorts of privacy-related features enabled, including blocking cookies and canvas fingerprinting, an advanced form of tracking devices.

FIGURE 7-5:
My website as seen in a Tor browser, with the Tor circuit information button clicked so as to show how Tor is hiding the user's point of origin. The image was generated using the Tor browser bundle running on a computer in New Jersey, USA, but because of Tor's security features, appears to the web server as if it were in the United Kingdom.

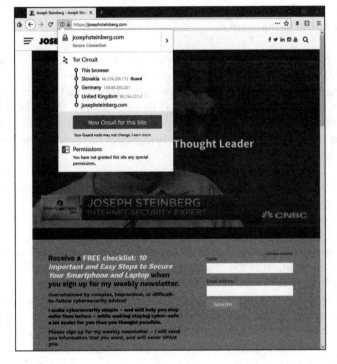

If Tor seems complicated, you can also utilize a reputable VPN service for similar purposes.

REMEMBER

By using browsing technology that makes it harder for sites to track you, they are less likely to establish as detailed profiles about you — and the less data about you that they have, the less data about you that can be stolen. Besides, you may not want those parties to build profiles about you in the first place.

WARNING

One technology that, despite its name, does not prevent tracking at anywhere near the level that do Tor or VPNs is the private mode offered by most web browsers. Unfortunately, despite its name, the private mode suffers from multiple serious weaknesses in this regard and does not come close to ensuring privacy.

Securing Data at Parties You Haven't Interacted With

Numerous entities likely maintain significant amounts of data about you, despite the fact that you've never knowingly interacted with them or otherwise authorized them to maintain such information.

For example, at least one major social media service builds de facto profiles for people who don't (yet) have accounts with the service, but who have been mentioned by others or who have interacted with sites that utilize various social widgets or other related technologies. The service can then use these profiles for marketing purposes — even, in some cases, without knowing the person's true identity, and without the person being aware of what is going on behind the scenes.

Furthermore, various information services that collect information from numerous public databases establish profiles based on such data — containing details that you may not even realize was available to the public.

Some genealogy sites utilize all sorts of public records and also allow people to update the information about other people. This ability can lead to situations in which all sorts of nonpublic information about you may be available to subscribers to the site (or people with free trial subscriptions) without your knowledge or consent. Such sites make finding people's mothers' maiden names or mothers' birthdays easy, which undermines the authentication schemes used by many organizations.

Besides family tree sites, various professional sites maintain information about folks' professional histories, publications, and so on. And, of course, credit bureaus maintain all sorts of information about your behavior with credit — such information is submitted to them by financial institutions, collection agencies, and so on.

While the Fair Credit Reporting Act may help you manage the information that the bureaus have about you, it can't help you remove negative information that appears in other venues, such as in old newspaper articles that are online. Besides the privacy implications of such, if any information in those articles provides the answer to challenge questions used for authentication, it can create security risks. In such cases, you may want to reach out to the provider of the data, explain the situation, and ask it to remove the data. In some cases, they will cooperate.

In addition, some businesses, such as insurance companies and pharmacies, maintain medical information about people. Typically, individuals have little control over such data. Of course, this type of data, which isn't under your complete control, can impact you. The bottom line is that many entities likely maintain significant amounts of data about you, even though you have never directly interacted with them.

It is the duty of such organizations to protect their data stores, but they do not always properly do so. As the Federal Trade Commission notes on its website, a data breach at the credit bureau Equifax, discovered in 2017, exposed the sensitive personal information of 143 million Americans.

The reality is that other than in the cases in which you can manually update records or request that they be updated, you can do little to protect the data in such scenarios.

Securing Data by Not Connecting Hardware with Unknown Pedigrees

While we have graduated from 720 kilobyte floppies to 2 terabyte USB drives, not much has changed conceptually since the 1980s in terms of the general danger of connecting data storage media with a questionable pedigree into a computer. If you connect a USB drive containing malware-infested files to your laptop, you may infect your laptop. Memory cards pose similar risks, as infected contents can lead to serious cybersecurity problems for any device into which the memory cards are inserted.

In addition, any time you connect a piece of hardware to a computer via a USB connection, you potentially enable communications between the two connected devices. Because of the way Plug and Play works, certain code on a USB device executes on a computer whenever the USB drive is first connected — and if that code is poisoned, you could be hacked as well.

The same holds true for other USB devices. Drivers are usually loaded upon connection, so a device with poisoned hardware or flash memory can create serious risk for any computer to which it is attached — and to any devices on the same network as that computer.

Furthermore, there are also dangerous USB devices designed to "fry" computers. Such devices charge themselves via the USB port, store the electricity in a capacitor, and then essentially fire it all out into the USB port in one big burst, permanently damaging electronics within the connected device in under a second.

Even phone chargers and the like can pose problems. Anything that connects to a USB port can potentially seek to communicate with the USB-port-enabled-device, and can potentially try to kill the USB-enabled device by overwhelming it with electricity.

TIP

When you travel, be sure to bring your chargers, USB drives, and memory cards.

» Discovering how often you need to change passwords — or not

» Storing passwords

» Finding alternatives to passwords

Chapter **8**

Passwords

Most people alive today are familiar with the concept of passwords and with the use of passwords in the realm of cybersecurity. Yet, there are so many misconceptions about passwords, and misinformation about passwords has spread like wildfire, often leading to people undermining their own security with poor password practices, sometimes even done in the name of improving cybersecurity.

In this chapter, you discover some best practices vis-à-vis passwords. These practices should help you both maximize your own security and maintain reasonable ease of use.

Passwords: The Primary Form of Authentication

Password authentication refers to the process of verifying the identity of users (whether human or computer process) by asking users to supply a password — that is, a previously-agreed-upon secret piece of information — that ostensibly the party authenticating would only know if they were truly the party who it claimed to be. While the term "password" implies that the information consists of a single word, today's passwords can include combinations of characters that don't form words in any spoken or written language.

Despite the availability for decades of many other authentication approaches and technologies — many of which offer significant advantages over passwords — passwords remain de facto worldwide standard for authenticating people online. Repeated predictions of the demise of passwords have been proven untrue, and the number of passwords in use grows every day.

Because password authentication is so common and because so many data breaches have resulted in the compromise of password databases, the topic has received significant media attention, with reports often spreading various misleading information. Gaining a proper understanding of the realm of passwords is important if you want to be cybersecure.

Avoiding Simplistic Passwords

Passwords only secure systems if unauthorized parties can't easily guess them, or obtain them from other sources. Criminals often guess or otherwise obtain passwords by

>> **Guessing common passwords:** It's not a secret that 123456 and password are common passwords — data from recent breaches reveals that they are, in fact, among the most common passwords used on many systems (see the nearby sidebar)! Criminals exploit such sad reality and often attempt to breach accounts by using automated tools that feed systems passwords one at a time from lists of common passwords — and record when they have a hit. Sadly, those hits are often quite numerous.

>> **Launching dictionary attacks:** Because many people choose to use actual English words as passwords, some automated hacker tools simply feed all the words in the dictionary to a system one at a time. As with lists of common passwords, such attacks often achieve numerous hits.

>> **Using people's own information:** Sadly, many people use their own names or birthdays as passwords. It is quite simple for criminals to attempt to use such information as passwords.

>> **Credential stuffing:** *Credential stuffing* refers to when attackers take lists of usernames and passwords from one site — for example, from a site that was breached and whose username password database was subsequently posted online — and feed its entries to another system one at a time in order to see whether any of the login credentials from the first system work on the second. Because many people reuse username and password combinations between systems, credential stuffing is, generally speaking, quite effective.

Password Considerations

When you create passwords, keep in mind that, contrary to what you may have often heard from "experts," more complex isn't always better. Password strength should depend on how sensitive the data and system are that the password protects. The following sections discuss easily guessable passwords, complicated passwords, sensitive passwords, and password managers.

Easily guessable personal passwords

As alluded to earlier, criminals know that many people use the name or birth date of their significant other or pet as a password, so crooks often look at social media profiles and do Google searches in order to find likely passwords. They also use automated tools to feed lists of common names to targeted systems one by one, while watching to see whether the system being attacked accepts any of the names as a correct password.

Criminals who launch targeted attacks can exploit the vulnerability created by such personalized, yet easily guessable, passwords. However, the problem is much larger: Sometimes, reconnaissance is done through automated means — so, even opportunistic attackers can leverage such an approach.

Furthermore, because, by definition, a significant percentage of people have common names, the automated feeders of common names often achieve a significant number of hits.

Complicated passwords aren't always better

To address the problems inherent in weak passwords, many experts recommend using long, complex passwords — for example, containing both uppercase and lowercase letters, as well as numbers and special characters.

Using such passwords makes sense in theory, and if such a scheme is utilized to secure access to a small number of sensitive systems, it can work quite well. However, employing such a model for a larger number of passwords is likely to lead to problems that can undermine security:

>> Inappropriately reusing passwords

>> Writing down passwords in insecure locations

>> Selecting passwords with poor randomization and formatted using predictable patterns, such as using a capital for the first letter of a complicated password, followed by all lowercase characters, and then a number

Hence, in the real world, from a practical perspective, because the human mind can't remember many complex passwords, using significant numbers of complex passwords can create serious security risks.

According to *The Wall Street Journal*, Bill Burr, the author of NIST Special Publication 800-63 Appendix A (which discusses password complexity requirements), admitted shortly before the turn of the new decade that password complexity has failed in practice. He now recommends using passphrases, and not complex passwords, for authentication.

Passphrases are passwords consisting of entire phrases or phrase-length strings of characters, rather than of simply a word or a word-length group of characters. Sometimes passphrases even consist of complete sentences. Think of passphrases as long (usually at least 25 characters) but relatively easy to remember passwords.

Different levels of sensitivity

Not all types of data require the same level of password protection. For example, the government doesn't protect its unclassified systems the same way that it secures its top-secret information and infrastructure. In your mind or on paper, classify the systems for which you need secure access. Then informally classify the systems that you access and establish your own informal password policies accordingly.

On the basis of risk levels, feel free to employ different password strategies. Random passwords, passwords composed of multiple words possibly separated with numbers, passphrases, and even simple passwords each have their appropriate uses. Of course, multifactor authentication can, and should, help augment security when it's both appropriate and available.

TIP

Establishing a stronger password for online banking than for commenting on a blog on which you plan to comment only once in a blue moon makes sense. Likewise, your password to the blog should probably be stronger than the one used to access a free news site that requires you to log in but on which you never post anything and at which, if your account were compromised, the breach would have zero impact upon you.

Your most sensitive passwords may not be the ones you think

When classifying your passwords, keep in mind that while people often believe that their online banking and other financial system passwords are their most sensitive passwords, that is not always the case. Because many modern online systems allow people to reset their passwords after validating their identities through email messages sent to their previously known email addresses, criminals who gain access to someone's email account may be able to do a lot more than just read email without authorization: They may be able to reset that user's passwords to many systems, including to some financial institutions.

Likewise, many sites leverage social-media-based authentication capabilities — especially those provided by Facebook and Twitter — so a compromised password on a social media platform can lead to unauthorized parties gaining access to other systems as well, some of which may be quite a bit more sensitive in nature than a site on which you just share pictures.

TIP

If you change email addresses, remember to change the address associated with any account that uses email messages for authentication or for resetting passwords. I recently purchased a domain formerly used by a since-acquired cybersecurity business, and was able to receive password-reset emails for accounts currently in use!

You can reuse passwords — sometimes

You may be surprised to read the following statement in a book teaching you how to stay cybersecure:

> *You don't need to use strong passwords for accounts that you create solely because a website requires a login, but that does not, from your perspective, protect anything of value.*

If you create an account in order to access free resources, for example, and you have nothing whatsoever of value stored within the account, and you don't mind getting a new account the next time you log in, you can even use a weak password — and use it again for other similar sites.

TIP

Essentially, think about it like this: If the requirement to register and log in is solely for the benefit of the site owner — to track users, market to them, and so on — and it doesn't matter one iota to you whether a criminal obtained the access credentials to your account and changed them, use a simple password. Doing so will preserve your memory for sites where password strength matters. Of course, if you use a password manager, you can use a stronger password for such sites.

Consider using a password manager

Alternatively, you can use a password manager tool, shown in Figure 8-1, to securely store your passwords. Password managers are software that help people manage passwords by generating, storing, and retrieving complex passwords. Password managers typically store all their data in encrypted formats and provide access to users only after authenticating them with either a strong password or multifactor authentication.

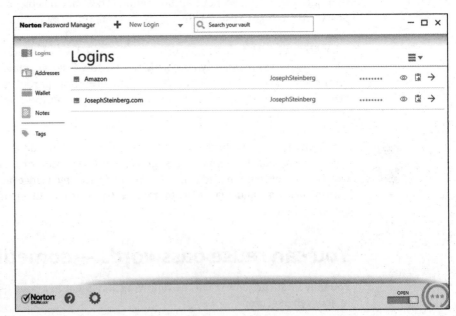

FIGURE 8-1:
A password
manager.

Such technology is appropriate for general passwords, but not for the most sensitive ones. Various password managers have been hacked, and if something does go wrong you could have a nightmare on your hands. Remember, when you store passwords in a password manager you are "putting multiple eggs into one basket," and that password managers are also treasure chests for hackers and on their radars. As such, of course, be sure to properly secure any device that you use to access your password manager.

Many password managers are on the market. While all modern mainstream password managers utilize encryption to protect the sensitive data that they store, some store passwords locally (for example, in a database on your phone), while others store them in the cloud.

Many modern smartphones come equipped with a so-called *secure area* — a private, encrypted space that is *sandboxed*, or separated, into its own running environment. Ideally, any password information stored on a mobile device should be stored protected in the secure area (see Figure 8-2).

FIGURE 8-2:
Secure Folder, the secure area app provided by Samsung for its Android series of phones, as seen in the Google Play Store.

Data that is stored in the secure area is supposed to be rendered by the operating system to be inaccessible to a user unless that user enters the secure area, which usually requires running a secure area app and entering a special password or otherwise authenticating. Devices also typically display some special symbol somewhere on the screen when a user is working with data or an app located in the secure area.

REMEMBER

Remember, though, that operating systems are not perfect, and sometimes bugs do create exploitable vulnerabilities. So even if you do trust the secure area, keep in mind that its security is not 100 percent guaranteed.

Creating Memorable, Strong Passwords

The following list offers suggestions that may help you create strong passwords that are, for most people, far easier to remember than a seemingly random, unintelligible mix of letters, numbers, and symbols:

>> **Combine three or more unrelated words and proper nouns, with numbers separating them.** For example, laptop2william7cows is far easier to remember than 6ytBgv%j8P. In general, the longer the words you use within the password, the stronger the resulting password will be.

>> **If you must use a special character, add a special character before each number; you can even use the same character for all your passwords.** (If you use the same passwords as in the previous example and follow this advice, the passwords is laptop%2william%7cows.) In theory, reusing the same character may not be the best way to do things from a security standpoint, but doing so makes memorization much easier, and the security should still be good enough for purposes for which a password is suitable on its own anyway.

>> **Ideally, use at least one non-English word or proper name.** Choose a word or name that is familiar to you but that others are unlikely to guess. Don't use the name of your significant other, best friend, or pet.

>> **If you must use both capital and lowercase letters (or want to make your password even stronger), use capitals that always appear in a particular location throughout all your strong passwords.** Make sure, though, that you don't put them at the start of words because that location is where most people put them. For example, if you know that you always capitalize the second and third letter of the last word, then laptop2william7kALb isn't harder to remember than laptop2william7kalb.

Knowing When to Change Passwords

Conventional wisdom — as you have likely heard many times — is that it is ideal to change your password quite frequently. The American Association of Retired Persons (AARP), for example, until recently recommended on its website that people (including the disproportionately older folks who comprise its membership) "change critical passwords frequently, possibly every other week."

Theoretically, such an approach is correct — frequent changes reduce risks in several ways — but in reality, it's bad advice that you shouldn't follow.

If you have a bank account, mortgage, a couple credit cards, a phone bill, a high-speed Internet bill, utility bills, social media accounts, email accounts, and so on, you may easily be talking about a dozen or so critical passwords. Changing them every two weeks would mean 312 new critical passwords to remember within the span of every year — and you likely have many more passwords on top of that figure. For many people, changing important passwords every two weeks may mean learning a hundred new passwords every month.

Unless you have a phenomenal, photographic memory, how likely is it that you'll remember all such passwords? Or will you simply make your passwords weaker in order to facilitate remembering them after frequent changes?

The bottom line is that changing passwords often makes remembering them far more difficult, increasing the odds that you'll write them down and store them insecurely, select weaker passwords, and/or set your new passwords to be the same as old passwords with minute changes (for example, password2 to replace password1).

REMEMBER

So, here is the reality: If you select strong, unique passwords to begin with and the sites where you've used them aren't believed to have been compromised, the cons of frequently changing the passwords outweigh the pros. Changing such passwords every few years may be a good idea. In reality, if a system alerts you of multiple failed attempts to log in to your account and you're not alerted of such activity, you can likely go for many years with no changes without exposing yourself to significant risk.

Of course, if you use a password manager that can reset passwords, you can configure it to reset them often. In fact, I've worked with a commercial password-management system used for protecting system administration access to sensitive financial systems that automatically reset administrators' passwords every time they logged on.

Changing Passwords after a Breach

If you receive notification from a business, organization, or government entity that it has suffered a security breach and that you should change your password, follow these tips:

>> Don't click any links in the message because most such messages are scams.

>> Visit the organization's website and official social media accounts to verify that such an announcement was actually made.

>> Pay attention to news stories to see whether reliable, mainstream media is reporting such a breach.

>> If the story checks out, go to the organization's website and make the change.

TIP

Do not change all your passwords after every breach you hear about on the evening news or read about online.

Ignore experts who "cry wolf" and tell you to change all your passwords after every single breach as a matter of "extra caution" or that it may not be necessary to change passwords, but that "it is better to be safe than sorry." If changing passwords is not necessary, doing so uses up your brainpower, time, and energy, and, whether you realize it or not, likely dissuades you from changing passwords if a situation arises in which you actually do need to make such changes.

After all, if after a breach you make unnecessary password changes and then find out that your friends who did not do so fared no worse than you, you may grow weary and ignore future warnings to change your password when doing so is actually necessary.

If you reuse passwords on sites where the passwords matter — which you should not be doing — and a password that is compromised somewhere is also used on other sites, be sure to change it at the other sites as well. In such a case, also take the opportunity when resetting passwords to switch to unique passwords for each of the sites.

Providing Passwords to Humans

On its website, the United States Federal Trade Commission (FTC) recommends the following:

> Don't share passwords on the phone, in texts, or by email. Legitimate companies will not send you messages asking for your password.

That sounds like good advice, and it would be, if it were not for one important fact: Legitimate businesses do ask you for passwords over the phone! So how do you know when it is safe to provide your password and when it is not?

Should you just check your caller ID? No. The sad reality is that crooks spoof caller IDs on a regular basis.

What you should do is never provide any sensitive information — including passwords, of course — over the phone unless you *initiated* the call with the party requesting the password and are sure that you called the legitimate party. It is far less risky, for example, to provide an account's phone-access password to a customer service representative who asks for it during a conversation initiated by you calling to the bank using the number printed on your ATM card than if someone calls you claiming to be from your bank and requests the same private information in order to "verify your identity."

Storing Passwords

Ideally, don't write down your passwords to sensitive systems or store them anywhere other than in your brain.

Storing passwords for your heirs

If you want to ensure that you have a copy of your most sensitive passwords (and perhaps any other passwords) written down somewhere — perhaps for your family in case something happens to you — write the passwords down and put the list in a safe deposit box or safe, and do not take the list out on a regular basis. Of course, if you want the list to be useful to your heirs, make sure to keep the list updated.

Some major technology providers, such as Facebook and Apple, also provide people with the ability to specify who should be given access to their accounts upon their deaths.

Storing general passwords

For less sensitive passwords, use a password manager or store them in an encrypted form on a strongly-secured computer or device. If you store your passwords on a phone, use the secure area. (For more on password managers and your phone's secure area, see the section "Consider using a password manager," earlier in this chapter.)

Transmitting Passwords

Theoretically, you should never email or text someone a password. So, what should you do if your child texts you from school saying that they forgot the password to their email, or the like?

TIP

Ideally, if you need to give someone a password, call that person and don't provide the password until you identify the other party by voice. If, for some reason, you must send a password in writing, choose to use an encrypted connection, which is offered by various chat tools. If no such tool is available, consider splitting the password and sending some via email and some via text.

Obviously, none of these methods are ideal ways to transmit passwords, but they certainly are better options than what so many people do, which is to simply text or email people passwords in clear text.

Discovering Alternatives to Passwords

On some occasions, you should take advantage of alternatives to password authentication. While there are many ways to authenticate people, a modern user is likely to encounter certain types:

>> Biometric authentication

>> SMS-based authentication

>> App-based one-time passwords

>> Hardware token authentication

>> USB-based authentication

Biometric authentication

Biometric authentication refers to authenticating using some unique identifier of your physical person — for example, your fingerprint. Using biometrics — especially in combination with a password — can be a strong method of authentication, and it certainly has its place. Two popular forms used in the consumer market are fingerprints and iris-based authentication.

While using a fingerprint to unlock a phone is certainly convenient, and looking at the screen is even more convenient, in many cases, mandating that phones be unlocked only after a user provides a strong password actually provides better security.

Before using biometric authentication, consider the following points:

>> **Your fingerprints are likely all over your phone.** You hold your phone with your fingers. How hard would it be for criminals who steal the phone to lift your prints and unlock the phone if you enable fingerprint based authentication using a phone's built-in fingerprint reader (see Figure 8-3)? If anything sensitive is on the device, it may be at risk. No, the average crook looking to make a quick buck selling your phone is unlikely to spend the time to unlock it — the crook will more than likely just wipe it — but if someone wants the data on your phone for whatever reason, and you used fingerprints to secure your device, you may have a serious problem on your hands (pun intended).

>> **If your biometric information is captured, you can't reset it as you can a password.** Do you fully trust the parties to whom you're giving this information to properly protect it?

>> **If your biometric information is on your phone or computer, what happens if malware somehow infects your device?** What happens if a server where you stored the same information is breached? Are you positive that all the data is properly encrypted and that the software on your device fully defended your biometric data from capture?

FIGURE 8-3:
A phone fingerprint sensor on a Samsung Galaxy S9 in an Otterbox case. Some phones have the reader on the front, while others, like the S9, have it on the back.

- **》 Masks create problems for facial recognition systems.** Most facial recognition systems will not work if a person is wearing a mask, as was required in many places during the COVID-19 pandemic.

- **》 Cold weather creates problems.** Fingerprints can't be read even through smartphone-compatible gloves.

- **》 Glasses, as worn by millions of people, pose challenges to iris scanners.** Some iris readers require users to take off their glasses in order to authenticate. If you use such authentication to secure a phone, you may have difficulty unlocking your phone when you're outdoors on a sunny day.

- **》 Biometrics can undermine your rights.** If, for some reason, law enforcement wants to access the data on your biometric-protected phone or other computer system, it may be able to force you to provide your biometric authentication, even in countries like the United States where you have the right to remain silent and not provide a password. Likewise, the government may be able to obtain a warrant to collect your biometric data, which, unlike a password, you can't reset. Even if the data proves you innocent of whatever the government suspects you have done wrong, do you trust the government to properly secure the data over the long term? (These types of issues are in the process of being addressed by various courts, and the final results may vary by jurisdiction.)

- **》 Impersonation is possible.** Some quasi-biometric authentication, such as the face recognition on some devices, can be tricked into believing that a person is present by playing to them a high-definition video of that person.

- **》 Voice-based authentication is no longer trustworthy.** It has become possible for criminals to undermine voice-based authentication using what has become known as deep fake technology, which is technology that uses artificial intelligence to impersonate a person either in an audio recording or video recording. Criminals have already successfully stolen money using deep-faked audio.

As such, biometrics have their place. Using a fingerprint to unlock features on your phone is certainly convenient but think before you proceed. Be certain that in your case the benefits outweigh the drawbacks.

SMS-based authentication

In *SMS (text message)–based authentication*, a code is sent to your cellphone. You then enter that code into a web or app to prove your identity. This type of authentication is, in itself, not considered secure enough for authentication when true multifactor authentication in required. Sophisticated criminals have ways of intercepting such passwords, and can sometimes even social–engineer phone companies in order to steal people's phone numbers, thereby, stealing their SMS messages. That said, SMS one-time passwords used in combination with a strong password are typically better than just using the password.

WARNING

Keep in mind, however, that, in most cases, one-time passwords are worthless as a security measure if you send them to a criminal's phishing website instead of a legitimate site. The criminal can replay them to the real site in real time.

App-based one-time passwords

One-time passwords generated with an app running on a phone or computer are a good addition to strong passwords, but they should not be used on their own. App-based one-time passwords are likely a more secure way to authenticate than SMS-based one-time passwords (see preceding section), but they can be inconvenient; if you get a new phone, for example, some one time password generation apps require you to reconfigure information at every one of the sites where you're using one-time passwords created by the generator app running on your smartphone. Even those that do not may require you to disable password generation on your old device in addition to enabling it on the new one.

As with SMS-based one-time passwords, if you send an app-generated one-time password to a criminal's phishing website instead of a legitimate site, the criminal can replay it to the corresponding real site in real time, undermining the security benefits of the one-time password in their entirety.

Hardware token authentication

Hardware tokens (see Figure 8-4) that generate new one-time passwords every x seconds are similar to the apps described in the preceding section with the major difference being that you need to carry a specialized device that generates the one-time codes. Some tokens can also function in other modes — for example, allowing for challenge-response types of authentication in which the site being logged into displays a challenge number that the user enters into the token in order to retrieve a corresponding response number that the user enters into the site in order to authenticate.

Although hardware token devices normally are more secure than one-time generator apps in that the former don't run on devices that can be infected by malware or taken over by criminals remotely, they can be inconvenient. They are also prone to getting lost, and are less likely to be quickly detected as missing as are phones. Many models are also not waterproof, leading to problems of such devices sometimes getting destroyed when people do their laundry after forgetting the devices in their pockets.

USB-based authentication

USB devices that contain authentication information — for example, digital certificates — can strengthen authentication. Care must be exercised, however, to use such devices only in combination with trusted machines — you don't want the device infected or destroyed by some rogue device, and you want to be sure that the machine obtaining the certificate, for example, doesn't transmit it to an unauthorized party.

Many modern USB-based devices offer all sorts of defenses against such attacks. Of course, you can connect USB devices only to devices and apps that support USB-based authentication. You also must carry the device with you and ensure that it doesn't get lost or damaged. And, as with other hardware keys, such devices are prone to being lost, and are not always waterproof.

Chapter **9**

Preventing Social Engineering Attacks

M ost, if not all, major breaches that have occurred in recent years have involved some element of social engineering. Do not let devious criminals trick you or your loved ones. In this chapter, you find out how to protect yourself.

Don't Trust Technology More than You Would People

Would you give your online banking password to a random stranger who asked for it after walking up to you in the street and telling you that they worked for your bank?

If the answer is no — which it certainly should be (and, if it is not, your security problems are much greater than just your cybersecurity) — you need to exercise the same lack of trust when it comes to technology. The fact that your computer shows you an email sent by some party that claims to be your bank instead of a random person approaching you on the street and making a similar claim is no reason to give that email your trust any more than you would give the stranger.

REMEMBER

Unless you are using an email security system that overcomes such issues with digital signatures and other security technologies, when you receive an email from someone, you are not actually receiving the email from that person. Your computer is simply telling you that another computer told it, based on what another computer told it, based on what another computer told it, and so on, that the person who is the "sender" actually sent you the included message.

In short, you don't give offers from strangers approaching you on the street the benefit of the doubt, so don't do so for offers communicated electronically — they may be even more risky.

Types of Social Engineering Attacks

Phishing attacks are one of the most common forms of social engineering attacks. (For more on phishing and social engineering, see Chapter 2.) Figure 9-1 shows you an example of a phishing email.

FIGURE 9-1:
A phishing email.

Phishing attacks sometimes utilize a technique called *pretexting* in which the criminal sending the phishing email fabricates a situation that both gains trust from targets as well as underscores the supposed need for the intended victims to act quickly. In the phishing email shown in Figure 9-1, note that the sender, impersonating Wells Fargo bank, included a link to the real Wells Fargo within the email, but failed to properly disguise the sending address.

Chapter 2 discusses common forms of social engineering attacks, including spear phishing emails, smishing, spear smishing, vishing, spear vishing, and CEO fraud. Additional types of social engineering attacks are popular as well:

>> **Baiting:** An attacker sends an email or chat message — or even makes a social media post that promises someone a reward in exchange for taking some action — for example, telling intended targets that if they complete a survey, they will receive a free item (see Figure 9-2). Or that if they perform such action, they will receive some free cryptocurrency. Sometimes such promises are real, but often they're not and are simply ways of incentivizing people to take a specific action that they would not take otherwise. Sometimes such scammers seek payment of a small shipping fee for the prize, sometimes they distribute malware, and sometimes they collect sensitive information. There is even malware that baits.

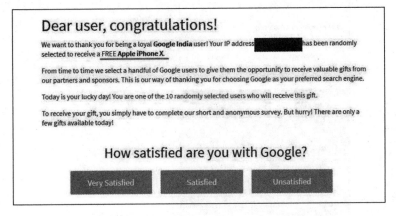

Dear user, congratulations!

We want to thank you for being a loyal **Google India** user! Your IP address ▇▇▇▇▇▇ has been randomly selected to receive a FREE **Apple iPhone X**.

From time to time we select a handful of Google users to give them the opportunity to receive valuable gifts from our partners and sponsors. This is our way of thanking you for choosing Google as your preferred search engine.

Today is your lucky day! You are one of the 10 randomly selected users who will receive this gift.

To receive your gift, you simply have to complete our short and anonymous survey. But hurry! There are only a few gifts available today!

How satisfied are you with Google?

| Very Satisfied | Satisfied | Unsatisfied |

FIGURE 9-2: Example of a baiting message.

WARNING

Don't confuse baiting with *scambaiting*. The latter refers to a form of vigilantism in which people pretend to be gullible, would-be victims, and waste scammers' time and resources through repeated interactions, as well as (sometimes) collect intelligence about the scammer that can be turned over to law enforcement or published on the Internet to warn others of the scammer. I have sometimes led scammers on when they call by listening to their spiel and then giving them the FBI's New York office contact information for their requested follow-up call.

>> **Quid pro quo:** The attacker states that they need the person to take an action in order to render a service for the intended victim. For example, an attacker may pretend to be an IT support manager offering assistance to an employee in installing a new security software update. If the employee cooperates, the criminal walks the employee through the process of installing malware.

>> **Social media impersonation:** Some attackers impersonate people on social media in order to establish social media connections with their victims. The parties being impersonated may be real people or nonexistent entities. The scammers behind the impersonation shown in Figure 9-3 and many other such accounts frequently contact the people who follow the accounts, pretending to be the account owners, and request that the followers make various "investments."

FIGURE 9-3:
An example of an Instagram account impersonating me, using my name, bio, and primarily photos lifted from my real Instagram account.

>> **Tantalizing emails:** These emails attempt to trick people into running malware or clicking on poisoned links by exploiting their curiosity, sexual desires, and other characteristics.

>> **Tailgating:** *Tailgating* is a physical form of social engineering attack in which attackers accompany authorized personnel as they approach a doorway that they, but not the attackers, are authorized to pass and tricks them into letting the attackers pass with the authorized personnel. The attackers may pretend to be searching through a purse for an access card, claim to have forgotten their card, or may simply act social and follow the authorized party in.

>> **False alarms:** Raising false alarms can also social engineer people into allowing unauthorized people to do things that they should not be allowed to. Consider the case in which an attacker pulls the fire alarm inside a building and manages to enter normally secured areas through an emergency door that someone else used to quickly exit due to the so-called emergency.

>> **Water holing:** Water holing combines hacking and social engineering by exploiting the fact that people trust certain parties, so, for example, they may click on links when viewing that party's website even if they'd never click on links in an email or text message. Criminals may launch a watering hole attack by breaching the relevant site and inserting the poisoned links on it (or even depositing malware directly onto it).

>> **Virus hoaxes:** Criminals exploit the fact that people are concerned about cybersecurity, and likely pay undeserved attention to messages that they receive warning about a cyberdanger. Virus hoax emails may contain poisoned links, direct a user to download software, or instruct a user to contact IT support via some email address or web page. These attacks come in many flavors — some attacks distribute them as mass emails, while others send them in a highly targeted fashion.

Some people consider scareware that scares users into believing that they need to purchase some particular security software (as described in Chapter 2) to be a form of virus hoax. Others do not because scareware's "scaring" is done by malware that is already installed, not by a hoax message that pretends that malware is already installed.

>> **Technical failures:** Criminals can easily exploit humans' annoyance with technology problems to undermine various security technologies. For example, research I performed nearly two decades ago showed that if a criminal impersonates a website that normally displays a security image in a particular area, but in the fake copy, places a "broken image symbol," many users will not perceive danger, as they are accustomed to seeing broken-image symbols and associate them with technical failures rather than security risks. There is no reason to believe that over the years anything has changed for the significantly better in this regard.

Six Principles Social Engineers Exploit

Social psychologist Robert Beno Cialdini, in his 1984 work published by Harper-Collins, *Influence: The Psychology of Persuasion*, explains six important, basic concepts that people seeking to influence others often leverage. Social engineers seeking to trick people often exploit these same six principles, so I provide a quick overview of them in the context of information security.

TIP

The following list helps you understand and internalize the methods crooks are likely to use to try to gain your trust:

» **Social proof:** People tend to do things that they see other respectable people doing.

» **Reciprocity:** People, in general, often believe that if someone did something nice for them, they owe it to that person to do something nice back.

» **Authority:** People tend to obey authority figures, even when they disagree with the authority figures, and even when they think what they are being asked to do is objectionable.

» **Likeability:** People are, generally speaking, more easily persuaded by people who they like than by others.

» **Consistency and commitment:** If people make a commitment to accomplish some goal and internalize that commitment, that commitment becomes part of their self-image. They are likely, therefore, to attempt to pursue their goal even if the original reason for pursuing the goal is no longer relevant.

» **Scarcity:** If people think that a particular resource is scarce, regardless of whether it actually is scarce, they will want it, and often take risks to obtain it, even if they don't actually need it.

Don't Overshare on Social Media

Oversharing information on social media arms criminals with material that they can use to social engineer you, your family members, your colleagues at work, and your friends. If, for example your privacy settings allow anyone with access to the social media platform to see your posted media, your risk increases. Many times, people accidentally share posts with the whole world that they actually intended to be visible and/or audible by only a small group of people.

Furthermore, in multiple situations, bugs in social media platform software have created vulnerabilities that allowed unauthorized parties to view media and posts that had privacy settings set to disallow such access.

Also, consider your privacy settings. Family-related material with privacy settings set to allow nonfamily members to view it may result in all sorts of privacy-related issues and leak the answers to various popular challenge questions used for authenticating users, such as "Where does your oldest sibling live?" or "What is your mother's maiden name?" And consider that romantic relationships can sour, too; there may be materials from previous relationships that you do not want a new partner to see, or vice versa.

WARNING

Don't rely on social media privacy settings to protect truly confidential data. Some social media platforms allow for granular protection of posted items, while others do not. Certain items, if shared, may help criminals social engineer you or someone you know. This list isn't meant to be comprehensive. Rather, it's meant to illustrate examples to stimulate your thinking about the potential risks of what you intend to post on social media before you go ahead and post it.

REMEMBER

Numerous other types of social media posts than the ones I list in the following sections can help criminals orchestrate social engineering attacks. Think about potential consequences before you post and set your posts' privacy settings accordingly.

Your schedule and travel plans

Details of your schedule or someone else's schedule may provide criminals with information that may help them set up an attack. For example, if you post that you'll be attending an upcoming event, such as a wedding, you may provide criminals with the ability to *virtually kidnap* you or other attendees — never mind incentivizing others to target your home with a break-in attempt when the home is likely to be empty. (*Virtual kidnapping* refers to a criminal making a ransom demand in exchange for the same return of someone who the criminal claims to have kidnapped, but who in fact, the criminal has not kidnapped.)

Likewise, revealing that you'll be flying on a particular flight may provide criminals with the ability to virtually kidnap you or attempt CEO-type fraud against your colleagues. They may impersonate you and send an email saying that you're flying and may not be reachable by phone for confirmation of the instructions so just go ahead and follow them anyway.

WARNING

Avoid posting about a family member's vacation or trip, which may increase risks of virtual kidnapping (and of real physical dangers to that person or that person's belongings).

Financial information

Sharing a credit card number may lead to fraudulent charges, while posting a bank account number can lead to fraudulent bank activity.

In addition, don't reveal that you visited or interacted with a particular financial institution or the locations where you store your money — banks, crypto-exchange accounts, brokerages, and so forth. Doing so can increase the odds that criminals will attempt to social engineer their way into your accounts at the relevant financial institution(s). As such, such sharing may expose you to attempts to breach your accounts, as well as targeted phishing, vishing, and smishing attacks and all sorts of other social engineering scams.

Posting about potential investments, such as stocks, bonds, precious metals, or cryptocurrencies, can expose you to cyberattacks because criminals may assume that you have significant money to steal. In some cases, if you make posts encouraging people to investor to perform other forms of investment-related activities, you may also run afoul of rules laws or of regulations of the SEC, CFTC, or other government bodies. You may even also open the door to criminals who impersonate regulators and contact you to pay a fine for posting information inappropriately.

Personal information

For starters, avoid listing your family members in your Facebook profile's About section. That About section links to their Facebook profiles and explains to viewers the nature of the relevant family relationship with each party listed. By listing these relationships, you may leak all sorts of information that may be valuable for criminals. Not only will you possibly reveal your mother's maiden name (challenge question answer!), you may also provide clues about where you grew up. The information found in your profile also provides criminals with a list of people to social engineer or contact as part of a virtual kidnapping scam.

Also you should avoid sharing the following information on social media, as doing so can undermine your authentication questions and help criminals social engineer you or your family:

>> Your father's middle name

>> Your mother's birthday

>> Where you met your significant other

>> Your favorite vacation spot

>> The name of the first school that you attended

>> The street on which you grew up

>> The type, make, model, and/or color of your first car or someone else's

>> Your or others' favorite food or drink

WARNING

Despite many years of industry-wide understanding that challenge questions of this sort are generally not suitable to be asked as a means of authenticating people. In early 2022, as part of the authentication process in use by a major financial institution, I was still being asked for my mother's birthday. Go figure.

Likewise, never share your Social Security number as doing so may lead to identity theft.

Information about your children

WARNING

Sharing information about your children can not only set you up for attacks, but put your children at great risk of physical danger. For example, photos of your children may assist a kidnapper. The problem may be exacerbated if the images contain a timestamp and/or *geotagging* — that is, information about the location at which a photograph was taken.

Timestamps and geotagging do not need to be done per some technical specification to create risks. If it is clear from the images where your kids go to school, attend after-school activities, and so on, you may expose them to danger.

In addition, referring to the names of schools, camps, day care facilities, or other youth programs that your children or their friends attend may increase the risk of a pedophile, kidnapper, or other malevolent party targeting them. Such a post may also expose you to potential burglars because they'll know when you're likely not to be home. The risk can be made much worse if a clear pattern regarding your schedule and/or your children's schedule can be extrapolated from such posts. Also avoid posting about a child's school or camp trip. And, if you feel you must post about it, wait until your child is back home after completing the trip.

Information about your pets

As with your mother's maiden name, sharing your current pet's name or your first pet's name can set you or others who you know up for social engineering attacks because such information is often used as an answer to authentication questions.

Work information

Details about with which technologies you work with at your present job (or a previous job) may help criminals both scan for vulnerabilities in your employers' systems and social engineer your colleagues. Yet many people's profiles on profession-focused social media sites contain a wealth of information about the systems in use at their employers — sometimes even effectively disclosing the public what security systems the employer is using, and is considering for use in the future.

Possible cybersecurity issues

Many virus hoaxes and scams have gone viral — and inflicted far more damage than they should have — because criminals exploit people's fear of cyberattacks and leverage the likelihood that many people will share posts about cyber-risks, often without verifying the authenticity of such posts.

Crimes and minor infractions

Information about a moving violation or parking ticket that you received not only presents yourself in a less-than-the-best light, but can inadvertently provide prosecutors with the material that they need to convict you of the relevant offense. You may also give crooks the ability to social engineer you or others — they may pretending to be law enforcement, a court, or an attorney contacting you about the matter — perhaps even demanding that a fine be paid immediately in order to avoid an arrest.

In addition to helping criminals social engineer you in a fashion similar to the moving violation case, information about a crime that you or a loved one commit-ted may harm you professionally and personally.

Medical or legal advice

If you offer medical or legal advice, people may be able to extrapolate that you or a loved one has a particular medical condition, or involved in a particular legal situation. And, if you offer incorrect advice, you could not only get yourself into hot water and legal troubles, but also contribute to unnecessary human suffering.

During the COVID-19 pandemic, social media platforms were regularly used to spread incorrect information — and this spread might have contributed both to increasing the number of coronavirus illnesses and deaths, and to prolonging the pandemic.

Your location

Your location or *check-in* on social media may not only increase the risk to yourself and your loved ones of physical danger, but may help criminals launch virtual kidnapping attacks and other social engineering scams.

In addition, an image of you in a place frequented by people of certain religious, sexual, political, cultural, or other affiliations can lead to criminals extrapolating information about you that may lead to all sorts of social engineering. Criminals are known, for example, to have virtually kidnapped a person who was in synagogue and unreachable on the Jewish holiday of Yom Kippur. They knew when and where the person would be walking to the temple, and called family members (at a time that they knew the person would be impossible to reach) claiming to have kidnapped the person. The family members fell for the virtual kidnapping scam because the details were right and they were unable to reach the "victim" by telephone in the middle of a synagogue service.

Your birthday

A happy birthday message to someone on social media may reveal the person's birthday. Folks who use fake birthdays on social media for security reasons have seen their precautions undermined in such a fashion by would be well-wishers.

Your "sins"

Anything that is "sin-like" may lead not only to professional or personal harm, but to blackmail-like attempts as well as social engineering of yourself or others depicted in such posts or media. If in doubt, be careful. Something you post that may be questionable today might be considered nothing short of repugnant in the future; old posts cause people personal and professional harm on a regular basis.

Leaking Data by Sharing Information as Part of Viral Trends

From time to time, a *viral trend* occurs, in which many people share similar content. Posts about the ice bucket challenge, your favorite concerts, and something about you today and ten years ago are all examples of viral trends. Of course, future viral trends may have nothing to do with prior ones. Any type of post that spreads quickly to large numbers of people is said to have "gone viral."

WARNING

While participating may seem fun — and "what everyone else is doing" — be sure that you understand the potential consequences of doing so. For example, sharing information about the concerts that you attended and that you consider to be your favorites can reveal a lot about you — especially in combination with other profile data — and can expose you to all sorts of social engineering risks.

Identifying Fake Social Media Connections

Social media delivers many professional and personal benefits to its users, but it also creates amazing opportunities for criminals — many people have an innate desire to connect with others and are overly trusting of social media platforms. They assume that if, for example, Facebook sends a message that Joseph Steinberg has requested that they become his friend, that the real "Joseph Steinberg" has requested such — when, often, that is not the case.

Criminals know, for example, that by connecting with you on social media, they can gain access to all sorts of information about you, your family members, and your work colleagues — information that they can often exploit in order to impersonate you, a relative, or a colleague as part of criminal efforts to social engineer a path into business systems, steal money, or commit other crimes.

One technique that criminals often use to gain access to people's "private" Facebook, Instagram, or LinkedIn information is to create fake profiles — profiles of nonexistent people — and request to connect with real people, many of whom are likely to accept the relevant connection requests. Alternatively, scammers may set up accounts that impersonate real people — and which have profile photos and other materials lifted from the impersonated party's legitimate social media accounts.

How can you protect yourself from such scams? The following sections offer advice on how to quickly spot fake accounts — and how to avoid the possible repercussions of accepting connections from them.

REMEMBER

Keep in mind that none of the clues in the following sections operates in a vacuum or is absolute. The fact that a profile fails when tested against a particular rule, for example, doesn't automatically mean that it is bogus. But applying smart concepts such as the ones I list in the following sections should help you identify a significant percentage of fake accounts and save yourself from the problems that can ultimately result from accepting connection requests from them.

Photo

Many fake accounts use photos of attractive models, sometimes targeting men who have accounts that show photos of women and women whose accounts have photos of men. The pictures often appear to be stock photos, but sometimes are stolen from real users.

WARNING

If you receive a social media connection request from someone who you don't remember ever meeting and the picture is of this type, beware. If you're in doubt, you can load the image into Google's reverse image search and see where else it appears.

You can also search on the person's name (and, if appropriate, on LinkedIn) or title to see whether any other similar photos appear online. However, a crafty impersonator may upload images to several sites. Obviously, any profile without a photo of the account holder should raise red flags. Keep in mind, though, that some people do use emojis, caricatures, and so on as profile photos, especially on nonprofessional-oriented social media networks.

Verification

If an account appears to represent a public figure who you suspect is likely to be verified (meaning it has a blue check mark next to the user's account name to indicate that the account is the legitimate account of a public figure), but it is not verified, that is a likely sign that something is amiss. Likewise, it is unlikely that a verified account on a major social media platform is fake. However, there have been occasions on which verified accounts of such nature have been taken over temporarily by hackers.

Friends or connections in common

Fake people are unlikely to have many friends or connections in common with you, and fake folks usually will not even have many secondary connections (Friends of Friends, LinkedIn second level connections, and so on) in common with you either.

Don't assume that an account is legitimate just because it has one or two connections in common with you; some of your connections may have fallen for a scam and connected with a fake person, and your contact's connecting with the fake account may be how the criminal found out about you in the first place. Even in such a scenario, the number of shared connections is likely to be relatively small as compared with a real, mutual connection, and the human relationship between the friends who did connect with the crook's profile may seem difficult to piece together.

You know your connections better than anyone else — exercise caution when someone's connection patterns don't make sense. You may want to think twice, for example, if people trying to connect with you seem to know nobody in the industry in which they work, but know three of your most gullible friends who live in three different countries and who do not know one another.

Relevant posts

Another huge red flag is when an account is not sharing material that it should be sharing based on the alleged identity of the account holder. If someone claims to be a columnist who currently writes for *Forbes*, for example, and attempts to but has never shared any posts of any articles that they wrote for *Forbes*, something is likely amiss.

Number of connections

A senior-level person, with many years of work experience, is likely to have many professional connections, especially on LinkedIn. The fewer connections that an account ostensibly belonging to a senior level person has on LinkedIn (the further it is from 500 or more), the more suspicious you should be.

Of course, every LinkedIn profile started with zero connections — so legitimate, new LinkedIn accounts may seems suspicious when they truly are not — but practical reality comes into play: How many of the real, senior-level people who are now contacting you didn't establish their LinkedIn accounts until recently? Of course, a small number of connections and a new LinkedIn account isn't abnormal for people who just started their first job or for people working in certain industries, in certain roles, and/or at certain companies — CIA secret agents don't post their career progress in their LinkedIn profiles — but if you work in those industries, you're likely aware of this fact already.

Contrast the number of connection with the age of an account and the number of posts it has interacted with or has shared — a person who has been on Facebook for a decade and who posts on a regular basis, for example, should have more than one or two Friends.

Industry and location

Common sense applies vis-à-vis accounts purporting to represent people living in certain locations or working in certain industries. If, for example, you work in technology and have no pets and receive a LinkedIn connection request from a veterinarian living halfway across the world whom you have never met, something may be amiss. Likewise, if you receive a Facebook friend request from someone with whom you have nothing in common, beware.

WARNING

Don't assume that any claims made in a profile are necessarily accurate and that if you share a lot in common, the sender is definitely safe. Someone targeting you may have discerned your interests from information about you that is publicly available online.

Similar people

If you receive multiple requests from people with similar titles or who claim to work for the same company and you don't know the people and aren't actively doing some sort of deal with that company, beware. If those folks don't seem to be connected to anyone else at the company who you know actually works there, consider that a potential red flag as well.

REMEMBER

You can always call, text, or email real contacts and ask whether they see that person listed in a staff directory.

Duplicate contact

If you receive a Facebook friend request from a person who is already your Facebook friend, verify with that party that that person is switching accounts. In many cases, such requests come from scammers.

Contact details

Make sure the contact details make sense. Fake people are far less likely than real people to have email addresses at real businesses and rarely have email addresses at major corporations. They're unlikely to have physical addresses that show where they live and work, and, if such addresses are listed, they rarely correspond with actual property records or phone directory information that can easily be checked online.

Premium status

Historically, criminals avoided paying for paying for premium service for their scam accounts. Because LinkedIn charges tens of dollars per month for its Premium service, for example, some experts have suggested that Premium status is a good indicator that an account is real because a criminal is unlikely to pay so much money for an account.

While it may be true that most fake accounts don't have Premium status, some crooks do invest in obtaining Premium status in order to make their accounts seem more real — especially if they plan to use the accounts to engage in targeted attacks. In some cases, they are paying with stolen credit cards, so it doesn't cost them anything anyway. So, remain vigilant even if an account is showing the Premium icon.

TIP

Keep in mind that some Premium services, such as Twitter Blue, are relatively inexpensive, and criminals may be even more inclined to purchase such "authenticity" as a result.

LinkedIn endorsements

Fake people are not going to be endorsed by many real people. And the endorsers of fake accounts may be other fake accounts that seem suspicious as well.

Group activity

Fake profiles are less likely than real people to be members of closed groups that verify members when they join and are less likely to participate in meaningful discussions in both closed and open groups on Facebook or LinkedIn. If they are members of closed groups, those groups may have been created and managed by scammers and contain other fake profiles as well.

Fake folks may be members of many open groups — groups that were joined in order to access member lists and connect with other participants with "I see we are members of the same group, so let's connect" type messages.

WARNING

In any case, keep in mind that on any social platform that has groups, being members of the same group as someone else is not, in any way, a reason to accept a connection from that person.

Appropriate levels of relative usage

Real people who use LinkedIn or Facebook heavily enough to have joined many groups are more likely to have filled out all their profile information. A connection request from a person who is a member of many groups but has little profile information is suspicious. Likewise, an Instagram account with 20,000 followers but only two posted photos that seeks to follow your private account is suspicious for the same reason.

Human activities

Many fake accounts seem to list cliché-sounding information in their profiles, interests, and work experience sections, but contain few other details that seem to convey a true, real-life human experience.

Here are a few signs that things may not be what they seem:

>> On LinkedIn, the Recommendations, Volunteering Experience, and Education sections of a fake person may seem off.

>> On Facebook, a fake profile may seem to be cookie cutter and the posts generic enough in nature that millions of people could have made the same post.

>> On Twitter, they may be retweeting posts from others and never share their own opinions, comments, or other original material.

>> On Instagram the photos may be lifted from other accounts or appear to be stock photos — sometimes none of which include an image of the actual person who allegedly owns the accounts.

TIP

The content within a user's social media profile may provide terms and phrases that you can search for in Google along with the person's name to help you verify whether the account truly belongs to a human being whose identity the profile alleges to represent.

Likewise, if you perform a Google image search on someone's Instagram images and see that they belong to other people, something is amiss.

Cliché names

Some fake profiles seem to use common, flowing American names, such as Sally Smith, that both sound overly American and make performing a Google search for a particular person far more difficult than doing so would be for someone with an uncommon name.

TIP

More often than occurs in real life, but certainly not always, bogus profiles seem to use first and last names that start with the same letter. Perhaps, scammers just like the names or, for some reason, find them funny.

Poor contact information

If a social media profile contains absolutely no contact information that can be used to contact the person behind the profile via email, telephone, or on another social platform, beware.

Skill sets

If skill sets don't match someone's work or life experience, beware. Something may seem off when it comes to fake accounts. For example, if someone claims to have graduated with a degree in English from an Ivy League university, but makes serious grammatical errors throughout their profile, something may be amiss. Likewise, if someone claims to have two PhDs in mathematics, but claims to be working as a gym teacher, beware.

Spelling

Spelling errors are common on social media. However, something may be amiss if folks misspell their own name or the name of an employer, or makes errors of this nature on LinkedIn (a professionally oriented network).

Age of an account

Does the age of the account make sense considering to whom the account allegedly belongs? If you come across an active Instagram account belonging to some attractive person whom you met on a dating site, and the account has shared many photos, but all of the photos were uploaded within the last few weeks, ask yourself if it makes sense that the person in question did not post photos before that date. You may have encountered a "catfish" as explained in Chapter 4.

Suspicious career or life path

People who seem to have been promoted too often and too fast or who have held too many disparate senior positions, such as VP of Sales, then CTO, and then General Counsel, may be too good to be true.

Of course, real people have moved up the ladder quickly and some folks (including myself) have held a variety of different positions throughout the course of their careers, but scammers often overdo it when crafting the career progression or role diversity data of a bogus profile. People may shift from technical to managerial roles, for example, but it is extremely uncommon for someone to serve as a company's VP of Sales, then as its CTO, and then as its General Counsel — roles that require different skill sets, educational backgrounds, and potentially, different certifications and licenses.

TIP

If you find yourself saying to yourself "no way" when looking at someone's career path, you may be right.

Level or celebrity status

LinkedIn requests from people at far more senior professional levels than yourself can be a sign that something is amiss, as can Facebook friend requests from celebrities and others about whose connection request you're flattered to have received.

It is certainly tempting to want to accept such connections (which is, of course, why the people who create fake accounts often create such fake accounts), but think about it: If you just landed your first job out of college, do you really think the CEO of a major bank is suddenly interested in connecting with you out of the blue? Do you really think that Ms. Universe, whom you have never met, suddenly wants to be your friend?

In the case of Facebook, Instagram, and Twitter, be aware that most celebrity accounts are verified. If a request comes in from a celebrity, you should be able to quickly discern if the account sending it is the real deal.

DO YOU NEED TO AVOID FAKE CONNECTIONS?

It should be noted, however, that if you use an account to share material with the public — and not for personal use — that there may be no problem of connecting with "fake people." The issue of fake connections focuses on cases in which by connecting you expose some information to the party to whom you are connecting that it otherwise would not have been able to obtain from you.

Using Bogus Information

Some experts have suggested that you use bogus information as answers to common challenge questions. Someone — especially someone whose mother has a common last name as her maiden name — may establish a new, substitute "mother's maiden name" to be used for all sites that ask for such information as part of an authentication process. There is truth to the fact that such an approach somewhat helps reduce the risk of social engineering.

What such advice does in a much stronger fashion, however, is reveal how poor challenge questions are as a means of authenticating people. Asking one's mother's maiden name is effectively asking for a password while providing a hint that the password is a last name!

Likewise, because in the era of social media and online public records, finding out someone's birthday is relatively simple, some security experts recommend creating a second fake birthday for use online. Some even recommend using a phony birthday on social media, both to help prevent social engineering and make it harder for organizations and individuals to correlate one's social media profile and various public records.

While all these recommendations do carry weight, keep in mind that, in theory, there is no end to such logic — establishing a different phony birthday for every site with which one interacts offers stronger privacy protections than establishing just one phony birthday, for example. But how many "birthdays" can one remember? And besides, all using multiple fake birthdays does is effectively transform the authentication-using-birthday into a authentication using a second password — albeit one that is weak and has only 366 possible values.

TIP

In general, however, creating and utilizing one fake birthday, one fake mother's maiden name, and so on is probably worthwhile and doesn't require much additional brainpower and mindshare over using just the true one. Be sure, however, not to mislead any sites where providing accurate information is required by law (for example, when opening a credit card account).

Using Security Software

Besides providing the value of protecting your computer and your phone from hacking, various security software may reduce your exposure to social engineering attacks. Some software, for example, filters out many phishing attacks, while other software blocks many spam phone calls. While using such software is wise, don't rely on it. There is a danger that if few social engineering attacks make it through your technological defenses, you may be less vigilant when one does reach you — don't let that happen.

While smartphone providers have historically charged for some security features, over time they have seen the value to themselves of keeping their customers secure. Today, basic versions of security software, including technology to reduce spam calls and to scan apps for malware, are often provided at no charge along with smartphone cellular-data service. Premium offerings still exist and are often worthwhile to use.

General Cyberhygiene Can Help Prevent Social Engineering

Practicing good cyberhygiene in general can also help reduce your exposure to social engineering. If, as so commonly happened during the COVID-19 pandemic, your children, for example, have access to your computer but you encrypt all your data, have a separate login, and don't provide them with administrator access, your data on the machine may remain safe even if criminals social engineer their way into your child's account.

Likewise, not responding to suspicious emails or providing information to potential scammers who solicit it can help prevent all sorts of social engineering and technical attacks.

4

Cybersecurity for Businesses, Organizations, and Government

Chapter **10**

Securing Your Small Business

Nearly everything I discuss in this book applies to both individuals and businesses. Small business owners and workers should be aware of some points that may not necessarily be important for individuals. This chapter discusses some such cybersecurity issues.

One important note: Small businesses tend to frequently lack proper cybersecurity, and as a result, I could probably write an entire series of books about improving the cybersecurity of small businesses. As such, this chapter isn't a comprehensive list of everything that every small business needs to know. Rather, it provides some cybersecurity "food for thought" for those running small businesses.

Making Sure Someone Is In Charge

Individuals at home are responsible for the security of their computers, but what happens when you have a network and multiple users? Somebody within the business needs to ultimately "own" responsibility for information security. That person may be you, the business owner, or someone else. But whoever is in charge must clearly understand that they are responsible.

REMEMBER

Confusion as to who within an organization is responsible for cybersecurity often leads to major cybersecurity headaches.

In many small businesses, the person in charge of information security will outsource some of the day-to-day activities that are involved with performing the cybersecurity function. Even so, that person is ultimately responsible for ensuring that necessary activities, such as installing security patches, happen — and happen on time. If a breach occurs, "I thought so-and-so was taking care of that security function" is not a valid excuse that will carry a lot of weight — although, sadly, we hear people trying to use it on a regular basis.

Watching Out for Employees

Employees, and the many cybersecurity risks that they create, can become major headaches for small businesses. Human errors are the No. 1 catalyst for data breaches. Even if you're reading this book and seeking to improve your cybersecurity knowledge and posture, your employees and coworkers may not have the same level of commitment as you do when it comes to protecting your data and systems.

As such, one of the most important things small business owners can do is to educate their employees. Education consists of essentially three necessary components:

>> **Awareness of threats:** You must ensure that every employee working for the business understands that they, and the business as a whole, are targets. People who believe that criminals want to breach their computers, phones, and databases, or want to otherwise steal their data, act differently than people who have not internalized such realities. While formal, regular training is ideal, even a single, short conversation conducted when workers start, and refreshed with periodic reminders, can deliver significant value in this regard.

>> **Basic information-security training:** All employees should understand certain basics of information security. They should, for example, know to avoid cyber-risky behavior, such as opening attachments and clicking on links found in unexpected email messages, downloading music or videos from questionable sources, inappropriately using public Wi-Fi, or buying products from unknown stores with too-good-to-be-true prices and no publicly known physical address.

Numerous related training materials (often free) are available online. That said, never rely on training in itself to serve as the sole line of defense against any substantial human risk. Remember, we know with certainty that many people still do stupid things even after receiving clear training to the contrary. Furthermore, training does nothing to address rogue employees who intentionally sabotage information security.

» **Practice:** Information security training should not be theoretical. Employees should be given the opportunity to practice what they have learned — for example, by identifying and deleting/reporting a test phishing email.

Incentivize employees

Just as you should hold employees accountable for their actions if things go amiss, you should also reward employees for performing their jobs in a cyber-secure fashion and acting with proper cyberhygiene. Positive reinforcement can go a long way and is almost always better received than negative reinforcement.

Furthermore, many organizations have successfully implemented reporting systems that allow employees to anonymously notify the relevant powers within the business of suspicious insider activities that may indicate a threat, as well as potential bugs in systems, that could lead to vulnerabilities. Such programs are common among larger businesses, but can also be of benefit to small companies and other organizations.

Avoid giving out the keys to the castle

There are countless stories of employees making mistakes that open the organizational "door" to hackers. Likewise, there have been numerus cases of disgruntled employees stealing data and/or sabotaging systems. The damage from such incidents can be catastrophic to a small business. Protect yourself and your business from these types of risks by setting up your information infrastructure to contain the damage if something does go amiss.

TIP

How can you do this? Give workers access to all the computer systems and data that they need in order to do their jobs with maximum performance, but do not give them access to anything else of a sensitive nature. Programmers shouldn't be able to access a business's payroll system, for example, and a comptroller doesn't need access to the version control system housing the source code of a company's proprietary software.

Limiting access can make a world of difference in terms of the scope of a data leak if an employee goes rogue. Many businesses have learned this lesson the hard way. Don't become one of them.

Give everyone separate credentials

Every employee accessing each and every system in use by the organization should have their own login credentials to that system. Do not share credentials!

Implementing such a scheme improves the ability to audit people's activities (which may be necessary if a data breach or other cybersecurity event happens) and also encourages people to better protect their passwords because they know that if the account is misused, management will address the matter with them personally rather than with a team. The knowledge that employees are going to be held accountable for their behavior for maintaining or compromising security can work wonders in a proactive sense.

Likewise, every person should have their own multifactor authentication capabilities — whether that be a physical token, a code generated on their smartphone, and so on.

Restrict administrators

System administrators typically have superuser privileges — meaning that they may be able to access, read, delete, and modify other people's data. It is essential, therefore, that if you — the business owner — are not the only superuser, that you implement controls to monitor what an administrator does. For example, you can log administrator actions on a separate machine that the administrator does not have access to.

Allowing access from only a specific machine in a specific location — which is sometimes not possible due to business needs — is another approach, as it allows a camera to be aimed toward that machine to record everything that the administrator does.

Limit access to corporate accounts

Your business itself may have several of its own accounts. For example, it may have social media accounts — a Facebook page, Instagram account, and a Twitter account — customer support, email accounts, phone accounts, and other utility accounts.

REMEMBER

Grant access only to the people who absolutely need access to those accounts (see preceding section). Ideally, every one of the folks to whom you do give access should have *auditable access* — that is, it should be easy to determine who did what with the account.

Basic control and audibility are simple to achieve when it comes to Facebook Pages, for example, as you can own the Facebook Page for the business, while providing other people the ability to write to the page. In some other environments, however, granular controls aren't available and you will need to decide between providing multiple people logins to a social media account or having them submit content to a single person (perhaps, even you) who makes the relevant posts.

The challenge of providing every authorized user of corporate social media accounts with their own account to achieve both control and audibility is exacerbated by the fact that all sensitive accounts should be protected with multifactor authentication. (See Chapter 7 for more on multifactor authentication.)

Some systems offer multifactor authentication capabilities that account for the fact that multiple independent users may need to be given auditable access to a single account. In some cases, however, systems that offer multifactor authentication capabilities do not blend well with multi-person environments. They may, for example, allow for only one cellphone number to which one-time passwords are sent via SMS. In such scenarios, you will need to decide whether to

>> **Use the multifactor authentication, but with a work-around.** For example, by using a VOIP number to receive the texts and configuring the VOIP number to forward the messages on to multiple parties via email (as is offered at no cost, for example, by Google Voice).

>> **Use the multifactor authentication with no work-around.** Configure the authorized users' devices not to need multifactor authentication for the activities that they perform.

>> **Use a form of multifactor authentication that does not need a work-around.** For example, one that allows multiple users to independently authenticate using different credentials and multifactor logins, and subsequently receive permission to act on the same account.

>> **Use a form of multifactor authentication that does not need a work-around, but does not multifactor separately for different users.** For example, allowing users to use separate initial authentication credentials, but use shared multifactor credentials such as by giving them a one-time code generator configured with the same seed (that is, configured to produce exactly the same one-time codes at exactly the same times).

>> **Not use the multifactor authentication, but instead rely solely on strong passwords**. This solution is not recommended.

>> **Find another work-around by modifying your processes, procedures, or technologies used to access such systems.**

>> **Utilize third-party products that overlay systems.** This is often the best option when available.

TIP

The last option is often the best option. Various content management systems, for example, allow themselves to be configured for multiple users, each with their own independent, strong authentication capabilities, and all such users have auditable access to a single social media account.

While larger enterprises almost always follow some variant of the last approach — both for management and security reasons — many small businesses tend to take the easy way out and simply not use strong, multifactor authentication in such cases. The cost of implementing proper security — both in terms of dollars and time — is usually quite low, so exploring third-party products should definitely be done before deciding to take another approach.

REMEMBER

The value of having proper security with auditability will become immediately clear if you ever have a disgruntled employee who had access to the company's social media accounts or if a happy and satisfied employee with such access is hacked.

Implement employee policies

Businesses of all sizes that have employees need an employee handbook that includes specific rules regarding employee usage of business technology systems and data. It is beyond the scope of this book to cover all elements of employee handbooks, but the following are examples of rules that businesses can implement to govern the use of company technology resources:

>> Company's employees are expected to use technology responsibly, appropriately, and productively, as necessary to perform their professional responsibilities.

>> The use of company devices, as well as company Internet access and email, as provided to employees by the company, are for job-related activities. Minimal personal use is acceptable provided that the employees using it as such does not violate any other rules described in this document and does not interfere with their work.

>> Employees are responsible for any computer hardware and software provided by the company, including for the safeguarding of such items from theft, loss, or damage.

>> Employees are responsible for their accounts provided by the company, including the safeguarding of access to the accounts.

>> Employees are strictly prohibited from sharing any company-provided items used for authentication (passwords, hardware authentication devices, PINs, and so on) and are responsible for safeguarding such items.

>> Employees are strictly prohibited from connecting any networking devices, such as routers, access points, range extenders, and so on, to company networks unless explicitly authorized to do so by the company's CEO. Likewise, employees are strictly prohibited from connecting any personal computers or electronic devices — including any Internet of Things (IoT) devices — to company networks other than to the Guest network, under the conditions stated explicitly in the Bring Your Own Device (BYOD) policy.

>> Employees are responsible to make sure that security software is running on all company-provided devices. Company will provide such software, but it is beyond company's ability to check that such systems are always functioning as expected. Employees may not deactivate or otherwise cripple such security systems, and must promptly notify company's IT department if they suspect that any portion of the security systems may be compromised, nonfunctioning, or malfunctioning.

>> Employees are responsible to make sure that security software is kept up to date. All company-issued devices come equipped with Auto-Update enabled; employees must not disable this feature.

>> Likewise, employees are responsible for keeping their devices up to date with the latest operating system, driver, and application patches when vendors issue such patches. All company-issued devices come equipped with Auto-Update enabled; employees must not disable this feature.

>> Performing any illegal activity — whether or not the act involved is a felony, a misdemeanor, or a violation of civil law — is strictly prohibited. This rule applies to federal law, state law, and local law in any area and at any time in which the employee is subject to such laws.

>> Copyrighted materials belonging to any party other than the company or employee may not be stored or transmitted by the employee on company equipment without explicit written permission of the copyright holder. Material that the company has licensed may be transmitted as permitted by the relevant licenses.

>> Sending mass unsolicited emails (spamming) is prohibited.

» The use of company resources to perform any task that is inconsistent with company's mission — even if such task is not technically illegal — is prohibited. This includes, but is not limited to, the accessing or transmitting sexually explicit material, vulgarities, hate speech, defamatory materials, discriminatory materials, images or description of violence, threats, cyberbullying, hacking-related material, stolen material, and so on.

» The previous rule shall not apply to employees whose job entails working with such material, only to the extent that is reasonably needed for them to perform the duties of their jobs. For example, personnel responsible for configuring the company's email filter may, without violating the preceding rule, email one another about adding to the filter configuration various terms related to hate speech and vulgarities.

» No company devices equipped with Wi-Fi or cellular communication capabilities may be turned on in China or Russia without explicit written permission from the company's CEO. Loaner devices will be made available for employees making trips to those regions. Any personal device turned on in those regions may not be connected to the Guest network (or any other company network).

» All use of public Wi-Fi with corporate devices must comply with the company's Public Wi-Fi policies. Ideally, companies should ban such use except in rare, specific types of cases.

» Employees must backup their computers by using the company's backup system as discussed in the company's backup policy.

» Employees may not copy or otherwise back up data from company devices to their personal computers, storage devices, or cloud-based repositories such as DropBox, Google Drive, Box, or any other such services.

» Any and all passwords for any and all systems used as part of an employees' job must be unique and not reused on any other systems. All such passwords must consist of three or more words, at least one of which is not found in the English dictionary, joined together with numbers or special characters or meet all the following conditions:

- Contain eight characters or more with at least one uppercase character

- Contain at least one lowercase character

- Contain at least one number

- Not contain any words that can be found in an English dictionary

- Names of relatives, friends, or colleagues may not be used as part of any password

>> Data may be taken out of the office for business purposes only and must be encrypted prior to removal. This rule applies whether the data is on hard drive, SSD, CD/DVD, USB drive, or on any other media or is transmitted over the Internet. It may not be taken out of the office by copying to employee cloud-storage accounts (such as Google Drive or Dropbox). Any and all data taken out of the business's infrastructure or infrastructure contracted for use by the business must be returned to the business (or at the company's sole discretion, destroyed) immediately after its remote use is complete or upon employee's termination of employment, whichever is sooner.

>> In the event of a breach or other cybersecurity event or of any natural or man-made disaster, no employees other than the company's officially designated spokesperson may speak to the media on behalf of the company.

>> No devices from any manufacturer that the FBI, the FCC, or other United States federal agencies have warned that they believe are potentially unsafe and/or that foreign governments are using to spy on Americans may be connected to any company network (including the guest network) or brought into the physical offices of the company. Nor should company data ever be stored or processed on such devices.

Enforce social media policies

Devising, implementing, and enforcing social media policies is important because inappropriate social media posts made by your employees (or yourself) can inflict all sorts of damage. They can leak sensitive information, violate compliance rules, and assist criminals to social engineer and attack your organization, expose your business to boycotts and/or lawsuits, and so on.

TIP

You want to make clear to all employees what is and is not acceptable use of social media. As part of the process of crafting the policies, consider consulting an attorney to make sure that you do not violate anyone's freedom of speech. You may also want to implement technology to ensure social media does not transform from a marketing platform into a nightmare.

Monitor employees

Regardless of whether or not they plan to actually monitor employees' usage of technology, companies should inform users that they have a right to do so. If an employee were to go rogue and steal data, for example, you do not want to have the admissibility of evidence challenged on the grounds that you had no right to monitor the employee. Furthermore, telling employees that they may be monitored reduces the likelihood of employees doing things that they are not supposed to do because they know that they may be monitored while doing such things. Of course, monitoring should be done only on employer-issued devices and networks. (This is discussed in more detail in the section on remote work that follows.)

Here is an example of text that you can provide to employees as part of an employee handbook or the like when they begin work:

> Company, at its sole discretion, and without any further notice to employee, reserves the right to monitor, examine, review, record, collect, store, copy, transmit to others, and control any and all email and other electronic communications, files, and any and all other content, network activity including Internet use, transmitted by or through its technology systems or stored in its technology systems or systems, whether onsite or offsite. Such systems shall include systems that it owns and operates and systems that it leases, licenses, or to which it otherwise has any usage rights.

> Furthermore, whether sent to an internal party, external party, or both, any and all email, text and/or other instant messages, voicemail, and/or any and all other electronic communications are considered to be Company's business records, and may be subject to discovery in the event of litigation and/or to disclosure based on warrants served upon company or requests from regulators and other parties.

Dealing with a Remote Workforce

While the concept of working remotely is not new, the number of people who actually work from home has skyrocketed since early 2020 when the novel coronavirus began to spread like wildfire throughout the world. The resulting COVID-19 pandemic has become, by far, the leading motivator for change vis-à-vis remote working. It quickly transformed the world from one in which nearly all people worked at locations chosen and administered by their employers, to one in which a significant percentage of the population worked solely from home. Even as people return to workplaces after the pandemic, many are still telecommuting from home some of the time.

While working remotely during a global pandemic may help people remain safe from invisible microscopic attackers, and may even offer various productivity and financial benefits to employers, the fact that remote workers must access important data and systems from geographically scattered environments not managed by their employers creates all sorts of cybersecurity concerns. Entire books could be written on such a topic — and probably will be. But for those who wish to learn what cybersecurity safeguards they can take while working from home, the following overview of some important ideas may prove useful.

Use work devices and separate work networks

If employees connect to employer networks, access employer systems, or work with employer data with their own personal devices, employers run serious risks of malware infections, data being stored in insecure locations, data being pilfered by nefarious parties, and all sorts of other cybersecurity nightmares. As such, if possible, all remote work should be done on computers and other types of computing devices that are owned by, managed by, and issued to employees by the employer.

Ideally, access to employer systems should also be conducted using Internet connections and networking equipment paid for and managed by the employer. And no personal devices should be connected. Employers might want to have the ability to remotely access such devices to monitor and/or wipe such devices in case they are lost or stolen. In many cases, however, such arrangements are either impractical or impossible, and as such, various other types of precautions should be taken.

If employees will be using their own Internet connections, for example, it is ideal that employers provide a network router to employees so that employees can connect that router to their home network routers, and thereby isolate the employer's equipment and data from the main network segment at home and all of its traffic.

TIP

While employees should not be connecting to employer networks with personal devices, if for some reason you or your employer choses to ignore such advice, at least make sure that any and all devices connecting to the employer network have up-to-date security software running on them. Employers should manage such software installations, and keep in mind that if any software an employer instructs an employee to install creates technical issues on the employee's personal device, the employer may be responsible to correct the problem.

WARNING

Of course, never, ever, attempt to monitor an employees' actions on their personal devices.

Set up virtual private networks

A virtual private network (VPN) provides remote workers with several significant benefits. It can prevent unauthorized parties from sharing any Internet connection back to the employer's network, and can prevent other parties connected to the same local network, as well as the Internet service provider for that connection, from seeing the contents of the VPN user's transmissions.

As such, a VPN from the separate network router to a special corporate remote-worker network (for those familiar with the term, this network would likely be a form of demilitarized zone [DMZ] — not fully trusted by the company, but yet not open to the public) may also ideal, especially if the user needs to use multiple corporate devices from the remote location, or in situations in which multiple employees may be working at that location. When network-to-network VPNs are not possible — or when only one user is using only one device — a connection directly from the user's remote corporate device may be appropriate.

In some cases, either type of VPN connection may actually be dangerous from a cybersecurity perspective, such as if an employer does not have the expertise or the capability to properly implement and supervise such a VPN. Even when no VPN is used, however, isolating work devices from any personal devices through the use of a separate network at the remote location (as described earlier) is ideal.

Of course, you can also subscribe to consumer-type VPN services, but these services are less ideal because these services do not connect the remote worker to the employer's infrastructure via a "secure tunnel" (think of a secured-by-encryption communication pathway over the insecure Internet); rather, they connect the employee to the VPN provider's systems over a secure tunnel and then communicate from the VPN provider's infrastructure to others on the Internet using potentially insecure transmissions.

WARNING

Employees should not connect their personal devices to an employer's VPN. Allowing people to connect as such is a recipe for a potential cybersecurity disaster.

Create standardized communication protocols

As discussed in Chapter 6, ideally, an organization should create standardized policies, procedures, and technologies for any video calls or chatting, and security should weigh heavily as a factor when such decisions are made. Relevant policies should include configuration requirements, such as requiring that all video calls require a password in order for someone to gain access, that virtual "waiting rooms" be utilized to prevent anyone from attending a meeting until admitted by the host, and that only users properly authenticated and signed into the communication platform be admitted into any non-public meetings.

Use a known network

When working from home, make sure that any network to which you connect wirelessly is using encryption and a strong Wi-Fi key (WPA2 or better). The reason for such advice is not only to ensure that communications cannot be monitored between your devices and the Wi-Fi access point or router, but also to ensure that you are connecting to the correct access point or router in the first place.

Hackers can set up "evil twin networks" with the same name as your network, for example, and if you receive a better signal from the evil twin access point, your device may connect to it rather than the intended, legitimate access point. Utilizing Wi-Fi security reduces the likelihood of such a problematic connection occurring, as the hacker is unlikely to have established the same encryption key. (And if somehow an attacker has your key, you have bigger problems than just this connection.)

Determine how backups are handled

Make sure you have a plan in place — and properly implemented — for how remote workers' systems and data will be backed up. Backups should be performed, managed, and administered by the employer. Do not rely on employees to back up employer data. If for some reason, despite all of the information provided earlier in this chapter, you find yourself in a situation in which employees are using personal devices for working remotely, be absolutely sure as their employer not to back up any personal contents of such devices.

Be careful where you work remotely

Keep in mind that working from home is likely to be less secure than working at a normal professional work location, not only for technical reasons, but also due to the people often present in the respective areas. Simply put, besides technical issues, as discussed elsewhere in this book, working remotely creates major concerns about "shoulder surfing." Ideally, therefore, remote employees should be working strictly from home and other locations with strongly controlled human access, and not from coffee shops, airports, libraries, public parks, sidewalks, and/or restaurants.

Also, it should be noted that with workers situated in the safety of their homes, unauthorized outsiders are far more unlikely to see what appears on the display of the employee's computer or hear sensitive information conveyed by the employee during voice-based phone calls, many organizations are rightfully still uncomfortable with their employees' children or significant others knowing all sorts of information that remote workers may handle and expose during work-at-home sessions.

TIP

Using a noise machine, such as those intended to produce background noise to help people fall asleep, or those used by psychologists, psychiatrists, and social workers for years to prevent people in waiting rooms from hearing the conversations taking place in treatment rooms, can be used to reduce the likelihood of sensitive information being overheard.

In addition, privacy screens for laptops can reduce the likelihood of anyone being able to read what appears on the display. Such screens allow displayed contents to be seen clearly when someone looks directly at them, but not when someone looks from the side.

Be extra vigilant regarding social engineering

Would-be cyberattackers know that remote workers make good targets not only because of the technical cybersecurity limitations present at the vast majority of home-office sites, but because of human weaknesses as well.

Unlike their in-office counterparts, for example, people working remotely cannot simply walk down the hall and ask someone about a particular request allegedly made by that person and received in a chat message or email. Remote workers are also more likely than in-office workers to deviate from normal business hours for their work schedules. And, such workers rarely benefit as much as do their in-office counterparts, from robust technology suites implemented to protect people from phishing and other social engineering attacks.

For those reasons as well as others, remote workers are believed by many to be more likely to be successfully social engineered by criminals than are otherwise similar people working in professional offices. Remote workers are more likely to open problematic emails, click on dangerous links, and/or otherwise inadvertently take action based on the request of a criminal. Think for a moment how likely you would be — if you were working remotely — to open a spear-phishing email made to look like it was sent by your boss with the subject, "Important Updates to Corporate Remote Working Policy."

As such, remote workers must be especially vigilant against social engineering attacks. To learn more about such attacks and how to defend against them, see Chapter 9.

Considering Cybersecurity Insurance

While cybersecurity insurance may be overkill for most small businesses, if you believe that your business could suffer a catastrophic loss or even fail altogether if it were to be breached, you may want to consider buying insurance. If you do pursue this route, keep in mind that nearly all cybersecurity insurance policies have *carve outs*, or exclusions — so make sure that you understand exactly what is covered and what is not and for what amount of damage you are actually covered. If your business fails because you were breached, a policy that pays only to have an expert spend two hours restoring your data is not going to be worth much.

REMEMBER

Cybersecurity insurance is never a replacement for proper cybersecurity.

In fact, to the contrary, insurers normally require that a business meet a certain standard of cybersecurity to purchase and maintain coverage. In some cases, the insurer may even refuse to pay a claim if it finds that the insured party was breached at least in part due to negligence on the insured's part or due to the failure of the breached party to adhere to certain standards or practices mandated by the relevant insurance policy.

CYBERSECURITY INSURANCE IS NOW AVAILABLE TO BUSIENSSES OF ALL SIZES

For many years, cybersecurity insurance (also known as cyber liability insurance) policies were available primarily to large businesses. Today, however, that is not the case; various companies now offer policies to smaller businesses, and some even offer policies to individuals.

Before obtaining any policy, it is critical to understand what the policy covers and what it does not cover. Policies for smaller entities and individuals typically vary quite a bit from those of larger enterprises in such regard.

In any event, do not discount the value of cybersecurity insurance. If a situation ever arises in which you need to make a claim, you are likely to be extremely happy to have previously obtained a policy — to put it mildly.

Complying with Regulations and Compliance

Businesses may be bound by various laws, contractual obligations, and industry standards when it comes to cybersecurity. Your local Small Business Administration office may be able to provide you with guidance as to what regulations potentially impact you. Remember, though, that there is no substitute for hiring a properly trained lawyer experienced with this area of law to provide professional advice optimized for your particular situation.

The following sections provide examples of several such regulations, standards, and so on that often impact small businesses.

Protecting employee data

You're responsible for protecting sensitive information about your employees. If you don't properly protect this information, you could end up in hot water with government regulators, with your employees, or in the eyes of the public.

For physical files, you should, in general, protect records with at least *double-locking* — storing the paper files in a locked cabinet within a locked room (and not using the same key for both). For electronic files, the files should be stored encrypted within a password-protected folder, drive, or virtual drive. Such standards, however, may not be adequate in every particular situation, which is why you should check with an attorney.

REMEMBER

Keep in mind that failure to adequately protect employee information can have severe effects: If your business is breached and a criminal obtains private information about employees, the impacted employees and former employees can potentially sue you, and the government may fine you as well. Remediation costs may also be much higher than the costs of proactive prevention would have been. And, of course, the impact of bad publicity on the business's sales may also be catastrophic — sometimes even forcing a business to fail!

Remember, employee personnel records, W2 forms, Social Security numbers, I9 employment eligibility forms, home addresses and phone numbers, medical information including COVID-19 test results and/or vaccination records and any other health-related information that you may maintain, vacation records, family leave records, and so on are all potentially considered private.

TIP

In general, if you're unsure as to whether some information may be considered private, err on the side of caution and treat it as if it is private.

PCI DSS

Payment Card Industry Data Security Standard (PCI DSS) is an information security standard for organizations that handle major credit cards and their associated information. The standard has been updated and expanded multiple times; the most current version is Version 3.2.1, published in May 2018.

While all companies of all sizes that are subject to the PCI DSS standard must be compliant with it, PCI does take into effect the different levels of resources available to different sized businesses. PCI Compliance has effectively four different levels. To what level an organization must comply is normally based primarily on how many credit card transactions it processes per year. Other factors, such as how risky the payments are that the company receives, also weigh in. The different levels are

>> **PCI Level 4:** Standards for businesses that process fewer than 20,000 credit card transactions per year

>> **PCI Level 3:** Standards for businesses that process between 20,000 and 1,000,000 credit card transactions per year

>> **PCI Level 2:** Standards for businesses that process between 1,000,000 and 6,000,000 credit card transactions per year

>> **PCI Level 1:** Standards for businesses that process more than 6,000,000 credit card transactions per year

Exploring PCI in detail is beyond the scope of this book. Entire books have been written on the topic, and various organizations offer classes dedicated to the topic. If you operate a small business and process credit card payments or store credit card data for any other reason, be sure to engage someone knowledgeable in PCI to help guide you. In many cases, your credit card processors will be able to recommend a proper consultant or guide you themselves.

Breach disclosure laws

In recent years, various jurisdictions have enacted so-called *breach disclosure laws,* which require businesses to disclose to the public if they suspect that a breach may have endangered certain types of stored information. Breach disclosure laws vary quite a bit from jurisdiction to jurisdiction, but in some cases, they may apply even to the smallest of businesses.

Be sure that you are aware of the laws that apply to your business. If, for some reason, you do suffer a breach, the last thing that you want is the government punishing you for not handling the breach properly. Remember: Many small businesses fail as the result of a breach; the government entering the fray only worsens your business's odds of surviving after a successful cyberattack.

The laws that apply to your business may include not only those of the jurisdiction within which you're physically located but the jurisdictions of the people you're handling information for.

GDPR

The *General Data Protection Regulation* (GDPR) is a European privacy regulation that went into effect in 2018 and applies to all businesses handling the consumer data of residents of the European Union, no matter the size, industry, or country of origin of the business and no matter whether the EU resident is physically located within the EU. It provides for stiff fines for businesses that do not properly protect private information belonging to EU residents. This regulation means that a small business in New York that sells an item to an EU resident located in New York may be subject to GDPR for information about the purchaser and, can, in theory, face stiff penalties if it fails to properly protect that person's data. For example, in July 2019, the United Kingdom's Information Commissioner's Office (ICO) announced that it intended to fine British Airways about $230 million and Marriott about $123 million for GDPR-related violations stemming from data breaches.

GDPR is complex. If you think that your business may be subject to GDPR, speak with an attorney who handles such matters.

TIP

Do not panic about GDPR. Even if a small business in the United States is technically subject to GDPR, it is unlikely that the EU will attempt to fine small American businesses that do not operate in Europe anytime soon; it has much bigger fish to fry. That said, do not ignore GDPR because eventually American small businesses may become targets for enforcement actions.

HIPAA

Federal law throughout the United States of America requires parties that house healthcare-related information to protect it in order to maintain the privacy of the individuals whose medical information appears in the data. The *Health Insurance Portability and Accountability Act* (HIPAA), which went into effect in 1996, provides for stiff penalties for improperly defending such information. Be sure to learn whether HIPAA applies to your business and, if so, ensure that you are properly protecting the data to which it applies according to industry standards or better. Many other jurisdictions around the world have regulations similar in concept to HIPAA.

Biometric data

If you utilize any forms of biometric authentication or for any other reason store biometric data, you may be subject to various privacy and security laws governing that data. Multiple states have already enacted laws in this regard, and others are likely to follow.

Anti-money laundering laws

Anti-money laundering laws seek to make it difficult for criminals to convert illegally obtained money into money that appears to have been legally obtained. While many anti-money laundering laws are applicable primarily to financial institutions, anyone utilizing cryptocurrency for performing transactions with unknown parties should be sure that their actions do not violate these laws.

International sanctions

Paying ransomware ransoms can sometimes in itself be a crime, especially in situations in which the criminals receiving the payments are under sanctions (meaning it is a federal crime to conduct any financial transactions with them). While, to date, people who have paid ransoms have not been prosecuted by the U.S. government for violating such laws, there are indications that tolerance for such violations may be waning.

Handling Internet Access

Small businesses face significant challenges related to Internet access and information systems that individuals rarely must think about, and must take various actions to prevent the emergence of various dangers. The following sections cover a few examples.

Segregate Internet access for personal devices

If you provide Internet access for visitors to your place of business, and/or for your employees to use with their personal smartphones and tablets while at work, implement this Internet access on a separate network from the network(s) used to run your business. Most modern routers offer such a capability, which is usually found somewhere in the configuration with a name like Guest network. (Likewise, as mentioned earlier in this chapter, remote home-based workers should be keeping their work and personal networks separate.)

Create bring your own device (BYOD) policies

If you allow employees to perform business activities on their own personal laptops or mobile devices, you need to create policies regarding such activity and implement technology to protect your data in such an environment.

Don't rely on policies. If you don't enforce policies with technology, you could suffer a catastrophic theft of data if an employee goes rogue or makes a mistake.

In general, small businesses should not allow bring your own device (BYOD) — even if doing so is tempting. In the vast majority of cases when small businesses do allow employees to use their own devices for work-related activities, data remains improperly protected, and problems develop if an employee leaves the organization (especially if the employee leaves under less than optimal circumstances).

Many Android keyboards "learn" about a user's activities as the user types. While such learning helps improve spelling correction and word prediction, it also means that in many cases, sensitive corporate information may be learned on a personal device and remain as suggested content when a user types on it even after the employee leaves the employer.

If you do allow BYOD, be sure to set proper policies and procedures — both for usage and for decommissioning any company technology on such devices, as well as for removing any company data when an employee leaves. Develop a full mobile device security plan that includes remote wipe capabilities, enforces protection of passwords and other sensitive data, processes work-related data in an isolated area of the device that other apps can't access (a process known as *sandboxing*), installs, runs, and updates mobile-optimized security software, prohibits staff from using public Wi-Fi for sensitive work-related tasks, prohibits certain activities from the devices while corporate data is on them, and so on.

Properly handle inbound access

One of the biggest differences between individuals and businesses using the Internet is often the need of the business to provide inbound access for untrusted parties. Unknown parties must be able to initiate communications that result in communications with internal servers within your business.

For example, if a business offers products for sale online, it must allow untrusted parties to access its website to make purchases (see Figure 10-1). Those parties connect to the website, which must connect to payment systems and internal order tracking systems, even though they are untrusted. (Individuals typically do not have to allow any such inbound access to their computers.)

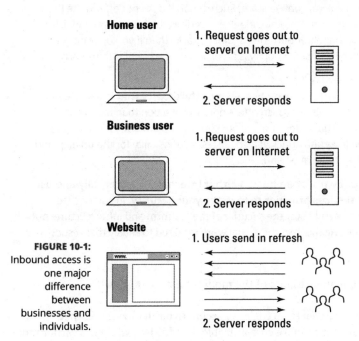

Home user

1. Request goes out to server on Internet

2. Server responds

Business user

1. Request goes out to server on Internet

2. Server responds

Website

1. Users send in refresh

2. Server responds

FIGURE 10-1: Inbound access is one major difference between businesses and individuals.

While small businesses can theoretically properly secure web servers, email servers, and so on, the reality is that few, if any, small businesses have the resources to adequately do so, unless they're in the cybersecurity business to begin with. As such, it is wise for small businesses to consider using third-party software and infrastructure, set up by an expert, and managed by experts, to host any systems used for inbound access. To do so, a business may assume any one or more of several approaches:

>> **Utilize a major retailer's website.** If you're selling items online, and sell only through the websites of major retailers, such as Amazon, Rakuten, and/or eBay, those sites serve as a major buffer between your business's systems and the outside world. The security armies at those companies defend their customer-facing systems from attacks. In many cases, such systems don't require small businesses to receive inbound communications, and when they do, the communications emanate from those retailers' systems, not from the public. Of course, many factors go into deciding whether to sell via a major

retailer — online markets do take hefty commissions, for example. When you weigh the factors in making such a decision, keep the security advantages in mind.

>> **Utilize a third-party hosted retail platform.** In such a case, the third party manages most of the infrastructure and security for you, but you customize and manage the actual online store. Such a model does not offer quite the same level of isolation from outside users as does the preceding model, but it does offer much greater buffering against attacks than if you operate your own platform by yourself. Shopify is an example of a popular third-party platform.

>> **Operate your own platform, hosted by a third party that is also responsible for security.** This approach offers better protection than managing the security yourself, but it does not isolate your code from outsiders trying to find vulnerabilities and attack. It also places responsibility for the upkeep and security of the platform on you.

>> **Operate your own system hosted either internally or externally and use a managed services provider to manage your security.** In such a case, you're fully responsible for the security of the platform and infrastructure, but you're outsourcing much of the actual work required to satisfy that responsibility to a third party.

Other models and many variants of the models I list exist as well.

While the models may step from easier to secure to harder to secure, they also step from less customizable to more customizable. In addition, while the earlier models may cost less for smaller businesses, the expense of the earlier models typically grows much faster than do the later ones as a business grows.

TIP

While using third-party providers does add some risks; the risk that a small business will be unable to properly implement and perpetually manage security is likely much greater than any security risk created by using a reliable third party. Of course, outsourcing anything to an unknown third party that you have done no due diligence on is extremely risky and is not recommended.

Protect against denial-of-service attacks

If you operate any Internet-facing sites as part of your business, make sure that you have security technology implemented to protect against denial-of-service (DoS) attacks. If you're selling via retailers, they likely have it already. If you're using a third-party cloud platform, the provider may supply it as well. If you're running the site on your own, you should obtain protection to ensure that someone can't easily take your site — and your business — offline. Various companies specialize in providing such protection.

Use https

If your business operates a website, be sure to install a valid TLS/SSL certificate so that users can communicate with it over a secure connection and know that the site actually belongs to your business.

TIP

Some security systems that protect against DoS attacks include a certificate as part of the package.

Use a VPN

As is discussed earlier in this chapter regarding home-based workers, if you intend to provide employees remote access to corporate systems, consider using a virtual private network (VPN) and multifactor authentication. In the case of remote access, the VPN should create an encrypted tunnel between your remote users and your business, not between users and a VPN provider. The tunnel both protects against people snooping on the communications between remote users and the business and also allows remote users to function as if they were in the company's offices, and utilize various business resources available only to insiders. Multifactor authentication is discussed in detail in Chapter 7. Of course, if you use third-party, cloud-based systems, the relevant providers should already have security capabilities deployed that you can leverage — do so.

Run penetration tests

Individuals rarely run tests to see whether hackers can penetrate into their systems, and neither do most small businesses. Doing so, however, can be valuable — especially if you are deploying a new system of some sort or upgrading network infrastructure. See Chapter 17 for more on penetration testing.

Be careful with IoT devices

Many businesses today utilize connected cameras, alarms, and so on. Be sure that someone is responsible for overseeing the security of these devices, which should be run on separate networks (or virtual segments) than any computers used to operate the business. Control access to these devices and do not allow employees to connect any unauthorized IoT devices to the business's networks. Ideally, purchase IoT devices only if they are made by a respectable manufacturer. Don't, for example, seek to get the least expensive connected cameras available online regardless of who made them and where they were made. For more on IoT devices, see Chapter 18.

Use multiple network segments

Depending on the size and nature of your business, isolating various computers onto different network segments may be wise. A software development company, for example, should not have developers coding on the same network that the operations folks use to manage payroll and accounts payable. (As is discussed earlier in this chapter, the same holds true for remote home-based workers. Their personal and work networks should be separated.)

Be careful with payment cards

If you accept credit and/or debit cards — and are not selling via a major retailer's website — make sure to speak with your processor about various anti-fraud technology options that may be available to you. And make sure you comply with PCI DSS as discussed earlier in this chapter.

Managing Power Issues

Use an uninterruptable power supply (UPS) on all systems that you can't afford to have go down even momentarily. Do not overload UPSs — make sure they can handle the total load needed for all of the devices plugged into them. Also, make sure the power supplies can keep the systems up and running for longer than any expected outage. If you're selling various goods and services via online retail, for example, you may lose current sales and future sales, as well as suffer reputational harm, if your ability to sell goes offline even for a short period of time.

LOCKING ALL NETWORKING EQUIPMENT AND SERVERS IN A VENTILATED CLOSET

You must control physical access to your systems and data if you want to protect them from unauthorized access. While individuals typically store computers in the open in their homes, businesses usually keep servers in locked racks or closets. You need to be sure, though, that any such rack or closet where you locate computer equipment is well ventilated, or your equipment may overheat and die. You may even need to install a small air conditioner in the closet if ventilation on its own does not sufficiently get rid of the heat generated by the equipment.

WARNING

Never let cleaning personnel enter the server closet unaccompanied — even for a moment. I personally witnessed a case in which a server actively and extensively used by dozens of people went down because an administrator allowed cleaning personnel to enter a server room unaccompanied only to find later that someone unplugged the relevant server from an uninterruptible power supply — a device that serves as both the entry point for power into the system as well as a battery backup — to plug in a vacuum cleaner.

Chapter **11**

Cybersecurity and Big Businesses

Many of the information security challenges facing large enterprises and small business are similar in nature. In fact, over the past decade, cloud-based offerings have brought to small businesses many well-protected systems sporting enterprise-class technologies, reducing some of the historical differences between firms of different sizes as far as the architecture of many major business systems is concerned. Of course, many security risks scale with enterprise size, but don't qualitatively differ based on the number of employees, partners, and customers that a business has, or based on the size of its information technology budget.

At the same time, however, bigger companies often face significant additional complications — sometimes involving orders of magnitude more complexity than the challenges facing small businesses. A large number of diverse systems spread across geographies and utilizing custom code, for example, often make securing a large enterprise quite difficult and complex — and such systems rarely if ever exist in the realm of small businesses.

Thankfully, however, larger firms tend to have significantly larger budgets to acquire defenses and defenders. Furthermore, despite the fact that all companies should, in theory, have formal information security programs, small business tend not to, while large businesses almost always do. This chapter explores some areas that disproportionately impact large companies.

Utilizing Technological Complexity

Large enterprises often have multiple offices and lines of business, many different information systems, complex business arrangements with partners and suppliers, and so on — all of which are reflected in much more complicated information infrastructure than typically exists in the case of smaller businesses. As such, large companies have a much larger *attack surface* — that is, they have many more potential points at which an attacker can attack them than do small businesses. The varied systems common in large business environments also usually mean that no individual, or even small number of people, can possibly be experts on all of them. Large firms use a blend of cloud and local systems, commercial-off-the-shelf and custom-built systems, numerous diverse technologies, complex network architectures, and so on — and their security teams must make sure that all of these work together in a secure fashion.

Managing Custom Systems

Large enterprises almost always have significant amounts of custom-built technology systems that are managed in-house. Depending on how they are deployed and utilized, these systems may require the same level of security patching that off-the-shelf software requires — which means that if security is to be maintained, internal folks and/or third-party contractors who helped build the systems need to manage the code from a security perspective, push out patches, and so on.

Furthermore, security teams must be involved with internal systems throughout the systems' entire life cycle — including phases such as initial investigation, analysis and requirements definition, design, development, integration and testing, acceptance and deployment, ongoing operations, and maintenance, evaluation, and disposal. They must also ensure that any third parties involved at any stages of system creation, implementation, or retirement and disposal adhere to proper security standards.

Simply put, security as an element of software development is a complicated and challenging matter. In fact, entire books have been written about delivering security during the software development life cycle, and various organizations even test competence levels and provide professional certifications in this area as well.

Continuity Planning and Disaster Recovery

While small businesses should have business continuity and disaster recovery plans (sometimes known as BCPs and DRPs) and should regularly test those plans as well, they typically have, at least from a formal perspective, rudimentary plans — at best. And that is being generous. In most cases, small businesses have no business continuity and disaster recovery plans other than identifying who will make decisions as to how to operate in the event of a disaster. Such a lack became obvious during the early days of the COVID-19 pandemic in 2020, during which many small businesses simply had to "wing it" as a result of having no plans as to what to do if employees could not make it to the office.

Large businesses, on the other hand, typically have much more formal plans in place — including detailed arrangements for resumption of work in case a facility becomes unavailable and so on. While many groups within large enterprises were hit hard by the COVID-19 pandemic's sudden work-at-home demands, many others were properly prepared and simply activated plans that they had already tested.

One point the COVID-19 pandemic should have made obvious to everyone, however, is that disasters do happen — and even serious disruptions can happen with far less warning than many folks might expect. Furthermore, hackers know that such disruptions, during which many business are flying by the seats of their pants and making all sorts of compromises when it comes to cybersecurity in order to ensure continuity of operations, are opportune times for hacking.

TIP

Prepare in advance. Remember, when it comes to cybersecurity, an ounce of prevention is worth many tons of cure.

Looking at Regulations

Large enterprises are often subject to many more regulations, laws, guidance, and industry standards than are small businesses. Besides all the issues that are described in the chapter on securing small businesses, for example, the following sections cover some other ones that may impact large enterprises.

Sarbanes Oxley

The Sarbanes Oxley Act of 2002, technically known as either the Public Company Accounting Reform and Investor Protection Act or the Corporate and Auditing Accountability, Responsibility, and Transparency Act, established many rules intended to help protect investors in public companies. Many of its mandates, for example, are intended to improve the accuracy, objectivity, and reliability of corporate statements and disclosures and to create formal systems of internal checks and balances within companies. SOX, as it is often known, mandated stronger corporate governance rules, closed various accounting loopholes, strengthened protections for whistle-blowers, and created substantial penalties (including jail time) for corporate and executive malfeasance.

As its name implies, all publicly held American companies are subject to SOX, as are companies outside of the United States that have registered any equity or debt securities with the United States Securities and Exchange Commission (SEC). In addition, any third party, such as an accounting firm, that provides accounting or other financial services to companies regulated by SOX, is itself mandated to comply with SOX, regardless of its location.

SOX has many implications on information security — both directly and indirectly. Two sections of SOX effectively mandate that companies implement various information security protections:

» **Section 302** of SOX addresses the corporate responsibility to utilize controls to ensure that the firm produces accurate financial reports and requires companies to implement systems to prevent any unauthorized tampering with corporate data used to create such reports — whether the tampering is done by employees or external folks.

» **Section 404** is perhaps the most controversial portion of SOX and certainly, for many businesses, the most expensive with which to comply. This section makes corporate managers responsible to ensure that the company has adequate and effective internal control structures and requires that any relevant shortcomings be reported to the public. Section 404 makes management responsible to ensure that the corporation can properly protect its data processing systems and their contents and mandates that the firm must make all relevant data available to auditors, including information about any potential security breaches.

In addition to these two areas in which SOX plays a role, information security professionals are likely to deal with many other systems that companies have implemented in order to comply with other SOX requirements. Such systems need protection as well as they themselves must adhere to SOX, too.

SOX is complicated — and public companies normally employ people who are experts in the relevant requirements. Information security professionals are likely to interface with such folks.

Stricter PCI requirements

The PCI DSS standards for protecting credit card information (see Chapter 10) include stricter mandates for larger companies (for example, those processing more credit card transactions) than for smaller firms. Also, keep in mind that from a practical perspective, larger firms are likely to have more processing terminals and more credit card data, as well as more diverse technology involved in their credit card processing processes — raising the stakes when it comes to PCI. Larger firms also face a greater risk of reputational damage: A violation of PCI DSS standards by a larger firm is far more likely to make the national news than if the same violation were made by a mom-and-pop shop.

Public company data disclosure rules

Public companies — that is, businesses owned by the public via their shares being listed on a stock exchange (or on various other public trading platforms) — are subject to numerous rules and regulations intended to protect the integrity of the markets.

One such requirement is that a company must release to the entire world at the same time various types of information that may impact the value of the company's shares. A publicly traded company cannot, for example, provide performance information to investment banks before disclosing exactly the same information to the media. In fact, anyone to whom a publicly traded company does release private (insider) information prior to the information's disclosure to the public at large — for example, the public company's accounting or law firms — is strictly prohibited from trading shares or any derivative based on that data. Illegally benefiting from such "insider information" is typically a felony — and even attempting to benefit as such can lead to a prison sentence in a federal penitentiary.

Because of the seriousness of protecting company data, large corporations often have all sorts of policies, procedures, and technologies in place to protect any data subject to such regulations — and to address situations in which some such data was inadvertently released.

Breach disclosures

Some breach disclosure rules exempt smaller businesses, but all require disclosures from large enterprises. Furthermore, large enterprises often have multiple departments that must interact and coordinate in order to release information about a breach — sometimes also involving external parties. Representatives of the marketing, investor relations, information technology, security, legal, and other departments, for example, may need to work together to coordinate the text of any release and may need to involve a third-party public relations firm and external counsel as well. Large enterprises also tend to have official spokespeople and media departments to which the press can address any questions.

Industry-specific regulators and rules

Various industry-specific rules and regulations tend to apply to larger firms more often than to small businesses. For example, the Nuclear Regulatory Commission (NRC), which is an independent federal agency that regulates nuclear power companies in the United States, regulates some major utilities, but few, if any, mom-and-pop shops will ever be subject to its regulations. Hence, only larger firms dedicate significant resources to ensuring compliance with its rules. In the world of NRC regulations, cybersecurity is an important element in governing various Supervisory Control and Data Acquisition systems (SCADA), which are computer-based control and management systems that speak to the controllers in components of a plant.

Likewise, with the exception of certain hedge funds and other financial operations, few small businesses are required to monitor and record all the social media interactions of their employees, the way major banks must do for certain workers.

As a result of industry specific regulations, many large businesses have various processes, policies, and technologies in place that yield data and systems requiring all sorts of information security involvement. Various states have also enacted breach disclosure rules. While such rules impact business of various sizes, they often place more onerous demands on larger organizations, as such firms are, in many cases, better equipped to quickly report breaches. It should be noted that in some cases, covering up a breach (or even *attempting* to cover up a breach) can expose an organization — and the individuals involved — to both civil and criminal liabilities.

Fiduciary responsibilities

While many small businesses don't have external shareholders to whom management or a board of directors may be fiduciarily responsible, most large corporations do have investors who may sue either or both parties if a cybersecurity breach harms the firm's value. Various laws require management and boards to ensure that systems are appropriately secured. In some cases, folks may even be able to be criminally charged if they were negligent. Even if senior executives are not charged after a breach, they may still suffer severe career and reputational damage for their failure to prevent it.

INSIDER TRADING AFTER A BREACH OCCURS AND BEFORE IT IS REPORTED

There have been instances in which, after a data breach occurred, but before it was reported to the public, executives of the breached entities have sold stock positions they held in the companies for which they worked. Such actions are not only reprehensible, they are often illegal as well, since advance knowledge of the breach is insider information not known to the public, and trading on such information is against the law.

One defense some executives have made for such behavior is that they were not personally aware of the relevant breach. While the public has the right to question the veracity of any such claims, it is certainly possible that a scenario could arise in which an executive honestly was unaware of the breach at the time the executive made a trade. For that reason and other reasons it is imperative that appropriate legal advice be obtained — not only immediately upon discovery of the breach vis-à-vis how to prevent potential issues related to accusations of insider trading, but also in advance in order to advise executives how to avoid such suspicions in the first place. (One method, for example, might be for executives who wish to sell stock to break up the position they which to sell into multiple subpositions and set up sales to occur automatically on a regular basis in order to liquidate those subpositions.)

Deep pockets

Because large enterprises have much deeper pockets than small businesses — in other words, they have a lot more money at their disposal — and because targeting mom-and-pop shops isn't usually as politically advantageous as targeting a large firm that exhibited some bad behavior, regulators tend to pursue compliance cases against large enterprises suspected of violations with much more gusto than they do against small businesses.

One exception to this rule is when it comes to cryptocurrency and other blockchain-related projects, as securities regulators have been increasingly targeting such operations in recent years even when such operations are relatively small.

Deeper Pockets — and Insured

Because larger organizations are more likely to have large amounts of cash and assets than small businesses, they make better targets for class action and various other forms of lawsuits than do mom-and-pop shops. Lawyers don't want to expend large amounts of time fighting a case if their target has no money with which to settle or may go bankrupt (and therefore not pay) in the case of a judgment. As a result, the odds that a larger enterprise will be targeted with a lawsuit if data leaks from it as a result of a breach are relatively high when compared with the odds that the same would happen to a much smaller business suffering a similar breach.

Considering Employees, Consultants, and Partners

Employees are often the weakest link in a business's security chain. Far more complex employment arrangements utilized by large enterprises — often involving unionized employees, non-unionized employees, directly hired contractors, contractors hired through firms, subcontractors, foreign workers in the United States, foreign employees outside of the United States, American employees outside the United States, and so on — threaten to make the problem even worse for larger business.

REMEMBER

Complexity of any sort increases the odds of people making mistakes.

With human errors being the No. 1 catalyst for data breaches, large enterprises must go beyond the human management processes and procedures of small businesses. They must, for example, establish and maintain streamlined processes for deciding who gets to access what and who can give authorization for what. They must establish simple processes for revoking permissions from diverse systems when employees leave, contractors complete their assignments, and so on.

Revoking access from departing parties is not as simple as many people might imagine. An employee of a large corporation might, for example, have access to multiple, unconnected data systems located in many different locations around the globe and that are managed by different teams from different departments. Identity and access management systems that centralize parts of the authentication and authorization processes can help, but many large enterprises still lack the totally comprehensive centralization necessary to make revoking access a single-step process. Cybersecurity professionals have often witnesses multiple situations in which accounts belonging to people who have left a large company have remained active for years after the individual left. Often, access was only terminated when the system itself was retired and shut down completely.

Dealing with internal politics

While all businesses with more than one employee have some element of politics, large businesses can suffer from conflicts between people and groups that are literally incentivized to perform in direct opposition to one another. For example, a business team may be rewarded if it delivers new product features earlier than a certain date — which it can do more easily if it skimps on security — while the information security team may be incentivized to delay the product release because it's incentivized to ensure that there are no security problems and not to get the product to market quickly.

REMEMBER

The only winners when there are conflicts between a firm's information security divisions and its business units are hackers.

Offering information security training

All employees should understand certain basics of information security. They should, for example, know to avoid cyber-risky behavior, such as opening attachments and clicking on links found in unexpected email messages, downloading music or videos from questionable sources, inappropriately using public Wi-Fi for sensitive tasks, or buying products from unknown stores with "too good to be true" prices and no publicly known physical address.

In large firms, however, most employees do not personally know most other employees. Such a situation opens the door for all sorts of social engineering attacks — bogus requests from management to send W2s, bogus requests from the IT department to reset passwords, and so on. Training and practice to make sure that such attacks cannot successfully achieve their aims are critical.

Today, it is also imperative that people be taught about deep fakes so that even if they hear the CEO's voice telling them to do something else, for example, they must not deviate from security protocols without verifying the authenticity of the request and authorization of its maker.

Replicated environments

Larger businesses often replicate environments not only in order to protect against outages, but also for maintenance purposes. As such, they often have three replicas for every major system in place: the production system (which may be replicated itself for redundancy purposes), a development environment, and a staging environment for running tests of code and patches.

REMEMBER

It is imperative not to mix these environments up. Never develop in the staging environment. And do not test in production before testing in staging. These may sound like obvious points, but deviations from such a scheme are still extremely common.

Looking at the Chief Information Security Officer's Role

While all businesses need someone within them to ultimately own responsibility for information security, larger enterprises often have large teams involved with information security and need someone who can oversee all the various aspects of information security management, as well as manage all the personnel involved in doing so. This person also represents the information security function to senior management — and sometimes to the board. Typically that person is the chief information security officer (CISO).

While the exact responsibilities of CISOs vary by industry, geography, company size, corporate structure, and pertinent regulations, most CISO roles share basic commonalities. In general, the CISO's role includes overseeing and assuming responsibility for all areas of information security. The following sections describe those areas.

Overall security program management

The CISO is responsible to oversee the company's security program from A to Z. This role includes not only establishing the information security policies for the enterprise, but everything needed to ensure that business objectives can be achieved with the desired level of risk management — something that requires performing risk assessments, for example, on a regular basis.

While, in theory, small businesses also have someone responsible for their entire security programs, in the case of large enterprises, the programs are usually much more formal, with orders of magnitude more moving parts. Such programs are also forever ongoing.

Test and measurement of the security program

The CISO is responsible to establish proper testing procedures and success metrics against which to measure the effectiveness of the information security plan and to make adjustments accordingly. Establishing proper security metrics is often far more complicated than one might initially assume, as defining "successful performance" when it comes to information security is not a straightforward matter.

Human risk management

The CISO is responsible for addressing various human risks as well. Screening employees before hiring them, defining roles and responsibilities, training employees, providing employees with appropriate user manuals and employee guides, providing employees with information security breach simulations and feedback, creating incentive programs, and so on all often involve the participation of the CISO's organization (along with human resources and other groups within the firm).

Information asset classification and control

This function of the CISO includes performing an inventory of informational assets, devising an appropriate classification system, classifying the assets, and then deciding what types of controls (at a business level) need to be in place to adequately secure the various classes and assets. Auditing and accountability should be included in the controls as well.

Security operations

Security operations means exactly what it sounds like. It is the business function that includes the real-time management of security, including the analysis of threats, and the monitoring of a company's technology assets (systems, networks, databases, and so on) and information security countermeasures, such as firewalls, whether hosted internally or externally, for anything that may be amiss. Operations personnel are also the folks who initially respond if they do find that something has potentially gone wrong.

Information security strategy

This role includes devising the forward-looking security strategy of the company to keep the firm secure as it heads into the future. Proactive planning and action is obviously a lot more comforting to shareholders than is reacting to attacks.

Identity and access management

This role deals with controlling access to informational assets based on business requirements, and includes identity management, authentication, authorization, and related monitoring. It includes all aspects of the company's password management policies and technologies, any and all multifactor authentication policies and systems, and any directory systems that store lists of people and groups and their permissions.

The CISO's identity and access management teams are responsible to give workers access to the systems needed to perform the workers' jobs and to revoke all such access when a worker leaves. Likewise, they manage partner access and all other external access.

Major corporations almost always utilize formal directory services systems of some sort — Microsoft's Active Directory, for example, is quite popular.

Data loss prevention

Data loss prevention includes policies, procedures, and technologies that prevent proprietary information from leaking. Leaks can happen accidentally — for example, a user may accidentally attach the wrong document to an email before sending the message — or through malice (for example, a disgruntled employee steals valuable intellectual property by copying it to a USB drive and taking the drive home just before resigning).

In recent years, some social media management functions have been moved into the data loss prevention group. After all, oversharing on social media often includes the de facto sharing by employees of information that businesses do not want going out onto publicly accessible social networks.

Fraud prevention

Some forms of fraud prevention may fall within the CISO's realm of responsibility. For example, if a company operates consumer-facing websites that sell products, the CISO may be responsible for minimizing the number of fraudulent transactions that are successfully completed using the websites.

Even when such responsibility doesn't fall within the purview of the CISO, the CISO is likely to be involved in the process, as anti-fraud systems and information security systems often mutually benefit from sharing information about suspicious users.

Besides dealing with combatting fraudulent transactions, the CISO may be responsible for implementing technologies to prevent rogue employees from perpetrating various types of schemes in order to steal money from the company — with the CISO usually focusing primarily on mechanisms that involve the use of computers.

Incident response plan

The CISO is responsible to develop and maintain the company's incident response plan. The plan should include not only the technical steps described in Chapters 12 and 13, but also detail who speaks to the media, who clears messages with the media, who informs the public, who informs regulators, who consults with law enforcement, and so on. It should also detail the identities (specified by job description) and roles of all other decision-makers within the incident response process.

Disaster recovery and business continuity planning

This function includes managing disruptions of normal operations through contingency planning and the testing of all such plans. While large businesses often have a separate DR and BCP team, the CISO almost always plays a major role in these functions — if not owns them outright — for multiple reasons:

>> **Keeping systems and data available is part of the CISO's responsibility.** As such, there is little difference from a practical perspective if a system goes down because a DR and BC plan is ineffective or because a DDoS attack hit — if systems and data are not available, it is the CISO's problem.

>> **CISOs need to make sure that BCP and DR plans provide for recovery in such a manner that security is preserved.** This is especially true because it is often obvious from major media news stories when major corporations may need to activate their continuity plans, and hackers know that companies in recovery mode make ideal targets.

Compliance

The CISO is responsible to ensure that the company complies with all with legal and regulatory requirements, contractual obligations, and best practices accepted by the company as related to information security. Of course, compliance experts and attorneys may advise the CISO regarding such matters, but ultimately, it is the CISO's responsibility to ensure that all requirements related to information security are at least met, if not exceeded.

Investigations

If (and, sadly, when) an information security incident occurs, the folks working for the CISO in this capacity investigate what happened. In many cases, they'll be the same folks who coordinate investigations with law enforcement agencies, consulting firms, regulators, or third-party security companies. These teams must be skilled in forensics and in preserving evidence. It does little good to know that some rogue employee stole money or data, if, as a result of your own mishandling of digital evidence during your investigation, you can't prove in a court of law that that is the case.

Physical security

Ensuring that corporate informational assets are physically secure is part of the CISO's job. This includes not only systems and networking equipment, but the transport and storage of backups, disposal of decommissioned computers, and so on.

In some organizations, the CISO is also responsible for the physical security of buildings housing technology and for the people within them. Regardless of whether this is the case, the CISO is always responsible to work with those responsible to ensure that information systems and data stores are protected with properly secured facilities sporting adequate security perimeters and with appropriate access controls to sensitive areas on a need-to-access basis.

Security architecture

The CISO and the CISO's team are responsible to design and oversee the building and maintenance of the company's security architecture. Sometimes, of course, CISOs inherit pieces of the infrastructure, so the extent to which they get to design and build may vary. The CISO effectively decides what, where, how, and why various countermeasures are used, how to design network topology, DMZs, and segments, and so on.

Geopolitical risks

It is the CISO's responsibility to ensure that any geopolitical risks that could impact the security of the organization's data and systems are properly addressed by management. If the company is outsourcing software development to an area of the world under threat of violence, for example, the CISO must point out the risks of such to the CEO.

TIP

The CISO must weigh geopolitical risks when it comes to investing in security technology offered by overseas companies. Are there risks to receiving support? Is the company subject to the manipulation of a hostile foreign government? Are the company's products banned, or likely to be banned in the future, by the U.S. government for its own use?

Ensuring auditability of system administrators

It is the CISO's responsibility to ensure that all system administrators have their actions logged in such a fashion that their actions are auditable, and attributable to the parties who took them.

Cybersecurity insurance compliance

Most large companies have cybersecurity insurance. It is the CISO's job to make sure that the company meets all security requirements for coverage under the policies that are in effect, so that if something does go amiss and a claim is made, the firm will be covered.

5

Handling a Security Incident (This Is a When, Not an If)

IN THIS PART . . .

Recognize signs that you may have suffered a security breach.

Understand when you may be impacted from someone else's security breach.

Recover from hacked email, social media accounts, computers, and networks.

Recover from ransomware and other forms of malware.

Understand the role other parties play in responding to the breach.

Find out what to do if your computer or mobile device is stolen.

Chapter **12**

Identifying a Security Breach

Despite valiant efforts to protect your computer systems and data, you may suffer some sort of breach. In fact, the odds that your data will — at some point — be somehow breached by someone are close to 100 percent. The only real question is whether the breach will take place on a device or network that you operate or one that is owned and operated by someone else.

Because you're ultimately responsible for maintaining your own computer systems, you need to be able to recognize the signs of a potential breach occurring of your equipment. If a hacker does manage to penetrate your systems, you need to terminate the attacker's access as quickly as possible. If your data has been manipulated or destroyed, you need to restore an accurate copy within a reasonable amount of time. If systems are malfunctioning, you need to stop them from performing inappropriate activities and get them back on track to deliver service as expected.

In this chapter, you learn about the typical symptoms of a breach. Armed with this knowledge, you can hopefully recognize if something is amiss so that you can take appropriate corrective actions, as discussed in the next chapter.

TIP

If you've already received notification from a third-party provider where you store data, or where others store data about you, that your data has been compromised or may have been compromised, refer to Chapter 14.

Identifying Overt Breaches

The easiest breaches to identify are those in which the attacker announces to you that you've been breached and provides proof of that accomplishment. Three of the most common overt breaches are those involving ransomware, defacement, and claimed destruction.

Ransomware

Ransomware is a form of malware that encrypts or steals data on a user's device and demands a ransom in order to restore the data to the user's control (see Figure 12-1). Typically, ransomware includes an expiration date with a warning to the tune of "pay within *x* hours or the data will be destroyed forever!" (See Chapter 2 for more on ransomware.)

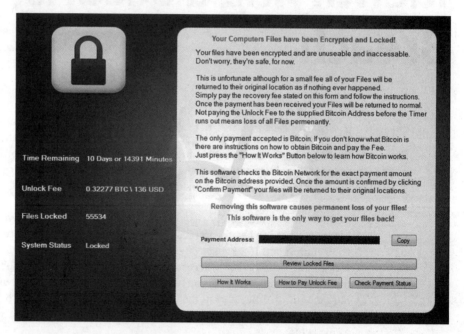

FIGURE 12-1:
A ransomware screen from an overt infection.

Obviously, if your device presents you with such a demand and important files that should be accessible to you aren't available because they're missing or encrypted, you can be reasonably sure that you need to take corrective action.

Over the past few years, ransomware has become increasingly dominant as a weapon of choice by financially-motivated cyberattackers, both in terms of opportunistic attacks and in terms of targeted attacks.

WARNING

One note: Some strains of bogus smartphone ransomware — yes, that is a real thing — display such messages but do not actually encrypt, destroy, or pilfer data. Before taking any corrective action — and certainly before paying any ransoms or ransom negotiation services — always check that ransomware is real.

Defacement

Defacement refers to breaches in which the attacker defaces the systems of the victim — for example, changing the target's website to display a message that the hacker hacked it (in an almost "virtual subway graffiti"-like sense) or a message of support for some cause, as is often the case with hacktivists (see Figure 12-2).

FIGURE 12-2:
A defaced website (ostensibly by the hacker group known as the Syrian Electronic Army).

If you have a personal website and it's defaced or if you boot up your computer and it displays a `hacked by <some hacker>` message, you can be reasonably certain that you were breached and that you need to take corrective action. Of course, the breach may have occurred at the site hosting your site, and not on your local computer — a matter that I discuss in Chapter 13.

Claimed destruction

Hackers can destroy data or programs, but so can technical failures or human errors. The fact that data has been deleted, therefore, doesn't necessarily mean that a system was breached. However, if some party claims responsibility, the odds that the problems are the result of a breach can skyrocket. (Although there have been instances in which parties falsely claimed responsibility for cyberattacks ostensibly in order to convince the public of their technical prowess.)

TIP

If someone contacts you, for example, and claims to have deleted a specific file or set of files that only a party with access to the system would know about, and those are the only files gone, you can be reasonably certain that the issue with which you are dealing is not a failure of hard disk sectors or solid-state disk chips.

Detecting Covert Breaches

While some breaches are obviously discernable to be breaches, many breaches are actually quite hard to detect. In fact, breaches are sometimes so hard to notice that various enterprises that spend tens of millions of dollars a year, or even hundreds of millions of dollars a year, on cybersecurity technology including systems that try to identify breaches have had breaches go undetected for significant periods of time — sometimes even for years! The following sections describe some symptoms that may indicate that your computer, tablet, or smartphone has been breached.

REMEMBER

Keep in mind that none of the following clues exists in a vacuum, nor does the presence of any individual symptom, on its own, provide a guarantee that something is amiss. Multiple reasons other than the occurrence of a breach may cause devices to act abnormally and to exhibit one or more of the ailments described in the following sections.

However, if a device suddenly seems to suffer from multiple suspicious behaviors or if the relevant issues develop just after you left the device unattended for some period of time in a public location, clicked on a link in an email or text message, downloaded and ran some software provided by a source with potentially deficient security practices, opened some questionable attachment, or did something else about which wisdom you now question, you may want to take corrective action, as described Chapter 13.

REMEMBER

When considering the likelihood that a system was breached, always keep in mind relevant circumstances. If problems start occurring after an operating system auto-update, for example, the likely risk level is much lower than if the same symptoms start showing up right after you click on a link in a suspicious email message offering you $1,000,000 if you process a payment being sent from a Nigerian prince to someone in the United States. Always maintain a proper, "chilled" perspective and do not panic. If something did go amiss, you can still take action to minimize the damage. Panicking will not make matters better, and it certainly may lead you into making errors and making things worse.

Your device seems slower than before

Malware running on a computer, tablet, or smartphone often impacts the performance of the device in a noticeable fashion. Malware that transmits data can also sometimes slow down a device's connection to the Internet or even to internal networks.

Keep in mind, however, that updates to a device's operating system or to various software packages can also adversely impact the device's performance, so don't panic if you notice that performance seems to be somewhat degraded just after you updated your operating system or installed a software upgrade from a trusted source. Likewise, if you fill up the memory on your device or install many processor and bandwidth intensive apps, performance is likely to suffer even without the presence of malware. More than once I have heard stories of IT support personnel who were summoned by users reporting suspicious performance problems only to discover that the users had opened many applications and dozens of browser tab windows.

You can see what is running on a Windows PC by pressing Ctrl + Shift + Esc and checking out the Task Manager window that pops up. On a Mac, use the Activity Monitor, which you can access by clicking the magnifying glass on the right side of the menu bar on the top of the screen and starting to type Activity Monitor. After you type the first few characters, the name of the tool should display, at which point you can press Enter to run it.

On Android devices, one of the three buttons or swipe actions on the bottom of the screen will usually load up a list of active applications (exactly which button varies between devices).

Your Task Manager doesn't run

If you try to run Task Manager on Windows (see Figure 12-3) or Activity Monitor on a Mac (see preceding section) and the tool does not run, your computer may be infected with malware. Various strains of malware are known to impact the ability of these programs to operate.

Your Registry Editor doesn't run

If you try to run Registry Editor on Windows (for example, by typing **regedit** at the Run prompt) and it does not run, your computer may be infected with malware. Various strains of malware are known to impact the ability of the Registry Editor to execute.

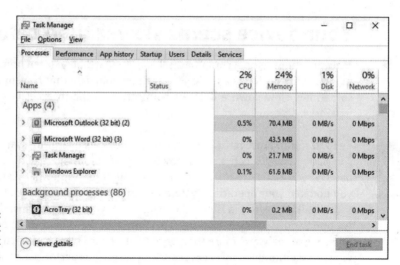

FIGURE 12-3:
The Microsoft
Windows Task
Manager.

WARNING

Note that you may receive a warning when running Registry Editor that it requires Administrator permissions. That warning is normal and not the sign of a problem. It also should remind you of the potentially serious consequences of making registry edits: Don't make any if you're not sure what you are doing. Technologists often consider making registry edits and edits to DNS servers as among the activities about which they most worry about making a mistake with potentially significant impact.

Your device starts suffering from latency issues

Latency refers to the time it takes for data to begin to travel after the instruction is issued to make it travel. If you're noticing delays that were not present before — especially if the delays seem significant — something may be amiss. Of course, you may also have a poor network connection, so check the network connection strength. If that connection is fine, it is still possible that your Internet provider or some other provider along the network path between yourself and the resources you are trying to access may be experiencing problems, and everything may be fine on your local device. However, if the latency issues appear from only one device or a particular set of devices and not from all devices connected to the same network and if rebooting the impacted device/s does not ameliorate the situation, your device/s may have been compromised.

TIP

If the device is using a wired network connection, be sure to test it with a new cable. If the problem goes away, the cause was likely a defective or damaged physical connection.

Your device starts suffering from communication and buffering issues

One highly visual symptom of communication-performance problems that can easily be discerned without much technical knowledge is if streaming videos seem to freeze while preloading future frames, or buffering, far more often than they did in the past (see Figure 12-4). While buffering is an annoyance that happens to most folks from time to time, if it is happening regularly on a connection that previously did not suffer on a regular basis from such an ailment or it's happening from only one or more particular devices using the connection but not on others even when connected wirelessly and situated in the same location or using the same physical network wire, it may be indicative of a compromised system. If the device is using a wired network connection, be sure to check any physical cables that may be causing network issues.

FIGURE 12-4: An example of communication problems while streaming video. Note the viewable portion of the rotating circle in the middle of the video image.

REMEMBER

Note that communication performance problems can also be a sign that someone is piggy-backing on your Internet connection (in other words, someone is sharing your connection without your knowledge), which is also a type of breach.

Your device's settings have changed

If you notice that some of your device's settings have changed — and you're certain that you did not make the change — that may be a sign of problems. Of course, some software makes setting changes, too (especially on classic computers, as opposed to smartphones), so changes may have a legitimate source as well. Most software, however, does not make major changes without notifying you. If you see dramatic settings changes, beware.

Your device is sending or receiving strange email messages

If your friends or colleagues report receiving emails from you that you did not send to them, something is likely amiss — this is especially true if the messages appear to be spam. Likewise, if you're receiving emails that appear to be from people who claim to have never sent the relevant messages, you may have suffered a breach.

REMEMBER

Keep in mind, however, that many other reasons (including other kinds of attacks on systems other than your own devices and accounts) can lead to spam appearing to have emanated from you. For example, some hacked systems that compromise a list of contacts send emails to some of the parties in that list from other parties in the list, rather than always from the owner from whom the contact list was pilfered.

Your device is sending or receiving strange text messages

If your friends or colleagues report receiving text messages or other smartphone-type communications from you that you did not send to them, your smartphone may have been breached. Likewise, if you're receiving messages that appear to be from people who claim to have never sent the relevant messages, you may have suffered a breach. As before, there could be other explanations for such a situation, and it is possible that some other system or collection of systems are the actual victims who have been breached.

New software (including apps) is installed on your device — and you didn't install it

If new programs or apps suddenly appear on your device and you did not install them, something may be amiss. While, especially in the case of some portable devices, the manufacturer or relevant service provider may occasionally install certain types of apps without your knowledge, if new apps suddenly appear, you should always look into the matter. Of course, if you are using a corporate device that is centrally managed, the system administrators may have "pushed down" an app to you, so check with them.

Do a Google search on the apps and see what reliable tech sites say about them. If the apps are not showing up on other people's devices, you may have a serious issue on your hands.

Keep in mind, however, that sometimes the installation routines of one program install other applications as well. It is relatively common, for example, for various programs that are offered for free to users in a limited-feature version to also install other programs that are comarketed alongside them. Normally, such installation programs ask for permission to install the additional programs, but such transparency is not mandated by law, and some applications do not afford users such choices.

If you let someone else your computer, that person may have installed something (legitimate or illegitimate). Of course, if you have configured your device to never install auto-updates, and not to accept new apps from any providers associated with your account, then the presence of a new app that you, yourself, did not install should be even more concerning.

Your device's battery seems to drain more quickly than before

Malware running in the background uses battery power and can help drain the battery of laptops, smartphones, and tablets. Keep in mind, however, that the performance of rechargeable batteries can deteriorate over time due to repeated draining and charging. So, if your three-year-old laptop that you use every day does not seem to be holding a charge quite as well as it did three years prior, that may not be indicative of anything other than natures conforming to the laws of physics.

Your device seems to run hotter than before

Malware running the background uses CPU cycles and can cause a device to run physically hotter than before. You may hear internal cooling fans going on louder or more often than you usually do, or you may feel that the device is physically hotter to the touch.

File contents have been changed

If the contents of files have changed without you changing them and without you running any software that you expect would change them, something may be seriously amiss. Of course, if you let other people use your computer and gave them access to the files in question, before blaming malware or a hacker, be sure to check with the people you let use the computer whether they made any changes either on purpose or by accident.

Files are missing

If files seem to have disappeared without you deleting them and without you running any software that you expect might delete them, something may be seriously amiss. Of course, technical failures and human mistakes can also cause files to disappear — and, if you let someone else use your computer, that person may be the culprit.

Websites appear different than before

If someone has installed malware that is *proxying* on your device — that is, sitting between your browser and the Internet and relaying the communications between them (while reading all the contents of the communications and, perhaps, inserting various instructions of its own) — it may affect how some sites display and/or cause some sites, apps, or features within either or both, to malfunction.

Your Internet settings show a proxy, and you never set one up

If someone has configured your device to use their server as a proxy, that party may be attempting to read data sent to and from your device and may try to modify the contents of your session or even seek to hijack it altogether.

Some legitimate programs do configure Internet proxies — but such proxy information should show up when the software is installed and initially run, not suddenly after you click on a questionable link or download a program from a less-than-trustworthy source. (See Figure 12-5.)

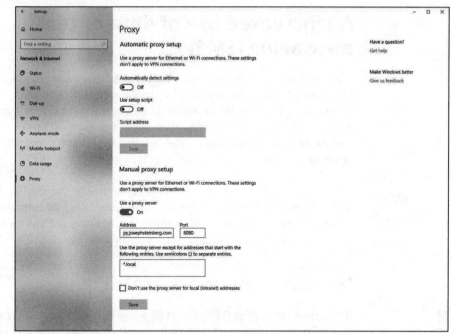

FIGURE 12-5:
Internet
connections
configured to use
a proxy. If you do
not use a proxy
and suddenly one
appears listed in
your Internet
settings,
something is
likely amiss.

Some programs (or apps) stop working properly

If apps that you know used to work properly on your device suddenly stop functioning as expected, you may be experiencing a symptom of either proxying or malware interfering with the apps' functionality.

TIP

Of course, if such a problem develops immediately after you perform an operating system update, the update is a far more likely source of the issue than is something more sinister (assuming, of course, that you did not install the update after downloading it from a questionable source).

Security programs have turned off

If the security software that you normally run on your device has suddenly been disabled, removed, or configured to ignore certain problems, it may be a sign that a hacker (or malware) has penetrated your device and has turned off its defenses to prevent both the attacker's efforts from being blocked as well as to ensure that you do not receive warnings as the attacker carries out various additional nefarious activities.

An increased use of data or text messaging (SMS)

If you monitor your smartphone's data or SMS usage and see greater usage figures than you expect, especially if that increase begins right after some suspicious event, it may be a sign that malware is transmitting data from your device to other parties. You can even check your data usage per app — if one of them looks like it is using way too much data for the functionality that it provides, something may be amiss.

WARNING

If you installed the app from a third-party app store, you can try deleting the app and reinstalling it from a more trusted source. Keep in mind, however, that if malware is on your device, reinstalling the app may not always fix the problem, even if the app was the original source of the infection.

Increased network traffic

If you monitor your device's Wi-Fi or wired network usage and see greater levels of activity than you expect, especially if that increase begins right after some suspicious event, it may be a sign that malware is transmitting data from your device to other parties.

TIP

On some systems, you can even check your data usage per app — if one or more apps look like they are using way too much data for the functionality that they provide, something may be amiss. If you installed the app in question from a less-than-reliable source, you can try deleting the app and reinstalling it from a more trusted source — but if malware is present on your device, reinstalling the app that it brought to the device may not always fix the problem, even if the app was, in fact, the original source of the infection.

TIP

You can check how much data your computer is using — and even how much each program is using — by installing a bandwidth monitor program on the device in question.

Keep in mind that different types of apps can use wildly different amounts of bandwidth. An app used for sending email messages, for example, should usually be using no more than a tiny fraction of the bandwidth used by someone's Netflix app if that user streams and watches shows and/or movies on a regular basis.

Unusual open ports

Computers and other Internet-connected devices communicate using "ports" that can be thought of as numbered ports virtually lined up along the device as if they were piers along the coast. Communications for different applications typically enter the device via different ports. Ports are numbered, and most port numbers should always be *closed* — that is, not configured to allow communications in.

TIP

If ports that are not normally open on your computer are suddenly open and you did not just install software that could be using such ports, it is usually indicative of a problem. If you use Windows — especially if you understand a little about networking — you can use the built-in `netstat` command to determine which ports are open and what is connecting to your device.

Your device starts crashing

If your computer, tablet, or smartphone suddenly starts to crash on a much more frequent basis than in the past, malware may be running on it. Of course, if you just upgraded your operating system, installed or updated drivers for hardware components, or installed some significant new software package, that is a more likely source for the problem.

WARNING

If you are regularly seeing screens like the Blue Screen of Death (see Figure 12-6) — or other screens indicating that your computer suffered a fatal error and must be restarted, you have a problem. It may be technical, or it may be due to corruption from malware or a hacker.

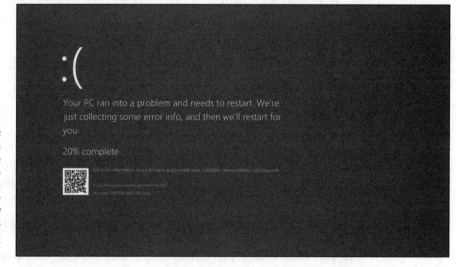

:(

Your PC ran into a problem and needs to restart. We're just collecting some error info, and then we'll restart for you.

20% complete

FIGURE 12-6: The modern version of the notorious Blue Screen of Death that appears after a severe crash of a computer running Microsoft Windows 10.

Your cellphone bill shows unexpected charges up to here

Criminals are known to have exploited compromised smartphones in order to make expensive overseas phone calls on behalf of a remote party proxying through the device. Likewise, they can use a breached device to send SMS messages to international numbers and can ring up various other phone charges in other ways.

Unknown programs request access

Most security software for computers warns users when a program first attempts to access the Internet. If you receive such warnings and you don't recognize the program that is seeking access, or you recognize the program but can't understand why it would need to access the Internet (for example, Windows Calculator or Notepad), something may be amiss.

External devices power on unexpectedly

If one or more of your external input devices (including devices such as cameras, scanners, and microphones) seem to power on at unexpected times (for example, when you're not using them), it may indicate that malware or a hacker is communicating with them or otherwise using them. There are attacks that are known to have involved criminals remotely turning on people's cameras and spying on them.

Your device acts as if someone else were using it

Malicious actors sometimes take over computers and use them via remote access almost as if they were sitting in front of the device's keyboard. If you see your device acting as if someone else is in control — for example, you see the mouse pointer moving or keystrokes being entered while you're not using your mouse or keyboard — it may be a sign that someone else is actually controlling the machine.

New browser search engine default

As part of several attack techniques, hackers are known to change the default search engine used by people browsing the web. If your own browser's default search engine changed and you did not change it, something may be amiss. (To check if your search engine changed, check the list of default applications by searching for "default apps" in the Windows search box.)

Your device password has changed

If the password to your phone, tablet, or computer changed without you changing it, something is wrong, and the cause is likely something serious.

Pop-ups start appearing

WARNING

Various strains of malware produce pop-up windows asking the user to perform various actions (see Figure 12-7). If you're seeing pop-ups, beware. Such malware is common on laptops, but it exists for some smartphones as well.

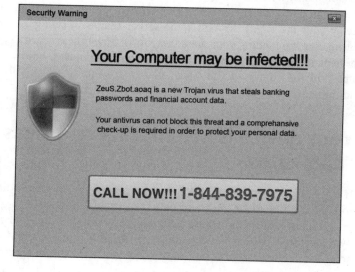

FIGURE 12-7:
This pop-up window from adware malware attempts to scare people into purchasing bogus security software.

Keep in mind that pop-ups that appear when you're not using a web browser are a big red flag, as are pop-ups advising you to download and install "security software" or to visit websites of questionable repute. Pop-ups should never appear on an Android device.

New browser add-ons appear

You should be prompted before any browser add-on is installed. If a new add-on is installed without your knowledge, it likely indicates a problem. Some malware is delivered in poisoned versions of various browser toolbars.

New browser home page

As part of several attack techniques, hackers are known to change the home page of users' browsers. If your own browser's home page changed and you did not change it, something may be amiss.

Your email from the device is getting blocked by spam filters

If email that you send from the device in question used to be able to reach intended recipients with no problem, but is suddenly getting blocked by spam filters, it may be a sign that someone or something altered your email configuration in order to relay your messages through some server that is allowing an attacker to read, block, or even modify, your messages, and which other security systems are flagging as problematic. There are also other possible causes, however, so if you cannot find the source of the issue, you may want to check with your network administrator, email provider, or Internet provider.

Your device is attempting to access "bad" sites

If you use your computer, tablet, or smartphone on a network that blocks access to known problematic sites and networks (many businesses, organizations, and government entities have such technology on both their internal and bring-your-own-device [BYOD] networks) and you find out that your device was trying to access such sites without your knowledge, your device is likely compromised.

You're experiencing unusual service disruptions

If your smartphone seems to be suddenly dropping calls in locations with good cellular signal, or if you find your device unable to make calls altogether at times when you appear to have ostensibly good signal strength, something may be amiss.

TIP

If you hear strange noises during your phone conversations, something may also be amiss, and someone may even be listening in to, joining, or recording, your conversations.

Keep in mind that in most cases, the symptoms described here emanate from technical issues unrelated to a breach. However, in some cases, a breach is the reason for such ailments. So, if you noticed the relevant symptoms shortly after you took some action that you now question or regret, you may want to consider whether you need to take corrective action (see Chapter 13).

Your device's language settings changed

People rarely change the language settings on their computers after performing the initial language setup procedure upon acquiring their devices or upon configuring a new keyboard, and few software packages change such settings either. So, if your computer is suddenly displaying menus and/or prompts in a foreign language or even has a language installed that you never installed, something is likely wrong.

You see unexplained activity on the device

If, on your device, you see emails in your Sent folder that you did not send, your device or email account was likely compromised. Likewise, if files that you're certain that you never downloaded appear in your Downloads folder, someone else may have downloaded them to your device.

You see unexplained online activity

If your social media account has social media posts that you're certain that neither you nor any app that you have authorized made, something is clearly amiss. It may be that your account was breached, and your devices are all secure, or it may be that one of your devices with access to the account was breached and became the conduit for the unauthorized access to your account.

The same is true if you see videos that you never ordered appearing in your previous rentals of a video streaming service, purchases that you never made appearing in your order history at an online retailer, and so on.

Your device suddenly restarts

While restarts are an integral part of many operating system updates, they should not happen suddenly outside the context of such updates. If your device is regularly rebooting without your approval, something is wrong. The only question is whether the problem emanates from a security breach or from some other issue.

TIP

It is generally a good idea to reboot your devices on a regular basis, as devices that are not rebooted for a long time are more likely to suffer from problems emanating from the repeated use of applications that do not properly release memory and other resources after completing their utilization of such resources.

You see signs of data breaches and/or leaks

Of course, if you know that some of your data has leaked, you should try to determine the source of the problem — and the process of checking obviously includes examining for signs of problems on all your smartphones, tablets, and computers.

You are routed to the wrong website

If you're sure that you typed in a correct URL, but were still routed to the wrong website, something is amiss. The problem may reflect a security breach elsewhere, but it could indicate that someone has compromised your device as well.

If the misrouting happens from only one or more particular devices, but not from others on the same network, the odds are that the devices in question were compromised. A hacker or malware could have configured poisoned routing tables on your device, for example. If you see that you are being incorrectly routed from multiple devices but only when they are connected to a particular network, or that a device that routes properly when connected to other networks routes improperly when connected to a particular network, networking equipment from that network, or a provider of routing services (such as DNS) to that network may have been compromised.

In any case, never perform any sensitive task (such as logging into a website) from a device that is routing you incorrectly. Even better, don't use the device at all (other than for debugging) until you figure out what is going on.

Your hard drive or SSD light never seems to turn off

If your hard drive or solid state drive (SSD) light remains on constantly, or near constantly, malware may be doing something to the drive. Of course, hard drive and SSD lights can come on for legitimate reasons when you are not actively using a computer — and, sometimes, a legitimate reason such as the system optimizing the disk in the background or performing a search for malware will cause the light to be on for quite some time — so don't panic if the light being on is the only sign that something might be amiss.

Other abnormal things happen

It is impossible to list all the possible symptoms that malware can cause a device to exhibit. So, if you keep in mind that parties are seeking to hack into your systems, and that anomalous behavior by your device may be a sign of problems, you increase your odds of noticing when something seems off — and, of properly responding to a breach if one does, in fact, occur.

Chapter **13**

Recovering from a Security Breach

O MG! It happened.

You've discovered that you've suffered a data breach.

Now what?

Read this chapter, which discusses how to respond in these types of situations.

An Ounce of Prevention Is Worth Many Tons of Response

REMEMBER

When it comes to recovering from a security breach, there simply is no substitute for adequate preparation. Simply put, no amount of post-breach expert actions can deliver the same level of protection as proper pre-breach prevention.

If you follow the various techniques described throughout this book about how to protect your electronic assets, you're likely to be in far better shape to recover from a breach than if you did not. Of course, preparation not only helps you reduce the risks of suffering a breach in the first place, but can also help you recover and help ensure that you can detect a breach if one occurs. Without proper preparation, you may not even be able to determine that a breach occurred, never mind contain the attack and stop it. (If you're unsure whether you've suffered a breach, see Chapter 12.)

Stay Calm and Act Now with Wisdom

A normal human reaction to a cyber breach is to feel outraged, violated, and upset. It is also normal to experience some level of panic. To properly respond to a breach, however, you need to think logically and clearly and act in an orderly fashion. Spend a moment to tell yourself that everything will be all right, and that the type of cyberattack with which you are dealing is one that most successful people and businesses will likely have to deal with at some point (or at many points).

WARNING

Likewise, don't act irrationally. Do not attempt to fix your problem by doing a Google search for advice. Plenty of people online provide bad advice. Even worse, plenty of rogue websites with advice on removing malware and stopping attacks deposit malware on computers accessing them! Obviously, do not download security software or anything else from questionable sites.

Also, keep in mind that you need to act ASAP. Stop whatever else you're doing and focus on fixing the problem. Shut down any programs that you're using, save (and back up onto media that you will scan for malware before you reuse) any open documents and so on, and get to work on recovering from the breach.

REMEMBER

When a breach occurs, time usually works against you. The sooner that you stop someone from stealing your files, corrupting your data, or attacking additional devices on your network, the better off you will likely be.

Bring in a Pro

Ideally, you should bring in a cybersecurity professional to help you recover. While this book gives you good guidance, when it comes to technical skills, there is simply no substitute for the years of experience that a good pro has.

TIP

You should apply the same logic and seek professional help when faced with a serious computer and data crisis as you would if any of the following were true:

» If you were seriously ill, you'd go to the doctor or hospital.

» If you were arrested and charged with a crime, you'd hire a lawyer.

» If the IRS sent you a letter that you're being audited, you'd hire an accountant.

Recovering from a Breach without a Pro's Help

TIP

If you do not have the ability to bring in a pro, the following steps are those that you should follow. These steps are essentially the ones most professionals follow:

1. **Figure out what happened (or is happening).**

2. **Contain the attack.**

3. **Terminate and eliminate the attack.**

Step 1: Figure out what happened or is happening

If possible, you want to figure out as much about the attack as possible so that you can respond accordingly. If an attacker is transferring files from your computer to another device, for example, you want to disconnect your device from the Internet ASAP.

That said, most home users do not have the technical skills to properly analyze and understand exactly what the nature of a particular attack may be — unless, of course, the attack is overt in nature (see Chapter 12).

Gather as much information as you can about

» What happened

» What information systems and databases were hit

» What could a criminal or other mischievous party do with the stolen material

» What data and programs have been affected

>> Who, besides yourself, may face risks because of the breach (this includes any potential implications for your employer)

>> What other parties (if any) need to be notified ASAP of the breach

REMEMBER

Do not spend a lot of time on this step — you need to take action, not just document — but the more information that you do have, the greater the chances that you will be able to prevent another similar attack in the future.

Step 2: Contain the attack

Cut off the attacker by isolating the attacker from the compromised devices. Containing may entail:

>> **Terminating all network connectivity ASAP:** To terminate network connectivity for all devices on a network, turn off your router by unplugging it. (*Note:* If you're in a business setting, this step is usually not possible.)

>> **Unplugging any Ethernet cables:** Understand, however, that a network-borne attack may have already spread to other devices on the network. If so, disconnect the network from the Internet and disconnect each device from your network until it is scanned for security problems.

>> **Turning off Wi-Fi on the infected device:** Again, a network-borne attack may have already spread to other devices on the network. If so, disconnect the network from the Internet and disconnect each device from your network by turning off Wi-Fi at the router and any access points, not just on the infected computer.

>> **Turning off cellular data:** In other words, put your device into airplane mode.

WHEN AN ATTACK GOES UNDETECTED

The lack of expertise in this area by the average person should not be surprising. Most businesses that are breached, including many with their own information security professionals on staff, do not even discover that they have been successfully breached until months after the attackers began attacking! Some experts estimate that, on average, businesses do not discover non-overt information-security compromises until somewhere between six months and a year have elapsed since the initial breach occurred!

>> **Turning off Bluetooth and NFC:** Bluetooth and NFC are both wireless communication technologies that work with devices that are in close physical proximity to one another. All such communications should be blocked if there is a possibility of infections spreading or hackers jumping from device to device.

>> **Unplugging USB drives and other removable drives from the system:** *Note:* The drives may contain malware, so do not attach them to any other systems.

>> **Revoking any access rights that the attacker is exploiting:** If you have a shared device and the attacker is using an account other than yours to which the attacker somehow gained authorized access, temporarily set that account to have no rights to do anything.

TIP

If, for some reason, you need Internet access from your device in order to get help cleaning it up, turn off all other devices on your network, to prevent any attacks from spreading over the network to your device. Keep in mind that such a scenario is far from ideal. You want to cut off the infected device from the rest of the world, not just sever the connections between it and your other devices.

Step 3: Terminate and eliminate the attack

Containing an attack (see preceding section) is not the same thing as terminating and eliminating an attack. Malware that was present on the infected device is still present after disconnecting the device from the Internet, for example, as are any vulnerabilities that a remote hacker or malware may have exploited in order to take control of your device. So, after containing the attack, it is important to clean up the system.

TERMINATING NETWORK CONNECTIVITY

While you can disconnect your Internet connection by physically unplugging from the router or network connection, you can also disable the connection on your device(s).

To terminate network connectivity on a Windows computer, follow these steps:

1. Choose Settings ➪ Network Connections.

2. Right-click on the relevant connection (or connections one at a time) and then click on Disable.

The following sections describe some steps to follow at this point:

Boot the computer from a security software boot disk

While most modern users will not have a security software boot disk, if you do have one, boot from it. If you do not have one, please skip to the next section.

1. Remove all USB drives, DVDs, CDs, floppies (yes, some people still have them), and any other external drives from your computer.

2. Insert the boot disk into the CD/DVD drive.

3. Shut down your computer.

4. Wait ten seconds and push the power button to start your computer.

5. If you are using a Windows computer and it does not boot from the CD, turn the machine off, wait ten seconds, and restart it while pressing the BIOS-boot button (different computers use different buttons, but most use some F-key, such as F1 or F2) to go into the BIOS settings and set it to boot from the CD if a CD is present, before trying to boot from the hard drive.

6. Exit the BIOS and Reboot.

If you're using a Windows PC, boot the computer in Safe Mode. Safe Mode is a special mode of windows that allows only essential system services and programs to run when the system starts up. To do this, follow these steps:

1. Remove all USB drives, DVDs, CDs, floppies (yes, some people still have them), and any other external drives from your computer.

2. Shut down your computer.

3. Wait ten seconds and push the power button to start your computer.

4. While your computer is starting, press the F8 key repeatedly to display the Boot Options menu.

5. When the Boot Options menu appears, select the option to boot in Safe Mode.

If you're using a Mac, boot it with Safe Boot. MacOS does not provide the full equivalent of Safe Mode. Macs always boot with networking enabled. Its Safe Boot does boot cleaner than a normal boot. To Safe Boot, follow these steps:

1. Remove all USB drives, DVDs, CDs, floppies (yes, some people still have them), and any other external drives from your computer.

2. **Shut down your computer.**

3. **Wait ten seconds and push the power button to start your computer.**

4. **While your computer is starting, hold down the Shift key.**

TIP

Older Macs (macOS versions 6–9) boot into a special superuser mode without extensions if a user presses the hold key during reboot. The advice to boot with Safe Boot applies only to Macs running more recent operating systems.

Backup

Hopefully you can ignore this section, because you paid attention to the advice in the chapter on backups, but if you have not backed up your data recently, do so now. Of course, backing up a compromised device is not necessarily going to save all your data (because some may already be corrupted or missing), but if you do not already have a backup, do so now — ideally by copying your files to an external USB drive that you will not attach to any other devices until it is properly scanned by security software.

TIP

Do not back up a potentially compromised device to your usual backup data store — keep that drive disconnected from the potentially compromised equipment. Back up to some other media. And, of course, do not overwrite any other backups with the backup of the compromised device.

Delete junk (optional)

At this point, you may want to delete any files that you do not need, including any temporary files that have somehow become permanent (a list of such files appears in the chapter on backups).

Why do the deletion now?

Well, you should be doing periodic maintenance, and, if you are cleaning up your computer now, now is a good time. The less there is for security software to scan and analyze, the faster it will run. Also, some malware hides in temporary files, so deleting such files can also directly remove some malware.

For users of Windows computers, one easy way to delete temporary files is to use the built-in Disk Cleanup utility:

1. **In Windows 10, in the search box on the taskbar, type disk cleanup.**

2. **Select Disk Cleanup from the list of results**

3. **Select the drive you want to clean up and then click OK.**

4. **Select the file types to get rid of and then click OK.**

5. **Click on Accessories (or Windows Accessories).**

6. **Click on Disk Cleanup.**

Run security software

Hopefully, you already have security software installed. If you don't, that may be the reason why you are dealing with the compromise in the first place! If you do have security software installed, run a full system scan. One important caveat: Security software running on a compromised device may itself be compromised or impotent against the relevant threat (after all, the security breach took place with the security software running), so, regardless of whether such a scan comes up clean, it may be wise to run the security software from a bootable CD or other read-only media, or, in cases of some products, from another computer on your home network.

TIP

Not all brands of security software catch all variants of malware. Security professionals doing a device "clean up" often run security software from multiple vendors.

If you are using a Mac and your Safe Boot includes Internet access, run the security software update routines prior to running the full scan.

Malware, or attackers, may add new files to a system, remove files, and modify files. They may also open communication ports. Security software should be able to address all of these scenarios. Pay attention to the reports issued by the security software after it runs. Keep track of exactly what it removed or repairs. This information may be important, if, for example, some programs do not work after the cleanup. (You may need to reinstall programs from which files were removed or from which malware-modified files malware was removed.) Email databases may need to be restored if malware was found within messages and the security software was unable to fully clean the mess up.

Security software report information may also be useful to a cybersecurity or IT professional if you end up hiring one at a later date. Also, the information in the report may provide you with clues as to where the attack started and what enabled it to happen, thereby also helping to guide you on preventing it from recurring.

TIP

Security Software often detects, and reports about, various non-attack material that may be undesirable due to their impact on privacy or potential to solicit a user with advertisements. You may, for example, see alerts that security software has detected tracking cookies or adware; neither is a serious problem, but you may want to remove adware if the ads bother you. In many cases you can pay to upgrade the software displaying the ads to a paid version that lacks ads. As far as recovering from an attack is concerned, these undesirable items are not a problem.

TIP

Sometimes, security software will inform you that you need to run an add-on in order to fully clean a system. Symantec, for example, offers its Norton Power Eraser, that it says "Eliminates deeply embedded and difficult-to-detect crimeware that traditional virus scanning doesn't always detect." If your security software informs you that you need to run such a scanner, you should do so, but make sure that you obtain it from the legitimate, official, original source. Also, never download or run any scanner of such a sort if you are told to do so not as the result of running security software. Plenty of rogue pop-ups will advise you similarly, but install malware if you download the relevant "security software."

Reinstall Damaged Software

There are experts who recommend uninstalling and reinstalling any software package that you know was affected by the attack, even if the security software fixed it. While doing so is not usually necessary, don't forget about this advice, as if you do detect any problems using the software after system recovery, you may need to go back and uninstall and reinstall.

Restart the system and run an updated security scan

For Windows computers, after you have cleaned the system, restart it in Safe Mode with networking using the procedure described above (but selecting Safe Mode with Networking rather than Safe Mode), run the security software, download all updates, and run the security software scan again. If there are no updates, then you do not need to rerun the security software.

If you are using a Mac, Safe Boot already included networking so there is no reason to repeat the scan. Install all relevant updates and patches. If any of your software has not been updated to its latest version and may contain vulnerabilities, fix this during the cleanup.

TIP

If you have the time to do so, run the security software full scan again after you have installed all the updates. There are several reasons for doing so, including the fact that you want it to check your system using its own most-up-to-date information on malware and other threats, as well as the fact that you want its heuristic analysis engine to have a baseline of what the system looks like with its latest updates.

Erase all potentially problematic System Restore points

System Restore is a useful tool, but it can also be dangerous. If a system creates a restore point when malware is running on a device, for example, restoring to that point will likely restore the malware! After cleaning up a system, therefore, be sure to erase all system restore points that may have been created when your system was compromised. If you are unsure if a restore point may be problematic, erase it. For most users, this means that it may be good to erase all system restore points. To do this:

1. Click the Start menu.
2. Click Control Panel.
3. Click All Control Panel Items.
4. Click Recovery.
5. Click Configure System Restore.
6. Follow the prompts to delete the relevant system restore points.

Restore modified settings

Some attackers and malware may modify various settings on your device. What page you see when you start your web browser — for example, your web browser home page — is one common item that malware commonly changes. It is important to change the browser page back to a safe page as the malware's starting page might lead to a page that reinstalls malware or performs some other nefarious task. The following sections walk you through the process for each browser.

REMEMBER

When using the phone or tablet versions of the browsers described in the following sections, the process will differ slightly, but should be simply discernable based on the instructions.

IN CHROME

To reset the Chrome browser:

1. Click the three-dot menu icon in the top-right corner.
2. Click Settings.
3. Scroll down to the On Startup section and configure it accordingly.

IN FIREFOX

To reset the Firefox browser:

1. Click the three-line menu icon in the top-right corner.

2. Click Options.

3. Click Home.

4. Configure the values in the New Windows and Tabs section accordingly.

IN SAFARI

To reset the Safari browser:

1. Click the Safari menu.

2. Click Preferences.

3. Select the General tab.

4. Scroll down to the Homepage field and configure it accordingly.

IN EDGE

To reset the Edge browser:

1. Click the three-dot menu icon in the top-right corner.

2. Click Settings.

3. Configure the Open Microsoft Edge with and Open new tabs with sections accordingly.

Rebuild the system

Sometimes it is easier, instead of following the aforementioned processes, to simply rebuild a system from scratch. In fact, because of the risk of security software missing some problem, or of user mistakes when performing the security cleanup, many experts recommend that, whenever possible, one should rebuild a system entirely after a breach.

Even if you plan to rebuild a system in response to a breach, it is still wise to run a security software scan prior to doing so as there are some rare forms of malware that can persist even after a restore (such as BIOS reprogramming malware, certain boot sector viruses, and so on), and to scan all devices on the same network as the compromised device at the time of the compromise or afterwards, so as to ensure that nothing bad can propagate back to the newly restored device.

Dealing with Stolen Information

If your computer, phone, or tablet was breached, it is possible that sensitive information on it was stolen. That data may be misused now or in the future, either by the party that stole it, or by another party to whom the original data thief sold or gave it.

As such, you should change any of your passwords that were stored on the device, for example, and check all accounts that were accessible from the device without logging in (due to your earlier setting of the device to "Remember Me" after a successful login) to ensure that nothing goes wrong. Obviously, if your passwords were stored in a strongly encrypted format the need to change them is less urgent than if they were stored in clear text or with weak encryption, but ideally, unless you are certain that the encryption will hold up for the long term, you should change them anyway.

TIP

If you suspect that information may have been taken that could be used to impersonate you, it may be wise also to initiate a credit freeze and file a police report. Keep a copy of the police report with you. If you are pulled over by a police officer who informs you that there is a warrant out for your arrest in some location where you have never been, for example, you will have proof that you filed a report that private information that could be used to steal your identity was stolen from you. Such a document may not prevent you from having problems entirely, but it certainly may make your situation better in such a scenario than it would be if you had no such proof.

If you believe that your credit or debit card information was stolen, contact the relevant party at the phone number printed on the back of your card, tell them that the number may have been compromised, and ask them to issue you a new card with a new number. Also check the account for any suspicious transactions.

Keep a log of every call you make, when you made it, with whom you spoke, and what occurred on the call. If the fact that information may have been stolen could impact other people you should, in most cases, notify them of what happened as well.

REMEMBER

The more sensitive that information is, the more important it is to take action and to take it quickly.

Here are some ways to think of information:

> **Not private, but can help criminals with identity theft:**
  - Names, address, and home telephone number.

- This type of information is really available to anyone who wants it, even without hacking you. (Consider that a generation ago this type of information was literally published in phone books and sent to every home that had a phone line.) That said, this type of information can be used in combination with other information to commit all sorts of crimes, especially if unsuspecting other people make mistakes (for example, by allowing someone with this information to open a library card without ever producing identification documents).

- Other public-record information: The price that you paid for your home, the names of your children, and so on. While this information is public record, a criminal correlating it with other information that may be lifted from your computer could create issues for you.

» **Sensitive:** Email addresses, cellphone numbers, credit card account numbers without the CVC code, debit cards account numbers that require a PIN to use or without a CVC code, ATM card numbers, student ID numbers, passport numbers, complete birthdays including the year, and so on. These items create security risks when compromised — for example, a stolen email address may lead to sophisticated phishing attacks that leverage other information garnered from your computer, attempts at hacking into the account, spam emails, and so on. Also, this type of stolen information may be used by a criminal as part of identity theft and financial fraud crimes, but may require combining multiple pieces of information in order to create a serious risk.

» **More sensitive:** Social Security numbers (or their foreign equivalents), passwords to online accounts, bank account numbers (when compromised by a potential criminal as opposed to when displayed on a check given to a trusted party), PINs, credit and debit card information with the CVC code, answers to challenge questions that you have used to secure accounts, and so on. These types of information can often be abused on their own.

Paying ransoms

If you have proper backups, you can remove ransomware the same way that you remove other malware. If any data gets lost in the process, you can restore it from backups.

If you have been hit with over ransomware and do not have proper backups, however, you may face a difficult decision. Obviously, it is not in the common interest for you to pay a ransom to a criminal in order get your data back, but in some cases, if your data is important to you, that may be the route that you need to go. In many cases, criminals will not even give you your data back if you do pay the ransom — so, by paying a ransom, you may not only waste money, but still suffer a permanent loss of your data. You will need to decide if you want to take that chance. (Hopefully, the information in the preceding few sentences will serve as a strong motivator for readers to back up proactively as discussed in the chapter on backups, rather than to rely on paying ransoms as a possible method of addressing ransomware attacks.)

REMEMBER

The best defense for home users against the impact of ransomware is to back up and keep the backups disconnected from anything else!

Before paying a ransom, consult an information security expert and a lawyer.

TIP

Consult a cybersecurity expert

Speaking with the cybersecurity expert is important, because some ransomware can be removed, and its effects undone, by various security tools. However, unless your security software tells you that it can undo the encryption done by ransomware, do not try to remove ransomware on your own once it has encrypted your data. Some advanced ransomware wipes the data permanently if it detects attempts to decrypt the data. Also, keep in mind that some advanced ransomware does not encrypt data, but rather removes it from the victim's device and only transmits it back if the ransom is paid. Such ransomware may be removable by security software, but security software cannot usually restore the data pilfered by the ransomware.

Consult a lawyer

Speaking with an attorney familiar with the relevant areas of law is important because, in some cases, paying a ransomware ransom can be a serious crime that could potentially land you in prison. Seriously!

While to date, the United States has not made it a crime to pay ransoms in general — although there are various ongoing efforts being made to influence legislators to enact such legislation — there are cases in which paying a ransom violates other laws.

For example, if criminals operating a particular ransomware system are under sanctions — meaning that it is a federal crime to conduct any financial transactions with them — it can be a felony to pay them a ransom in order to obtain access to your own data. While individuals have not, to date, been prosecuted by the U.S. government under such laws, at the end of the Trump administration's term, the federal government threatened to begin doing so, and regardless of who is in power, such enforcement is likely to become reality at some point in the not-so-distant future. After all, if sanctioned parties can easily become rich by perpetrating cybercrimes, and nobody is prosecuted for participating in the transactions that enrich them, what good are sanctions in the first place?

CYBER LIABILITY INSURANCE AND RANSOMS

Many cyber liability insurance policies cover ransomware ransom payments, and many do not. So, if you are securing an insurance policy in order to protect yourself against ransomware risks, make sure you have actually purchased an appropriate policy.

Also keep in mind that in some cases, paying a ransom may be illegal under federal law, or the laws of another jurisdiction. In such cases, an insurance company can potentially refuse to pay a ransom that it otherwise would have had to pay. As such, do not rely on cyber liability insurance to provide adequate protection from ransomware. Make sure you also act diligently to prevent problems.

Likewise, eventually, we may see prosecution of ransom payers under federal statues related to wire fraud and/or money laundering.

TIP

While the FBI generally officially recommends against paying ransoms, it is not the party that suffers the consequences of losing data when ransoms are not paid — the ransomware victims are. As such, many parties ignore the FBI's advice. Should the law mandate that ransoms not be paid, the FBI's instructions could potentially change from advice to a legal requirement.

Learning for the future

It is important to learn from breaches. If you can figure out what went wrong, and how a hacker managed to get into your systems (either directly or by using malware), you can institute de facto policies and procedures for yourself to prevent future such compromises. A cybersecurity professional may be able to help you vis-à-vis doing so.

Recovering When Your Data Is Compromised at a Third Party

Nearly all Internet users have received notification from a business or government entity (or both) that personal data was potentially compromised. How you address such a scenario depends on many factors, but the following sections tell you the essentials of what you need to know.

Reason the notice was sent

Multiple types of data breaches lead to organizations sending notifications. Not all of them represent the same level of risk to you, however. Notifications may be sent when a company has

- ➤ Knowledge that an unencrypted database containing personal information was definitely stolen

- ➤ Knowledge that an encrypted database containing personal information was definitely stolen

- ➤ Detected unauthorized activity on a computing device housing your information

- ➤ Detected unauthorized activity on a computing device, but not the one that houses your information (but on one connected to the same or logically connected network)

- ➤ Detected the theft of credit or debit card numbers as can occur with a skimming device or the hacking of a point-of-sale credit card processing device

- ➤ Discovered that there were, or may have been, improperly discarded computers, hard drives, or other storage media or paper-based information

- ➤ Discovered that there was, or may have been, improperly distributed information, such as sensitive information sent to the wrong parties, unencrypted email sent to authorized parties, and so on

In all these cases, action may be warranted. But if a company notifies you that an unencrypted database of passwords including yours was stolen, the need to act is more urgent than if it detects unauthorized activity on a system on the same network as another machine containing only an encrypted version of your password.

Scams

Criminals see when a breach receives significant attention and often leverage the breach for their own nefarious purposes. One common technique is for crooks to send bogus emails impersonating the breached party. Those emails contain instructions for setting up credit monitoring or filing a claim for monetary compensation for the pain and inconvenience suffered due to the breach. Of course, the links in such messages point to phishing sites, sites that install malware, and other destinations to which you do not want to go.

Criminals also act quickly. In February 2015, for example, Better Business Bureaus across the United States started reporting complaints of emails impersonating Anthem, Inc., less than one day after the health insurance company announced that it had suffered a breach.

Passwords

One of the types of breaches most commonly reported in the mass media involves the theft of password databases. Modern password authentication systems are designed to provide some protection in case of a breach. Passwords are usually stored in a *hashed format*, meaning that they are stored with one-way encryption. When you enter your password during an attempt to log in, what you type is hashed and then compared with the relevant hash value stored in the password database. As such, your actual password is not stored anywhere and is not present in the password database. If a hacker steals a password database, therefore, the hacker does not immediately obtain your password.

At least that is how things are supposed to work.

In reality, however, not all authentication systems are implemented perfectly; hashed password databases have multiple exploitable weaknesses, some of which can help criminals decipher passwords even when they're hashed. For example, if a criminal looks at the database and sees that the hashed password for many people is the same, it is likely to be a common password (maybe even "password"), which often can be cracked quickly. There are defenses against such attacks, but many authentication systems do not use them.

As such, if you are notified by a company that it has been breached and that an encrypted version of your password was stolen, you should probably reset the password. You don't need to panic, though. In most cases, your password was likely protected by the hashing (unless you selected a common, weak password, which, of course, you should not have). If, for some reason, you have reused the compromised password on other sites that you don't want have unauthorized parties to log in as you, you should reset your password there as well and don't reuse the new password this time!

REMEMBER

Keep in mind that every so often hash functions are rendered obsolete and vulnerable. So, if a party is using outdated software, the hashed versions of passwords may be far less secure than necessary.

Payment card information

If your credit card information or debit card information may have been compromised, take the following measures:

>> **Leverage credit monitoring services.** Breached firms often give those people potentially affected by the relevant breaches a free year or two of credit monitoring. While one should never rely on such services to provide full protection against identity theft, using such services does have benefit. Being that the cost to you is only a few minutes of time to set up an account, you should probably do so.

>> **Monitor your credit reports.** If you see any new accounts that you did not open, immediately contact the party involved. Remember, when it comes to fraud, the earlier that you report a problem, the less aggravation you are likely to suffer from it.

>> **Set up text alerts.** If your card issuer offers the capability to set up text alerts, use the feature. That way, you'll be notified when charges are made and can act quickly if something appears to be amiss.

>> **Check your monthly statements.** Make sure that you continue to receive your account's statements as you did before and that they are not being misdirected to someone else.

>> **Switch to e-statements.** If possible, set up your account to receive electronic monthly statements rather than physical statements and make sure that you receive an email and/or text message when each and every statement is issued. Of course, be sure to properly protect the email account and smartphone to which such messages are sent.

Government-issued documents

If your passport, driver's license, or other government-issued identity document has been compromised, you should contact the agency that issued the relevant document and ask how you should proceed. Document everything that you're told, including details as to who told you what, and when they did so. Keep a log of all calls that you make and what transpired on those calls.

You should also check online on the agency's website to see whether it offers instructions for such scenarios. In some cases, agencies will advise you to replace the document, which may necessitate a physical visit to an agency office. In other cases, the agency will advise you to do nothing, but will tag your account so that if the document is used for identification at other government agencies, those checking the ID will know to be extra vigilant (which, in itself, might be a reason to replace the document so that you do not encounter any extra aggravation when using it as ID).

School or employer-issued documents

If your school or employer ID information is compromised, you should immediately notify the issuer. Not only could the compromised information be used to social engineer your school or employer, but it may potentially be used to obtain sensitive information about you from either one, or to otherwise get you into trouble.

Social media accounts

If any of your social media accounts is compromised, immediately contact the relevant social media provider. All major platforms have mechanisms to address stolen accounts because all major platforms have had to deal with stolen accounts numerous times. Keep in mind that you may be asked to provide government ID to prove your identity as part of the account recovery process.

In such a situation, it is also often a good idea to warn people with whom you are connected on the compromised social media platform of the potential misuse of your account. If you make fully public posts on the platform housing the compromised account, you may wish to notify the public at large.

You can notify people via your non-compromised social media accounts that the compromised account has been compromised, so that if the party that took over the accounts attempts to perpetrate a scam using the account (such as by posting some request for money or the like), fewer people will fall prey. You can also use email, texting, or the phone to contact individual parties who may be put at risk.

6

Backing Up and Recovery

Chapter **14**

Backing Up

W hile backing up your data sounds like a simple concept — and it is — actually implementing an efficient and effective backup routine is a bit more complicated. To properly back up, not only do you need to know about your backup options, but you also need to think about many other details, such as the location of your backups, encryption, passwords, and boot disks. In this chapter, you find out about all those backup details and more.

Backing Up Is a Must

In the context of cybersecurity, *backing up* refers to creating an extra copy, or extra copies, of data (that may consist of data, programs, or other computer files) in case the original is damaged, lost, or destroyed.

Backing up is one of the most important defenses against the loss of data, and, eventually, it's likely to save you from serious aggravation, as nearly everyone, if not everyone, will, at some point, want to access data to which they no longer have access.

In fact, such scenarios occur on a regular basis. Sometimes, they're the result of human error, such as a person inadvertently deleting a file or misplacing a computer or storage device. Sometimes, they're the result of a technical failure, such as a hard drive dying or an electronic device falling into water. And sometimes, they're the result of ransomware attacks or other hostile hacker action. And when it comes to ransomware, an ounce of prevention — having all of your valuable data backed up and ready to restore in an efficient manner — is often worth many tons of cure.

Sadly, many people believe that they back up all their data only to find out when something goes wrong that they do not have proper backups. Don't let that happen to you. Be sure to back up on a regular basis — often enough that if you had to restore from a backup, you would not panic. In general, if you're in doubt as to whether or not you are backing up often enough, you aren't.

TIP

Do not think of backups as being there for you if you ever lose data. Think of them being there for you *when* you lose data. At some point, essentially every person who uses electronic devices on a regular basis will lose data.

Backing Up Data from Apps and Online Accounts

While most of this chapter focuses on backing up data that resides on your laptop or other local computer data store, it is also important to back up data that resides not within your own "infrastructure," but which other parties house for you as a result of using their systems.

REMEMBER

If you store any data in the cloud or use a third-party service to host any of your systems or data, the party that owns the physical and/or virtual systems on which your data resides may or may not back it up — often without your knowledge or approval. If you store data on a Google Drive, for example, you have absolutely no control over how many copies Google makes of your data. Likewise, if you use a third-party service such as Facebook, any data that you upload to the social media giant's servers — regardless of the privacy settings you set for the uploads (or possibly even if you deleted them) — may be backed up by Facebook to as many backups as the firm so desires, in as many different locations as the firm desires.

In some cases, third-party backups resemble drive backups. While the provider has your data backed up, only you — the party who "owns" the data — can actually read it in an unencrypted form from the backup. In other cases, however, the backed-up data is available to anyone who has access to the backup.

That said, most major third parties have robust redundant infrastructure and backup systems in place, meaning that the odds that data stored on their infrastructure will remain available to users is extremely high when compared with data in most people's homes. However, risks still remain.

SMS texts

Your cellular service provider may provide backup capabilities for your SMS text messages, and your phone's operating system may provide general device backup features that include all SMS messages within the backups. If not, or if you choose not to use such backups, various apps can be downloaded from Google Play and Apple App Store that provide such features specifically.

Social media

Every major social media platform allows you to download all of your respective social media account's data. While many people seem to think that there is no reason to back up such data (after all, they reason, the social media provider does its own backups of all account data), there are actually good reasons to do so.

First, if your social media account were somehow breached and taken over by a hacker, and that hacker deleted material from the account, you may have difficulty getting the material back — even if you successfully regain access to the account. This is true even if the social media provider actually has a backup in its possession of your original data; remember, restoring your data is not its highest priority.

Second, there is no guarantee that social media providers will remain in business forever. People are fickle, and while certain mainstay platforms may seem now to be "too big to fail," that is most definitely not the case. Not that many years ago, MySpace was the dominant platform, with few people knowing about something called "The Face Book." How things have changed!

And while MySpace is still around in some form, Friendster, which had over 100 million users, and Yik Yak, which had a valuation of over $400 million, have vanished, taking with them to the history books any access to the data that they once held for people. Also gone are Google Plus and Vine, and while the companies that last operated them still exist as tech giants (Vine was acquired by Twitter), the platforms are dead and the material that was on them is no longer easily accessible.

Third, a social media provider itself may be hacked, or otherwise go offline. Not that long ago, the right-wing social media network, Parler, for example, went offline completely for a period of many months. People who wanted to access their accounts could not do so.

While the exact mechanisms of backing up data vary between platforms, there is typically a function within the settings or help menus called Download Account Data or something of the like. You should periodically use it.

WhatsApp

WhatsApp, which was acquired by Facebook (now known as Meta) in 2014, is arguably the world's most popular tool for communication; its operator claims that the tool has more than 2 billion users worldwide.

To back up your Android device's WhatsApp data, go into the Settings menu in the top-right corner of your screen, tap Chats, tap Chat Backup, and either tap BACKUP to manually back up, or configure the appropriate settings for periodic automatic backups. On Apple devices, you can reach the Chat Backup feature by tapping Settings at the bottom-right corner of the screen, tapping Chats, and then tapping Chat Backup.

Google Photos

If you use Google Photos, you can also separately configure Google to sync copies of your photos and videos on your phone to storage space in the cloud (Google Drive). To do so, click your profile photo that appears in the top-right corner of the screen in the Google Photos app, click Photos Settings, Click Backup & Sync, and turn on the feature accordingly.

Other apps

Many other apps offer backup capabilities. Look through the app's settings options, or check help forums online, if you have difficulty finding such features.

TIP

If you back up app data and store the backups on your laptop's local hard disk or solid state drive (SSD), and then back up that laptop drive as described in the following sections, you will have copies of your app backups within your laptop backups. If you typically use apps on a smartphone, ideally don't back up to only that device.

Backing Up Data on Smartphones

Both Google and Apple offer automatic syncing of data; using such a feature keeps a copy of your most recent data and also simplifies transferring your data when you upgrade to a new phone. Such syncing, however, also means that if you delete data, the deletions also sync. As such, you should still back up.

Android

Android provides two ways to back up your data and apps: automatic backups and by backing up manually.

Automatic backups

On Android versions 9 and later you can easily set up automatic backups as follows:

1. **Tap the Google One app to open it.**
2. **Tap Storage.**
3. **In the device backup section, tap "Set up data backup."**
4. **Tap "Manage backup."**
5. **Set up what you want backed up, and how often, etc.**

Depending on your phone's current configuration, you may receive additional instructions (such as to update a Google app necessary for the backups to run). If you do, follow such instructions. You may also be asked to allow Google apps to have access permissions needed to run the backups. Once your first backup has run you will see "On" listed below the data types that have been backed up.

Manual backups

You can run manual backups on Android at any point simply by opening the Settings app, tapping System, and then tapping Backup. Some Android phone manufacturers have slightly different menu schemes, so just search through the menus for the Backup or Backup Now option.

Apple

Apple offers several built-in ways to back up your iPhone (or other iOS device).

Backing up to iCloud

To back up your device to iCloud, run the Settings app, and tap your name at the top of the screen. You will then see an option for iCloud — tap it. You will then see a switch to turn on automatic backups to iCloud as well as a button to immediately launch a manual backup.

Backing up using iTunes

Apple lets you backup your Apple device to a Windows PC or to a Mac.

To back up on Windows:

1. **Run iTunes**

2. **Connect your device to your computer. (On modern Apple devices this is normally done using a USB to lighting cable — the USB side goes into the computer and the Lighting side goes into the Apple device.)**

   iTunes will start. If you have configured your device to require a password to unlock it this is when you will be prompted to enter it.

3. **Find where your device is displayed as an icon in iTunes and select it.**

4. **Click Summary.**

   Optionally (but you know what you should do) turn on "Encrypt local backup" and create a password to protect your backup.

5. **Click Back Up Now.**

To back up on a Mac:

1. **On modern Macs running the macOS Catalina operating system or later, open a Finder window.**

   Note: If you are using a Mac running an older version of macOS (macOS-Mojave or earlier) you will first need to open iTunes, then follow Steps 2–4 that follow.

2. **Connect your device to your Mac using a USB to lighting cable and enter your device password if prompted.**

3. **Select the icon for your iPhone as seen on your computer.**

   Optionally (but you know what you should do) turn on "Encrypt local backup" and create a password to protect your backup.

4. **Click Back Up Now.**

Conducting Cryptocurrency Backups

Because cryptocurrency (see Chapter 1) is tracked on a ledger and not stored in a bank, backing up cryptocurrency involves backing up the private keys used to control the addresses in the ledger at which one has cryptocurrency, not backing up the cryptocurrency itself. Often, for security reasons, keys are not maintained electronically. They're printed on paper and stored in a bank vault or fireproof safe.

For those who use hardware wallets to store the keys to their cryptocurrency, the backup for the wallet device is often a *recovery seed*, which is a list of words that allows the device to re-create the keys needed for the relevant addresses. It is generally accepted that, for security reasons, the list of words should be written down on paper and stored in a bank vault and/or safe — not stored electronically.

REMEMBER

In most cases, anyone who obtains either aforementioned form of backup can easily transfer to themselves all of the related cryptocurrency — in which case you would likely have no way to recover what was taken.

Backing Up Passwords

Anytime that you back up lists of passwords, make sure to do so in a secure manner. For important passwords that do not change often and are not likely to be needed on an urgent basis, consider making no digital records of them at all. Instead, write them down on a piece of paper and put that paper in a bank safe deposit box.

Looking at the Different Types of Backups

Backups of your data can be categorized in many different ways. One important way of distinguishing various types of backups from one another is based on what is actually being backed up when a backup process runs. The following sections look at the different types of backups based on that approach.

Full backups of systems

A *full system backup* is a backup of an entire system, including the operating system, programs/apps, settings, and data. The term applies whether the device being backed up is a smartphone or a massive server in a data center.

Technically speaking, a full system backup includes a backup of all drives attached to a system, not just those mounted inside of it — although if some drives are attached to the system only from time to time and are not needed for the primary use of the system, some might exclude the contents of such drives from full system backups, especially if they're attached to other systems, or are backed up as part of the backup of other systems. For most home users, however, a full system backup means exactly what it sounds like: Backing up everything.

A full system backup is sometimes known as a *system image* because it essentially contains an image of the system as it existed at a particular point in time. If a device that you have an image of fails, you should be able to use the system image to re-create the entire system as it was at the time that the backup was made. When you use the rebuilt system, it should function exactly as the previous system did at the time of the backup.

WARNING

Full system backups typically do *not* include backing up any material that is accessible to a system via a network share. So, if your computer has a network drive mounted as N:, for example, a full system backup run on the device may not include the data you have stored on N:.

TIP

Full system backups are the form of backup that typically is fastest to restore an entire system from, but they take longer to create than other forms of backup. They also usually require more storage space.

One important caveat: Because a system backup includes settings, hardware drivers, and so on, restoring from a system image does not always work well if you restore to a different device than the one that was originally backed up. If you imaged a laptop that runs Windows 7 as its operating system, for example, and then acquired a newer device intended to run Windows 11, which has different hardware in it, a restored system image of the first device may not work well on the newer device. The reverse is even more likely to be true: If you keep an old computer in your closet "just in case" and that just-in-case situation turns into reality, your attempts to restore the image from a newer machine to the older machine may fail fully or in part.

TIP

System images are sometimes referred to as *ghosts* (with ghost also being the verb for creating such images), especially among techies. The name originates from one of the original disk cloning software packages for PCs.

WARNING

It is important to note that some backup software packages offer "full system backups" that do not truly image everything on a system. Always read the "fine print" when software provides information about a backup option.

Original system images

One special case of system images is the original system image, also known as a *factory image*.

Many modern computing devices, whether laptops, tablets, or smartphones, come equipped with a factory image that can be restored. This means that when you acquire the device, it comes with an image of the original configuration that you receive — including the operating system, all the original software, and all the default settings — stored in a hidden partition or other storage mechanism not normally accessible to users.

At any point in time, you can perform a *factory reset* and set your device to look identical to the way that it did when it was new. When you do so, the device restores from the hidden image.

WARNING

Three important caveats:

>> Some computers allow users to manually overwrite factory images if they so desire. It is highly recommended that you not do so. If you need more storage space, obtain it elsewhere.

>> Some devices overwrite the factory reset image with new images in the event of certain operating system upgrades.

>> If you factory reset a computer, all security updates installed since the factory image was originally created will not be present on the restored device. Be sure to update your system ASAP after restoring and before going online for any other purpose!

Later system images

Some systems also create periodic images that you can restore from without having to go back to the original factory settings. Windows 10 and Windows 11, for example, have such capabilities built in.

WARNING

Never restore from an image unless you know that any problems that developed and caused you to need to restore did so after that image was made.

Original installation media

Original installation media is for programs that you acquire and install after you purchased your device. If software came on a DVD, CD, or USB drive, saving the physical media that it came on allows you to reinstall the software in case of a problem.

Keep in mind, however, that if any updates for the software were issued and installed subsequent to the original installation, you will need to redownload and reinstall the updates. Doing so may happen automatically upon reinstallation, or it may require manual effort.

Downloaded software

If you've acquired programs since you purchased your device, it's likely that some or all of them were delivered to you via digital download.

When software is delivered as a download, the downloader does not receive a physical copy. However, if you received software via a download, you can store a copy of the installation file that you downloaded on one or more of many different types of media, such as a thumb drive or a CD or DVD. Alternatively, you can store the copy on a hard drive, but be sure to back up that drive if it is part of your computer infrastructure.

In addition, some stores that sell downloadable software maintain copies of the software for you in a *virtual locker* so that you can download it at a later date. Such "backups" are useful, but be sure that you know how long the store will maintain the product in your locker. Some people have had serious problems because they relied on such "backups" only to find out that the software was not available to them at the time that they needed it.

TIP

For music and video files, the vendor's retention period is often theoretically forever, or at least as long as the material is available to purchase by others. For software, as new versions are released and old versions are *sunsetted* (the technical term for a software vendor phasing out and, ultimately, terminating support for an obsolete version of its software), the retention period may be far shorter.

Full backups of data

An alternative to performing a full backup of the entire system is to perform a full backup of the data on the system, but not of software and the operating system. (Configuration settings for both the operating system and various installed programs are often stored in data folders and included in such backups.) Performing a full data backup allows users to restore all of their data in one shot if something goes wrong. Depending on the tool used to perform the backup, users may be able to restore a subset of the data as well — for example, by choosing to restore only one particular file that they accidentally deleted.

Restoring from a full data backup will not restore applications. If a system has to be rebuilt entirely, recovering from full backups of data likely requires prior restorations to factory settings (or a later image of the computer) and reinstallation of all software. That is certainly more tedious than simply restoring from a system image. At the same time, it is also far more portable. The recovery can usually be done without any problems on many devices that vary quite a bit from the original device. Reduce the likelihood of your restored system suffering a security breach by updating the reinstalled software with the latest patches immediately after the relevant installations.

Incremental backups

Incremental backups are backups made after a full backup and that contain copies of only the portion of data (or, in the case of a system backup, the portion of the entire system) that has changed since the preceding backup (full or incremental) was run.

Incremental backups normally run much faster than full backups because, on most systems, the vast majority of data files do not change on a regular basis. For the same reason, incremental backups also use less storage space than do full backups.

To recover data, however, restoration must be done from the last full backup plus all the incremental backups performed since that last full backup.

If you decide to use incremental backups, consider limiting the number of such backups that you create after a full backup. For example, if you did only one full backup on the first day of the calendar month and performed incremental backups on all subsequent days until the next month began, then if something went wrong on the last day of the month, you would potentially need to restore from as many as 30 backups in order to recover your files.

Many people (and many businesses as well) choose to do full system backups on one of the days of the weekend and then do incremental backups during each other day of the week, thereby finding a happy medium between the efficiency gains during the backup process and the potential for a tedious recovering process.

Differential backups

Differential backups contain all the files that changed since the last full backup. (They are similar to the first in a series incremental backups run after a full backup.) A series of differential backups therefore requires more time to run and uses more storage space than incremental backups, but less than the same number of full backups. Recovering from differential backups can be faster and simpler than doing so from incremental backups because a restore needs to be done from only the last full backup and last differential backup.

If you decide to use differential backups, consider how many backups you should be making before making the next full backup. If the differential backup starts to grow quite large, there will not be much performance gains while making the backup, and any restoration will take far longer than if done from just a full backup.

Many people (and many businesses as well) choose to do full system backups on one of the days of the weekend, and then do differential backups during each other day of the week.

Mixed backups

Incremental and differential backups are made in conjunction with full backups, as shown in Table 14-1.

TABLE 14-1 ## A Comparison of Full, Incremental, and Differential Backups

	Full Backup	Incremental Backup	Differential Backup
Backup #1	All data	—	—
Backup #2	All data	Changes from Backup #1	Changes from Backup #1
Backup #3	All data	Changes from Backup #2	Changes from Backup #1

TIP

Do not mix incremental and differential backups within the same backup scheme, as doing so can create complexity and lead to confusion and costly mistakes.

Continuous backups

Continuous backups refers to backups that run continuously. Every time that a change is made to data (or to a system and data), a backup of that change is made.

WARNING

Continuous backups are great in case of a hard drive failure in the primary system — the backup is available and up-to-date — but do little in the case of a malware infection or data destruction, as the malware typically propagates to the backup as soon as it infects the primary system.

One exception are complex backup systems that log each backup action and have the ability to reverse them. These backups can undo problematic portions of backups to the point that they occurred.

The process of continuously backing up is sometimes known as *syncing* (or *synchronizing*). You may see it described as such on your electronic devices or within various software packages.

Partial backups

Partial backups are backups of a portion of data. As opposed to full backups, partial backups do not back up all elements of data from a system. If a system were to be completely hosed, for example, you would have no way to fully recover all of its data contents from partial backups made earlier of that system.

Partial backups can be implemented in a full incremental-like model in which the first backup in a series includes all the elements that are part of the set included in the partial backup, and subsequent backups in the series include only items from that set that have changed.

Partial backups can also be implemented as always full-like — in which case, all elements of the set included in the partial backup are backed up each time, regardless of whether or not they have changed since the last backup.

Partial backups are not intended to be full backups in case of a malware attack or the like. They are useful, however, in other situations, such as one in which a particular set of files needs to be backed up separately due to the needs of a particular individual or group or due to the sensitivity of the material. For example, while the IT department may do full and incremental backups of all files on a shared network drive, the accountants who need constant access to a particular set of spreadsheets stored on that drive — and would be unable to work if those files become inaccessible — may set up their own backups of just those files. They can use their backups if something goes wrong when they are on the road or working from home on the weekend, without the need to bother members of the technical support department to work unnecessarily on a Sunday.

Folder backups

Folder backups, are similar to partial backups in situations where the set of items being backed up is a particular folder. While backup tools can facilitate folder backups, to the chagrin of many cybersecurity professionals and IT departments, many users perform such backups in an ad hoc fashion by manually making a copy of hard drive (or SSD) folders to USB drives at the end of each workday and consider such backups to be sufficient protection in case of problems.

Theoretically, of course, such backups work and can be used to recover from many problems. Reality dictates, however, that ad hoc backup procedures almost never result in proper backups: People forget on some days to back up or do not back up because they're hurried, neglect to back up some materials that they should have backed up, store the backups on insecure devices in insecure locations, or lose the devices on which the backups are stored — you get the idea!

If you want to be sure that you have proper backups when you need them — and, at some point, you are likely to need them — do not rely on ad hoc folder backups.

Never back up a folder onto the same drive as the original folder resides. If the drive fails, you will lose both the primary source of data as well as the backup copy.

Drive backups

A *drive backup* is similar to a folder backup, but for situations where an entire drive is being backed up instead of only a folder. Ad hoc backups of drives do afford some protection, but rarely deliver sufficient protection against risks of losing data.

Never store the backup of a drive on the same drive as the one being backed up. If the drive fails, you will lose the primary source of data and the backup copy.

Virtual drive backups

One special case of drive backup is that in which a person or organization uses an encrypted virtual drive. For example, users may store their files within a BitLocker drive on Windows. BitLocker is a utility built in to many version of Windows that allows users to create a *virtual drive* that appears as any other drive to the user when it is in use, but appears as one giant encrypted file when not in use. To access the drive, the user must unlock it, normally by entering a password.

Backing up such drives is often accomplished by simply including the encrypted file within the full, incremental, folder, or drive backup. As such, all contents of the encrypted drive are copied without being referred to by name and remain inaccessible to anyone who does not know how to open the encrypted drive. Many backups tools offer drive backups in addition to more structured forms of backup.

Some software packages refer to the creation of an image of an entire disk as *cloning*.

While such a scheme protects the contents of the encrypted drive as they live in backups by using the same encryption as was used for the primary copies, note several caveats:

>> **Even if one small change was made to a single file within the virtual drive, the entire encrypted file will be changed.** As such, a 1KB change could easily lead to an incremental backup having to back up an entire 1TB file.

>> **The backup is useless for recovery unless someone knows how to unlock the encrypted drive.** While encryption may be a good defense mechanism against unauthorized parties snooping on sensitive files in the backup, it also means that the backup is not, on its own, fully usable for recovery. It is not hard to imagine problems developing as a result — for example, if someone attempting to utilize a backup several years after it was originally made forgets the access code, or if the person who created a backup is unavailable at the time that someone needs to restore from it.

>> **As with all encrypted data, there is a risk that as computers become more powerful — and, especially, as quantum computing takes hold — today's encryption may not offer sufficient protection against brute force attacks.** While production systems will, no doubt, be upgraded with better encryption capabilities over time (as they already have been since the 56-bit encryption of the 1990s), backups that were made with old encryption technology and keys may become vulnerable to decryption by unauthorized parties. Hence, encryption may not forever protect your sensitive data contained in backups. You must store such backups in a secure location or destroy them when they are no longer needed.

Exclusions

Some files and folders do not need to be backed up unless you are imaging a disk (in which case the image must looks exactly like the disk). Operating system paging files and other temporary files that serve no purpose if a system is restored, for example, need not be backed up.

The following are examples of some such files and folders that you can exclude from backups on a Windows 10 machine. If you're using backup software, the software likely comes with a built-in list of default exclusions that may resemble this list:

>> **The Recycle Bin,** which effectively temporarily backs up deleted files in case users change their minds about deleting them

- » **Browser caches,** which are temporary Internet files from web browsers, such as Microsoft Edge or Internet Explorer, Firefox, Chrome, Vivaldi, or Opera

- » **Temporary folders,** which are often called Temp or temp and reside in c:\, in the user directory, or in the data directory of software

- » **Temporary files,** which are usually named *.tmp or *.temp

- » **Operating system swap files,** such as pagefile.sys

- » **Operating system hibernation-mode system image information,** such as hyberfil.sys

- » **Backups** (unless you want to back up your backups), such as Windows File History

- » **Operating system files backed up during an operating system upgrade,** as usually found in C:\Windows.old on Windows computers that have had their operating systems upgraded

- » **Microsoft Outlook cache files (*.ost),** but Outlook local data stores (*.pst) should be backed up (in fact, in many cases, they may be the most critical files in a backup)

- » **Performance log files** in directories called PerfLogs

- » **Junk files** that users create as personal temporary files to hold information, such as a text file in which users type a phone number that someone dictated to them, but that the users have since entered into their smartphone directory

To conserve storage space, some backup engines will also back up only one copy of an identical file that appears in two places instead creating two "links" to the contents of that file in the backup. Sometimes such a feature appears as an option in an Exclusions settings section.

In-app backups

Some applications have built-in backup capabilities that protect you from losing your work if your computer crashes, power fails, or you don't have battery power left.

One such program is Microsoft Word, which offers users the ability to configure how often files should be saved for AutoRecover. For most people, this feature is quite valuable. I even benefited from this feature while writing this book!

While the mechanism of configuring AutoRecover varies between some versions of Word, in most modern versions, the process is the following or something similar: Choose File ⇨ Options ⇨ Save and configure the options according to your taste.

In-app backups usually take just seconds to configure, normally run without your being actively involved, and can save you a lot of aggravation. In almost all cases, you should enable the feature if it exists.

Figuring Out How Often You Should Backup

No simple one-size-fits-all rule applies as to how often you should backup your system and data. In general, you want to ensure that you never lose enough work that it would cause you significant heartache.

Performing a full backup every day requires the most amount of storage space for backups and also takes the most time to run. However, doing so means that more total copies of data are available — so, if a backup were to go bad at the same time as the primary data store, less data is likely to be lost — and fewer backups are required to perform a system or data restoration.

Performing a full backup everyday may be feasible for many individuals, especially those who can run the backups after work hours or while they are asleep at night. Such a strategy offers the best protection. With storage prices plummeting in recent years, the cost of doing so, which was once prohibitive for most individuals, is now affordable to most folks.

Some people and organizations choose to perform a weekly full backup and couple that backup with daily incremental or differential backups. The former strategy provides the fastest backup routine; the latter offers the faster recovery routine and reduces the number of backups needed in order to perform a restore to a maximum of two instead of seven.

In addition, consider using manual backups or an automated in-app backup scheme if you are working on important materials during the day. Using the in-app automated backups in Word, for example, can protect you from losing hours of work if your computer crashes. Likewise, copying documents to a second location can prevent losing significant work if your hard drive or SSD fails.

For apps that do not have in-app-auto-backup capabilities, some folks have suggested periodically using the Windows or Mac Send menu option to send to themselves via email copies of files that they are working on. While doing so is clearly not a formal backup strategy, it does provide a way of backing up work during the day between regular backups and often does so offsite, ensuring that if one's computer were to die suddenly, an entire day's worth of work would not be lost.

TIP

In general, if you are not sure if you are backing up often enough, you probably aren't.

Exploring Backup Tools

You can use multiple types of tools to create, manage, and restore from backups. Tools can automate various types of backups, for example, or can manage the process of a perpetual syncing backup. Backup tools come in wide variety of price ranges, depending on their robustness and scalability.

Backup software

Backup software is software designed specifically to run and manage backups and restorations from backups. You can find multiple vendors of such software, with exact features varying between products and between the platforms that they support (for example, features may vary between Windows and Mac versions of the same backup software package). Some offerings are intended for home users, some for large enterprises, and others for pretty much every level in between.

You can use backup software to manually or automatically backup — that is, you can configure it to backup specific systems, data, drives, or folders at specific times, using different backup models, such as full, incremental, and so on.

WARNING

Backups can run only if a machine is on. So, be sure that your device to be backed up is on at those times! (Some backup software can be configured in cases of a missed backup to run the backup the next time that the device is booted or is idle.)

TIP

Backup software can take some time to set up, but after you do so, it can often make the process of creating proper backups much easier than any other method of backing up.

Ideally, you should configure your systems to automatically back up at specific times to make sure that you actually back up and don't neglect doing so while you do any of the many things that come up in life.

WARNING

Do not confuse these manual and automatic options with manual and automated task copying.

If you just worked on some important project or spent many hours creating some new work on your computer, however, you may want to kick off an extra manual backup to protect your work and the time that you invested in it.

Beware of bogus backup software! Unscrupulous parties offer free backup software that contains malware of various severity, ranging from annoying adware to data-stealing infectors. Make sure that you obtain your backup software (as well as any other software that you use) from a reliable source.

Drive-specific backup software

Some external hard drives and solid state devices come with built-in backup software. Such software is often extremely intuitive and easy to use, and users may find it the most convenient way to set up their backup routines.

Three caveats, however:

>> Remember not to leave the drive connected to the system holding the primary data store.

>> If you use drive-specific versions of backup software, you may need to purchase all your backup drives from the same manufacturer in order not to complicate backup and restore procedures.

>> Drive-specific software is less likely to support newer technologies as they emerge from other vendors than is general backup software.

Windows Backup

Windows comes equipped with basic backup software built in. The software sports several features, and, for many people, may be sufficient. Using Windows Backup is certainly better than not backing up at all.

You can configure Windows Backup in two places:

>> In the Settings App, in the Update and Security Section.

>> Via the traditional Control Panel, which can be run from the Start Menu. Backup and Restore is an item in the traditional All Items view or in the System and Security section of the modern view.

Additionally, a Windows File Backup utility automatically backs up files as you modify them. You can access its configuration options via the Control Panel File History option. If you have plenty of disk space and work efficiently, make sure that your files are backed up quite often.

For more on restoring files from Windows File History, see Chapter 15.

Smartphone/tablet backup

Many devices come equipped with the ability to automatically sync your data to the cloud — a process that allows you to restore the data to a new device if your device is lost or stolen. Even devices that do not have this feature built in almost always can run software that effectively delivers these features for a specific folder tree or drive.

Using the sync feature provides great protection, but it also means that your data is sitting *in the cloud* — which, simply means that it is on someone else's computer — and potentially accessible to both the cloud-service provider (in the case of most smartphones, the provider would be Apple or Google), as well as to any government agencies that demand access to the relevant data while armed with a warrant, rogue insiders, or hackers who manage to somehow obtain access to it.

As discussed earlier, syncing also typically means that if you delete something on your device, it gets deleted from the synced copy (which means syncing is not sufficient on its own as a means of backing up).

REMEMBER

Even if you haven't committed any crimes, the government may still demand your data as part of data collection procedures related to crimes committed by other people. Even if you trust the government not to abuse your data, the government itself has had several breaches and data leaks, so you have good reason not to trust it to adequately protect your information from being stolen by other parties who may abuse it.

Before you decide whether or not to use the sync, think about the pros and cons.

Manual file or folder copying backups

Manual backups are exactly what they sound like: backups performed manually, often by people copying files, folders, or both from their primary hard drive (or solid-state drive) to a network folder or thumb drive.

WARNING

Manual backups have their purpose, but using them on their own is not usually a good backup strategy. People inevitably do not perform such backups as frequently as they should, do not properly store such backups, and often do not back up all the items they should be storing copies of.

Automated task file or folder copying backups

Automated-task backups are essentially manual backups on steroids; they are manual backups that are run by a computer automatically instead of by people manually kicking them off. While automating the backup process reduces the risk of forgetting to back up or not backing up due to someone being hurried, file and folder copying is still risky because if some sensitive information is, for some reason, not stored in the proper folder, it may not be backed up.

One possible exception is the case of virtual drives. If users automate the process of copying of the file containing the entire drive on which they store all of their data files, such backups may be sufficient. For most home users, however, setting up an automated copying routine is not a practical solution. Using backup software is a far simpler, and better, option.

Creating a Boot Disk

If you ever need to re-create your system, you will need the ability to boot the computer, so as part of the backup process, you should create a boot table disk. For most smartphones and tablets, creating a boot disk is not an issue because resetting the device to factory settings will make it bootable.

Such simplicity is not, however, always the case with computers, so when you perform your first backup you should ideally make a bootable disk that you know is safe to boot from (in other words, no malware and so on). Most backup software packages will walk you through this process, and some computer manufacturers will do the same on your initial startup of the system. Various security software packages are distributed on bootable CDs, DVDs, and/or USB drives as well.

Knowing Where to Back Up

For backups to have any value, they must be properly stored so they can be quickly and easily accessed when needed. Furthermore, improper storage of backups can severely undermine the security of information contained within the backups. You've probably heard stories of unencrypted backup tapes that contained sensitive information on them getting lost or stolen.

That said, there is not a one-size-fits-all approach to proper storage of backups. You can back up in different places, which results in different storage locations.

Local storage

Storing a *local copy* of your backup — meaning somewhere near a home computer or readily accessible to the owner of a smartphone, tablet, or laptop — is a good idea. If you accidentally delete a file, you can quickly restore it from the backup.

That said, you should never keep all your backups local. If you store your backups in your house, for example, and your house were to be severely damaged in a natural disaster, you could simultaneously lose your primary data store (for example, your home computer) and your backups.

Backups should always be stored in a secure location — not on a bookshelf. A fireproof and waterproof safe bolted down to the floor or fastened to the wall are two good options.

Also, keep in mind that hard drives and other magnetic media are less likely to survive certain disasters than solid-state drives, thumb drives, and other devices containing memory chips.

Offsite storage

Because one of the purposes of backing up is to have the ability to preserve data (and systems) even if your primary copy is destroyed, you want to have at least one backup *offsite* — meaning in a different location than your primary data store.

Opinions differ as to how far away from the primary store the backup should be kept. Essentially, the general rule is to keep the backups far away enough that a natural disaster that severely impacts the primary site would not impact the secondary.

Some people store a backup copy of their data in a fireproof and waterproof bag inside a safe deposit box. Bank safes typically survive natural disasters, so even if the bank is relatively close to the primary site, the backup is likely to survive even if it cannot be retrieved for several days.

Cloud

Backing up the cloud offers the benefits of offsite storage. If you lose all your equipment and systems to a natural disaster, for example, a copy of your data will almost always still exist in the cloud. Also, from a practical standpoint, the odds are that the information-security team at any major provider of cloud storage has much greater knowledge of how to keep data secure than do most individuals and have at their disposal tools that the average person cannot afford to purchase or license.

At the same time, cloud-based backup has its drawbacks.

When using cloud-based backup, you are relying on a third-party to protect your data. While that party may have more knowledge and better tools at its disposal, its primary concern is not you. If a breach occurs, for example, and large customers are impacted, its priorities may lie in addressing their concerns before addressing yours. Also, major sites are often major targets for hackers because they know that such sites contain a treasure trove of data, far greater than what they may be able to lift from your home PC. Of course, if the government serves the cloud provider a warrant, law enforcement agents may obtain copies of your backups — even, in some cases, if the warrant was served because it has demonstrated probable cause only that someone else (and not you) committed a crime.

That said, for most people, cloud-based backup makes sense, with the pros outweighing the cons, especially if you encrypt your backups, thereby making their contents inaccessible to the cloud provider.

When it comes to computers, *cloud* really means "someone else's computers." Anytime you store sensitive data, including sensitive data within in backups, in the cloud, you're really storing it on some physical computer belonging to someone else. The cloud provider may offer better security than you can offer yourself, but do not expect that your using the cloud will somehow magically eliminate cybersecurity risks.

Network storage

Backing up to a network drive offers a blend of features from several of the prior locations for storing backups.

Like a local backup, a network backup is normally readily available, but perhaps at a slightly lower speed.

Like an offsite backup, if the network server on which the backup is located is offsite, the backup is protected from site problems at the primary data's site. Unlike offsite backup, however, unless you know for sure that the files are offsite, they may be in the same facility as the primary data.

Like cloud backup, network based backup can be restored to other devices on your network. Unlike cloud backup, it may be accessible to only devices on the same private network (which, may be a problem, or, in some situations, a good thing from a security standpoint).

Also, network storage is often implemented with redundant disks and with automatic backups, offering better protection of your data that many other storage options.

TIP

If you use network storage for backups, make sure that whatever mechanism you are using to run the backup (for example, backup software) has the proper network permissions to write to the storage. In many cases, you may need to configure a login and password.

Mixing locations

There is no reason to only back up to one location. From the perspective of restoring data quickly, the more places that you have your data securely backed up, the better. In fact, different locations provider different types of protection optimized for different situations.

Keeping one copy local so that you can quickly restore a file that you accidentally delete, as well as maintaining a backup in the cloud in case of natural disaster, for example, makes sense for many people.

Keep in mind, however, that if you do store backups in multiple locations you need to make sure all the locations are secure. If you can't be sure about the security of some form of backup, beware and do not back up there just because "the more backups, the better."

TIP

As different backup locations provide different strengths and weaknesses, utilizing multiple backup locations can protect you better against more risks than using just one site.

Knowing Where Not to Store Backups

Never, ever, store backups attached to your computer or network, unless you have another backup that you are willing to recover in case of a malware attack. Ransomware that infects your computer and renders the files on it inaccessible to you may do the same to your attached backup.

WARNING

After backing up, never leave backup hard drives or solid-state drives connected to the systems or networks that they are backing up. Any malware that infects the primary system can spread to the backups as well. Removing your backup from being connected to the material that it is backing up can make all the difference between quickly recovering from a ransomware attack and having to pay an expensive ransom to a criminal.

If you back up to write-once, read-many-times type media, which is most commonly found today in the form of CD-Rs and DVD-Rs, it is safe to leave the backup in an attached drive after you have finalized the backup recording and set the disk to read-only.

TIP

Always consider the environment and weather patterns when deciding where to store backups. You might be amazed at how many people have lost data after storing hard drives on the floor of basements that were prone to flooding.

Encrypting Backups

Backups can easily become a weak point in the data protection security chain. People who are diligent about protecting their personal information, and organizations that are careful to do the same with their confidential and proprietary information, often fail to afford the same level of protection to the exact same data when it resides in backups rather than in its primary location.

How often do we hear news stories, for example, of sensitive data put at risk because it was present in an unencrypted form on backups tapes that were lost or stolen?

TIP

In general, if you're not sure if you should encrypt your backup, you probably should.

Be sure to encrypt your backups if they contain any sensitive information, which, in most cases, they do. After all, if data is important enough to be backed up, the odds are pretty good that at least some of it is sensitive and should be encrypted.

Just be sure to properly protect the password needed to unlock the backups. Remember, it may be a while before you actually need to use the backups, so do not rely on your memory, unless you practice using that password on a regular basis to test the backups.

TIP

From a practical standpoint, many professional system administrators who deal with multiple backups every day have never seen a backup that did not need to be encrypted.

Also, keep in mind that if encryption methods used to protect backups go obsolete, the backups should be replaced with backups re-encrypted with better encryption. This issue is likely going to become a major headache for many organizations as quantum computing (discussed in Chapter 18) matures.

Testing Backups

Many folks have thought that they had proper backups only to discover at the time that they needed to restore that the backups were corrupted. Hence, testing backups is critical.

While, theoretically, you should test every backup that you make and test that every single item within the backup can be restored, such a scheme is impractical for most people. Do, however, test the first backup that you make with any software, check the auto-recover files the first time that you use Word, and so on.

Some backup software comes with the capability to *verify* backups — that is, after making a backup, it checks that the original data and data in the backups match. Running such verification after making a backup adds significant time to the backup process, but is well worth running if you can do so because it helps ensure that nothing was improperly recorded or otherwise became corrupted during the backup process.

WARNING

If you do not test that your backups actually work, you may be in for a terribly nasty surprise if you ever do need to restore from them.

Disposing of Backups

People and organizations often store backups for long periods of time — sometimes preserving materials for so long that the encryption used to protect the sensitive data on backup media is no longer sufficient to adequately protect the information from prying eyes.

As such, it is imperative that, from time to time, you either destroy your backups or re-create them.

REMEMBER

Both hardware and software formats change over time. If you backed up to tapes in the 1980s, to Bernoulli Boxes in the early 1990s, or to Zip drives in the late 1990s, you may have difficulty restoring from the backups today because you may have problems obtaining the necessary hardware, compatible drivers, and other software needed to read the backups on a modern computer.

Likewise, if you backed up data along with various DOS programs or early Windows 16-bit executables needed to process the contents of those backups, you may be unable to restore from the backups to many modern machines that may be unable to run the executables. Obviously, if you did a full system image of a machine 20 years ago, you are going to have difficulty restoring from the image today (you may be able to do so using virtual machines — something well beyond the technical skill level of most users).

Even some older versions of data files may not work easily. Word documents from the mid-1990s, for example, which can be infected with various forms of malware, do not open in modern versions of Word unless a user enables such access, which may be difficult or impossible to do in certain corporate environments. Files formats utilized specifically by software that has long since disappeared entirely from the market may be even harder to open.

As such, old backups may not have much value to you anyway. So, once a backup is no longer valuable or once its data protection may be at risk of compromise, get rid of it.

How should you dispose of the backup tapes, disks, and so on? Can you just throw them in the trash?

No. Do not. Doing so can totally undermine the security of the data in the backups.

Instead, utilize one of the following methods:

>> **Overwriting:** Various software programs will write over every sector of the storage media several times (the actual number of times depends on the security level that the user specifies), making subsequent recovery of data from the decommissioned media difficult, if not impossible.

>> **Degaussing:** Various devices containing strong magnets can be used to physically render data on magnetic media (such as hard drives and floppy disks) inaccessible by exposing the media to a strong magnetic field.

>> **Incineration:** Burning storage media in a high-temperature fire is often enough to destroy it. Do not attempt this on your own. If you want to pursue such a method, find a professional with experience. The incineration process varies based on the type of media involved.

>> **Shredding:** Cutting the media into tiny pieces. Ideally, such media should be totally pulverized into dust. In any case, shredding using an old-fashioned shredder that cuts media into strips is generally not considered secure disposal of media that has not been previously overwritten or degaussed.

TIP

I can't overstate the importance of properly storing and disposing of backups. Serious data leaks have resulted from backup media that was lost after being stored for quite some time.

Chapter **15**

Resetting Your Device

C hapter 14 talks about backing up and why backing up is a critical component of any and every cybersecurity plan. The odds are close to 100 percent that, at some point, you will lose access to some file to which you still need access, and restoring from a backup will be a "lifesaver." In this chapter, I discuss resetting your computer and teach you what you need to know to successfully reset your device so that it's (almost) as good as new.

Exploring Two Types of Resets

Sometimes, the easiest way to restore — and to help ensure that none of the problems that forced you to restore in the first place remain — is to start over by resetting your device to factory settings and reinstalling your apps and copying your data files from a backup.

However, even resets that are called "factory resets" often do not really set the device back to an identical state as that in which it came; some significant changes that have been made in the ensuing time will not be undone. For example, in many cases, if the BIOS of a device was updated since the device was acquired, a "factory reset" will not reset the BIOS back to its original state. And, as is discussed later, if any updates that were downloaded also updated the "factory image" used for restoration to factory settings, the restored computer will have those updates as well.

From a security perspective, this is important to understand, for at least two important reasons:

>> Any malware that infects the BIOS may not be removed by a factory reset.

>> If you have physical installation media (for example, a CD or DVD) for any software that you installed on the device previously, and you plan to install it again from such media and download and install updates to that software online after installing the version on the media, you must keep in mind that in some rare cases the versions on the media may not be compatible with the BIOS that is now in the device, and the installations could potentially fail.

TIP

Some forms of malware can survive a factory reset. So, if your device was infected with malware, be sure to address that problem even if you plan to reset your device. Or consult with an expert.

In addition, there will likely be times when your device crashes — that is, it becomes unresponsive and stops functioning normally. Such occasions can be scary for many nontechnical users, who assume that they may lose their data. Performing the proper type of reset in such occasions, however, is quite simple and will almost always preserve the user's files (although files currently being worked on may be preserved as they were last saved).

Resets come in two major flavors — soft and hard. It is critical to know the difference between them before you use either type.

Soft resets

A *soft reset* is the equivalent of physically turning a device off and then turning it back on. A soft reset does *not* wipe programs, data, or malware, and does not reset most previously set configuration elements.

TIP

One common use of soft resets is to restart a device if it crashes and becomes unresponsive. It can also be useful after a Blue Screen of Death-type of crash.

Older devices

Most modern computing devices have a soft reset capability, but some older devices do not. In such devices, however, the battery is often removable, so removing the battery and cutting off all power to the device (in other words, make sure to unplug it from the "mains") achieves the same desired effect.

Windows computers

Most Windows computers can be soft reset by holding down the Power button (for ten seconds or so) to do a shutdown. Holding down the button cuts off power to the computer from both the battery and any connected AC adapters/mains (even if the battery is connected and fully charged) and shuts it down.

TIP

After the device shuts down, wait ten seconds and press the Power button once to restart the computer. I know it will restart even if you don't wait the ten seconds, but waiting the ten seconds reduces the risks of rare electrical damage that occur from turning a device off and then on. (At a high level, and oversimplified, the damage occurs from an overload of electrical current if you send new current into the device while some of the current that was previously there before it was turned off has not fully left the scene because it was stored within capacitors and present even for a few seconds after being unplugged.)

Mac computers

Various models of Mac computers can be soft reset through different means:

>> Hold down the Power button for about five seconds, and the Mac should shut down completely. Let go of the Power button, wait a few seconds, and press it once again, and the Mac should reboot. On some Macs pressing and holding the Power button may display a menu, in which case you should press R for Reboot and reboot directly, rather than shutting down and restarting the device.

>> Press and hold the Control + ⌘ key together with the Power button.

>> Press and hold the TouchID button until the Mac reboots.

Android devices

The way to soft reset an Android device varies between manufacturers. One of the following methods is likely to work:

>> Press and hold the Power button until you see a shutdown/restart menu and then press Restart. (Or press Power Off, wait a few seconds, and then press the Power button again to turn the phone back on.)

>> Press and hold the Power button. If no menu appears, keep holding the Power button for 2 minutes. At some point the phone should turn off — when it does, wait 10 seconds and turn it back on.

>> If you have a removable battery, remove it, wait ten seconds, put it back in, and turn on the phone.

iPhones

The way to soft reset an iPhone varies based on the model. In general, one of the following methods will work:

>> Press and release the Volume Up button, then press and release the Volume Down button, and then press and hold the Side button (the Power button) until the Apple logo appears on the screen. Wait for the device to reboot.

>> Press and hold the Power button. While still holding it, press and hold the Volume Down button. When a Slide To Power Off prompt and slider appears on the screen, slide the slider to the right and turn the device off. Wait ten seconds and press the Power button to turn it back on.

>> Press and hold the Power button, and, while still doing so, press and hold the Volume Down button. Continue to hold both buttons as the iPhone powers off and back on. Release both buttons when the Apple logo appears on the screen and wait for the device to reboot.

WARNING

If you are using some versions of the iPhone X, following this option for performing a soft reset could end up calling emergency services (911 in the United States) because holding these particular buttons for longer than five seconds may be preprogrammed to issue an SOS signal from the device.

Hard resets

Hard resets reset a device to its factory image or to something similar. (For more on factory image, see Chapter 14.)

If you want to recover to the original factory image — to effectively reset your device to the way it was when it was new — you need to follow the instructions for your particular device.

WARNING

Hard resets are almost always irreversible. Once you run a hard reset and a device is set back to its factory settings, you typically cannot undo the reset. Anything that you previously installed on the device (other than BIOS updates and the like as discussed earlier in this chapter), and any data that you stored on it is likely gone forever. (Advanced tools may, in some cases, be able to recover some of the material, but such recoveries are often incomplete, and, in many cases, impossible altogether.) As such, do not run a hard reset until you are sure that you have back-ups of all the material that you need on the device that you are hard resetting.

Also keep in mind the following:

» In some cases, a factory reset will not reset your device to the way it was when it was new because during operating system updates, the recovery image was updated as well. Factory resetting such a device will set the device to the way the device would have looked (or quite similar to the way it would have looked) when it was new had you purchased it with the new operating system.

» After performing a factory reset, one or more (or possibly all) patches and other security updates that you have installed on the device may be gone — meaning that your device is more likely than not vulnerable to various compromises. So, immediately after restoring you should run the operating system update process (repetitively — until it finds no needed updates) as well as the update process for any security software (also repetitively until it finds no needed updates). Only after those steps have been completed should you begin to install other software or perform any other online activities.

Resetting a modern Windows device

Your modern Windows device likely offers one or more ways to reset it. The following sections describe three major ways.

METHOD 1

1. **In the Start menu, click on Settings or PC Settings, depending on your operating system version.**

2. **In Windows Settings, click on Update and Security.**

The Windows Update screen appears.

3. **Click on Recovery in the menu on the left side of the Window.**

4. **Click on the Get Started button in the Reset this PC section at the top of the window.**

At this point, you may be prompted to install the original installation CD on which you received Windows 10. If you receive that message, do so. If you do not receive it — and most users don't — just continue.

Windows then offers you two choices. Both remove programs and apps and reset settings to their defaults:

- **Keep my files:** Selecting this option leaves your data files intact (as long as they are stored in data folders).

- **Remove everything:** Selecting this option removes all your data files along with the apps and programs (this is the factory reset option).

5. **Select either reset option.**

If you're performing a full reset because your system was infected by malware or your data files may otherwise have been corrupted, ideally select Remove everything and restore your data files from a clean backup.

If you select to remove your files along with everything else, Windows presents you with two choices:

- **Just remove my files:** Selecting this option erases your files, but does not perform any drive cleaning. This means that someone who gains access to the drive may be able to recover the data that was in the files — in full or in part — even after the files are deleted by the rest. This option runs relatively quickly.

- **Remove files and clean the drive:** Selecting this option not only removes all your data files, it wipes the drive — that is, writes over every 1 or 0 in your file — to dramatically reduce the likelihood that anyone in the future could recover any data from the deleted files. Cleaning a drive is time-consuming; if you select this option the restore can take much longer than if you select the first option.

If you are resetting the system so that you can use a clean system after recovering from a malware infection, there is no reason to clean the drive. If you are wiping it before giving it to someone else, fully cleaning the drive is a good idea. (In fact, some would argue that you should wipe the entire drive with even better wiping technology than is provided through the reset option discussed in this chapter.)

At this point, you may receive a warning message. If your computer originally had a different operating system and was upgraded to Window 10, resetting the system will remove the recovery files created during the upgrade that allow you to downgrade back to the previously running operating system — meaning that if you reset the system you will have a Windows 10 computer that cannot be easily downgraded to another operating system. In most cases, this warning is not a significant issue — Windows 10 is relatively mature, and few people who upgrade to Windows 10 as of the data of this book's publishing choose to downgrade.

Of course, if you are resetting the system because it is not working properly after you performed an upgrade to Windows 10, do not proceed with the reset. Downgrade it to the older version of Windows using the relevant tool.

You then will see a final warning message that tells you that the computer is ready to reset — and which communicates what that means. Read what it says. If you do not want any of the things that it says will happen to happen, do not proceed.

6. **When you are ready to proceed, click on the Reset button.**

You can probably go out for coffee. A reset takes quite some time, especially if you chose to clean your drive.

7. **After a while, if you receive a prompt asking you whether you want to continue to Windows 10 or to perform troubleshooting, click on Continue.**

METHOD 2

If you're *locked out* of your computer, meaning that it boots to a login screen, but you cannot log in — for example, if a hacker changed your password — you can still factory reset the machine:

1. **Boot your PC.**

2. **When the login screen appears, click on the Power icon in the bottom right-hand corner.**

You are prompted with several choices. Do not click on them yet.

3. **Without clicking any choices, first hold down the Shift key and then click on Restart.**

A special menu appears.

4. **Click on Troubleshoot.**

5. **Select Reset This PC.**

6. **Select Remove Everything.**

WARNING

Read the warnings, and understand what the consequences of running a hard reset are before you run it. This reset is likely irreversible.

METHOD 3

This method may vary a bit between various computer manufacturers.

To reset your device:

1. **Turn on your computer and boot into Windows 10.**

If you have more than one operating system installed on your computer, select the Windows 10 installation that you want to reset. If all you have is one operating system — as is the case for most people — you won't have to select it because it will boot automatically.

2. **While the computer is booting, press and hold down the F8 key to enter the boot menu.**

3. In the boot menu on the Advanced Boot Options screen that appears, click on **Repair Your Computer** and press **Enter**.

4. If you're prompted to choose a keyboard layout, do so and then click on **Next**.

5. Select your username, type your password, and click on **OK**.

6. From the System Recovery Options menu that appears, click on the **System Image Recovery** link and follow the onscreen prompts to do a factory reset.

TIP

If your menus appear differently after pressing F8 in the last step, look through them for a Factory Reset option.

Resetting a modern Android device

Modern Android devices come equipped with a Factory Reset feature, although the exact location of the activation option for it varies based on the device's manufacturer and operating system version.

I show you several examples of how to activate a hard reset on several popular devices. Other devices are likely to have similar options.

SAMSUNG GALAXY SERIES RUNNING ANDROID 11

On popular Samsung Galaxy phones running Android version 11 (the latest version of Android as of this writing), you can access the factory reset option by following these instructions:

1. Run the Settings app.

2. From the main Settings menu, click on **General Management**.

3. Click on **Reset**.

4. Click on **Factory Data Reset**.

5. Follow the instructions presented with the relevant warning.

SAMSUNG TABLETS RUNNING ANDROID 11

The popular Samsung series of tablets have menu structures for hard-resetting that are similar to those used for the Galaxy series, although with a different look and feel.

1. Run the Settings app.

2. From the main Settings menu, click on **General Management**.

3. **In the General Management menu, click on Reset.**

4. **Click on Factory Data Reset.**

5. **Follow the instructions at the warning to continue.**

HUAWEI DEVICES RUNNING ANDROID 8

Huawei phones, which are popular throughout Asia, but discouraged from use by Americans due to questions about Chinese government influence in the manufacturer, can be reset using the following steps (or similar steps, in case of operating system version differences):

1. **Run the Settings app.**

2. **From the main settings menu, click on System.**

3. **In the System menu, click on Reset.**

4. **In the Reset menu, click on Factory Data Reset.**

5. **Follow the instructions at the warning to continue.**

Resetting a Mac

Before you hard reset a Mac, you should perform the following steps:

1. **Sign out of iTunes.**

2. **De-authorize any apps that are locked to your Mac.**

   Sign out of them so that you can relog-in from the newly restored device, which those systems may see as if it were a different device.

3. **Sign out of Messages.**

4. **Sign out of iCloud.**

   You can do this in the System Preferences app. You will need to put in your password.

While a hard reset will work without the preceding three steps, performing the steps can prevent various problems when you restore.

After you're signed out of iTunes, Messages, and iCloud:

1. **Restart your Mac in Recovery Mode by restarting your Mac and holding down the Command and R keys while it reboots.**

   You may be presented with a screen asking you in what language you want to continue. If you are, select your preferred language — for the sake of this book, I assume that you have selected English.

2. **Run the Disk Utility.**

3. **In the Disk Utility screen, select your device's main volume and click on Unmount then Erase.**

4. **Erase any other disks in the device.**

5. **Exit the Disk Utility by clicking Quit Disk Utility in the Disk Utility menu.**

6. **Click on Reinstall macOS and follow the steps to reinstall the operating system onto the primary disk within your Mac.**

Resetting an iPhone

To hard reset a modern iPhone:

1. **Run the Settings app and choose General ⇨ Reset ⇨ Erase All Content and Settings.**

2. **If you're asked for your Apple ID and Password to confirm the erasure, enter them.**

3. **When you see a warning and a red Erase iPhone (or iPad) button, click on it.**

Rebuilding Your Device after a Hard Reset

After you hard reset a device, you should

» Install all security updates

» Install all the programs and apps that you use on the device — and any relevant updates

» Restore your data from a backup

WARNING

After you restore a device, any updates or configuration changes you made in order to address security concerns are likely gone. Make sure to have a list of such changes prior to the reset so that you have a plan of action in place when you restore.

Chapter **16**

Restoring from Backups

B acking up is a critical component of any and every cybersecurity plan. After you reset a device to its factory settings as part of the recovery process (see Chapter 15), you can restore your data and programs so that your device will function as normal.

Because most people do not have to restore from backups regularly and because restoration is typically done after something "bad" happened that forced the restoration to be necessary, many folks first experience the process of restoring from backups when they are quite stressed. As such, people are prone to making mistakes during restoration, which can lead to data being lost forever. Fortunately, this chapter shows you how to restore.

You Will Need to Restore

The odds are close to 100 percent that, at some point, you will lose access to some file to which you still need access, and restoring from a backup will be a lifesaver. But restoring is not necessarily simple. You need to contemplate various factors before performing a restoration. Proper planning and execution can make the difference between recovering from lost data and losing even more data.

TIP

Restoring from backups is not as simple as many people think. Take the time to read this chapter before you perform a restore.

Wait! Do Not Restore Yet!

You noticed that some data that you want to access is missing. You noticed that a file is corrupted. You noticed that some program is not running properly. So, you should restore from a backup, right? Wait!

WARNING

Restoring without knowing why the problem occurred in the first place may be dangerous. For example, if you have a malware infection on your computer, restoring while the malware is still present won't remove the threat, and, depending on the type of malware and backup, may lead to the files in your backup becoming corrupted as well. If the malware corrupts the primary data store, you may lose your data and have nowhere from which to restore it!

For example, people who tried to restore data from backups on external hard drives have lost data to ransomware. The moment the external drive was connected to the infected computer, the ransomware spread to the backup and encrypted it as well!

WARNING

Malware can spread to cloud-based storage as well. Merely having the backup in the cloud is not a reason to restore before knowing what happened.

Even in the case of backups that are on read-only media, which malware cannot infect, attempting to restore before neutralizing the threat posed by the infection can waste time and potentially give the malware access to more data to steal.

Before you restore from any backups, make sure to diagnose the source of the problem that is causing you the need to restore. If you accidentally deleted a file, for example, and know that the problem occurred due to your own human error, by all means go ahead and restore. But if you're unsure what happened, apply the techniques described in Chapters 12 and 13 to figure out what you need to do to make your computer safe and secure prior to restoring from the backup.

Restoring Data to Apps

As discussed in Chapter 14, many apps and social media accounts provide their own backup and restore mechanisms. Typically the restore functions can be found in the same places within the apps' respective configuration settings as the backups.

In any event, if, when making your backups, you took note of where the restore functions are and wrote that information down, you should be in good shape to go. If not, look on the support pages for that app.

Restoring from Full Backups of Systems

A *full system backup* is a backup of an entire system, including the operating system, programs/apps, settings, and data. The term applies whether the device being backed up is a smartphone or a massive server in a data center.

As such, the restoration process recreates a system that is effectively identical to the one that was backed up at the time that it was backed up. (This is not totally true in the absolute sense — the system clock will show a different time than the original system, for example — but it is true for the purposes of learning about system restoration.)

Restoring to the computing device that was originally backed up

System restoration from a system image works best when systems are restored to the same computing device from which the original backup was made. If your system was infected with malware, for example, and you restore to the same device from an image created before the malware infection took place, the system should work well. (Of course, you would lose any work and other updates done since that time, so hopefully you backed them up using one of the methods in Chapter 14.)

WARNING

Full system restores are often irreversible. And if a restore fails, as can happen if a backup is corrupted or for any one or more of a number of reasons including some discussed in the next section, you could have a system that is unusable in its present form. Be absolutely sure that you want to run a full system restore before you actually run one.

Restoring from a full system backup is likely the fastest way to restore an entire system, but the process can take dramatically longer than restoring just a few files that were corrupted. It is also far more likely to lead to accidentally erasing settings or data created since the last backup. As such, use a full system restore only when one is truly needed.

TIP

If you accidentally delete a bunch of files or even folders, do not perform a full system restore. Just restore those files from a backup using one of the techniques described later in this chapter.

Restoring to a different device than the one that was originally backed up

REMEMBER

System restoration from an image often won't work on a system with totally different hardware components than the system that was originally imaged. In general, the more different a system is from the system that was imaged, the more problems that you may encounter.

Some of those problems may autocorrect. If you restore a system with drivers for one video card to a system with another video card, for example, the restored system should realize that the wrong drivers are installed and simply not use them. Instead, it defaults to the operating system's built-in drivers and allows you to install the drivers for the correct card (or, in some cases, automatically download them or prompt you to do so).

Some problems may not autocorrect. For example, if the computer that was backed up used a standard USB-connected keyboard and mouse and the device to which you are restoring uses some proprietary keyboard that connects differently, it may not work at all after the restore; you may need to attach a USB keyboard to the system to download and install the drivers for your proprietary keyboard. Such situations are becoming increasingly rare due to both standardization and improvements in modern operating systems, but they do exist.

Some problems may not be correctable. If you try to restore the system image of a Mac to a computer designed to run Windows, for example, it won't work.

TIP

Some backup software packages allow you to configure a restore to either install separate drivers or search for drivers that match the hardware to which the restoration is being done to replace those found in the backup that are unsuitable. If you have such feature and have difficulty restoring without it, you may want to try it.

A full system backup may or may not include a backup of all content on all drives attached to a system, not just those mounted inside of it. (Theoretically, all such drives should be included in a system image, but the term *system image* is often used to mean an image of the internal hard drives and SSDs.)

TIP

If a device for which you have an image fails, you should be able to use the system image to re-create the entire system as it was at the time that the backup was made. When you use the rebuilt system, it should function exactly as the previous system did at the time of the backup.

Original system images

If you want to recover to the original factory image of a system prior to restoring your data and programs, see Chapter 15, which is dedicated to performing such restorations.

After performing such a factory reset, one or more (or possibly all) patches and other security updates that you have installed on the device may be gone. Your device is likely vulnerable to various compromises. Immediately after restoring, you should, therefore, run the operating system update process (repetitively until it finds no needed updates) as well as the update process for any security software (also repetitively until it finds no needed updates).

Only after those steps are completed should you install other software, restore your data, or perform any other online activities.

Later system images

Before you restore from any system image, you must ascertain that whatever problem occurred that necessitated the restoration will not remain, or be restored, during the restoration. If your computer was infected with ransomware, for example, and you remove the malware with security software, but need to restore the criminally encrypted files from a backup, you do not want to end up restoring the ransomware along with the data.

If you know for certain that an image was made prior to the arrival of the problem, go ahead and use it. If in doubt, if possible, restore to an extra device and scan it with security software prior to performing the actual restoration. If you do not have an extra device to which you can restore and are unsure as to whether the backup is infected, you may want to hire a professional to take a look.

Installing security software

After you restore from a system image (whether factory settings or a later image), the first thing that you should do is check whether security software is installed. If it is not, install it. Either way, make sure to run the auto-updates until the software no longer needs updates.

TIP

Install security software before attempting to do anything online or read email. If you do not have security software in place before you perform such tasks, performing them could lead to a security breach of your device.

If you have the security software on CD, DVD, or USB drive, install it from there. If you created a USB drive or other disk with the security software on it, you can install it from there. If not, copy the security software to the hard drive from wherever you have it and run it.

Original installation media

For programs that you acquire and install after you purchased your device, you can reinstall them after you restore the original system image or even a later image that was created before the software was installed.

TIP

If you reinstall software from a CD, DVD, or USB drive any updates to the software that were released after the CD, DVD, or USB drive image was created will not be installed. Be sure to either configure your program to auto-update or manually download and install such updates. In some cases, software installation routines may also ask you whether you want them to automatically perform a check for updates immediately upon the completion of the installation. In general, answering affirmatively is a wise idea.

Downloaded software

The way that you reinstall programs that you previously purchased and installed at some point after you purchased your device depends on where the software is located:

TIP

>> **If you have a copy of the software on a thumb drive,** you can reinstall from the drive by connecting it into your device, copying the files to your hard drive, and running the install.

If there is any possibility that the thumb drive is infected with malware — for example, you're restoring due to a malware infection and may have inserted the thumb drive into your infected computer at some point in the past — make sure to scan it with security software before you run or copy anything from it. Do so from a device with security software running that will prevent infections from spreading upon connection from the drive to the machine being used for scanning.

>> **If you copied the software to a DVD, USB drive, or CD,** you can install from that disc. Make sure to install all necessary updates.

>> **If the purchased software can be redownloaded from a virtual locker,** do so. In some cases, software that is redownloaded will have been automatically upgraded to the latest release. In other cases, it will be the same version as you originally purchased, so make sure to install updates.

>> **If the software is downloadable from its original source** (public domain software, trialware that you activate with a code, and so on), feel free to redownload it. In some cases — for example, if newer versions require paying an upgrade fee — you may need to download the version that you had previously. In any case, make sure to install all updates for the version that you do install.

Restoring from full backups of data

In many cases, it makes sense to restore all the data on a device:

>> **After a restore from a factory image:** After restoring from a factory image and reinstalling all necessary software, your device will still have none (or almost none) of your data on it, so you need to restore all your data.

>> **After certain malware attacks:** Some malware modifies and/or corrupts files. To ensure that all your files are as they should be, after an infection, restore all your data from a backup. Of course, this assumes that you have a recent enough backup from which to do so without losing any work.

>> **After a hard drive failure:** If a hard drive fails, in full or in part, you will want to move your files to another drive. If you have a separate drive for data than for the operating system and programs — as many people do — performing a full restore of data is the easiest way to restore.

>> **When transitioning to a new, similar device:** Restoring from a backup is an easy way to ensure that you put all your data files onto the new device. Because some programs store settings in user data folders, copying the files directly or performing a selective restoration from a backup is usually a better way to go. But as people sometimes inadvertently leave out files when using such a technique, full restorations are sometimes used.

>> **After accidental deletions:** People occasionally accidentally delete large portions of their data files. One easy way to restore everything and not worry about whether everything is "back to the way that it should be" is to do a full restore of all data.

Unlike restoring from a full system backup, restoring from a full data backup won't restore applications. If a system has to be rebuilt entirely, recovering from full backups of data likely requires prior restorations to factory settings (or a later image of the computer) and reinstallation of all software.

TIP

The multi-step process of restoring from a factory image and then reinstalling applications and restoring data may seem more tedious than simply restoring from a more recent system image, but it also usually proves to be far more portable. Recovery can usually be done on devices that vary quite a bit from the original device, using images of those devices (or onto a new device), followed by the reinstallation of programs and the restoration of data.

Restoring from Incremental Backups

Incremental backups are backups made after a full backup and contain copies of only the portion of the contents being backed up that have changed since the preceding backup (full or incremental) was run.

TIP

Some simplistic backup software products use incremental and differential backups internally, but hide the internal workings from users. All users do is select which files or file types to restore and, if appropriate, which versions of those files, and the system works like magic hiding the merging of data from multiple backups into the resulting restoration.

Incremental backups of data

In many cases of home users, *incremental backup* refers to incremental backups of data. To recover data that was backed up using an incremental backup scheme requires multiple steps:

1. **A restoration must be done from the last full data backup.**

2. **After that restoration is complete, restoration must be performed from each incremental backup performed since that last full backup.**

Failing to include any of the incremental backups necessary in Step 2 may lead to corrupt data, missing data, data being present that should not be, or inconsistent data.

WARNING

Most modern backup software will warn (or prevent) you if you try to skip any incremental backups during an incremental restoration. Such software, however, sometimes does not, however, tell you if you're missing the final backup or backups in a series.

Incremental backups of systems

Incremental system backups are essentially updates to system images (or partial system images in the case of partial backups) that bring the image up to date as of the data that the backup was made. The incremental system backup contains copies of only the portion of the system that changed since the preceding backup (full or incremental) was successfully run.

To restore from an incremental backup of a system:

1. **A restoration must be done from the last full system backup.**

2. **After that restoration is complete, restoration must be performed from each incremental backup performed since that system image was created.**

Failing to include any of the incremental backups necessary in Step 2 may lead to corrupt of missing programs, data, operating system components, and incompatibility issues between software. Most modern backup software will warn (or prevent) you if you try to skip various incremental backups during a restore from an incremental backup. They often do not, however, tell you if you're missing the final backup or backups in a series.

Differential backups

Differential backups contain all the files that changed since the last full backup was successfully run. (They are similar to the first in a series incremental backups run after a full backup.)

TIP

While creating a series of differential backups usually takes more time than creating a series of incremental backups, restoring from differential backups is usually much simpler and faster.

To recover from a differential backup:

1. **Perform a restoration from the last full system backup.**

2. **After that restoration is complete, perform a restoration from the most recent differential backup.**

Be sure to restore from the last differential backup and not from any other differential backup.

TIP

Many backup systems won't warn you if you attempt to restore from a differential backup other than the latest one. Be sure to double-check before restoring that you're using the latest one!

Table 16-1 shows the comparative restoration processes from full, incremental, and differential backups.

TABLE 16-1 **Restoration Processes**

	Full Backup	Incremental Backup	Differential Backup
After Backup #1	Restore from Backup #1	Restore from Backup #1 (Full)	Restore from Backup #1 (Full)
After Backup #2	Restore from Backup #2	Restore from Backups #1 and #2	Restore from Backups #1 and #2
After Backup #3	Restore from Backup #3	Restore from Backups #1, #2, and #3	Restore from Backups #1 and #3
After Backup #4	Restore from Backup #4	Restore from Backups #1, #2, #3, and #4	Restore from Backups #1 and #4

Continuous backups

Some continuous backups are ideal for performing system restore. Similar to a system image, they allow you to restore a system to the way that it looked at a certain point in time. Others are terrible for performing restores because they allow restoration to only the most recent version of the system, which often suffers from the need to be rebuilt in the first place.

In fact, the normal use of continuous backups is to address equipment failures, such as a hard drive suddenly going caput — not the rebuilding of systems after a security incident. Furthermore, because continuous backups constantly propagate material from the device being backed up to the backup, any malware that was present on the primary system may be present on the backup.

Partial backups

Partial backups are backups of a portion of data. Likewise, partial backups are not intended to be full backups in case of a malware attack or the like. They are useful, however, in other situations, and you should be aware of how to restore from them.

If you have a particular set of files that are extremely sensitive and need to be backed up and stored separately from the rest of your system, you may use a partial backup for that data. If something happens and you need to rebuild a system or restore the sensitive data, you will need that separate partial backup from which to do the restore.

Digital private keys that provide access to cryptocurrency, email encryption/decryption capabilities, and so on, for example, are often stored on such backups along with images of extremely sensitive documents.

Often, partial backups of sensitive data are performed to USB drives (or, in cases of less up-to-date environments, writeable DVDs, CDs, or even floppy disks!) that are then locked in safes or safe deposit boxes. Restoring from the backup would, in such cases, demand that the restorer obtain the physical USB drive (or other form of media), which could mean a delay in restoration. If the need to restore arises at 6 p.m. Friday, for example, and the drive is in a safe deposit box that is not available until 9 a.m. Monday, the desired material may remain inaccessible to the user for almost three days.

Make sure that you store your partial backups in a manner that will allow you to access the backed-up data when you need it.

Another common scenario for specialized partial backups is when a network-based backup is used — especially within a small business — and users need to ensure that they have a backup of certain material in case of technical problems while traveling. Such backups should never be made without proper authorization. If permission has been obtained and a backup has been created, a user on the road who suffers a technical problem that requires restoration of data can do the restore by copying the files from the USB drive or other form of media (after, presumably, decrypting the files using a strong password or some form of multifactor authentication).

Folder backups

Folder backups are similar to partial backups because the set of items being backed up is a particular folder. If you performed a folder backup using a backup tool, you can restore it using the techniques described in the preceding section.

The restore process is different if, however, you created the relevant backup by simply copying a folder or set of folders to an external drive (hard drive, SSDs, USB drive, or network drive). Theoretically, you simply copy the backup copy of the folder or folders to the location of the original folder. However, doing so will potentially overwrite the contents of the primary folder, so any changes made since the backup will be lost.

Drive backups

A *drive backup* is similar to a folder backup, but an entire drive is backed up instead of a folder. If you backed up a drive with backup software, you can restore it via that software. If you backed up a drive by copying the contents of the drive somewhere else, you will need to manually copy them back. Such a restore may not work perfectly, however. Hidden and system files may not be restored, so a bootable drive backed up and restored in such a fashion may not remain bootable.

Virtual-drive backups

If you backed up an encrypted virtual drive, such as a BitLocker drive that you mount on your computer, you can restore the entire drive in one shot or restore individual files and folders from the drive.

Restoring the entire virtual drive

To restore the entire virtual drive in one shot, make sure the existing copy of the drive is not mounted (you will probably get an error message if you try to restore it while it is mounted, but do not rely on that). The easiest way to do so is to boot your computer and not mount any Bitlocker drives.

If your computer is booted already and the drive is mounted, simply dismount it:

1. **Choose Startup ➪ This PC.**

2. **Locate the mounted Bitlocker drive.**

The drive appears with an icon of a lock indicating that it is encrypted.

3. **Right-click on the drive and select Eject.**

Once the drive is dismounted, it disappears from the This PC list of drives.

After the drive is unmounted, copy the backup copy of the drive to the primary drive location and replace the file containing the drive.

You can then unlock and mount the drive.

Restoring files and/or folders from the virtual drive

To restore individual files or folders from the virtual drive, mount the backup as a separate virtual drive and copy the files and folders from the backup to the primary as if you were copying files between any two drives.

TIP

Ideally, you should back up the backup of the virtual drive before mounting it and copying files and/or folders from it and mount it read-only when you mount it.

TIP

Always unmount the backup drive after copying files to the primary. Leaving it mounted — which inherently means that two copies of a large portion of your file system are in use at the same time — can lead to human mistakes.

Dealing with Deletions

One of the problems of restoring from any restore that does not entirely overwrite your data with a new copy is that the restore may not restore deletions.

For example, if after making a full backup, you delete a file, create ten new files, modify two data files, and then perform an incremental backup, the incremental backup may or may not record the deletion. If you restore from the full backup and then restore from the incremental, the restore from the incremental should delete the file, add the ten new files, and modify the two files to the newer version. In some cases, however, the file that you previously deleted may remain because some backup tools do not properly account for deletions.

Even when this problem happens, it is not usually critical. You just want to be aware of it. Of course, if you've deleted sensitive files in the past, you should check whether a restoration restored them to your computer. (If you intend to permanently and totally destroy a file or set of files, you should also remove it/them from your backups.)

Excluding Files and Folders

Some files and folders should not be restored during a restoration. In truth, they should not have been backed up in the first place unless you imaged a disk, but in many cases, people do back them up anyway.

The following are examples of some such files and folders that can be excluded from typical restorations done on a Windows 10 machine. If you're using backup software, the software likely excluded these files when creating the backup. If you are copying files manually, you may have backed them up.

>> Contents of the Recycle Bin

>> Browser caches (temporary Internet files from web browsers, such as Microsoft Edge or Internet Explorer, Firefox, Chrome, Vivaldi, or Opera)

>> Temporary folders (often called Temp or tem and reside in C:\, in the user directory, or in the data directory of software

>> Temporary files (usually files named *.tmp or *.temp)

>> Operating system swap files (pagefile.sys)

>> Operating system hibernation-mode system image information (hyberfil.sys)

IN-APP BACKUPS

Some applications have built-in backup capabilities that protect you from losing your work if your computer crashes, power fails and you don't have battery power left, and other mishaps.

Some such applications will automatically prompt you to restore documents that would otherwise have been lost due to a system crash or the like. When you start Microsoft Word after an abnormal shutdown of the application, for example, it provides a list of documents that can be autorecovered — sometimes even offering multiple versions of the same document.

>> Backups (unless you want to back up your backups) such as Windows File History backup

>> Operating system files backed up during an operating system upgrade (usually found in C:\Windows.old on Windows computers that have had their operating systems upgraded)

>> Microsoft Outlook cache files (*.ost — note that Outlook local data stores [*.pst] should be backed up; in fact, in many cases they may be the most critical files in a backup)

>> Performance log files in directories called PerfLogs

>> Junk files that users create as personal temporary files to hold information (for example, a text file in which users type a phone number that someone dictated to them, but which the users have since entered into their smartphone directory)

Understanding Archives

The term *archive* has multiple meanings in the world of information technology. I describe the relevant meanings in the following sections.

Multiple files stored within one file

Sometimes multiple files can be stored within a single file. This concept was addressed with the concept of virtual drives earlier in this chapter and in Chapter 13. However, storing multiple files within one file does not necessitate the creation of virtual drives.

You may have seen files with the extension .ZIP, for example. *ZIP files*, as such files are called, are effectively containers that hold one or more compressed files. Storing multiple files in such a container allows for far easier transfer of files (a single ZIP file attached to an email is far easier to manage than 50 small individual files). It also reduces the amount (sometimes significantly) of disk space and Internet bandwidth necessary to store and move the files.

There are other forms of ZIP files that have the file extension .ZIPx. These files have been compressed with even more advanced compression mechanisms than standard .ZIP files, but are not able to be opened by many computers unless special software is installed in addition to the operating system. In addition to ZIP files, there are many other forms of compressed containers of files, and the files containing them have many different extensions, but ZIP is — by far — the type most people will encounter the most often.

If you need to restore files from a ZIP or similar archive, you can either extract all the files from the archive to your primary source, or you can open the archive and copy the individual files to your primary location as you would with any files found in any other folder.

Archive files come in many different formats. Some appear automatically as folders within Windows and Mac file systems and their contents as files and folders within folders. Others require special software to be viewed and extracted from.

Old live data

Sometimes old data is moved off of primary systems and stored elsewhere. Storing old data can improve performance. For example, if a search of all email items means searching through 25 years' worth of messages, the search will take far longer than a search through just the last 3 years. If nearly all relevant results will always be within the last few years, the older emails can be moved to a separate archive where you can access and search them separately if need be.

If you use archiving, factor that in when restoring data. You want to ensure that archives are restored to archives and that you don't accidentally restore archives to the primary data stores.

Also, keep in mind that even if you believe that data is not needed on a regular basis, you may be subject to regulations regarding its storage and safety. There are two primary aspects to this point. First, never delete an archive just because you have restored from it. Some data may be required to be retained for certain periods of time or even, in some cases, indefinitely, and the archive may have been created for that reason. Second, certain data may be subject to security and privacy regulations for as long as it is stored and wherever it is stored — sometimes restoring old data can bring with it security and privacy requirements.

Old versions of files, folders, or backups

The term *archives* is also sometimes used to refer to old versions of files, folders, and backups even if those files are stored on the primary data store. Someone who has ten versions of a contract, for example, that were executed at different points in time, may keep all the Word versions of these documents in an Archive folder. Archiving of this sort can be done for any one or more of many reasons. One common rationale is to avoid accidentally using an old version of a document when the current version should be used.

If you're archiving, factor that in when restoring data. Restore all the archives to their proper locations. You may see multiple copies of the same file being restored; don't assume that that is an error.

Restoring Using Backup Tools

Restoring using backup software is similar to the process of backing up using backup software. To restore using the backup software that was utilized to create the backups from which you are restoring, run the software (in some cases, you may need to install the software onto the machine, rather than run it from a CD or the like) and select Restore.

When you restore, make sure that you select the correct backup version to restore from.

WARNING

Beware of malware masquerading as bogus restoration prompts! Various forms of malware present bogus prompts advising you that your hard drive has suffered some sort of malfunction and that you must run a restore routing to repair data. Only run restores from software that you obtained from a reliable source and that you know that you can trust!

Many modern backup software packages hide the approach used to back up — full, differential, incremental, and so on — from users and instead allow users to pick which version of files they want to restore.

If you're restoring using the specialized backup and recovery software that came with an external hard drive or solid-state device that you use to back up your device, attach the drive, run the software (unless it runs automatically), and follow the prompt to restore.

Such software is usually simple to use; restoration typically works like a simplified version of that done using other backup software (see preceding section).

REMEMBER

Disconnect the drive from the system after performing the restore!

Restoring from a Windows backup

To restore from a Windows backup to the original locations from which the data was backed up, follow these steps:

1. Choose Start ⇨ Settings ⇨ Update & Security ⇨ Backup.

2. Click Restore files from a current backup.

3. In the File System viewer, browse through different versions of your folders and files or type and search for the name of the file you're looking for.

4. Select what you want to restore.

5. Click Restore.

Restoring to a system restore point

Microsoft Windows allows you to restore your system to the way it looked at a specific time at which the system was imaged by the operating system:

1. Click the Start button and select Settings.

2. Choose Control Panel ⇨ System and Maintenance ⇨ Backup and Restore.

3. Click Restore My Files to restore your files or Restore All Users' Files to restore all users files (assuming that you have permissions to do so).

Restoring from a smartphone/tablet backup

Many portable devices come equipped with the ability to automatically sync your data to the cloud, which allows you to restore the data to a new device if your device is lost or stolen. Even devices that do not have such a feature built in almost always can run software that effectively delivers such features for a specific folder tree or drive.

When you start an Android device for the first time after a factory reset, you may be prompted if you want to restore your data. If you are, restoring is pretty straightforward. Answer yes. While the exact routines may vary between devices and manufacturers, other forms of restore generally follow some flavor of the following process:

To restore contacts from an SD card:

1. **Open the Contacts App.**

If there is an import feature, select it and jump to Step 4.

2. **Select Settings from the main menu (or click the Settings icon).**

If you aren't displaying all contacts, you may need to click the Display menu and select All Contacts.

3. **Select Import/Export Contacts (or, if that option is not available, select Manage Contacts and then select Import Contacts on the next screen).**

4. **Select Import from SD Card.**

5. **Review the file name for the backup of the Contact list then click OK.**

Contacts are often backed up (or exported to) VCF files.

To restore media (pictures, videos, and audio files) from an SD card:

1. **Using File Manager, open the SD card.**

2. **Click to turn on check boxes next to the file or files that you want to restore.**

3. **To copy files to the phone's memory, go to the menu and select Copy⇨Internal Storage.**

4. **Select the folder to which you want to copy the files or create the folder and move into it.**

5. **Select Copy Here.**

Restoring from manual file or folder copying backups

To restore from a manual file or folder copy, just copy the file or folder from the backup to the main data store. (If you are overwriting a file or folder, you may receive a warning from the operating system.)

REMEMBER

Disconnect the media on which the backup is located from the main store when you are done.

Utilizing third-party backups of data hosted at third parties

If you utilized the backup capabilities of a third-party provider at which you store data in the cloud or whose cloud-based services you utilize, you may be able to restore your relevant data through an interface provided by the third-party provider.

If you use a third-party cloud-based-service provider and you have not performed backups, you may still be able to restore data. Contact your provider. The provider itself may have backed up the data without notifying you.

TIP

While you should never rely on your cloud service provider performing backups that you did not order, if you are in a jam and contact the provider, you may (or may not) be pleasantly surprised to find out that they do have backups from which you can restore.

Returning Backups to Their Proper Locations

After you restore from a physical backup, you need to return it to its proper location for several reasons:

» You do not want it to be misplaced if you ever need it again.

» You do not want it to be stolen.

» You want to ensure that you do not undermine any storage strategies and procedures intended to keep backups in different locations than the data stores that they back up.

Network storage

Ideally, when restoring from a network-based backup, you should mount the network drive as read-only to prevent possible corruptions of the backup. Furthermore, be sure to disconnect from the network data store once you are done performing the restoration.

TIP

Make sure that whatever mechanism you are using to run the restore (for example, backup software) has the proper network permissions to write to the primary data storage location.

Restoring from a combination of locations

There is no reason to back up to only one location. Restoration, however, typically will utilize backups from only one location at a time. If you do need to restore from backups that are physically situated at more than one location, be extremely careful not to restore the wrong versions of files as some of the files may exist on multiple backups.

Restoring to Non-Original Locations

When it comes to restoring data, some folks choose to restore to locations other than original locations, test the restored data, and then copy or move it to the original locations. Such a strategy reduces the likelihood of writing over good data with bad data, and is recommended when practical and possible.

You can make a bad day worse if you lose some of your data and discover that your backup of the data is corrupted. If you then restore from that backup over your original data and thereby corrupt it, you lose even more of your data.

Never Leave Your Backups Connected

WARNING

After restoring, never leave backup hard drives or solid-state drives connected to the systems or networks that they are backing up. Any future malware infections that attack the primary system can spread to the backups as well. Removing your backup from being connected to the material that it is backing up can make all the difference between quickly recovering from a ransomware attack and having to pay an expensive ransom to a criminal.

If you back up to write-once read-many-times media, such as CD-Rs, it is theoretically safe to leave the backup in an attached drive after you finalize the restoration, but you still should not do so. You want the backup to be readily available in its proper location in case you ever need it in the future.

Restoring from Encrypted Backups

Restoring from encrypted backups is essentially the same as restoring from non-encrypted backups except that you need to unlock the backups prior to restoration.

Backups that are protected by a password obviously need the proper password to be entered. Backups protected by certificates or other more advanced forms of encryption may require that a user possess a physical item or digital certificate in order to restore. In most cases, security conscious home users protect their backups with passwords. If you do so (and you should), do not forget your password.

Testing Backups

Many folks have thought that they had proper backups only to discover when they needed to restore that the backups were corrupted. Hence, testing backups is critical.

While theoretically you should test every backup that you make and test every single item within the backup can be restored, such a scheme is impractical for most people. But do test the first backup that you make with any software, check the auto-recover files the first time that you use Word, and so on.

Some backup software comes with the capability to verify backups — that is, after making a backup, it checks that the original data and data in the backups matches. Running such verification after making a backup adds significant time to the backup process. However, it's well worth running if you can do so because it helps ensure that nothing was improperly recorded or otherwise corrupted during the backup process.

Restoring Cryptocurrency

Restoring cryptocurrency after it is erased from a computer or some other device it was stored on is totally different than any of the restore processes described in this chapter.

Technically speaking, cryptocurrency is tracked on a ledger, not stored anywhere, so the restoration is not done to restore the actual cryptocurrency, but rather to restore the private keys needed in order to control the address (or addresses) within the respective ledger (or ledgers) at which the cryptocurrency is "stored."

Hopefully, if you lost the device on which your cryptocurrency is stored, you have the keys printed on paper that is stored in a safe or safe deposit box. Obtain the paper, and you have your keys. Just don't leave the paper lying around; put it back into the secure location ASAP. (If you keep the paper in a safe deposit box, consider performing the restoration technique at the bank so that you never take the paper out of the safe deposit box area.)

If you store cryptocurrency at an exchange, you can restore your credentials to the exchange through whatever means the exchange allows. Ideally, if you properly backed up your passwords to a secure location, you can just obtain and use them.

For those who use hardware wallets to store the keys to their cryptocurrency, the backup for the wallet device is often a *recovery seed*, which is a list of words that allows the device to re-create the keys needed for the relevant addresses. It is generally accepted that the list of words should be written down on paper and stored in a bank vault and/or safe, not stored electronically.

Booting from a Boot Disk

If you ever need to boot from a boot disk that you created (as might be necessary during a system reset and restore process), boot your system, go into the BIOS settings, and set the boot order to start with the disk from which you want to boot. Then restart the system.

WARNING

When you have booted, be sure to change the system back to boot from the internal hard drive or SSD first rather than the USB drive. Leaving a system with a configuration to boot first from a USB drive is a security risk on multiple accounts; anyone who has physical access to the device can potentially (intentionally or inadvertently) infect it with malware, for example, by installing an infected USB drive and booting from it.

7

Looking toward the Future

Chapter **17**

Pursuing a Cybersecurity Career

With a global shortage of competent cybersecurity professionals, there has never been a better time to pursue a cybersecurity career — especially because the shortage seems to grow with the passage of time. In fact, since the publication of the first edition of this book, the demand for qualified cybersecurity professionals has skyrocketed, fueled in part by the combination of a dramatic upsurge in high-profile, quality-of-life-impacting ransomware attacks, and the sudden and dramatic increase in remote working caused by the COVID-19 pandemic, but that is likely to continue well into the future.

To put it simply, there just aren't enough qualified cybersecurity professionals to fill all of the cybersecurity rolls that need to be filled, and the number of jobs that need to be filled continues to grow faster than the number of people able to fill those jobs. As a result of the insufficient supply of cybersecurity professionals to satisfy the demand for people with relevant skills, compensation packages earned by cybersecurity professionals have been, and continue to be, among the best among technology workers.

In this chapter, you find out about some of the professional roles in the cybersecurity field, potential career paths, and certifications.

Professional Roles in Cybersecurity

Cybersecurity professionals have a wide range of responsibilities that vary quite a bit based on their exact roles, but most, if not all, ultimately work to help either protect data and systems from being compromised, or, in the case of certain government positions, to breach the systems and compromise the data of adversaries.

No one, single career path called "cybersecurity" exists. The profession has many nuances, and different paths along which people's careers can progress. Also, note that the position titles of many jobs that focus on information security in general, or on cybersecurity in particular, sometimes simply say "security" rather than "cybersecurity," "information security," or "IT security."

Security engineer

Security engineers come in multiple types, but the vast majority are hands-on technical folks who build, maintain, and debug information security systems as part of organizational (corporate, government, or nonprofit) projects. Security engineers working in the professional services arms of vendors may also help ensure that software being deployed at clients is done so in a secure fashion.

Security manager

Security managers are typically mid-level management within larger enterprises who have responsibility for some specific area of information security. One security manager, may, for example, be responsible for all of a firm's security training, and another may be responsible for overseeing all of its Internet-facing firewalls. People in security manager positions typically perform less hands-on, technically detailed security activities than do the folks who report to them.

Security director

Security directors are the people who oversee information security for an organization. In smaller firms, the director is usually the de facto chief information security officer (CISO). Larger firms may have several directors responsible for various subsets of the firm's information security program; such folks, in turn, usually report to the CISO.

Chief information security officer (CISO)

The *CISO* is the person responsible for information security throughout an organization. You can think of the CISO role as being that of the chief of staff of the organization's information-security defensive military. The CISO is a senior, C-level management position. Serving as a CISO usually requires significant management knowledge and experience, in addition to an understanding of information security.

Security analyst

Security analysts work to prevent information security breaches. They review not only existing systems, but study emerging threats, new vulnerabilities, and so on in order to ensure that the organization remains safe.

Security architect

Security architects design and oversee the deployment of organizational information security countermeasures. They often have to understand, design, and test complex security infrastructures and regularly serve as the security team member who is involved in projects outside of the security department as well — for example, helping to design the security needed for a custom application that an organization is designing and building or helping to guide networking folks as the latter design various elements of corporate IT networking infrastructure.

Security administrator

Security administrators are hands-on folks who install, configure, operate, manage, and troubleshoot information security countermeasures on behalf of an organization. These folks are the ones to whom nontechnical professionals often refer when they say "I am having a problem and need to call the security guy or security gal."

Security auditor

Security auditors conduct security audits — that is, they check that security policies, procedures, technologies, and so on are working as intended and are effectively and adequately protecting corporate data, systems, and networks.

Cryptographer

Cryptographers are experts at and work with encryption, as used to protect sensitive data. Some cryptographers work to develop encryption systems to protect sensitive data, while others, known as *cryptanalysts,* do the opposite: analyzing encrypted information and encryption systems in order to break the encryption and decrypt the information.

As compared to other information security jobs, cryptographers disproportionately work for government agencies, the military, and in academia. In the United States, many government jobs in cryptography require U.S. citizenship and an active security clearance. Cryptographers are also involved in preparing for the quantum computing era, as discussed in Chapter 18.

Vulnerability assessment analyst

Vulnerability assessment analysts examine computer systems, databases, networks, and other portions of the information infrastructure in search of potential vulnerabilities. The folks working in such positions must have explicit permission to do so. Unlike penetration testers, described in the next section, vulnerability assessors don't typically act as outsiders trying to breach systems, but as insiders who have access to systems and have the ability to examine them in detail from the start.

Ethical hacker

Ethical hackers attempt to attack, penetrate, and otherwise compromise systems and networks on behalf of — and with the explicit permission of — the technologies' owners in order to discover security vulnerabilities that the owners can then fix. Ethical hackers are sometimes referred to as *penetration testers* or *pen-testers*. While many corporations employ their own ethical hackers, a significant number of folks who work in such positions work for consulting companies offering their services to third parties.

Security researcher

Security researchers are forward-looking folks who seek to discover vulnerabilities in existing systems and potential security ramifications of new technologies and other products. They sometimes develop new security models and approaches based on their research.

WARNING

As far as ethics are concerned, and as far as the law in many jurisdictions are concerned, a "security researcher" who hacks an organization without explicit permission from that organization is not a security researcher or an ethical hacker, but simply someone breaking the law.

Offensive hacker

Offensive hackers attempt to break into adversaries' systems to either cripple the systems or steal information. In the United States of America, it is illegal for a business to go on the offensive and attack anyone — including striking back at hackers who are actively trying to penetrate the organization. As such, all legal offensive hacking jobs in the United States are government positions, such as with intelligence agencies and the armed forces. If you enjoy attacking and are not satisfied with just ethical hacking, you may wish to pursue a career with the government or military. Many offensive hacking positions require security clearances.

Software security engineer

Software security engineers integrate security into software as it is designed and developed. They also test the software to make sure it has no vulnerabilities. In some cases, they may be the coders of the software itself.

Software source code security auditor

Software source code security auditors review the source code of programs in search of programming errors, vulnerabilities, violations of corporate policies and standards, regulatory problems, copyright infringement (and, in some cases, patent infringement), and other issues that either must be, or should be, resolved.

Security consultant

There are many different types of *security consultants.* Some, like me, advise corporate executives on security strategy, serve as expert witnesses, or help security companies grow and succeed. Others are hands-on penetration testers. Others may design or operate components of security infrastructure, focusing on specific technologies. When it comes to security consulting, you can find positions in just about every area of information security.

Security expert witness

Security expert witnesses are typically people with many years of experience in the area of security about which they are asked to testify, and who are trusted by a judge to provide "expert opinions" vis-à-vis matters being litigated.

Security specialist

The title *security specialist* is used to refer to people serving in many different types of roles. All the various roles, however, tend to require at least several years of professional experience working in the information security field.

Incident response team member

The *incident response team* consists of the de facto first responders who deal with security incidents. Team members seek to contain and eliminate attacks, while minimizing the damage from them. They also often perform some of the analysis into what happened — sometimes determining that nothing requires any corrective activity. You can think of incident responders as roughly the equivalent of cybersecurity firefighters — they deal with dangerous attacks, but sometimes get called in to verify that there is no fire.

Forensic analyst

Forensic analysts are effectively digital detectives, who, after some sort of computer event, examine data, computers and computing devices, and networks to gather, analyze, and properly preserve evidence and deduce what exactly happened, how it was possible to happen, and who did it. You can think of forensic analysts as roughly the equivalent of law enforcement and insurance company inspectors who analyze properties after a fire to determine what happened and who might be responsible.

Cybersecurity regulations expert

Cybersecurity regulations experts are knowledgeable in the various regulations related to cybersecurity and help ensure that organizations comply with such regulations. They are often, but not always, attorneys who have prior experience working with various compliance-type matters.

Privacy regulations expert

Privacy regulations experts are knowledgeable in the various regulations related to privacy and help ensure that organizations comply with such regulations. They are often, but not always, attorneys who have prior experience working with various compliance-type matters.

Exploring Career Paths

People should consider their long-term goals as they plan their careers. For example, if you're looking to become a CISO, you may want to work in a variety of different hands-on positions, earn an MBA, and pursue promotions and certifications in areas of information security management, while if you want to become a senior architect, you'll likely be better off focusing on promotions into various roles involved in security analysis and design, doing penetration testing, and earning technical degrees. The following sections give examples of some potential career paths.

Career path: Senior security architect

In the United States, security architects typically earn well over $100,000 — and, in some markets, considerably more — making this type of position quite attractive. While every person's career path is unique, one typical framework for becoming a senior security architect might be to follow a career path similar to the following:

1. **Do one of the following:**

   - Earn a bachelor's degree in computer science.

   - Earn a degree in any field and pass an entry-level certification exam in cybersecurity (for example, Security+).

   - Obtain a technical job while without a degree and demonstrate proficiency in the relevant technologies used as part of the job.

2. **Work as a network administrator or systems administrator and gain hands on security experience.**

3. **Obtain a slightly more focused credential (for example, CEH).**

4. **Work as a security administrator — preferably administering a range of different security systems over a period of several years.**

5. **Earn one or more general security certifications (for example, CISSP).**

6. **Become a security architect and gain experience in such a role.**

7. **Earn an advanced security architecture certification (for example, CISSP-ISSAP).**

8. **Become a senior level security architect.**

WARNING

Do not expect to become a senior-level architect overnight; it often takes a decade or more of relevant experience to achieve such a position.

Career path: CISO

In the United States, chief information security officers typically earn $150,000 or more (a lot more in certain industries), but the jobs can be quite stressful (which might explain why many CISOs leave their positions after just a couple of years) — CISOs are responsible for corporate information security — which often involves dealing with emergencies, and often involves few accolades when things go well, but tremendous criticism when things go amiss. While every person's career path is unique, one typical framework for becoming a CISO might be to follow a career path similar to the following:

1. **Earn a bachelor's degree in computer science or in information technology.**

2. **Do one of the following:**

   - Work as a systems analyst, systems engineer, programmer, or in some other related hands-on technical position.

   - Work as a network engineer.

3. **Migrate toward security and work as a security engineer, security analyst, or security consultant — taking on various different roles within an organization, or as a consultant to organizations, thereby exposing oneself to various different areas of information security.**

4. **Obtain general certifications in information security (for example, CISSP).**

5. **Migrate toward management of security by becoming the manager of a security operations team. Ideally, over time, manage multiple information security teams, each that deals with different areas of information security that the others.**

6. **Do one of the following:**

   - Earn a master's degree in cybersecurity (ideally with a focus on information security management).

   - Earn a master's in computer science (ideally with a focus on cybersecurity).

   - Earn a master's in information systems management (ideally, with a focus on information security).

   - Earn an MBA.

7. **Do one of the following:**

   - Become a divisional CISO (de facto or de jure).

   - Become the CISO of a relatively small business or nonprofit organization.

8. **Obtain an advanced information security credential focused on information security management (for example, CISSP-ISSMP).**

9. **Become the CISO of a larger business.**

WARNING

The path to becoming a CISO can easily take a decade, or even decades, depending on the size of the organization in which the CISO serves.

Starting Out in Information Security

Many folks who work in information security began their careers in other areas of information technology. In some cases, the folks were first exposed to the amazing world of cybersecurity while serving in technical positions. In other situations, people took technical jobs not directly tied to information security, but did so with the intent of developing various skills and using the positions as stepping stones into the world of security.

TIP

Jobs in the fields of risk analysis, systems engineering and development, and networking are often good entry points. An email administrator, for example, is likely to learn plenty about email security and possibly also about the architecture of secure network designs and securing servers in general. People developing web-based systems are likely to learn about web security as well as about secure software design. And system and network administrators are going to learn about the security of the items that they are responsible to keep alive and healthy.

Some of the technical jobs that can help prepare you for cybersecurity-related roles include

- Programmer (also known as a coder)
- Software engineer
- Web developer
- Information systems support engineer (technical support hands-on specialist)
- Systems administrator
- Email administrator
- Network administrator
- Database administrator
- Website administrator

Some nontechnical positions can also help prepare people for careers in the nontechnical roles of information security. Here are some examples:

- Auditor
- Law enforcement detective
- Attorney focusing on cybersecurity-related areas of law

>> Attorney focusing on regulatory compliance

>> Attorney focusing on privacy-related areas of law

>> Risk-management analyst

Exploring Popular Certifications

Recognized cybersecurity certifications and, to a lesser degree, certificates showing successful completion of cybersecurity courses, can prove to an employer that your cybersecurity knowledge meets certain standards and help you advance along your desired career path.

Many different information-security certifications are on the market today. Some focus on specific technologies or areas of information security, while others are more broad. While it is beyond the scope of this book to explore each and every possible certification available today, the following are five of the more popular — and better recognized — vendor-neutral certifications that may be ideal for folks relatively early in their cybersecurity careers.

TIP

The competent certifying bodies regularly update their certification requirements and curricula in order to keep up with the constantly changing world of cybersecurity, so always obtain a current study guide when preparing for a certification exam.

CISSP

The Certified Information Systems Security Professional (CISSP) certification, initially launched in 1994, covers a broad range of security-related domains, delving into details in some areas more than in others. It provides employers with the comfort of knowing that workers understand important aspects of more than just one or two areas of information security; as components of information security are often highly interconnected, broad knowledge is valuable, and becomes absolutely necessary as one ascends the information-security management ladder.

The CISSP is intended to be pursued by people with several years of experience in the information security field — in fact, while you can take the CISSP exam without experience, you won't actually receive the credential until you work in the field for the required number of years. As a result, folks possessing CISSP credentials, who always have several years of experience under their belts, often command higher salaries than do both uncertified peers and other counterparts who hold other certifications.

The CISSP credential, issued by the highly regarded (ISC)2 organization, is both vendor neutral and more evergreen than many other certifications. Study materials and training courses for CISSP exam are widely available, and tests are administered in more locations, and on more dates, than are most other, if not all other, cybersecurity certifications. Multiple add-ons to the CISSP are available for those interested in proving their mastery of information security architecture (CISSP-ISSAP), management (CISSP-ISSMP), and engineering (CISSP-ISSEP).

(ISC)2 requires that holders of the CISSP credentials accept to abide by a specific Code of Ethics and that they perform significant continuing education activities in order to maintain their credentials, which must be renewed every three years.

REMEMBER

The CISSP is not intended to test hands-on technical skills — and it does not do so.

People looking to demonstrate mastery of specific technologies or areas of technology — for example, penetration testing, security administration, auditing, and so on — may want to consider pursuing either a more technically focused, general certification or some specific product and skill certifications.

CISM

The well-regarded Certified Information Security Manager (CISM) credential from the Information Systems Audit and Control Association (ISACA) has exploded in popularity since its inception about two decades ago. Emanating from an organization focused on audit and controls, the CISM credential is, generally speaking, a bit more focused than is the CISSP on policies, procedures, and technologies for information security systems management and control, as typically occurs within large enterprises or organizations.

As with the CISSP, to earn a CISM, a candidate must have several years of professional information-security work experience. Despite the differences between the CISSP and CISM — with the former delving deeper into technical topics and the latter doing similarly for management-related topics — the two offerings also significantly overlap. Both are well respected.

CEH

The Certified Ethical Hacker (CEH), offered by the International Council of E-Commerce Consultants (EC-Council), is intended for people with at least two years of professional experience who are intent on establishing their credibility as ethical hackers (in other words, penetration testers).

CEH is a practical exam that tests candidates' skills as related to hacking: from performing reconnaissance and penetrating networks to escalating privileges and stealing data. This exam tests a variety of practical skills, including attack vehicles, such as various types of malware; attack techniques, such as SQL injection; cryptanalysis methods used to undermine encryption; methods of social engineering in order to undermine technical defenses via human error; and how hackers can evade detection by covering their tracks.

EC-Council requires CEH credential holders to acquire a significant number of continuing education credits in order to maintain a CEH credential — something quite important for an exam that tests practical knowledge — especially when you consider how rapidly technologies change in today's world.

Security+

Security+ is a vendor-neutral general cybersecurity certification that can be valuable especially for people early in their careers. It is offered and administered by the well-respected, technology-education nonprofit, CompTIA. While there is, technically speaking, no minimum number of years of professional experience required in order to earn a CompTIA Security+ designation, from a practical perspective, most people will likely find it easier to pass the exam after working in the field, and gaining practical experience, for a year or two.

The Security+ exam typically goes into more technical detail that either the CISSP or the CISM, directly addressing the knowledge needed to perform roles such as those related to entry-level IT auditing, penetration testing, systems administration, network administration, and security administration; hence, CompTIA Security+ is a good early-career certification for many folks. Anyone earning the Security+ designation since 2011 must earn continuing education credits in order to maintain the credential.

GSEC

The Global Information Assurance Certification Security Essentials Certification (GSEC) is the entry-level security certification covering materials in courses run by the SANS Institute, a well-respected information-security training company.

Like Security+, GSEC contains a lot more hands-on practical material than the CISM or CISSP certifications, making this certification more valuable than the aforementioned alternatives in some scenarios and less desirable in others. Despite being marketed as entry-level, the GSEC exam is, generally speaking, regarded as more difficult and comprehensive than the test required to earn a Security+ designation. All GSEC credential holders must show continued professional experience or educational growth in the field of information security in order to maintain their credentials.

Verifiability

The issuers of all major information security credentials provide employers with the ability to verify that a person holds any credentials claimed. For security reasons, such verification may require knowledge of the user's certification identification number, which credential holders typically do not publicize.

WARNING

If you earn a certification, be sure to keep your information in the issuer's database up to date. You do not want to lose your certification because you did not receive a reminder to submit continuing education credits or to pay a maintenance fee.

Ethics

Many security certifications require credential holders to adhere to a code of ethics that not only mandates that holders comply with all relevant laws and government regulations, but also mandates that people act appropriately even in manners that exceed the letter of the law.

WARNING

Be sure to understand such requirements. Losing a credential due to unethical behavior can obviously severely erode the trust that other people place in a person and can inflict all sorts of negative consequences on your career in information security.

Overcoming a Criminal Record

While a criminal record does not prevent someone from obtaining many cybersecurity-related jobs, a criminal record may be an insurmountable barrier when it comes to obtaining certain positions. Anything that prevents someone from obtaining a security clearance, for example, would disqualify that individual from working in certain government and government-contractor roles.

In some cases, the nature, timing, and age at which one committed past crimes may weigh heavily in an employer's decision. Some information-security organizations may be perfectly fine with hiring a reformed, former teenage hacker, for example, but may be averse to hiring someone who was convicted of a violent crime as an adult. Likewise, people who served time in prison for a computer crime they committed two decades ago, but whose records have since been clean, may be viewed quite differently by a potential employer than someone who was just recently released from prison after serving a sentence for a similar crime.

Overcoming Bad Credit

People unfamiliar with the security industry might not think that a poor credit score should be a relevant factor weighed by potential employers, but in some cases, it is. This is because in the case of government positions requiring a clearance, credit reports are reviewed as part of the relevant background check process; clearances can be denied if reviewers fear that the applicant is either not reliable, or is more likely than other people to be tempted to sell information because the applicant is having financial problems.

TIP

If you are applying for a position requiring a clearance and have a poor credit score as a result of factors beyond your control, you may wish to proactively discuss the matter with the relevant parties.

Looking at Other Professions with a Cybersecurity Focus

Besides working directly in cybersecurity, there are many opportunities to work in fields that interface directly with cybersecurity professionals, and which benefit from the global increase in attention to cybersecurity. Lawyers may decide, for example, to specialize in cybersecurity-related laws or on firms' compliance with privacy regulations, and law enforcement personnel may develop expertise in the forensics that are utilized investigating cybercrimes.

The bottom line is that cybersecurity has created, is creating, and will continue to create for the foreseeable future many lucrative professional opportunities for people in multiple fields. You need not be a technical genius to benefit from the discipline's boom. If you find cybersecurity fascinating, you may want to explore the rewarding opportunities that it may offer you.

Chapter **18**

Emerging Technologies Bring New Threats

The world has undergone a radical transformation in recent decades, with the addition of the benefits digital computing power to just about every aspect of human lives. Within the course of just one generation, Western society has evolved from single-purpose film cameras, photocopiers, closed circuit television, and radio-wave based music broadcast receivers to connected devices sporting the features of all these devices and many more — all within a single device.

Simultaneously, new, advanced computing technology models have emerged, creating tremendous potential for even greater incorporation of technology into daily lives. Offerings that would have been considered unrealistic science fiction just a few years ago have become so totally normal and ubiquitously deployed today that children don't always believe adults when the latter explain how much the world has changed in recent years. In fact, not only are transformative changes produced by the advent of new technologies continuing to occur on a near constant basis, but the rate at which they arrive and impact human society seems to be constantly accelerating.

While new technologies and resulting digital transformations of the human experience often provide wonderful benefits, they almost always bring along with them great information security risks. In this chapter, you discover some technologies that are rapidly changing the world and how they are impacting cybersecurity. This list of emerging technologies is by no means comprehensive. Technologies constantly evolve and therefore constantly create new information security challenges.

Relying on the Internet of Things

Not that long ago, the only devices that were connected to the Internet were classic computers — desktops, laptops, and servers. Today, however, is a different world.

From smartphones and security cameras to coffeemakers and exercise equipment, electronic devices of all types now have computers embedded within them, and many of these computers are constantly and perpetually connected to the Internet. The *Internet of Things (IoT)*, as the ecosystem of connected devices is commonly known, has been growing exponentially over the past few years.

And, ironically, while consumers see many such connected devices marketed to them in stores and online, the vast majority of IoT devices are actually components of commercial and industrial systems. In fact, some experts even believe that as much as 99 percent of connected nontraditional-computer devices live in commercial and industrial environments. The reliability of utilities, factories and other manufacturing facilities, hospitals, and most other elements of the backbone of today's economic and social existence depends heavily on having stable, secure technology.

Of course, any and all computing devices — whether classic computers or smart devices of other types — can suffer from vulnerabilities and are potentially hackable, and exploitable for nefarious purposes. Internet-connected cameras, for example, which are designed to allow people to watch homes or businesses from afar, can potentially allow unauthorized hackers to watch the same video feeds. Furthermore, such devices can be commandeered for use in attacking other devices. In fact, in October 2016, the Mirai Botnet attack leveraged many infected IoT devices in unison, and took the popular Dyn DNS service offline. *DNS* is the system that converts human-names for computers into machine-understandable Internet Protocol numeric addresses (IP addresses). As a result of the attack on Dyn, many high-profile websites and services, including Twitter, Netflix, GitHub, and Reddit, suffered de facto outages as people could not reach the sites because the names in the URLs of the sites could not be translated to their proper Internet addresses.

Likewise, IoT creates tremendous potential for serious sabotage. Consider the possible effects of hacking an industrial system involved in the manufacturing of some medical equipment. Could people die if bugs or backdoors were inserted into the code that runs on the computer embedded within the device and then is exploited once the device were in use?

REMEMBER

Hacks undermining systems controlled by connected devices are possible — even when such systems are not connected to the public Internet.

Critical infrastructure risks

One special case of IoT risks are systems (including control systems) at providers of national critical infrastructure. Ransomware attacks in May 2021, for example, caused both fuel and meat shortages in parts of the United States one after the other, after a fuel pipeline operator and a meat processing company were both independently forced to go offline and temporarily halt operations.

REMEMBER

Hacking is not just about money or data — it can produce tremendous impacts on the humane experience. Sometimes, even killing people.

Could you see hackers demanding ransoms in exchange for not releasing video from people's home security cameras? Could you see hackers demanding ransoms in exchange for not causing people's refrigerators to turn off and ruin their food — or even find criminals who turn off fridges when people leave for work and turn them on before the victims return home, causing food to spoil in an effort to poison targeted individuals?

STUXNET

One of the first and most significant attacks on connected devices to date was Stuxnet. Sometime in 2009 or 2010, malware now known as Stuxnet crippled an Iranian uranium refinement facility that was suspected by Western analysts of then having been used by Iran to enrich uranium for potential use in building nuclear weapons. The sophisticated cyberattack is widely believed to have been launched by a joint team of cyberwarriors from the United States and Israel.

Stuxnet targeted the Siemens industrial control systems that the Iranians were using to operate and manage uranium-refining centrifuges. The malware caused the control systems to send improper instructions to the centrifuges while reporting that everything was running properly. The cyberattack is believed to have both inappropriately increased and decreased the speed of centrifuges. The inappropriate changes of speed caused the centrifuges' aluminum tubes to suffer from unexpected stress and to expand as a result, eventually causing them to come in contact with other portions of the machine and severely damage the device. There is little doubt that Stuxnet's operational success will motivate other cyberwarriors to launch similar types of attacks in the future.

Computers on wheels: modern cars

On that note, consider that today's cars are highly computerized — digital displays may be the obvious visible sign of changes since the era of manual gauges, but underneath the hood (pun intended), there is far more that is hackable. In fact, modern vehicles have computer systems involved with nearly all of their systems.

Nearly every vehicle made in within the past decade are effectively smart cars. And as they become more common, could criminals potentially hack them and cause crashes? Or blackmail people into paying ransoms in exchange for not crashing their cars? Before answering that question, consider that security researchers have demonstrated on more than one occasion how hackers can take control of some vehicles and cause brakes to stop working.

Compound that fact with the increasing availability of various self-driving functions — from cruise control to self-parking to highway self-driving to fully self-driving — all of which are becoming more and more common with the passage of time. What will the level of danger be when fully self-driving cars and self-driving trucks are the norm? It should be pretty clear that the stakes and risks to human life and welfare will only grow as technology advances.

REMEMBER

IoT opens up a world of possibilities. It also dramatically grows the attack surface that criminals can exploit and increases the stakes if cybersecurity is not properly maintained.

Using Cryptocurrencies and Blockchain

A *cryptocurrency* is a digital asset (sometimes thought of as a digital currency) designed to work as a medium of exchange that uses various aspects of cryptography to control the creation of units, verify the accuracy of transactions, and secure financial transactions.

Modern cryptocurrencies allow parties who do not trust one another to interact and conduct business without the need for a trusted third party. Cryptocurrencies utilize *blockchain technology* — that is, their transactions are recoded on a distributed ledger whose integrity is protected through the use of multiple techniques that are supposed to ensure that only accurate transactions will be respected by others viewing a copy of the ledger.

Because cryptocurrencies are tracked via lists of transactions in ledgers, there are technically no cryptocurrency wallets. The currency is virtual and not stored anywhere, even electronically. Rather, cryptocurrency owners are the parties who control the various addresses on the ledger that have cryptocurrency associated with them after performing all the transactions to date on the ledger.

For example, if Address 1 has 10 units of a cryptocurrency and Address 2 has 5 units of a cryptocurrency and a transaction is recorded showing that Address 1 sent 1 unit of cryptocurrency to Address 2, the result is that Address 1 has 9 units of cryptocurrency and Address 2 has 6 units of cryptocurrency.

To ensure that only legitimate owners of cryptocurrency can send money from their addresses, cryptocurrencies typically utilize a sophisticated implementation of PKI where every address has its own public-private key pair, with the owner being the only one to possess the private key. Sending cryptocurrency from an address requires the signing of the outgoing transaction with its associated private key.

Because anyone with knowledge of the private key associated with a particular ledger address can steal whatever amount of cryptocurrency is recorded in the ledger as belonging to that address, and because cryptocurrencies are both liquid and difficult to track back to their real-life human or organizational owners, criminals often attempt to steal cryptocurrencies via hacking. If a crook obtains the private key to a cryptocurrency address from someone's computer, the crook can quickly and easily transfer the victim's cryptocurrency to another address that the criminal controls. In fact, if the criminal obtains the key in any way, they can steal the cryptocurrency without hacking anything. All the criminal has to do is issue a transaction sending the money to some other address and sign the transaction with the private key.

Because cryptocurrencies are not managed centrally, even if such a theft is detected, the legitimate owner has little hope of recovering their money. Reversing a transaction would, in most cases, require an unachievable consensus of a majority of operators within the cryptocurrency's ecosystem and is exceedingly unlikely to happen unless enough cryptocurrency was stolen to undermine the integrity of the entire currency. Even in such cases, the forking of a new cryptocurrency may be required to achieve such a reversal, and many operators will still likely reject the undoing of transactions as being an even greater threat to the integrity of the cryptocurrency than is a major theft.

Besides providing hackers with an easy way to steal money, cryptocurrencies have also facilitated other forms of cybercrimes. Most ransoms demanded by ransomware, for example, are required to be paid in cryptocurrency. In fact, cryptocurrency is the lifeblood of ransomware. Unlike payments made by wire transfer or credit card, smartly made cryptocurrency payments are exceedingly hard to trace back to real life people and are effectively irreversible once a transaction has settled.

Likewise, criminals have the ability to *mine* cryptocurrency — that is, to perform various complex calculations needed to both settle cryptocurrency transactions and create new units of the cryptocurrency — by stealing processing power from others. Cryptomining malware, for example, surreptitiously commandeers infected computers' CPU cycles to perform such calculations and, when new units of cryptocurrency are generated, transfers control of them to the criminals operating the malware. Cryptocurrency mining provides a simple way for criminals to monetize their hacking. Hacked computers can thus be used to "print money" without the involvement of victims as is typically needed for many other forms of monetization, such as ransomware.

Criminals have also benefited from the dramatic rise in the value of cryptocurrency. For example, those who accepted Bitcoin as payment for ransomware ransoms several years ago and who did not entirely cash out their cryptocurrency enjoyed amazing returns — sometimes growing their dollar-value holdings by a factor of hundreds or even thousands. Some such criminals likely cashed out a portion of their cryptocurrencies during the market frenzies of the past few years, and may be sitting on small fortunes that they are now investing in creating new cybercrime technologies.

TIP

The blockchain technology that serves as the underlying engine that powers cryptocurrencies also has potential uses within cybersecurity countermeasures. A distributed database may prove to be a better way to store information about backup servers and redundant capabilities than are existing structures because the distributed nature dramatically increases the number of points of failure necessary to take down the entire system. Likewise, distributed defenses against DDoS (distributed denial-of-service) attacks may prove to be both more effective and cost efficient than the present model of using single massive infrastructures to fight such attacks.

Blockchain also offers a way to create transparent records of transactions or of activities — transactions that are viewable by anyone, but not modifiable by anyone, and with only authorized parties able to create appropriate new transactions.

Cloud-Based Applications and Data

A generation ago, people, businesses, and organizations all stored all of their data (or close to it) on their own storage devices located within their own facilities, or on the hard drives of their own laptops. Applications were nearly always run from local machines or from servers located on local networks and were not accessible from other places across the Internet.

The world of computing, however, has changed. Dramatically.

The advent of cloud computing has meant that large amounts of data are stored by third-party providers, and apps are run from servers managed by third parties. Of course, such changes impact cybersecurity in a big way.

REMEMBER

There is no magic "cloud." When you store data "in the cloud," you are simply storing it on someone else's Internet-accessible server.

As data is no longer located strictly "within the castle walls," but rather, often situated in locations that are totally not under the control of the data's owners, precautions have to be taken in selecting vendors and in encrypting the data so that the hosting providers themselves (or any hackers that breach such providers) cannot access the data. That said, keep in mind that major providers of cloud storage or popular cloud apps — even if they are known to have suffered from various cybersecurity vulnerabilities and/or breaches — typically secure their operations, apps, and data far better than well over 99 percent of individuals.

When compared with most individuals, major cloud providers provide *much* better cybersecurity. For example, while Google provides encryption for files stored in Google Drives, Google maintains the decryption keys to such data. But users of Drive can deploy inexpensive apps such as BoxCrypt, Cryptomator, and/or others to provide additional encryption that Google cannot easily undo.

WARNING

Contingencies need to be established in case a provider temporarily goes down, or in some cases, even out of business altogether. If you rely on a cloud based application to read, write, and edit documents, for example, and your locality is expecting a potential Internet-connection-threatening weather event, you should make sure that you have local copies/caches available of any documents that you might need to edit as well as the local version of apps to do so.

Optimizing Artificial Intelligence

"Alexa."

"Siri."

"Hey, Google."

We all know to "who" these names refer, yet, do we really know what artificial intelligence (AI) is? *Artificial intelligence*, technically speaking, refers to the ability of an electronic system to perceive its environment and take actions that maximize its likelihood of achieving its goals, even without prior knowledge about the specifics of the environment and the situation in which it finds itself.

If that definition sounds complicated, it is. The definition of AI from a practical perspective seems to be a moving target. Concepts and systems that were considered to be forms of AI a decade or two ago — for example facial recognition technologies — are often treated as classic computer systems today. Today, most people use the term artificial intelligence to refer to computer systems that learn — that is, they mimic the way that humans learn from past experiences to take specific courses of action when encountering a new experience. Instead of being preprogrammed to act based on a set of specific rules, artificially intelligent systems look at sets of data to create their own sets of generalized rules and make decisions accordingly. The systems then optimize their own rules as they encounter more data and see the effects of applying their rules to that data.

AI is likely to ultimately transform the human experience at least as much as did the Industrial Revolution. The Industrial Revolution, of course, replaced human muscles with machines — the latter proving to be faster, more accurate, less prone to becoming tired or sick, and less costly than the former. AI is the replacement of human brains with computer thinking — and it will eventually also prove to be much faster, more accurate, and less prone to illness or sleepiness than any biological mind.

The era of AI has several major impacts on cybersecurity:

>> An increased need for cybersecurity

>> The use of AI as a security tool

>> The use of AI as a hacking tool

Increased need for cybersecurity

As artificially intelligent systems become increasingly common, the need for strong cybersecurity grows dramatically. Computer systems can make increasingly important decisions without the involvement of humans, which means that the negative consequences of not adequately securing computer systems could increase dramatically. Imagine if a hospital deployed an artificially system to analyze medical images and report diagnoses. If such a system or its data were hacked, incorrect reports could occur and cause people to suffer or even die. Unfortunately, such a problem is no longer theoretical (see the nearby sidebar).

Of course, such research represents just the tip of the iceberg. Industrial AI systems can be manipulated to alter products in ways that increase danger, and artificially intelligent transportation technology designed to optimize routes and improve safety could be fed data that increase danger or create unnecessary delays.

AI CAN ALREADY FALSIFY MRI IMAGES AND PRODUCE INCORRECT MRI RESULTS

In 2019, Israeli researchers found that AI technology could successfully modify medical images in such a way that it would consistently trick both radiologists and AI systems designed to diagnose medical conditions based on scans, including reporting cancer when none existed and overlooking it when it did. Even after the researchers told the radiologists involved that AI was being used to manipulate the scan images, the radiologists were still unable to provide correct diagnoses and incorrectly found cancer in 60 percent of the normal scans to which tumors had been artificially added and did not find cancer in 87 percent of the scans from which the AI had digitally removed tumors.

Furthermore, because evildoers can undermine the integrity of artificially intelligent systems without hacking the systems but rather by simply introducing hard-to-find small changes into large data sets and because the decisions made by artificially intelligent systems are not based on predefined rules known to the humans who create the system, protecting all elements of such systems becomes critical. Once problems are introduced, humans and machines will likely not be able to find them or even know that something is amiss.

The bottom line is that for AI projects to be successful, they must include heavy-duty cybersecurity.

Use as a cybersecurity tool

One of the biggest challenges facing cybersecurity operations professionals today is that it is practically impossible to dedicate sufficient time to analyze and act on all alerts produced by cybersecurity technologies. One of the first major uses for AI in the realm of cybersecurity is as an agent that helps prioritize alerts. This agent first learns how systems are typically used and what types of activities are anomalous, as well as which old alerts actually indicated serious issues rather than benign activities or minor issues. Future iterations of such artificially intelligent systems will likely involve the AI itself actually acting upon the alerts rather than referring them to humans.

Use as a hacking tool

AI is not just a defensive tool; it can also be a powerful weapon in the hands of attackers. For obvious reasons, I don't provide details in this book as to how to use AI to launch advanced attacks, but I do discuss several general examples.

AI systems can, for example, be used to scan and analyze other systems in order to find programming errors and configuration mistakes. AI systems may also be used to analyze organization charts, social media, corporate websites, press releases, and so on in order to design — and perhaps even implement — maximally effective social engineering attacks.

AI can also be utilized to undermine authentication systems. For example, a system that is given a recording of a person saying many different things may be able to trick a voice-based authentication system by mimicking the relevant human — even if the authentication system asks the AI to enunciate words for which the AI has no recording of the human speaking.

REMEMBER

The bottom line is that when it comes to the use of AI as a cybersecurity tool, it's likely a spy-versus-spy battle between cyberattackers and cyberdefenders, with each trying to build better and better AIs so as to defeat one another.

Where Was This Laptop Really Made? Supply Chain Risks

Over the past few years, supply chain risks have emerged in both hardware and software. *Supply chain risks* refer to the risks that one or more parties along the path of development of an item may modify that item in a way that introduces risks down the line. If a network switch is made by a Chinese manufacturer closely associated with the communist regime in the People's Republic of China, for example, there may be concerns that someone at the factory loaded malware on the computer's bootable SSD or hard drive, or inserted a physical "bug" into the device.

Likewise, hackers can — and have — breached systems that provide users with legitimate software updates and added malware to the distribution sets so that people updating their devices inadvertently installed spyware.

While various government agencies have begun to act against some risky manufacturers, the reality remains that chips and other components within nearly all modern computers are sourced from providers operating factories in questionable locations. Likewise, many modern pieces of software include code from libraries written by third parties — and those codebases themselves might include code from other libraries. As such, it is often not simple to determine from where *all* elements within a device or piece of software originally came, making the challenge of ensuring supply chain security quite complex.

Nothing Is Trustworthy: Zero Trust

Zero trust refers to a security model that has become an increasingly popular approach to information security. Instead of guarding the digital perimeter of an entity through the use, for example, of cybersecurity countermeasures and then trusting computers located within the perimeter, in the case of a zero trust approach, an individual or an organization deems all devices not to be inherently trusted. The same holds true for users — they are not inherently trusted either. Accessing a system from an internal device and a valid account is not enough to prove to the respective system that the request should be honored.

Effectively, zero trust assumes that organizational networks and devices may have been compromised by unauthorized parties, and that legitimate users may be anywhere, so every single request for a resource must be properly authenticated and authorized, regardless of where the request is made or by whom, and regardless of whether the request originated from a human using a device or from a bot or other computer process running on its own.

In addition, in a zero trust model, the default is not to provide authorization for resources. Authorization should only be granted if the party requesting the resource has an actual, legitimate need for that resource.

The zero trust model has become increasingly popular as technological and societal changes, such as cloud computing, remote workforces, supply chain risks, the proliferation of BYOD (bring your own device), modern cyberattack techniques, and vulnerabilities in IoT devices, have rendered impotent the old model of fortifying the perimeter. Today, there simply rarely is any true, well-defined perimeter.

Genius Computers Are Coming: Quantum Supremacy

While today's encryption algorithms seem quite powerful, most are in danger of soon becoming impotent. In fact, nearly every piece of data that is presently protected through the use of encryption may become vulnerable as quantum computers advance and become more prevalent.

Quantum computers are devices that leverage advanced physics to perform computing functions in ways that are simply not achievable using the types of electronic computers with which we are all familiar. Quantum physics is not a simple matter, and the details of how quantum computers physically work is way beyond the scope of this book.

For our purposes, think of quantum computers as machines that are able to leverage advanced physics in order to create huge multi-dimensional representations of data that the devices can then instantly analyze simultaneously in order to find desired values within the massive representations, rather than by evaluating possible options one by one as do today's computers. Instead of spending years trying every possible decryption key one by one, quantum computers will soon be sufficiently advances as to be able to simultaneously look for a working decryption key within an astronomical number of possibilities.

How fast can quantum devices perform advanced math requiring the analysis of immense amounts of data? Google's early-generation quantum computer, Sycamore, recently performed a complex mathematical calculation in 200 seconds that various groups of experts estimate would have taken the world's then most powerful classic supercomputer, IBM Summit, somewhere between several days and 10,000 years to complete. That's 200 seconds for an early version of a quantum computer versus days, years, or centuries for the world's most powerful supercomputer.

Quantum computers may transform brute-force attempts at cracking encryption from processes that can take many lifetimes to perform into yielding instant results.

To address this risk, quantum-safe encryption algorithms are being developed, but deployment will take time and money, as there is so much to replace and upgrade. And, even that won't fully solve the problem.

REMEMBER

It is not just data created in the future that is at risk — any data backups or communication sessions conducted across the Internet that have been captured by unauthorized parties and stored — could be exposed in the future if the sole protection that they benefit from now is encryption.

Experiencing Virtual Reality

Virtual reality refers to an experience taking place within a computer-generated reality rather than within the real world. Current virtual reality (VR) technology typically requires users to wear some sort of headset that displays images to the user and that blocks the user's vision of the real world. (In some cases, in lieu of wearing a headset, a user enters a special room equipped with a projector or multiple projectors, which achieves a similar effect.) Those images, combined with sounds and, in some cases, physical movements and other human-sensible experiences, cause the user to experience the virtual environment as if they were actually physically present in it. A person using VR equipment can usually move, look, and interact with the virtual world.

VR typically incorporates at least visual and audio components, but may also deliver vibrations and other sensory experiences. Even without additional sensory information, a human may experience sensations because the human brain often interprets what it sees and hears in a virtual environment as if it were real. For example, people riding a roller coaster in a virtual environment may feel their stomachs drop when the roller coaster makes a sharp drop, even though, in reality, they are not moving.

Immersive virtual environments can be similar to or completely different from what a person would experience in the real world. Popular applications of VR already include tourism (for example, walking through an art museum without actually being there), entertainment (first-person vantage point gaming), and educational purposes (virtual dissection).

VR systems, of course, are computer-based and, as a result, have many of the same security issues as other computer-based systems. But virtual reality also introduces many new security and privacy concerns:

>> Can someone hack VR ecosystems and launch visual attacks that trigger seizures or headaches? (Flashing strobe lights in various cartoons and other displays have been known to cause seizures.)

>> Can others make decisions about your physical abilities based on your performance in VR applications? Can governments, for example, refuse to issue drivers' licenses to people who perform poorly in VR driving games? Can auto insurance companies surreptitiously gather data about people's driving habits in the VR world and use it to selectively raise rates?

>> Can hackers digitally vandalize a virtual environment — substituting obscene content for art, for example, in a museum offering virtual tours?

>> Can hackers impersonate an authority figure, such as a teacher in a virtual classroom, by creating an avatar that looks similar to one used by that person and thereby trick other users into taking harmful actions (for example, by asking people for the answers to their tests, which the crooks then steal and pass off as their own to the real teacher)?

>> Likewise, can hackers impersonate a coworker or family member and thereby obtain and abuse sensitive information?

>> Can hackers modify virtual worlds in ways that earn them money in the real world — for example, by adding tolls to enter various places?

>> Can hackers steal virtual currency used in various virtual worlds?

>> Can hackers usurp control over a user's experience to see what they experience or even to modify it?

In theory, when it comes to new risks created by virtual reality, I can compile a list that would take up an entire book — and time will certainly tell which risks emerge as real-world problems.

Transforming Experiences with Augmented Reality

Augmented reality refers to technology in which computer-generated images sounds, smells, movements, and/or other sensory material are superimposed onto a user's experience of the real world, transforming the user's experience into a composite of both actual and artificial elements. Augmented reality (AR) technology can both add elements to a user's experience — for example, showing a user the name of a person above the person's head as that individual approaches the user — as well as remove or mask elements, such as converting Nazi flags into black rectangles with the words "Defeat hate" written on them.

AR is likely to become a major part of modern life over the next decade. It will introduce many of the risks that virtual reality does, as well as risks associated with the merging of real and virtual worlds, such as configuring systems to improperly associated various elements in the real world with virtual data.

As with all emerging technologies, time will tell. If you decide to invest in AR or VR technology, be sure to understand any relevant security issues.

POKÉMON GO

Pokémon Go is an augmented reality game for mobile devices that was first released in July 2016 as a result of a collaboration between Niantic, Nintendo, and The Pokémon Company. The game, which is free to play but offers in-game items for a fee, became an immediate hit and was downloaded more than half a billion times by the end of 2016. It uses a mobile device's GPS to locate, capture, battle, and train virtual creatures, called Pokémon, which appear on the device's screen within the context of the player's real-world location, superimposed on the image that would result if players were aiming their camera at some area within the field of view.

As of early 2019, the game is believed to have been downloaded more than 1 billion times and to have generated more than $3 billion in worldwide revenue.

8

The Part of Tens

IN THIS PART . . .

Find out how you can improve your cybersecurity without breaking the bank.

Learn from others' mistakes.

Learn when and how to safely use extremely convenient public Wi-Fi.

Chapter **19**

Ten Ways to Improve Your Cybersecurity without Spending a Fortune

N ot all security improvements require a large outlay of cash. In fact, many of the things you can do to greatly improve your security are free and require little effort. In this chapter, you discover ten ways you can quickly improve your cybersecurity without spending a lot of money.

Understand That You Are a Target

TIP

Attitude may be the most important element of keeping yourself cyber-safe. People who believe that hackers want to breach their computers, smartphones, and other smart devices, and that criminals want to steal their data, act differently than people who do not grasp the true nature of the threat.

Internalizing today's reality will help introduce into you a healthy level of skepticism, as well as impact your attitude and behavior around cybersecurity in numerous other positive ways — many of which you may not even consciously notice.

For example, if you believe that you're a target of cyberattackers, you're less likely to blindly trust that emails that you receive from your bank were actually sent by the bank, and as such, you're less likely to fall prey to phishing scams than are people who believe that they are not targets. You may feel that you already know not to trust such emails, but what if an email were to arrive was from your boss and instruct you to ship a laptop to some address? Or you heard your boss's voice tell you that you should do so — and didn't think for a moment about that fact that criminals know how to make targeted deep fakes that can impersonate voices?

People who believe that criminals are after their passwords and PINs are also more likely to better protect these sensitive pieces of data than are people who believe that crooks "have no reason to want" their data.

Use Security Software

All computer devices (laptops, phones, tablets, and so on) that house sensitive information or that will be attached to networks with other devices do need security software. Several popular, inexpensive packages include antivirus, firewall, antispam, and other beneficial technologies.

Portable devices should have tracking and remote wipe capabilities and software optimized for mobile systems; remember to enable such features as soon as you get the device. Many phones come with security software preinstalled by providers — make sure you enable and use it.

Encrypt Sensitive Information

Store all sensitive data in an encrypted format. If you have doubts as to whether something is sensitive enough to warrant encryption, it probably does, so err on the side of caution and encrypt.

Encryption is built in to many versions of Windows, and plenty of free encryption tools are available as well. It is amazing how much sensitive data that has been compromised could have remained secure if the parties from which it was stolen had used free encryption tools.

Also, never transmit sensitive information unless it is encrypted. Never enter sensitive information to any website if the site is not using TLS encryption (this type of encryption is sometimes called SSL, even though the SSL protocol was replaced by TLS many years ago), as evidenced by the page loading with HTTPS, and not HTTP, a difference easily seen by looking at the URL line of a web browser. Encryption involves complex mathematical algorithms, but you don't need to know any of the details in order to utilize and benefit from encryption.

TIP

Be aware, however, that the era of quantum computing — that is, of new types of computers that use quantum physics to store data and perform calculations rather than bits consisting of strictly a 0 or 1 — is likely to render many of today's encryption mechanisms obsolete and cause data encrypted with today's technologies to become vulnerable to exposure. How soon such so-called "quantum supremacy" arrives is unknown, and experts have wildly different opinions as to how many years it will take. So pay attention to updates offered by vendors over the next few years that ensure that their products are "quantum safe."

Also be aware of the two major families of encryption algorithms that are used today (in addition to the ostensibly "quantum safe" encryption mechanisms that are emerging):

» **Symmetric:** You use the same secret key to encrypt and decrypt.

» **Asymmetric:** You use one secret key to encrypt and another to decrypt. (This is the type that quantum computing most threatens.)

Most simple encryption tools utilize symmetric encryption, and all you need to remember is a password to decrypt your data. Throughout the course of your professional career, however, you may encounter various asymmetric systems that require you to establish both a public key and a private key. The public key is shared with the world, and the private key is kept secret. Asymmetric encryption helps with sending data:

» If you want to send information to John so that only John can read it, encrypt the data with John's public key so that only John can read it, because he is the only party who has John's private key.

» If you want to send information to John and want John to know that you sent it, encrypt the data with your own private key and therefore, John will decrypt it with your public key and know that you sent it because only you have the private key that goes along with your public key.

» If you want to send information to John in a format that only John can read and in a format that John will know that you sent it, encrypt with both your own private key and john's public keys.

In reality, because asymmetric is processor intensive, it is rarely used for encrypting entire conversations, but rather it is utilized to encrypt special *session keys* —that is, to convey to the parties to a conversation the keys that they need for symmetric encryption. Subsequent communications between the parties are conducted using symmetric encryption using the keys securely communicated using asymmetric encryption.

Back Up Often

Back up often enough that if something goes wrong, you won't panic about how much data you lost because your last backup was days ago.

TIP

Here is the general rule: If you're not sure whether you're backing up often enough, you probably aren't. No matter how convenient doing so may seem, do not keep your backups attached to your computer or even to your computer network (see Chapter 14). If you do keep backups attached in such a fashion, you run a serious risk that if ransomware or other malware somehow manages to infect your network, it can corrupt the backups as well, which would undermine the reason for backing up in the first place! This risk is not theoretical. Many ransomware victims who were calm upon initially discovering that they had been breached because they had recently backed up their device panicked when they discovered that the backups had also been corrupted by the ransomware!

Ideally, you should have backups stored both onsite and offsite. Onsite storage of backups lets you restore quickly. Offsite storage of backups helps ensure that backups are available even when a site becomes inaccessible or something else devastates all the computer equipment and digital data at a particular site. And make sure you regularly test that your backups actually work. As many parties have sadly learned the hard way, backing up is worthless if you can't actually restore from your backups.

Do Not Share Login Credentials

Every person accessing an important system should have their own login credentials. Ideally, you should not share passwords for online banking, email, social media, and so on, with your children or significant other — get everyone their own login.

REMEMBER

Implementing such a scheme not only improves the ability to track down the source of problems if they occur, but perhaps more important in the case of families, creates a much greater sense of responsibility and encourages people to better protect their passwords.

Use Proper Authentication

You have likely heard the conventional wisdom to use complex passwords for all systems, but do not overdo it. If using too many complex passwords is causing you to reuse passwords on multiple sensitive systems or to write down passwords in insecure locations, consider other strategies for forming your passwords, such as combining words, numbers, and proper names, such as custard4tennis6Steinberg. See Chapter 8 for more details.

TIP

For extremely sensitive systems, if stronger forms of authentication, such as multifactor authentication, are available, take advantage of the offerings and use them.

For systems to which passwords do not really matter — such as when accounts are required only so that the site operator can track you, but not to secure anything of value to you — consider using weak, easy-to-remember passwords. Don't waste brainpower where it does not need to be used. You can even reuse such passwords on multiple such sites, but of course, never use such passwords on any sites where security is actually of concern to you.

Alternatively, use a password manager, but ideally do not use a password manager for your most sensitive passwords — keep them in your head — because you don't want to put all your eggs in one basket. If you must write such passwords down for other people to use in case something happened to you, write them down on paper and store them in a fire-and-water-resistant bag in a safe deposit box or safe.

Use Social Media Wisely

Oversharing on social media posts has caused, and continues to cause, many problems, such as leaking sensitive information, violating compliance rules, and assisting criminals to carry out both cyber and physical attacks. Be sure that your phone does not autocorrect anything to sensitive material when posting. Also, don't accidentally cut and paste anything sensitive into a social media window. You would probably be amazed at how often errors of this type occur.

Segregate Internet Access

Nearly all modern Wi-Fi routers allow you to run two or more networks. If your router offers you such a feature, use it. If you work from home, for example, consider connecting your laptop to the Internet via a different Wi-Fi network than the one that your children use to browse the web and play video games. As discussed in Chapter 4, look for the Guest feature in your router's configuration pages — that is where you will typically find the ability to set up the second network (often referred to as the Guest network). Many people use the Guest network not only for guests, but also for their children who connect devices to the Internet.

Use Public Wi-Fi Safely (Or Better Yet, Don't Use It!)

While public Wi-Fi is a great convenience that most people utilize regularly, it also creates serious cybersecurity risks. As such, if your phone allows you to create an Internet hotspot to which your other devices can connect, use that method of connecting to the Internet and forgo the use of all public Wi-Fi. Sometimes, however, using a personal hotspot is impossible — you may be located underground, for example, or in some other area to which cellular signals do not penetrate.

Cybersecurity practitioners who preach that people should refrain from using public Wi-Fi in such situations are about as likely to succeed in their effort as they would be if they instructed people to abandon insecure computers and revert back to using typewriters. In such situations, therefore, if you absolutely must connect to public Wi-Fi, it is important that you already know how to use public Wi-Fi safely and understand multiple techniques for improving your odds of defending yourself against mischievous parties (see Chapter 7) and do so before you find yourself needing to connect. So check out Chapter 21 before you need to use it.

Hire a Pro

Especially if you're starting or running a small business, getting expert advice can be a wise investment. An information-security professional can assist you in designing and implementing your approach to cybersecurity. The minimal cost of a small amount of professional help may pay for itself many times over in terms of time, money, and aggravation saved down the road.

REMEMBER

The folks who will attack you — cybercriminals and other hackers — have, and utilize, technical expertise. If you'd hire a lawyer if you were charged with a crime, go to a doctor if you suffered a serious injury, or hire an accountant if the IRS notified you that it was auditing you, hire a cybersecurity pro.

Chapter **20**

Ten (or So) Lessons from Major Cybersecurity Breaches

Learning from the experiences of others can save people from unnecessary pain and suffering. In this chapter, I discuss seven breaches that teach several important lessons. I specifically chose these breaches because they directly impacted either myself or a member of my family and, due to the breaches' respective magnitudes, are likely to have impacted you and yours as well.

Marriott

In November 2018, Marriott International disclosed that hackers had breached systems belonging to the Starwood hotel chain as far back as 2014 and had remained in the systems until September 2018 — about two years after Marriott acquired Starwood.

At the time of the disclosure, Marriott estimated that the breach may have impacted as many as 500 million customers and that the data compromised ranged from just the name and contact information for some customers to far more detailed data (including passport numbers, travel data, frequent traveler numbers, and so on) for others. Marriott also estimated that 100 million people's credit card numbers — along with expiration dates, but without CVC codes — were compromised, but that data was in an encrypted database, and Marriott saw no clear indication that the hackers who had obtained the data were able to decrypt it.

Evidence suggests that the attack against Marriott was carried out by a Chinese group affiliated with the Chinese government and was launched in an effort to gather data on U.S. citizens. If such an attribution is correct, the Marriott breach would likely be the largest known breach to date by a nation-state funded organization of personal, civilian data.

In July 2019, the Information Commissioner's Office of the United Kingdom (ICO) announced that it intended to impose a fine of the equivalent of $123 million on Marriott as a penalty for the failure to properly protect consumer data as mandated by the European Union's General Data Protection Regulation (GDPR). (See Chapter 10 for more on GDPR.) According to an SEC filing by Marriott, the firm intends to appeal the penalty once the fine is formally filed, which had not happened at the time of writing.

While many lessons can be learned from the Marriott incident, two stand out:

>> **When anyone acquires a company and its information infrastructure, a thorough cybersecurity audit needs performed.** Vulnerabilities or active hackers within the acquired firm can become a headache to the new owner, and government regulators may even seek to hold the acquiring company responsible for the failures of a firm that it acquires.

As the UK's Information Commissioner, Elizabeth Denham, put it: "The GDPR makes it clear that organizations must be accountable for the personal data they hold. This can include carrying out proper due diligence when making a corporate acquisition, and putting in place proper accountability measures to assess not only what personal data has been acquired, but also how it is protected."

Don't rely on acquired companies to disclose cybersecurity problems; they may not be aware of potentially serious issues.

REMEMBER

>> **From an intelligence perspective, foreign governments — especially those engaged in competition with the United States and other Western powers — value data about civilians.** Such governments may seek to find and use information to blackmail folks into spying, look for people with

financial pressure who may be amenable to accepting money in exchange for illegal services, and so on. Remember, with the cost of data storage so low, and the arrival of encryption-busting quantum computing on the horizon, foreign governments may be storing huge amounts of encrypted data as well with the hope of decrypting it in the not-so-distant future. Because businesses and people typically do not encrypt most of their data, any data that is encrypted is likely to be of relative importance, so, any party that believes that it will be able to decrypt and view the contents now or in the future has a strong motive to collect such data.

Target

In December 2013, the giant retail chain Target disclosed that hackers had breached its systems and compromised about 40 million payment card numbers (a combination of credit and debit card numbers). Over the next few weeks, Target revised that figure. Altogether, the breach may have impacted as many as 110 million Target customers, and the information accessed may have included not only payment card information, but other personally identifiable information (such as names, addresses, telephone numbers, and email addresses) as well.

Hackers entered Target by exploiting a vulnerability in a system used by a third-party HVAC contracting company that was servicing Target, and that had access to the retail company's point-of-sale systems. As a result of the breach, Target's CEO and CIO both resigned, and the company estimated that the breach inflicted about $162 million of damage to the firm.

Two lessons from the Target incident stand out:

>> **Management will be held responsible when companies suffer cyberattacks.** Professional reputations and personal careers can be harmed.

>> **A person or organization is only as cybersecure as the most vulnerable party having access to its systems.** Like a weak link in a strong chain, an inadequately secured third party with access to one's systems can easily undermine millions of dollars in cybersecurity investment. Home users should consider the moral of the Target story when allowing outsiders to use their home computers or networks. You may be careful with your personal cyberhygiene, but if you allow people who are not careful to join your network, malware on their devices can potentially propagate to your machines as well.

Sony Pictures

In November 2014, a hacker leaked confidential data stolen from the Sony Pictures film studio, including copies of as-of-yet-unreleased Sony films, internal emails between employees, employees' compensation information, and various other personal information about employees and their families. The hacker also wiped many computers within Sony's information infrastructure.

The leak and wiping occurred after hackers had been stealing data from Sony for as long as a year — potentially taking as much as 100 terabytes of material; Sony's executives also apparently dismissed as spam various demands that the hackers had communicated via email. Sony's cybersecurity plan, procedures, and counter-measures either did not detect the large volume of data being transferred out, or took grossly insufficient action upon detection.

After the breach, a party claiming to be the hackers threatened to carry out physical terrorist attacks against theaters showing Sony's then-upcoming film, *The Interview*, a comedy about a plot to assassinate North Korean leader Kim Jong-un. With the attackers' credibility and capabilities clearly asserted via the breach, cinema operators took the threat seriously, and many major American movie theater chains stated that they would not show *The Interview*. As a result, Sony canceled the film's formal premiere and theatrical release, instead offering the film only as a downloadable digital release followed by limited theatrical viewings.

While some cybersecurity experts were at least initially skeptical about the attribution, the United States government blamed North Korea for the hack and subsequent threats and, in September 2018, brought formal charges against a North Korean citizen that it claimed was involved with carrying out the hack while working for the North Korean equivalent of the Central Intelligence Agency.

Here are two lessons that stand out:

>> Depending on what technology Sony actually had in place, this breach either shows the need for implementing data loss prevention technology or shows that cybersecurity technology can be terribly ineffective, if not utilized properly.

>> Nation-states may use cyberattacks as a weapon against businesses and individuals whom they view as harmful to their goals, interests, and aspirations.

U.S. Office of Personnel Management

In June 2015, the U.S. Office of Personnel Management (OPM), which manages personnel processes and records for the U.S. federal government, announced that it had been the victim of a data breach. While the office initially estimated that far fewer records were compromised, the eventual estimate of the number of stolen records was more than 20 million.

The stolen records included personally identifiable information, including Social Security numbers, home addresses, dates and places of birth, and so on, of both current and former government employees, as well as of people who had undergone background checks, but who were never employed by the government. While the government initially believed that the contents of sensitive SF-86 forms — which contain all sorts of information used in background checks for security clearances — were not compromised, it ultimately disclosed that such data may have been accessed and stolen, meaning that the attackers may have obtained a treasure trove of private information about people with all sorts of security clearances. The OPM breach is believed to actually be a combination of more than one breach — one likely began around 2012 and was detected in March 2014 and another began in May 2014 and was not detected until April 2015.

Many lessons can be learned from the OPM incident, but two stand out:

>> **Government organizations are not immune to serious breaches** — and even after being breached once, may still remain vulnerable to subsequent breaches. Furthermore, like their civilian counterparts, they may not detect breaches for quite some time and may initially underestimate the impact of a particular breach or series of breaches.

>> **Breaches at an organization can impact people whose connections with the organization have long since ended** — some folks may not even remember why the organization had their data. The OPM breach impacted people who had not worked at the government in decades or who had applied for clearances many years prior, but who never ended up working for the government.

Anthem

In February 2015, Anthem, the second-largest health insurer in the United States, disclosed that it had been the victim of a cyberattack that had compromised personal information of almost 80 million current and former customers. Data that was stolen included names, addresses, Social Security numbers, dates of birth, and employment histories. Medical data was not believed to have been pilfered, but the stolen data was sufficient to create serious risks of identity theft for many people.

The breach — likely the largest in the history of the American healthcare industry — was believed to have initially taken place sometime in 2014, when one worker at a subsidiary of the insurer clicked on a link in a phishing email.

Two lessons stand out:

>> **The healthcare industry is increasingly being targeted.** (This is also apparent from the tremendous number of ransomware attacks directed at hospitals in recent years, as discussed in Chapter 3.)

>> **While people often imagine that breaches of major corporations require sophisticated James Bond-like techniques, the reality is that many, if not most, serious breaches are actually achieved using simple, classic techniques.** Phishing still works wonders for criminals. Human mistakes are almost always an integral element of a serious breach.

Colonial Pipeline and JBS SA

In May 2021, in a world already suffering from the COVID-19 pandemic, two major companies suffered significant ransomware breaches, both of which yielded significant societal impacts.

Colonial Pipeline

On May 7, 2021, Colonial Pipeline, a major operator of fuel pipeline infrastructure in the United States and a carrier of fuel to almost half of the United States' East Coast, was hit with a ransomware attack. Technologists at the firm quickly realized that the malware infection might have potentially adversely impacted various computer systems used for managing pipelines. Therefore, for safety reasons, Colonial Pipeline shut down its operations, stopping the flow of fuel to several heavily populated portions of the U.S. East Coast. The shutdown led to fuel shortages in numerous areas, and fuel prices, already on the rise, spiked upward. In some cases, airlines even had to change schedules as a result of fuel procurement issues.

Colonial Pipeline — possibly acting under the direct guidance of law enforcement — paid a ransom of almost $4.5 million in Bitcoin to the criminals operating the ransomware, and the evildoers released a decryption tool to the company. Shortly thereafter, the FBI recovered a large portion, but not all, of the payments made to the hackers.

The immediate aftermath of the Colonial Pipeline ransomware attack led the President of the United States, as well as the Governor of the U.S. state of Georgia and the Federal Motor Carrier Safety Administration to declare states of emergency. Later in 2021, the federal government offered a $10 million reward for information leading to the capture of those responsible for the attack. While law enforcement has strong suspicions as to the identities of those responsible, as of the time this book went to print, the parties responsible for the Colonial Pipeline attack remain at large.

JBS

On May 30, just a few weeks after the Colonial Pipeline attack, JBS S.A., a Brazilian meat-processing company that supplies approximately 20 percent of the world's meat for human consumption through itself and its international subsidiaries, was hit with a ransomware attack that disrupted beef and pork production in multiple countries, including the United States, Canada, and Australia. The attack caused meat shortages in some places, and the forced the U.S. government to delay its release of data about wholesale beef and pork prices. JBS paid $11 million in Bitcoin as a ransom and resumed operations on June 2.

One great lesson learned from these two high-profile ransomware attacks stands out:

>> **Cybersecurity is not just about computer data or about money — it is necessary in order to maintain our quality of life.** People who had to sit for hours in lines for gasoline during the shortage caused by the Colonial Pipeline hack, or who had planned to barbecue on a beautiful spring weekend but, who as a result of the JBS hack, could not find any meat in their local stores, experienced firsthand how cyberattacks can impact daily life. And other people across the nation saw news reports showing such repercussions as well. Furthermore, it should be clear that, as we humans become increasingly reliant on technology, the extent to which cyberattacks can affect our quality of life also rises.

Chapter **21**

Ten Ways to Safely Use Public Wi-Fi

U ntil relatively recently, there were many occasions during which someone might reasonably want to use public Wi-Fi for connecting to the Internet.

Until the arrival of 4G (the fourth generation of cellular networks), for example, the speed of Wi-Fi connections typically dwarfed the speed of cellular connections. Likewise in many locations, cellular connections were not available, and even if they were, they were only available from phones and cellular-enabled tablets, not from laptops. Furthermore, cellular data plans were typically expensive, especially for travelers leaving the service areas of their providers, so even if you could share your cellphone connection with your laptop, there were financial reasons not to do so.

Today, however, the situation has changed. 4G is ubiquitous, and even faster 5G is available in many areas, making cellular connections fast enough for nearly all types of online activities conducted by the typical adult for work or pleasure. (Certain types of gaming may still be an issue.) The cost of mobile data plans offering sufficient amounts of high speed for people to conduct normal business and personal activities while on the road have dropped dramatically, as has the cost of features that allow sharing of cellular connections from one's phone to one's laptop. In other words, in many more cases than just a few years ago, it is possible to leverage a cellular network rather public Wi-Fi without making any significant sacrifice, and in such cases, it is almost always safer to choose cellular over Wi-Fi.

That said, there are still some situations in which you may need to use public Wi-Fi rather than a cellular connection, such as if you are visiting a client in a facility underground where there are no cellular signals, and if Wi-Fi is provided for visitors because of the lack of cellular service. If you are in a situation in which you do need to use public Wi-Fi, you should understand that you can do several things to protect yourself while using it. In this chapter, you discover ten ways to keep yourself and your devices safe while accessing Wi-Fi in public.

WARNING

Keep in mind that you should never use the Wi-Fi provided by a party who you have reasons to suspect may be trying to hack you, unless you are using a throw-away device and not accessing any accounts whose security you care about.

Use Your Cellphone as a Mobile Hotspot

As mentioned in the introduction to this chapter, if you have an unlimited cellular data plan, and have a good cellular signal, you can avoid the many risks of public Wi-Fi by transforming your cellphone into a mobile hotspot and connecting your laptop and any other devices that lack cellular data service to your cellphone, rather than to public Wi-Fi. If doing so is an option, it almost always pays to choose it.

Turn Off Wi-Fi Connectivity When You're Not Using Wi-Fi

Turning off Wi-Fi connectivity will prevent your device from (without notifying you) connecting to a network with the same name as one you have previously connected to. Criminals can, and have, set up Wi-Fi access points with names similar to popular public Wi-Fi networks, in an effort to lure people into connecting to poisoned networks that route their victims to phony sites or distribute malware to connected devices. As an added bonus, turning off Wi-Fi will also conserve battery power. At a minimum, turn off AutoConnect to any public Wi-Fi networks.

Don't Perform Sensitive Tasks over Public Wi-Fi

Do not bank online, shop online, or access medical records online while using a public Wi-Fi connection. Consider not logging into anything that requires you to type a password — especially if there are cameras in the area in which you are working.

Don't Reset Passwords When Using Public Wi-Fi

You should avoid resetting any passwords over public Wi-Fi. In fact, for the reasons mentioned previously about cameras and people seeing what you are doing, you should refrain from resetting any passwords while in a public location, regardless of whether or not you're using public Wi-Fi.

Use a VPN Service

If you can't use a cellular connection and must use the public Wi-Fi connection for a sensitive task despite the recommendation not to do so, at least consider using a VPN service, which adds multiple security benefits. Many popular VPN services are available today.

There is a tradeoff to using a VPN service, however. You may notice that your communications are slightly slower or suffer from greater latency than without the VPN running. Also, consider through which countries you are routing traffic, as in some cases, there may be legal issues that arise.

Use Tor

If you don't want your browsing history to be tracked by anyone, consider browsing using Tor (see Chapter 4), which bounces your communications through many servers and makes tracking exceedingly difficult. There are even Tor browsers for smartphones. Like a VPN, Tor may slow down your communications.

Use Encryption

Use HTTPS instead of HTTP for all web pages that offer it, to prevent other users on the network from seeing the content of your communications. Likewise, do not access any email service that does not encrypt messages during delivery.

REMEMBER

You should be using encryption even when working on your home and work network, but doing so is even more important when using public Wi-Fi.

Turn Off Sharing

If you're using a computer or device that shares any of its resources, turn off any and all shares before connecting to the public Wi-Fi. If you're unsure if your device shares resources, check it. Don't assume that it does not.

Have Information Security Software on Any Devices Connected to Public Wi-Fi Networks

For computers security packages must include, at a minimum, antivirus and personal firewall capabilities. For smartphones and tablets, use an app designed specifically to secure such devices. And, of course, make sure that the security software is up to date before connecting to public Wi-Fi.

Understand the Difference between True Public Wi-Fi and Shared Wi-Fi

It is critical to understand that not all public Wi-Fi is equally risky. There is usually a much lower risk of being misrouted to phony sites or of malware being delivered to your device if you use the password-protected Guest network of a well-run business whose office you are visiting, for example, than if you use unprotected free Wi-Fi offered by a public library. That does not mean that you should fully trust either network, however; even a well-run company may be hacked, and other guests at the site using the same network as you also pose risks to you.

Index

A

access control, as component of Crime Prevention Through Design (CPTD), 99

access devices, 125, 127

access management, 208, 211–212

accounts

  accessing of only when you're in safe location, 126

  audible access to corporate accounts, 179

  limiting access to corporate accounts on social media, 178–180

  monitoring of, 122

  reporting suspicious activity on, 122

  securing data associated with user accounts, 119–130

  securing of, 117–134

  securing of external accounts, 118–119

  setting appropriate limits regarding, 126

  use of alerts on, 127

advanced attacks, 43–45

advanced persistent threats (APTs), 45

adware, 37–38

adware malware, 37–38

alarms, 100, 155

Alcoa, hacking of, 53

alerts

  responding to fraud alerts, 127

  setting up text alerts for payment card information, 256

  signing up for from bank, 89

  triggering fraud alerts, 127

  use of on your accounts, 127

algorithms (for encryption), 355

Allegheny Technologies, hacking of, 53

Amazon AppStore, as reputable app store, 120

American Association of Retired Persons (AARP), on passwords, 143

Android devices, 265, 291, 296–297

Anthem, Inc., 255, 363–364

anti-money laundering laws, 193

Apple, backing up data on, 265–266

Apple App Store, as reputable app store, 120

apps

  backing up data from, 262–264

  cloud-based, 342–343

archives, understanding of, 312–314

artificial intelligence (AI), 343–346

assets, 74–75, 211

asymmetric algorithm, for encryption, 355

ATM cards, cautions with, 88

attacks. *see also* cyberattacks

  advanced attacks, 43–45

  blended attacks, 42, 45

  brute-force attacks, 42, 46

  buffer overflow, 48

  calculated attacks, 42

  credential attacks, 42

  credential stuffing, 136

  denial-of-service (DoS) attacks, 24, 196

  dictionary attacks, 42, 136

  distributed denial-of-service (DDoS) attacks, 21, 24–26

  injection, 46–47

  malformed URL, 47

  man-in-the-middle attacks, 21, 31

  opportunistic attacks, 44

  poisoned web page attack, 39–40

  poisoned web service attacks, 39–40

  rootkits, 45

  semi-targeted attacks, 45

  session hijacking, 47

  social engineering attacks, 42, 152–155

  targeted attacks, 44–45

  wiper attacks, 27

audible access, to corporate accounts, 179

augmented reality, transforming experiences with, 350

authentication

biometric authentication, 123, 146–148

cautions with authentication by Google, 66

digital certificates, as form of, 123

hardware tokens, as form of, 123, 149–150

knowledge-based authentication, 123

multifactor authentication, 89, 122–124, 179–180

password authentication, 135–136

SMS (text message)-based authentication, 148–149

USB-based authentication, 150

using proper authentication, 357

voice-based authentication, 148

Authy (app), 124

automated-task backups, 280–281

AutoRecover (Microsoft Word), 276

AutoUpdate (Windows), 125

availability, as part of CIA triad, 21

B

B2B International, 26

backup power, as physical security method, 101

backup software, 278–281

backup/backing up

from apps and online accounts, 262–264

automated-task backups, 280–281

as basic element of protection, 75, 76, 79

boot disks, 281

cloud-based backup, 282–283

continuous backups, 272–273, 308

cryptocurrency, 267

defined, 261

differential backups, 271–272, 307–308

disposing of, 286–287

downloaded software, 270

drive backups, 274, 309

drive-specific backup software, 279

encryption of, 283, 285

exclusions from, 275–276

folder backups, 273–274, 309

frequency of, 277–278

full backups of data, 270–271, 272, 305–306, 308

full system backup, 267–268, 301–306

importance of, 261–262

importance of doing so often, 356

in-app backups, 276–277, 312

incremental backups, 271, 272, 306–310, 308

knowing where not to store backups, 284–285

knowing where to backup, 282–284

later system images, 269

manual backups, 280

mixed backups, 272

mixing locations, 284

network storage, 283–284

never leaving backups connected, 318

original installation media, 269–270

original system images, 269

partial backups, 273, 308–309

passwords, 267

for remote workforces, 187

restoring from, 299–320

restoring using backup tools, 314–317

returning of to their proper locations, 317–318

risks from, 101

smartphone/tablet backup, 265–266, 280

storage of, 356

storage of local copy of, 282

testing of, 286, 319

third-party backups, 262

tools for, 262, 279–281

types of, 267–277

virtual drive backups, 274–275, 310

Windows backup, 279

bad guys, 50–55

baiting, as type of social engineering attack, 153–154

balance of power, as political ramification of cybersecurity, 19–20

banking, online, 88–89

battery, drain speed of, 227

big data, impact of on cybersecurity, 12

biometric authentication, 123, 146–148

biometric data, laws governing, 193

birthday, cautions in sharing of, 161

BitLocker, 274

black hat hackers, 55

blended attacks, 42, 45

blended malware, as cyberattack, 38

blockchain technology, 340–342

blue hat hackers, 56

bogus information, use of, 170

bogus press releases and social media posts, as technique of cyberattackers, 58

bogus smartphone ransomware, 221

boot disks, 281, 320

botnets, 26

breach disclosure laws, 191–192, 205–206

breaches. *see also* hacking

  Anthem, Inc., 363–364

  Colonial Pipeline, 364–365

  covert breaches, 222–237

  discovery of, 241–242

  human errors as No. 1 catalyst for, 176, 208

  identification of, 219–237

  JBS, 365

  lawsuits from, 207

  lessons from, 359–365

  Marriott International, 359–361

  not using professional to help recover from, 241–247

  overt breaches, 220–222

  preventing of, 239–240

  recovering from, 239–257

  Sony Pictures, 362

  Target, 361

  United States Office of Personnel Management (OPM), 363

  using professional to help recover from, 240–241

Bring Your Own Device (BYOD) policy, 181, 194

browser, 86, 125

browser add-ons, impact of covert breach on, 233

browser home page, impact of covert breach on, 234

brute-force attacks, 42, 46

buffer overflow attacks, 48

buffering, impact of covert breach on, 225

Burr, Bill (author), 138

business continuity plans (BCPs), 203, 213

business data theft, 32–33

business risks, as mitigated by cybersecurity, 22

C

calculated attacks, 42

car computers, 340

carve outs, 189

cellphone numbers, 86, 129

CEO fraud, as cyberattack, 28–29

certifications

  adherence to code of ethics as required by, 335

  Certified Ethical Hacker (CEH), 333–334

  Certified Information Security Manager (CISM), 333

  Certified Information Systems Security Professional (CISSP), 332–333

  in cybersecurity, 332–335

  digital certificates as form of authentication, 123

  Global Information Assurance Certification Security Essentials Certification (GSEC), 334–335

  Security+, 334

  TLS/SSL certificate, 197, 354–355

  verifiability of, 335

Certified Ethical Hacker (CEH), 333–334

Certified Information Security Manager (CISM), 333

Certified Information Systems Security Professional (CISSP), 332–333

Cheat Sheet, 4

chief information security officer (CISO), 210–215, 324–325, 329–330

China, as known for performing cyberespionage, 126

CIA triad, 21

Cialdini, Robert Beno (social psychologist), 156

claimed destruction, as overt breach, 221–222

class action lawsuits, from data breaches, 207

classified information, 94

giving everyone his or her own credentials, 178

implementing cybersecurity policies for, 180–183

incentivizing of, 177

limiting access of, 177–178

monitoring of, 183–184

protecting employee data, 190

watching out for, 176–184

employer-issued documents, compromise of, 257

encryption

of all private information, 87

of backups, 283, 285

end-to-end encryption, 87

for guest users, 78

one-way encryption, 255

ransomware as often encrypting user files, 35–36, 220

of sensitive information, 354–356

use of, 86, 102, 140, 370

of virtual drives, 274–275, 309

of Wi-Fi network, 77

endpoints, 75, 79

end-to-end encryption, 87

environmental risk mitigation, as physical security method, 100–101

ethical hacker, role of, 326

ethics, code of, 335

evil twin networks, 187

expunged records, as no longer really expunged, 65

external accounts, securing of, 118–119

external disasters, 62–63

F

Facebook

authentication capabilities provided by, 139

basic control and audibility on, 179

for business, 179

cautions in listing family members on, 158–159

celebrity accounts as verified on, 169

criminals as creating fake profiles on, 162

number of connections on as red flag, 164

red flags on, 42, 164, 167

use of to find someone's mother's maiden name, 85

factory image, 269

Fair Credit Reporting Act (FCRA), 64, 132–133

fake profiles, on social media, 162–169

false alarm, as type of social engineering attack, 155

family tree sites, cautions with, 132

Federal Trade Commission (FTC), 133, 144

fiduciary responsibilities, of big businesses, 206

files, 228

financial information, cautions in sharing of, 158

financial risks, as mitigated by cybersecurity, 22

fingerprint sensors, 146–148

Firefox, 87, 249

firewall/router, as basic element of protection, 76–78

folder backups, 273–274, 309

forced policy violations, 34

forensic analyst, role of, 328

fraud alerts, 127

fraud prevention, 212

frequency, of backups, 277–278

full backups of data, 270–271, 272, 305–306, 308

full system backup, 267–268, 301–306

G

genealogy sites, cautions with, 132

General Data Protection Regulation (GDPR), 192, 360

geopolitical risks, 214

Global Information Assurance Certification Security Essentials Certification (GSEC), 334–335

good guys, as relative term, 50–51

goods, stealing of as technique of cyberattackers, 59

Google, cautions with authentication by, 66

Google Chrome, 87, 248

Google Drive, data storage on, 262

Google Photos, backing up, 264

Google Play, as reputable app store, 120

Google Voice, 86, 129, 179

government-issued documents, compromise of, 256–257

green hat hackers, 56

grey hat hackers, 56

guessing passwords, 136

guest network capability, 78

H

hackers

 black hat hackers, 55

 blue hat hackers, 56

 ethical hacker, 326

 green hat hackers, 56

 grey hat hackers, 56

 history of teenage hackers, 52

 offensive hacker, 326–327

 white hat hackers, 55

hacking. *see also* breaches

 of Alcoa, 53

 of Allegheny Technologies, 53

 by nations, 52–53

 reasons of rogue insiders for, 55

 reasons of terrorists for, 54–55

 of SolarWorld, 53

 by states, 52–53

 of U.S. organizations by People's Liberation Army (PLA) of China, 53

 use of artificial intelligence (AI) as tool of, 345–346

 of Westinghouse, 53

hacktivism, as political ramification of cybersecurity, 18

hacktivists, defined, 54

hard resets, 292–298

hardware, evaluating security measures regarding, 82

hardware tokens, as form of authentication, 123, 149–150

hashed format, 255

Health Insurance Portability and Accountability Act (HIPAA), 114, 192

home computers, potential problems of regarding cybersecurity, 72

HTTPS, 127, 197, 354–355

Huawei devices running Android 8, hard resets on, 297

human errors, 60–62, 110, 176, 208

humans, as Achilles heel of cybersecurity, 60–61, 83

I

iCloud, backing up using, 266

icons, explained, 4

identity and access management, 211–212

impersonation, as cyberattack, 27–29, 154

in the cloud, defined, 280

in-app backups, 276–277, 312

inbound access, handling of, 194–196

incident response plan, 213

incident response team member, role of, 328

incineration, as way of disposing of backups, 287

incremental backups, 271, 306–310, 308

incremental system backups, 306–307

indirect financial fraud, as way to monetize cyberattackers actions, 56, 57–59

industry-specific regulations and rules, for big businesses, 206

Influence: The Psychology of Persuasion (Cialdini), 156

information

 bogus information, 170

 classified information, 94

 credit card information, 58, 120–121, 121–122

 dealing with stolen information, 250–253

 financial information, 158

 insider information, 58

 personal information, 158–160

 private information, 120

 sensitive information, 120, 124, 125, 251, 354–356

 stolen information, 250–253

 that is not private but can help criminals with identity theft, 250–251

information asset classification and control, 211

Information Commissioner's Office of the United Kingdom (ICO), 360

information security

mistakes, learning from, 80

mixed backups, 272

mobile device location tracking, potential consequences of, 66–67

mobile devices

  defined, 95

  fake malware on, 38

  keeping of up to date, 125

  potential problems of regarding cybersecurity, 73

  security for, 101–102

  taking inventory of physical security regarding, 97

  using your own, 124

mobile hotspot, using your cellphone as, 368

mobile workforces, impact of on cybersecurity, 11

multifactor authentication, 89, 122–124, 179–180

multiple network segments, use of, 198

N

National Socialist Party of America v. Village of Skokie, 50–51

nations, hacking by, 52–53

natural disasters, risk from, 62–63

Network Address Translation, 77

network connectivity, terminating of on Windows computer, 243–247

network infrastructure poisoning, as cyberattack, 40

network sniffing, 42

network storage of backup, restoring from, 317–318

network traffic, 230

networking equipment, potential problems of regarding cybersecurity, 74

networks

  evil twin, 187

  known, 186–187

  for remote workforces, 185, 186–187

  security of, 106–108

9/11, learnings from, 63

noise machines, 188

nonmalicious threats, dealing with, 60–67

Nuclear Regulatory Commission (NRC), 206

O

offensive hacker, role of, 326–327

Office of Personnel Management (OPM) (US), cybersecurity breach, 363

official apps/websites, use of, 120

one-way encryption, 255

online accounts, backing up data from, 262–264

online banking, 88–89

Opera, privacy mode, 87

opportunistic attacks, 44

original installation media, 269–270, 304

original system images, 269, 303

overwriting, as way of disposing of backups, 287

P

padlock icon, meaning of, 127

pandemics, 63

partial backups, 273, 308–309

partners, considerations described in big businesses, 208–210

passphrases, defined, 138

password authentication, 135–136

password managers, 140–142, 357

passwords

  AARP (American Association of Retired Persons) on, 143

  alternatives to, 146–150

  app-based one-time ones, 149

  avoid maintaining default passwords, 90

  avoid sharing of, 356

  avoid simplistic ones, 136–137

  avoiding simplistic, 136–137

  backing up, 267

  capturing of using malware, 42

  cautions with resetting of when using public Wi-Fi, 369

  changing of after breach, 144

  classification of, 139

  complicated ones as not always better, 138

  considerations described, 137–142

  considerations for, 137–142

  creating memorable, strong ones, 142

R

ransoms, paying of, 251–253

ransomware, 35–36, 56, 59, 220–221

recovering, defined, 80

Registry Editor, impact of covert breach on, 223–224

regulations
  for big businesses, 203–207
  on biometric data, 193
  breach disclosure laws, 191–192, 205–206
  cybersecurity regulations expert, 328
  General Data Protection Regulation (GDPR), 192
  Health Insurance Portability and Accountability Act (HIPAA), 192
  industry-specific regulations and rules, 206
  Payment Card Industry Data Security Standard (PCI DSS), 191, 205
  private regulations expert, 328
  public company data disclosure rules, 205
  Sarbanes Oxley Act of 2002 (SOX), 203–204
  Small Business Administration as source of guidance on, 190
  for small businesses, 190–193

regulatory issues, 113–114

remote access technologies, impact of on cybersecurity, 11

remote workforces, 184–188

renovations, contingencies during, 101

replicated environments, use of, 209–210

resets, 289–298

responding, defined, 80

restarting systems, 247

restoring
  from archives, 312–314
  from backups, 301–314
  booting from boot disk, 320
  cautions described, 300
  from combination of locations, 318
  to computing device that was originally backed up, 301
  cryptocurrency, 319–320
  dealing with deletions in, 311
  to different device than one that was originally backed up, 302
  from differential backups, 307–308
  of downloaded software, 304–305
  from drive backups, 309
  from encrypted backups, 319
  entire virtual drive, 310
  excluding files and folders in, 311–312
  files and/or folders from virtual drive, 310
  from folder backups, 309
  from full backups of data, 305–306
  from full backups of systems, 301–306
  from incremental backups, 306–310
  from incremental backups of data, 306
  from incremental backups of systems, 306–307
  installing security software, 303–304
  of later system images, 303
  from manual file or folder copying backups, 316
  of modified settings in Safari, 248–249
  need for, 299
  to network storage, 317–318
  to non-original locations, 318
  of original installation media, 304
  of original systems images, 303
  from partial backups, 308–309
  returning backups to their proper locations, 317–318
  from smartphone/tablet backup, 315–316
  to system restore point, 315
  testing backups, 319
  using backup tools, 314–317
  utilizing third-party backups of data hosted at third parties, 317
  from virtual-drive backups, 310
  from Windows backup, 315

reusing passwords, 139–140

risks
  addressing of through various methods, 67
  from backups, 101
  environmental risk mitigation, 100–101
  financial risks, 22
  human risk management, 211

identification of, 74–75

insiders as posing greatest risk, 102–103

from manmade environmental problems, 63

as mitigated by cybersecurity, 20–22

from natural disasters, 62–63

from pandemics, 63

personal risks, 22

physical danger, 22

privacy risks, 22

professional risks, 22

protecting against, 75–80

realizing insiders pose greatest risks, 102–103

from social media, 66

rogue groups, 52

rogue insiders, reasons of for hacking, 55

root your phone, cautions with, 120

rooting smartphones, 120

rootkits, 45

RSA SecureID one-time password generator hardware token, 149–150

S

Safari, 87, 249

Samsung Galaxy Series running Android 11, hard resets on, 296

Samsung tablets running Android 11, hard resets on, 296–297

sanctions, as political ramification of cybersecurity, 18–19

sandboxing, 141, 194

SANS Institute, 334

Sarbanes Oxley Act of 2002 (SOX), 203–204

scambaiting, 153–154

scams, 254–255

scareware, as cyberattack, 36

schedule, cautions in sharing of, 157–158

school-issued documents, compromise of, 257

script kiddies (a.k.a. skids or kiddies), 51

Section 302 (SOX), 204

Section 404 (SOX), 204

secure area, 141

Security+, 334

security administrator, role of, 325

security analyst, role of, 325

security architect, role of, 325

security architecture, 214

security auditor, role of, 325

security breaches. *see also* hacking

Anthem, Inc., 363–364

Colonial Pipeline, 364–365

covert breaches, 222–237

discovery of, 241–242

human errors as No. 1 catalyst for, 176, 208

identification of, 219–237

JBS, 365

lawsuits from, 207

lessons from, 359–365

Marriott International, 359–361

not using professional to help recover from, 241–247

overt breaches, 220–221

preventing of, 239–240

recovering from, 239–257

Sony Pictures, 362

Target, 361

United States Office of Personnel Management (OPM), 363

using professional to help recover from, 240–241

security consultant, role of, 327

security director, role of, 324

security engineer, role of, 324

security expert witness, role of, 327

security guards, as physical security method, 100

security manager, role of, 324

security measures, evaluating yours, 71–74, 80–83–78

security operations, 211

security program, 210–211

security questions, cautions with, 66

security researcher, role of, 326

security software, 76, 79, 125, 170–171, 246–247, 303–304, 354, 370

security specialist, role of, 327

security subscription renewal notifications, fake, 39

About the Author

Joseph Steinberg serves as a cybersecurity expert witness and as cybersecurity advisor to both businesses and governments around the world. He has led organizations within the cybersecurity industry for nearly 25 years, has been calculated to be one of the top three cybersecurity influencers worldwide, and has written books ranging from *Cybersecurity For Dummies* to the official study guide from which many chief information security officers (CISOs) study for their certification exams.

Steinberg is known for offering keen insights and unique perspectives on cybersecurity, artificial intelligence (AI), and the potential impact of technological developments on human society. He amassed millions of readers as a regular columnist for *Forbes* and *Inc.* magazines; today, his independent column receives millions of monthly views, making it one of the most read columns in the fields of cybersecurity and AI. His opinions are also frequently cited in books, law journals, security publications, and general interest periodicals.

Steinberg is one of only a few people worldwide to hold the suite of advanced information security certifications: CISSP, ISSAP, ISSMP, and CSSLP, indicating that he possesses a rare, robust knowledge of information security that is both broad and deep. His cybersecurity-related inventions are cited in well over 500 U.S. patent filings.

In addition to his primary work, Steinberg currently serves as a senior policy analyst at the Global Foundation for Cyber Studies and Research think tank, as a cybersecurity expert member of *Newsweek* magazine's Expert Forum, and as an advisor to the WonderKey Collective nonprofit that provides technology and related resources to underserved and underfunded communities across the United States. Steinberg also presently serves on the Cybersecurity Council of CompTIA, the world's largest technology trade association and its second-largest related certifying body.

He is an alumnus of NYU's Courant Institute of Mathematical Sciences. Joseph can be reached at https://JosephSteinberg.com.

Dedication

All of the educational and professional experiences that I have enjoyed in my life — and even my life itself — would likely not have been possible had my forebears not made the brave decision over a century ago to leave their entire known worlds behind and immigrate to the United States of America.

With the belief that the United States was truly a land of both opportunity and tolerance, and that they and their families, somehow, through hard work and perseverance, would ultimately flourish in their new home, my forebears, often alone and always with few possessions, journeyed on crowded steamliners to a land whose terrain, climate, culture, and language they did not at all know.

And, yet, in this great country and because of its greatness — in the only nation in human history born not out of its residents' common history, but rather, to deliver to people on their inherent right to life, liberty, and the pursuit of happiness — my forebears not only saw their many years of struggle ultimately yield an unimaginably better life for themselves and their descendants, but also became proud Americans themselves.

While we often take our current situations for granted, I know that any success that I ever achieve is built upon my grandparents' and great grandparents' endurance of extremely difficult circumstances; in fact, had they not been so brave so as to leave their homes to an unknown land, they would likely have ultimately been murdered by the Nazis along with their many relatives who chose to remain behind, I would not be here today, and you would not be reading this book. And I know that the same fate would also have met them (and me) had America not been the land of opportunity, a sanctuary that, while imperfect, uniquely allows refugees willing to put in effort to build great lives.

And so, I dedicate this book in memory of my grandparents and great grandparents — those who I met and those who died long before I was born — whose bravery and sacrifice is why I am here today. And, as I finish writing the second edition of *Cybersecurity For Dummies* in a place where I benefit from comforts, freedoms, and rights that my forebears several generations ago could not have even imagined enjoying, I also remind myself of how lucky I am to be an American.

Author's Acknowledgments

Cybersecurity is of paramount importance in today's world, but for obvious reasons, few if any modern-day adults learned from their parents or in school about mitigating against today's major cybersecurity risks. Couple such a lack of formal education with the combination of information overload, the proliferation of oft-repeated impractical advice, overused and misused technical jargon, and the constant barrage of news stories about cyberattacks and breaches, and it is no surprise that, when it comes to cybersecurity, many folks rightfully feel confused, fatigued, and scared. To put it simply, when it comes to cybersecurity, even Noble Prize-winning geniuses are often dummies.

As a result, there has never been a greater need for a book that brings basic, practical cybersecurity knowledge to "nontechnical" people than there is today. It was with the aim of satisfying that need in mind that Wiley initially approached me about writing the first edition of this book, and it was the importance of delivering on such a goal that led me to accept the opportunity.

Thankfully, our combined efforts paid off: the first edition of this book became a best seller, significantly exceeding sales projections. And, with that in mind, Wiley approached me to write a second edition, updating the book to both reflect two years of developments in the world of cybersecurity, and the many new cybersecurity challenges created by transformative societal changes facilitated by the COVID-19 pandemic.

You are holding the result of our second joint effort.

On that note, I would like to thank Elizabeth Stilwell and the team at Wiley for giving me the opportunity to, once again, collaborate with their team to provide the public with a book it so desperately needs. I would also like to thank my editor, Katharine Dvorak, and my technical reviewer, Daniel Smith, whose input and guidance helped improve the book that you are now holding, optimized it for readability, and ensured that it delivers to you its maximum informational value.

Thank you also to the many members of my immediate and extended family who gave me support and encouragement throughout the time-intensive process of bringing this book to reality.

And, finally, as I mentioned in the first edition, while there were no cybersecurity classes when I went to school, several great professors helped me hone my understanding of the building blocks of computer science that I ultimately assembled and applied in order to develop expertise in my field. I wish to single out and specifically recognize two of my instructors, Matthew Smosna and Aizik Leibovitch, both of who, unfortunately, did not live to see either edition of this book published, but whose influence on my thinking resonates throughout it.

Publisher's Acknowledgments

Acquisitions Editor: Elizabeth Stilwell
Managing Editor: Michelle Hacker
Project Editor: Katharine Dvorak
Technical Editor: Daniel Smith

Production Editor: Mohammed Zafar Ali
Cover Image: © Fotomay/Shutterstock

Take dummies with you everywhere you go!

Whether you are excited about e-books, want more from the web, must have your mobile apps, or are swept up in social media, dummies makes everything easier.

Find us online!

dummies.com

dummies
A Wiley Brand

Leverage the power

Dummies is the global leader in the reference category and one of the most trusted and highly regarded brands in the world. No longer just focused on books, customers now have access to the dummies content they need in the format they want. Together we'll craft a solution that engages your customers, stands out from the competition, and helps you meet your goals.

Advertising & Sponsorships

Connect with an engaged audience on a powerful multimedia site, and position your message alongside expert how-to content. Dummies.com is a one-stop shop for free, online information and know-how curated by a team of experts.

- Targeted ads
- Video
- Email Marketing
- Microsites
- Sweepstakes sponsorship

20 MILLION PAGE VIEWS EVERY SINGLE MONTH

15 MILLION UNIQUE VISITORS PER MONTH

43% OF ALL VISITORS ACCESS THE SITE VIA THEIR MOBILE DEVICES

700,000 NEWSLETTE SUBSCRIPTION TO THE INBOXES OF

300,000 UNIQUE INDIVIDUALS EVERY WEEK

# of dummies

Custom Publishing

Reach a global audience in any language by creating a solution that will differentiate you from competitors, amplify your message, and encourage customers to make a buying decision.

- Apps
- Books
- eBooks
- Video
- Audio
- Webinars

Brand Licensing & Content

Leverage the strength of the world's most popular reference brand to reach new audiences and channels of distribution.

For more information, visit dummies.com/biz

PERSONAL ENRICHMENT

Staying Sharp	Facebook	Guitar	Investing	Beekeeping	Digital Photography
9781119187790	9781119179030	9781119293354	9781119293347	9781119310068	9781119235606
USA $26.00	USA $21.99	USA $24.99	USA $22.99	USA $22.99	USA $24.99
CAN $31.99	CAN $25.99	CAN $29.99	CAN $27.99	CAN $27.99	CAN $29.99
UK £19.99	UK £16.99	UK £17.99	UK £16.99	UK £16.99	UK £17.99

Meditation	Pregnancy	Samsung Galaxy S7	iPhone	Crocheting	Nutrition
9781119251163	9781119235491	9781119279952	9781119283133	9781119287117	9781119130246
USA $24.99	USA $26.99	USA $24.99	USA $24.99	USA $24.99	USA $22.99
CAN $29.99	CAN $31.99	CAN $29.99	CAN $29.99	CAN $29.99	CAN $27.99
UK £17.99	UK £19.99	UK £17.99	UK £17.99	UK £16.99	UK £16.99

PROFESSIONAL DEVELOPMENT

 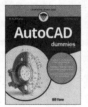     

Windows 10	AutoCAD	Excel 2016	QuickBooks 2017	macOS Sierra	LinkedIn	Windows 10
9781119311041	9781119255796	9781119293439	9781119281467	9781119280651	9781119251132	9781119310563
USA $24.99	USA $39.99	USA $26.99	USA $26.99	USA $29.99	USA $24.99	USA $34.00
CAN $29.99	CAN $47.99	CAN $31.99	CAN $31.99	CAN $35.99	CAN $29.99	CAN $41.99
UK £17.99	UK £27.99	UK £19.99	UK £19.99	UK £21.99	UK £17.99	UK £24.99

SharePoint 2016	Fundamental Analysis	Networking	Office 2016	Office 365	Salesforce.com	Coding
9781119181705	9781119263593	9781119257769	9781119293477	9781119265313	9781119239314	9781119293323
USA $29.99	USA $26.99	USA $29.99	USA $26.99	USA $24.99	USA $29.99	USA $29.99
CAN $35.99	CAN $31.99	CAN $35.99	CAN $31.99	CAN $29.99	CAN $35.99	CAN $35.99
UK £21.99	UK £19.99	UK £21.99	UK £19.99	UK £17.99	UK £21.99	UK £21.99

dummies.com

dummies
A Wiley Brand

Learning Made Easy

ACADEMIC

Algebra I dummies
2nd Edition
Mary Jane Sterling

9781119293576
USA $19.99
CAN $23.99
UK £15.99

Basic Math & Pre-Algebra dummies
2nd Edition
Mark Zegarelli

9781119293637
USA $19.99
CAN $23.99
UK £15.99

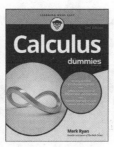

Calculus dummies
2nd Edition
Mark Ryan

9781119293491
USA $19.99
CAN $23.99
UK £15.99

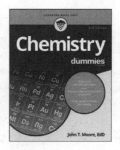

Chemistry dummies
2nd Edition
John T. Moore, EdD

9781119293460
USA $19.99
CAN $23.99
UK £15.99

Physics I dummies
2nd Edition
Steven Holzner, PhD

9781119293590
USA $19.99
CAN $23.99
UK £15.99

1,001 Practice Questions
SAT dummies
Ron Woldoff

9781119215844
USA $26.99
CAN $31.99
UK £19.99

Organic Chemistry I dummies
2nd Edition
Arthur Winter

9781119293378
USA $22.99
CAN $27.99
UK £16.99

Statistics dummies
2nd Edition
Deborah J. Rumsey, PhD

9781119293521
USA $19.99
CAN $23.99
UK £15.99

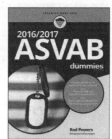

2016/2017
ASVAB dummies
Rod Powers

9781119239178
USA $18.99
CAN $22.99
UK £14.99

Includes Online Practice Tests
1,001 Practice Questions
Praxis Core dummies
Carla Kirkland
Chan Cleveland

9781119263883
USA $26.99
CAN $31.99
UK £19.99

Available Everywhere Books Are Sold

Small books for big imaginations

GETTING STARTED WITH **Coding**
Get Creative with Code!
Camille McCue, PhD

9781119177173
USA $9.99
CAN $9.99
UK £8.99

MODDING **Minecraft**™
Build Your Own Minecraft Mods!
Sarah Guthals, PhD
Stephen Foster, PhD
Lindsey Handley, PhD

9781119177272
USA $9.99
CAN $9.99
UK £8.99

MAKING **YouTube** VIDEOS
Star in Your Own Video!
Nick Willoughby

9781119177241
USA $9.99
CAN $9.99
UK £8.99

DESIGNING **Digital Games**
Create Games with Scratch™!
Derek Breen

9781119177210
USA $9.99
CAN $9.99
UK £8.99

GETTING STARTED WITH **Raspberry Pi**™
Program Your Raspberry Pi™!
Richard Wentk

9781119262657
USA $9.99
CAN $9.99
UK £6.99

EXPERIMENTING WITH **Science**
Think, Test, and Learn!

9781119291336
USA $9.99
CAN $9.99
UK £6.99

CREATING **Digital Animations**
Animate Stories with Scratch™!
Derek Breen

9781119233527
USA $9.99
CAN $9.99
UK £6.99

GETTING STARTED WITH **Engineering**
Think Like an Engineer!
Camille McCue, PhD

9781119291220
USA $9.99
CAN $9.99
UK £6.99

WRITING **Computer Code**
Learn the Language of Computers!
Chris Minnick and Eva Holland

9781119177302
USA $9.99
CAN $9.99
UK £8.99

Unleash Their Creativity